The Modern Language Review

APRIL 2014   VOLUME 109   PART 2

General Editor
Professor Derek Connon

English Editor
Professor Andrew Hiscock

French Editor
Dr Alison Williams

Italian Editor
Professor Jane Everson

Hispanic Editor
Professor Derek Flitter

Germanic Editor
Professor Katrin Kohl

Slavonic Editor
Dr Katharine Hodgson

Assistant Editor
Dr John Waś

MODERN HUMANITIES RESEARCH ASSOCIATION

The Modern Humanities Research Association

was founded in Cambridge in 1918 and has become an international organization with members in all parts of the world. It is a registered charity number 1064670, and a company limited by guarantee, registered in England number 3446016. Its main object is to encourage advanced study and research in modern and medieval European languages, literatures, and cultures by its publication of journals, book series, and its Style Guide.

Further information about the activities of the Association and individual membership may be obtained from the Hon. Secretary, Dr Barbara Burns, School of Modern Languages and Cultures, University of Glasgow, Glasgow G12 8RS, UK, email membership@mhra.org.uk, or from the website at www.mhra.org.uk

The Association's publications, including most back volumes, are available in print or electronically. Full details are available from www.mhra.org.uk

The Modern Language Review

The *Modern Language Review* is one of five journals available to members of the Modern Humanities Research Association in return for a composite membership subscription payable in advance through the Assistant Treasurer. (Associate membership is open to graduates for four years after their first degree, and postgraduate membership is also available.) Some other publications of the MHRA are available to members at special rates.

The *Modern Language Review* and other journals published by the MHRA may be ordered from JSTOR (http://about.jstor.org/csp).

ISSN 0026–7937 (Print)
ISSN 2222–4319 (Online)
© 2014 The Modern Humanities Research Association

All rights reserved. No part of this publication may be reproduced in any material form (including photocopying or storing it in any medium by electronic means) without the prior written permission of the copyright owner, except in accordance with the provisions of the Copyright, Designs and Patents Act 1988, or under the terms of a licence permitting restricted copying issued in the UK by the Copyright Licensing Agency Ltd, Saffron House, 6–10 Kirby Street, London EC1N 8TS, England, or in the USA by the Copyright Clearance Center, 222 Rosewood Drive, Danvers, Mass. 01923. Application for the written permission of the copyright owner to reproduce any part of this publication must be made to the General Editor.

DISCLAIMER

Statements of fact and opinion in the content of the *Modern Language Review* are those of the respective authors and contributors and not of the journal editors or of the Modern Humanities Research Association (MHRA). MHRA makes no representation, express or implied, in respect of the accuracy of the material in this journal and cannot accept any legal responsibility or liability for any errors or omissions that may be made.

TYPESET BY JOHN WAŚ, OXFORD

Guidelines for Contributors to *MLR*

The *Modern Language Review* publishes articles and book reviews in English on any aspect of modern and medieval European (including English and Latin American) languages, literatures, and cultures (including cinema). The journal does not publish correspondence. We are glad to receive general and comparative articles as well as those on language-specific topics. We encourage submissions from postgraduates. Articles should be submitted to the appropriate section editor in one typescript copy together with an identical electronic copy sent as an email attachment. Articles should conform precisely to the conventions of the *MHRA Style Guide*, 3rd edn, 2013 (ISBN 978-1-78188-009-8), obtainable from www.style.mhra.org.uk, price £6.50, US$13, €8; an online version of the *Guide* is also available from the same address. Authors should provide an abstract of their articles with keywords highlighted in bold type. This abstract should not exceed 100 words. At the end of articles and reviews contributors should include, in this order, their affiliation or location; name as it is to be printed; name and postal address for correspondence; and email address. Simple references should be incorporated into the text (see *MHRA Style Guide*, 10.2). Double spacing should be used throughout, including quotations and footnotes, which should be in the same large size of type as the rest of the article. Articles are typically about 8000 words in length including footnotes, but longer and shorter ones are also welcome. Quotations and references should be carefully checked. Quotations from languages covered by the journal, and from Latin and Greek, should be given in the original language. Latin and Greek passages should normally be translated or at least paraphrased; usually this is not required in the case of modern languages, though it may be helpful where dialects or early forms of the language are cited. However, since the journal has a broad readership, please provide translations or paraphrases of quotations within comparative or general articles (except for modern French). If in doubt, consult the appropriate section editor.

The *Modern Language Review* regrets that it must charge contributors for the cost of corrections in proof which the Editor in his or her discretion thinks excessive. Contributors should keep a copy of their typescript. Typescripts not accepted for publication will not normally be returned. If your article is accepted, you will be asked to supply a definitive version of it both in hard copy and as an email attachment. Authors should ensure that there is no discrepancy between the computer file and the printout.

It is a condition of publication in this journal that authors of articles and reviews assign copyright, including electronic copyright, to the MHRA. *Inter alia*, this allows the General Editor to deal efficiently and consistently with requests from third parties for permission to reproduce material. The journal has been published simultaneously in printed and electronic form since January 2001. Permission, without fee, for authors to use their own material in other publications, after a reasonable period of time has elapsed, is not normally withheld.

On publication of each issue of the journal authors will receive, by email, the finalized PDF of their contribution as it appears in the printed volume. Physical offprints are not supplied. Authors of articles will also receive a complimentary copy of the printed issue in which the article appears.

Articles and books for review should be sent to the Editor concerned:

General and Comparative. Professor Derek Connon, Department of French, Swansea University, Swansea, SA2 8PP (d.f.connon@swansea.ac.uk).
English and American. Professor Andrew Hiscock, School of English, Bangor University, Bangor, LL57 2DG (mhraassistant@bangor.ac.uk).
French. Dr Alison Williams, Department of French, Swansea University, Swansea, SA2 8PP (a.j.williams@swansea.ac.uk).
Italian. Professor Jane Everson, School of Modern Languages, Literatures and Cultures (Italian), Royal Holloway, University of London, Egham, TW20 0EX (j.everson@rhul.ac.uk).
Hispanic. Professor Derek Flitter, School of Modern Languages, Queen's Building, University of Exeter, Exeter EX4 4QH (d.w.flitter@exeter.ac.uk).
German, Dutch, and Scandinavian. Professor Robert Vilain, School of Modern Languages, University of Bristol, 17 Woodland Road, Bristol, BS8 1TE (robert.vilain@bristol.ac.uk).
Slavonic and Eastern European. Dr Katharine Hodgson, School of Modern Languages, Queen's Building, University of Exeter, Exeter EX4 4QH (k.m.hodgson@exeter.ac.uk).

CONTENTS

ARTICLES PAGE

Petrarch's *De vita solitaria*: Samuel Daniel's Translation *c.* 1610
By JESSICA STOLL 313

The Courtesan and the Bed: Successful Tricking in Middleton's *A Mad World, my Masters*
By KATE AUGHTERSON 333

'The Senses of Primitive Man': Joseph Conrad, W. H. R. Rivers, and Representing the Other in 'The End of the Tether'
By ANDREW PURSSELL 357

Mediterranean Mediations: Language and Cultural (Ex)change in BnF, MS fr. 19152
By T. S. MENDOLA 375

Galdós, Shakespeare, and What to Make of *Tormento*
By GARETH J. WOOD 392

Medieval Humour? Wolfram's *Parzival* and the Concept of the Comic in Middle High German Romances
By STEFAN SEEBER 417

After the *Flâneur*: Temporality and Connectivity in Wilhelm Genazino's *Belebung der toten Winkel* and *Das Glück in glücksfernen Zeiten*
By ANNE FUCHS 431

Evgenii Popov: A New Gogol' for a New Russia?
By DAVID GILLESPIE 447

Thesaurus of the Unspeakable: *Thanatopraxis* in Kharkiv's Tales of Trauma
By TANYA ZAHARCHENKO 462

REVIEWS

Georges Vigarello, *The Metamorphoses of Fat: A History of Obesity* (ANNA JENKIN) . 482
Medicine and Narration in the Eighteenth Century, ed. by Sophie Vasset (CLARK LAWLOR) 483
Tobias Boes, *Formative Fictions: Nationalism, Cosmopolitanism, and the Bildungsroman* (MICHAEL MINDEN) 484
Daniel Cottom, *International Bohemia: Scenes of Nineteenth-Century Life* (ANDREW J. COUNTER) 486
Matthew Potolsky, *The Decadent Republic of Letters: Taste, Politics, and Cosmopolitan Community from Baudelaire to Beardsley* (RICHARD HIBBITT) 487
Modernism and the Orient, ed. by Zhaoming Qian (SHUANGYI LI) 489
Jeremy Tambling, *Literature and Psychoanalysis* (LUCIANO PARISI) 491
Robert Baker, *In Dark Again in Wonder: The Poetry of René Char and George Oppen* (MICHAEL KINDELLAN) 492
Konstantina Georganta, *Conversing Identities: Encounters between British, Irish and Greek Poetry, 1922–1952* (GONDA VAN STEEN) 494
A Critical Edition of the Complete Poems of Henry Howard, Earl of Surrey, ed. by William McGaw (ANDREW HISCOCK) 495
Andrew Hadfield, *Edmund Spenser: A Life* (ELIZABETH HEALE) 497

Martin Wiggins, *Drama and the Transfer of Power in Renaissance England* (NICHOLAS GRENE) 498
Gregory Lynall, *Swift and Science: The Satire, Politics, and Theology of Natural Knowledge, 1690–1730* (BREAN S. HAMMOND) 499
William F. Engel, *Early Modern Poetics in Melville and Poe: Memory, Melancholy and the Emblematic Tradition* (DAVID E. E. SLOANE) 501
K. M. Newton, *Modernizing George Eliot: The Writer as Artist, Intellectual, Proto-Modernist, Cultural Critic* (JOSIE BILLINGTON) 502
A Historical Guide to Henry James, ed. by John Carlos Rowe and Eric Haralson (RICHARD SALMON) 503
Wyndham Lewis and the Cultures of Modernity, ed. by Andrzej Gąsiorek and others (RANDALL STEVENSON) 505
Steven Belletto, *No Accident, Comrade: Chance and Design in Cold War American Narratives* (DAVID SEED) 506
Kathryn Hume, *Aggressive Fictions: Reading the Contemporary American Novel* (BRIAN JARVIS) 508
The Fabliaux: A New Verse Translation, trans. by Nathaniel Dubin, intro. by R. Howard Bloch (GLYN S. BURGESS) 509
1511–2011, Philippe de Commynes: droit, écriture. Deux piliers de la souveraineté, ed. by Joël Blanchard (JELLE HAEMERS) 510
Fiction and the Frontiers of Knowledge in Europe, 1500–1800, ed. by Richard Scholar and Alexis Tadié (SÍOFRA PIERSE) 511
Jean Donneau de Visé, *Les Costeaux; ou, Les Marquis frians*, ed. by Peter William Shoemaker (DEREK CONNON) 513
Mark Darlow, *Dissonance in the Republic of Letters: The Querelle des Gluckistes et des Piccinnistes* (DEREK CONNON) 513
Cecilia Feilla, *The Sentimental Theater of the French Revolution* (CATRIN FRANCIS) . 514
Carolina Armenteros, *The French Idea of History: Joseph de Maistre and his Heirs, 1794–1854* (FRANCESCO MANZINI) 515
Mapping Memory in Nineteenth-Century French Literature and Culture, ed. by Susan Harrow and Andrew Watts (ANDREW J. COUNTER) 517
Daniel Sipe, *Text, Image, and the Problem with Perfection in Nineteenth-Century France: Utopia and its Afterlives* (GREG KERR) 518
Sonia Kruks, *Simone de Beauvoir and the Politics of Ambiguity* (CATHERINE RODGERS) 519
Carol Mavor, *Black and Blue: The Bruising Passion of 'Camera Lucida', 'La Jetée', 'Sans soleil', and 'Hiroshima mon amour'* (CATHERINE RODGERS) 520
Joseph Salmons, *A History of German: What the Past Reveals about Today's Language* (MARTIN DURRELL) 522
Georg Albert, *Innovative Schriftlichkeit in digitalen Texten: Syntaktische Variation und stilistische Differenzierung in Chat und Forum* (ALAN SCOTT) 523
Schreiben und Streichen: Zu einem Moment produktiver Negativität, ed. by Lucas Marco Gisi and others (ANDREAS KRAMER) 525
Heights of Reflection: Mountains in the German Imagination from the Middle Ages to the Twenty-First Century, ed. by Sean Ireton and Caroline Schaumann (THEODORE ZIOLKOWSKI) 526
Literarische Entdeckungsreisen: Vorfahren — Nachfahrten — Revisionen, ed. by Hansjörg Bay and Wolfgang Struck (DIRK GÖTTSCHE) 528
Popular Revenants: The German Gothic and its International Reception 1800–2000, ed. by Andrew Cusack and Barry Murnane (MICHAEL MINDEN) 531
Doerte Bischoff, *Poetischer Fetischismus: Der Kult der Dinge im 19. Jahrhundert* (FLORIAN KROBB) 532

Contents

Sarah Bowden, *Bridal-Quest Epics in Medieval Germany: A Revisionary Approach* (ANNETTE VOLFING)	534
'The Chronicle of Prussia' by Nicolaus von Jeroschin: A History of the Teutonic Knights in Prussia, 1190–1331, trans. by Mary Fischer (ALASTAIR MATTHEWS)	535
Handbuch kultureller Zentren der Frühen Neuzeit: Städte und Residenzen im alten deutschen Sprachraum, ed. by Wolfgang Adam and Siegrid Westphal (JOHN L. FLOOD)	537
Avi Lifschitz, *Language and Enlightenment: The Berlin Debates of the Eighteenth Century* (H. B. NISBET)	539
Gottlieb Wilhelm Rabener, *Briefwechsel und Gespräche*, ed. by E. Theodor Voss with Jan Müller (K. F. HILLIARD)	540
Jon Helgason, *Schriften des Herzens: Briefkultur des 18. Jahrhunderts im Briefwechsel zwischen Anna Louisa Karsch und Johann Wilhelm Ludwig Gleim*, trans. by Jana Mohnike (K. F. HILLIARD)	543
Karina Becker, *Der andere Goethe: Die literarischen Fragmente im Kontext des Gesamtwerks* (OSMAN DURRANI)	544
Who Is This Schiller Now? Essays on his Reception and Significance, ed. by Jeffrey L. High and others (OSMAN DURRANI)	545
German Women's Writing of the Eighteenth and Nineteenth Centuries: Future Directions in Feminist Criticism, ed. by Helen Fronius and Anna Richards (ROBERT GILLETT)	547
Mattias Pirholt, *Metamimesis: Imitation in Goethe's 'Wilhelm Meisters Lehrjahre' and Early German Romanticism* (MARTIN SWALES)	548
Roland Reuß, *'Im Freien?' Kleist-Versuche* (K. F. HILLIARD)	550
Johann Peter Hebel und die Moderne, ed. by Achim Aurnhammer and Hanna Klessinger (ROBERT GILLETT)	552
Sabine Becker, *Literatur im Jahrhundert des Auges: Realismus und Fotografie im bürgerlichen Zeitalter* (J. J. LONG)	554
The German Bestseller in the Late Nineteenth Century, ed. by Charlotte Woodford and Benedict Schofield (DIRK GÖTTSCHE)	555
Benedict Schofield, *Private Lives and Collective Destinies: Class, Nation and the Folk in the Works of Gustav Freytag* (FLORIAN KROBB)	556
Hillary Hope Herzog, *Vienna is Different: Jewish Writers in Austria from the 'fin de siècle' to the Present*; *Nexus: Essays in Jewish Studies*, vol. 1, ed. by William Collins Donahue and Martha B. Helfer (ANDREA REITER)	558
A Poet's Reich: Politics and Culture in the George Circle, ed. by Melissa S. Lane and Martin A. Ruehl (CHRISTOPHE FRICKER)	560
Lisa Marie Anderson, *German Expressionism and the Messianism of a Generation* (CAITRÍONA NÍ DHÚILL)	562
David Horton, *Thomas Mann in English: A Study in Literary Translation* (RITCHIE ROBERTSON)	563
Alan Corkhill, *Spaces for Happiness in the Twentieth-Century German Novel: Mann, Kafka, Hesse, Jünger* (INGO CORNILS)	565
Matthias Schuster, *Franz Kafkas Handschrift zum 'Schloss'* (RITCHIE ROBERTSON)	567
Kafka for the Twenty-First Century, ed. by Stanley Corngold and Ruth V. Gross (JULIAN PREECE)	568
Schriftsteller und Widerstand: Facetten und Probleme der inneren Emigration, ed. by Frank-Lothar Kroll and Rüdiger von Voss (WILLIAM J. DODD)	570
Brecht and the GDR: Politics, Culture, Posterity, ed. by Laura Bradley and Karen Leeder (IAN WALLACE)	571
Sara Jones, *Complicity, Censorship and Criticism: Negotiating Space in the GDR Literary Sphere* (KAREN LEEDER)	572

Verena Paul, *'Schreiben mit gespaltener Feder'*: *Peter Rühmkorfs ästhetisch-politisches Doppelengagement* (RÜDIGER GÖRNER)	574
Frauke Matthes, *Writing and Muslim Identity: Representations of Islam in German and English Transcultural Literature, 1990–2006* (TOM CHEESMAN)	575
The Concise CineGraph: Encyclopaedia of German Cinema, ed. by Hans-Michael Bock and Tim Bergfelder (ERICA CARTER)	577
The Many Faces of Weimar Cinema: Rediscovering Germany's Filmic Legacy, ed. by Christian Rogowski (ERICA CARTER)	579
Anna Kuxhausen, *From the Womb to the Body Politic: Raising the Nation in Enlightenment Russia* (URSULA STOHLER)	582
Taboo Pushkin: Topics, Texts, Interpretations, ed. by Alyssa Dinega Gillespie; Joe Peschio, *The Poetics of Impudence and Intimacy in the Age of Pushkin*; Svetlana Evdokimova, *Pushkin's Historical Imagination* (JAMES RANN)	584
Muireann Maguire, *Stalin's Ghosts: Gothic Themes in Early Soviet Literature* (ROGER COCKRELL)	586
Eric Laursen, *Toxic Voices: The Villain from Early Soviet Literature to Socialist Realism* (MAX ANLEY)	588
Abstracts of Articles, Vol. 109, Part 2 (April 2014)	590

PETRARCH'S *DE VITA SOLITARIA*: SAMUEL DANIEL'S TRANSLATION c. 1610

Most of Petrarch's life appears far from solitary. He was busy and famous from a young age: at thirty-seven, he was asked to be Poet Laureate by both the University of Paris and the Roman Senate, and accepted the latter. Nevertheless, within the tradition of his work in English translation, his most famous persona as a writer and thinker is to be found in the *Canzoniere*: the melancholic lover who bemoans his misfortune alone. Any consideration of English translations of Petrarch's work would rightly open with Chaucer, Wyatt, and Surrey's introduction of the sonnet form, developed later by the Elizabethans Sidney and Shakespeare.[1] However, reading Petrarch's Italian poetry alongside his work in Latin sheds another light on his interest in solitude. In several of his Latin works Petrarch presents a pleasant, rural solitary life, away from the city but comfortable and not at all isolated: this vision is especially clear in his *De vita solitaria*.[2]

In 1336 Petrarch climbed Mont Ventoux. In *Familiarum rerum libri* he observed that this moment was a turning point for his thought, but the solitude that he experienced there took longer to find full expression in his writing.[3] Ten years later, in Lent 1346, he completed the first draft of *De vita solitaria*, a long letter to his friend and patron Philippe de Cabassolles, Bishop of Cavaillon. Petrarch lived in his diocese while in exile from 1345 to 1346, and finally presented him with the treatise in 1366.[4]

The treatise is divided into two books. In the first, Petrarch contrasts the life of the *occupatus* (busy man) with that of the *solitarius* (solitary man) and deliberates on contemporary morals in Italy, before advocating the superiority of solitary life. In the second book he writes an 'encyclopaedia of solitude', describing the lives of solitary men and women drawn from classical, mytholo-

---

[1] Francesco Petrarca, *Canzoniere*, ed. by Marco Santagata (Milan: Mondadori, 1996); *Canzoniere*, trans. by Anthony Mortimer (London: Penguin, 2002); see e.g. Anthony Mortimer, *Petrarch's 'Canzoniere' in the English Renaissance* (Amsterdam: Rodopi, 2005). Patricia Thomson, 'Sonnet 15 of Samuel Daniel's *Delia*: A Petrarchan Imitation', *Comparative Literature*, 17 (1965), 151–57, comments on Daniel's response to the *Canzoniere*.

[2] All references to *De vita solitaria* are to Petrarch, *Prose*, ed. by Guido Martellotti and others (Milan: Ricciardi, 1955), pp. 285–591; all English translations, sometimes lightly adapted, are from *The Life of Solitude*, trans. by Jacob Zeitlin (Urbana: University of Illinois Press, 1924). Further references to Martellotti will be identified by the abbreviation P and to Zeitlin by the abbreviation LoS.

[3] In P, pp. 810–1025 (esp. pp. 830–32).

[4] B. L. Ullman, 'The Composition of Petrarch's *De vita solitaria* and the History of the Vatican Manuscript', in *Studies in the Italian Renaissance* (Rome: Edizioni di Storia e Letteratura, 1955), pp. 139–80 (p. 153).

gical, biblical, and hagiographical traditions.[5] He also discusses the practices of non-Christian solitaries. These solitary lives allow Petrarch to create a vision of a studious solitude, 'densely populated' with friends.[6] As Brian Vickers notes: 'his diatribe is really directed not against the human race but against all the dirt, noise and corruption of city life. Nor is solitude to be taken literally, for he envisages his retreat to peace and quiet being accompanied by some sympathetic friends and well supplied with books.'[7]

De vita solitaria enjoyed success throughout Europe in the fourteenth and fifteenth centuries. Today, it survives in 120 manuscripts—the largest number of any of Petrarch's works, along with *De remediis utriusque fortunae*—and it was printed in nine early modern editions, including three as a single text.[8] Spanish and Italian translations appeared in the fifteenth century,

An English version was slow to come, but nevertheless, *The Prayse of Private Life* has been dated around 1610, and seems likely to be the work of Samuel Daniel, who presented it to Margaret Clifford, Countess Dowager of Cumberland. We know this from a contemporary manuscript, and a title leaf in private ownership.[9] This manuscript appears to be the one that Lady Cumberland's daughter, Lady Anne Clifford, read in 1619, and which William Ford transcribed in 1810.[10] The title leaf comes from another source. The relationship between the two items is uncertain: one may have been copied from the other, or both from a third (now missing) source, or all from separate sources.[11] What is clear is that at least two copies of this text circulated in the seventeenth century. Despite its being attributed to Harington in 1930, their evidence suggests that Samuel Daniel is the probable author.[12]

Daniel's perspective differs markedly from Petrarch's. For Daniel, solitude

---

[5] Armando Maggi, '"You Will Be my Solitude": Solitude as Prophecy (*De vita solitaria*)', in *Petrarch: A Critical Guide to the Complete Works*, ed. by Victoria Kirkham and Armando Maggi (Chicago: University of Chicago Press, 2009), pp. 179-195 (p. 187).

[6] Ibid., p. 180.

[7] 'Leisure and Idleness in the Renaissance: The Ambivalence of *Otium*', *Renaissance Studies*, 4 (1990), 1-37, 107-54 (p. 111).

[8] Maggi, 'You Will Be my Solitude', p. 180; on the editions see *LoS*, pp. 16-17.

[9] Kendal Record Office WD/Hoth/A988/21 and the Pitcher leaf.

[10] All references are to *The Letters and Epigrams of Sir John Harington together with 'The Prayse of Private Life'*, ed. by Norman Egbert McClure (Philadelphia: University of Pennsylvania Press, 1930); McClure edits Ford's transcript, BL Add. MS 30161. There are a few lines missing from the start of Book II in Kendal Record Office WD/Hoth/A988/21 that are present in Ford's transcript. See John Pitcher, 'Margaret, Countess of Cumberland's *Prayse of Private Life*, Presented by Samuel Daniel', in *In the Prayse of Writing: Early Modern Manuscript Studies*, ed. by Susan P. Cerasano and Steven May (London: British Library, 2012), pp. 114-44, for a detailed examination of the manuscripts; pp. 119-25 on Kendal Record Office WD/Hoth/A988/21; pp. 127-33 on Ford's transcript; and pp. 125-27 on the Pitcher leaf.

[11] Pitcher, 'Margaret, Countess of Cumberland's *Prayse of Private Life*', pp. 126-27.

[12] See ibid., pp. 115-16, for a summary of debate, and pp. 138-40 for a new argument for Samuel Daniel's authorship. *The Prayse of Private Life* has not been published with an attribution to Daniel; for practical purposes, I quote from McClure's edition, identified by the abbreviation *LESJH*.

does not lead to a pleasurable life, but permits it to be endured; furthermore, being solitary means living alone, without any company, and the pleasure of study is reduced in importance. *The Prayse of Private Life* opens with comparisons of the solitary and busy life, written in a Horatian manner. Daniel translates this part of *De vita solitaria* closely; indeed, he was sufficiently drawn to this sequence to add a chapter to it (his Chapter 28, discussed below). However, towards the end of Book I and especially in his final chapter, he presents his own definition of the solitary life with increasing clarity. Daniel suggests that a Christian can live most appropriately (and is least likely to sin) by acknowledging that everyone is alone in this world. He or she should therefore spend the brief time allotted there thinking upon death and the eternal life that may ensue in heaven. Solitude is the only way of avoiding worldly vanities.

However, *The Prayse of Private Life* is most distinct from Petrarch in *De vita solitaria* through Daniel's adaptation of Book II, which comprises eighteen chapters, in comparison with fifty-two in the original. Daniel supports his advice to meditate upon eternal life with a host of classical and mythological exemplary figures, although he introduces the book with a chapter containing a handful of biblical personae. He proposes ancient figures as models for present-day readers to contemplate. His Book II is concise: by removing Petrarch's examples from early and medieval Christian traditions as well as from other religions, *The Prayse of Private Life* suggests that solitude is principally a classical idea. This emphasis complements contemporary work such as that of Montaigne, translated into English by Daniel's teacher, John Florio. It is 'likely that Daniel learns both French and Italian' in Oxford with Florio, who would later become Daniel's brother-in-law; Frances Yates suggests that Daniel 'surveyed the work with admiration'.[13] Daniel's interest in Petrarch thus far exceeds the most frequent use to which Petrarch's work was put in early modern England: his sonnets were a 'favoured source' for translation exercises into English in the early modern period.[14]

However, this use of Petrarch's work may offer a clue as to why Daniel translated this text: of his famous *Epistles* of 1603, he dedicates two to Lady Cumberland and her daughter, Lady Anne Clifford; two further epistles are sent to Lucy, Countess of Bedford and Henry Wriothesley, Earl of Southampton, both of whom also learnt Italian with Florio.[15] The court's burgeoning interest in learning Italian, frequently tutored by Florio, suggests that interest in Petrarch was growing; an increased desire to read his Latin works would have been

---

[13] Jason Lawrence, '*Who the Devil taught thee so much Italian?' Italian Language Learning and Literary Imitation in Early Modern England* (Manchester: Manchester University Press, 2005), p. 10; Frances Yates, *John Florio: The Life of an Italian in Shakespeare's England* (Cambridge: Cambridge University Press, 1934), p. 222.

[14] Lawrence, '*Who the Devil taught thee so much Italian?*', p. 30; pp. 32–36 on translations of Petrarch's Italian as language-learning exercises.

[15] Ibid., p. 8.

a natural development.[16] It is most likely that Lady Cumberland—who did not know other languages, according to her daughter—asked Daniel, Florio's former pupil, to put one of Petrarch's most popular Latin treatises into English, perhaps after having heard about it from him.[17] After all, Daniel's own knowledge of Latin was excellent; he did not need a translation to read Petrarch.

None the less, Daniel was not the first to begin the work of putting *De vita solitaria* into English. In 1577 Roger Baynes translated and paraphrased a few short passages from it in *The Praise of Solitarinesse*.[18] This work cannot be said to constitute a translation: it is a Platonic dialogue set on a Venetian gondola, both generically and structurally distinct from *De vita solitaria*. In the first two-thirds of Baynes's text the characters discuss the nature of virtue, principally quoting Plato. Only in the final third of the dialogue does Baynes begin to use *De vita solitaria*, in a discussion of how conducive solitary and busy lives are to virtue. Baynes translates a comparison between the two ways of life, frequently has his characters quote *sententiae* found in *De vita solitaria*, and paraphrases a selection of Petrarch's classical solitary lives.[19] No full, accurate English translation of *De vita solitaria* appeared until 1924.[20]

From these brief observations, it is clear that Daniel and Baynes were interested in the same moments in *De vita solitaria*—the comparative lives of the *occupatus* and the *solitarius*, and the classical figures who led solitary existences. Although Daniel does not follow Baynes's translations, he might have sought out *De vita solitaria* on the strength of *The Praise of Solitarinesse*. This article offers detailed assessment of Daniel's translation practices: the first part studies his translation of *De vita solitaria* as a whole; the second examines his translation patterns at closer hand through analysis of selected chapters.

How Samuel Daniel Translates 'De vita solitaria'

A brief examination of the two texts demonstrates how far Daniel recast the treatise in his draft for his Puritan patron, Margaret, Countess of

[16] See ibid., pp. 40–41, on Daniel's translations of Petrarch's sonnets.

[17] Lady Anne Clifford, *Lives of Lady Anne Clifford, Countess of Dorset, Pembroke and Montgomery (1590–1676) and of her Parents Summarized by Herself*, ed. by J. P. Gilson (London: Roxburghe Club, 1916), p. 19.

[18] Baynes, *The Praise of Solitarinesse* (London: Coldocke and Bynneman, 1577). See *LoS*, p. 17, for a brief summary of the translation history. See Andrés Navarro Lázaro, 'El primer humanism romanceado: la traduccíon castellana del *De vita solitaria* de F. Petrarca', in *Líneas Actuales de Investigacíon Literaria*, ed. by Verónice Arenas Lozano and others (Valencia: Universitat de València, 2004), pp. 281–90; for Tito Vespasiano Strozzi's fifteenth-century Italian translation see *La vita solitaria di Francesco Petrarca: volgarizzamento inedito del secolo XV*, ed. by Antonio Ceruti (Bologna: Romagnoli, 1879).

[19] *The Praise of Solitarinesse*, comparison, pp. 54–56; quotations from e.g. Terence, p. 74; solitary lives, pp. 66–68, 70–74.

[20] This is *The Life of Solitude*, trans. by Jacob Zeitlin.

Cumberland.²¹ He adds Latin *sententiae* while simplifying the variety of Petrarch's reference. He removes Petrarch's biographical context and many of his anecdotes; Daniel thus presents solitude as a moral way of life.

The most noticeable innovation in Book I complements Daniel's focus on classical lives in Book II, which I discuss below: here he adds Latin *sententiae* to the ends of chapters.²² At least seventeen out of the thirty-three *sententiae* which he adds to the chapters of Book I are drawn from Seneca, and three further ones are from Cicero, another writer who influenced the neo-Stoics. In changing the original like this, Daniel situates his translation within a popular trend in early modern England: most memorably, Francis Bacon's father Nicholas had Senecan—and other—quotations stencilled around the Great Hall at Gorhambury.²³ He equally places the thought of *De vita solitaria* within Senecan traditions. In *The Prayse of Private Life* Daniel finishes Book I's chapters with *sententiae* in three ways: first, by simply adding the *sententia* to the end of Petrarch's chapter, sometimes with a translation, as in Chapters 2, 4, 5, 6, 9, 12, 13, 15, 18, 27, and 29. Second, he replaces Petrarch's ending, either with a short translation or else with a sentence or two to introduce the *sententia*, e.g. in Chapters 3, 7, 8, 9, 11, 16, 17, 21, 24, 25, 30, and 32. Third, he reduces Petrarch's chapter significantly, as in Chapters 10, 14, 19, 20, 22, 23, and 26; Daniel ends his Chapter 22, the most pronounced example, with a quotation from Seneca taken from the middle of Petrarch's chapter. In Chapter 13 he reuses a quotation that had occurred early in Petrarch's chapter. Chapter 28—the chapter he wrote imitating Petrarch—and Chapter 33, modelled along neo-Stoic lines, also end with *sententiae*, as do Chapters 4 and 16 of Book II. The unfinished Chapter 31 suggests that *sententiae* were important to Daniel's methods of composition: it is structured around a list of *sententiae* with short notes; perhaps he had intended to reflect more upon their implications. The decision to add *sententiae* is an important one: Seneca is the central classical thinker within early modern traditions of Christian neo-Stoicism, which clustered initially around Justus Lipsius; in 1600s England Florio's Montaigne circulates, which also draws on this tradition (as well as many others). By highlighting this classical writer, whose presence signals a significant body of contemporary response, Daniel enabled his reader to locate Petrarch's arguments within this intellectual trend. He emphasized the strands of Petrarch's translation which would appeal to his patron; both Lady Cumberland and her

---

²¹ Richard T. Spence, 'Clifford, Margaret, Countess of Cumberland (1560–1616)', in *Oxford Dictionary of National Biography*, online edition (Oxford: Oxford University Press, 2004) <http://www.oxforddnb.com/> [accessed 9 August 2013]. Further references are identified by the abbreviation *ODNB*.

²² Michael Wyatt, 'Other Petrarchs in Early Modern England', in *Petrarch in Britain: Interpreters, Imitators and Translators over 700 Years*, ed. by Martin McLaughlin and Letizia Panizza (Oxford: Oxford University Press, 2007), pp. 203–16 (p. 214).

²³ Robert Tittler, 'Bacon, Sir Nicholas (1510–1579)', in *ODNB*.

daughter Lady Anne Clifford would have been familiar with Seneca's works, a copy of which rests under Lady Anne's right hand in *The Great Picture*.[24] By doing this, he also begins to place Petrarch's vernacular work in a neo-Stoic light: through the *sententiae*, *De vita solitaria* is principally underpinned by Stoic philosophy, but Daniel equally includes an Italian *sententia* from the *Canzoniere* and another from elsewhere in *De vita solitaria*.[25] The introduction of such maxims for moral reflection places Daniel's consideration of solitude clearly within long traditions of Stoic thought. Because these general maxims are quoted principally from classical authors, and always finish chapters, they imbue examples given elsewhere in the treatise with a degree of authority. They summarize the knowledge that the reader has gained and thus remind him or her of what has been learnt.

Because the treatise's messages are supported by such maxims, Daniel suggests that such moral suggestions might be of use in many situations, including for the reader. This implication is compounded because he removes the first person when it is clearly identifiable as Petrarch, as well as references to Petrarch's dedicatee and reader, Philippe de Cabassolles. The most important excisions from Book I to this end are the Prologue (*P*, pp. 286–94; *LoS*, pp. 97–102) and 1st Tractate, Chapters 1 and 2 (*P*, pp. 296–98; *LoS*, pp. 105–07), both of which address his dedicatee directly. Daniel also cuts 5th Tractate, Chapter 1 (*P*, pp. 362–66; *LoS*, pp. 154–57) from Book I, in which Petrarch discusses Quintilian's views on solitude and offers the reader advice. In Book II, two principal excisions remove Petrarch's epistolary context. The most important is perhaps 10th Tractate, Chapters 1 and 2 (*P*, pp. 558–68; *LoS*, pp. 293–300; between Chapters 10 and 11 in Daniel), in which Petrarch persuades his dedicatee to solitude and discusses his friends, before describing his ideal conditions for solitude. Daniel also cuts 10th Tractate, Chapter 9 (*P*, pp. 586–90; *LoS*, pp. 314–16), in which Petrarch commends solitude and concludes.

Daniel's removal of the personal narrator does not stop there. He removes personal anecdotes throughout, especially Petrarch's opinions and brief appeals to his dedicatee.[26] The treatise's original context is hidden. Although

---

[24] *The Great Picture*, by Jan van Belcamp (1650, Abbot Hall, Kendal; centre panel: 254×254 cm; side panels: 254×119.38 cm).

[25] The endings of Chapters 4 and 6: 'Un bel muorire tutta la vita honora' (*Canzoniere*, ed. by Satagata, poem 207) and 'Deo servire, libertas est' (*P*, p. 568).

[26] Similar excisions of personal addresses occur throughout Book I, for example: in Chapter 11 Petrarch's comment on how he has refrained from satire becomes a general comment on behaviour apt for satire (3rd Tractate, Chapter 2, *P*, p. 324; *LoS*, p. 126); between Chapters 12 and 13 Daniel removes 3rd Tractate, Chapter 4, on the dangers of the busy life and why the writer has chosen the retired life (*P*, pp. 326–28; *LoS*, pp. 129–30); in Chapter 13 Daniel removes the writer-persona's assertion that he will not stray from his argument for too long at the beginning of the 4th Tractate (*P*, pp. 328–30; *LoS*, p. 131); between Chapters 17 and 18 Daniel removes the end of 4th Tractate, Chapter 5 (*P*, p. 342; *LoS*, p. 140), when Petrarch justifies his digression on Plotinus, and opens the next chapter with a joke with the addressee; in the middle of Chapter 19 Daniel removes the moment

Daniel often preserves the second person, he addresses a general reader. For example, Petrarch's Book I, 3rd Tractate, Chapter 1 begins:

En, pater, unius occupati et unius otiosi hominis unum diem ante oculos tuos posui. (*P*, p. 318)

Behold, father, I have placed before your view a single day of an individual man of action and an individual man of leisure. (*LoS*, p. 122)

In his Chapter 10 Daniel rewrites:

Hetherto we have described, as well the busie as the Solitarie Man: beholde them seriously, and by consideringe their contrarie qualities, you may conceive how all Men live. (*LESJH*, p. 335)

In taking away Petrarch's addressee, Daniel removes the most animated narratorial moments in *De vita solitaria*. However, he does preserve the first person of *De vita solitaria*'s opening, which does not reveal much about the narrator:[27]

Certenly I thinke, that everie Christian vertuously resolved (and by age overtaken) ought not ymploy himselfe in other affaires then suche as concerne his owne soule and the Service of God, who is the ende of all. (*LESJH*, p. 325)

Equally, in Chapters 14 and 23 he preserves much of Petrarch's first-person narrative. In both of these chapters Petrarch's 'I' remains relatively impersonal, his observations read as precepts. Daniel usually uses the first person to advance or nuance the argument. His solitude is ascetic; anecdotes, conversation, and friendship are less important to his vision of solitude than the universal status of being alone in the world, preparing for death. Daniel especially stresses the universal need to extinguish desire, which ultimately means rejecting not just town life, but all life: 'Noe life at all is desiderable and all that this world promiseth is meere deceipte and troomperie' (*LESJH*, p. 360). Whereas Petrarch presents his philosophy as—in part—based on his

in 4th Tractate, Chapter 8, when Petrarch decides to 'figere hic animum [...] et cogitare' ('arrest the current of my thought at this point and reflect') (*P*, pp. 350–52; *LoS*, p. 146).

[27] Minor examples of deictic 'I' in Book I include: in Chapter 10, 'This onely I add' (*LESJH*, p. 335); in Chapter 11, 'Notwithstandinge I suppose a few examples' (*LESJH*, p. 337), 'Well I knowe', 'yet I feare', 'I doe also so thinke', 'I mislike not reasons wittily framed', 'I commende', 'I forget not', 'I suppose', 'I certenly thinke' (*LESJH*, p. 338); in Chapter 13, 'I exhort not' (*LESJH*, p. 339); in Chapter 15, 'I woulde wishe' (*LESJH*, p. 341); in Chapter 16, 'Albeit I have heretofore commended Solitude, yet will I add' (*LESJH*, p. 341); in Chapter 17, 'Where they are I know not' (*LESJH*, p. 342); in Chapter 20, 'I meane' (*LESJH*, p. 344); in Chapter 21, 'We reade that' (*LESJH*, p. 346); in Chapter 25, 'Surely as ofte as I have heard the question propounded, rarely did I see' (*LESJH*, p. 350); in Chapter 32, 'I saye that' (*LESJH*, p. 358), 'I finde', 'I wishe thoughe hope thereof I can no more' (*LESJH*, p. 360), 'whereof I have discoursed'. The same is true for the second-person pronoun, e.g. in Chapter 30: 'But happily you aske to what purpose we neede be troubled?' (*LESJH*, p. 355).

own experience, Daniel's generalizing tendencies imply that his treatise could well be relevant to the reader's own way of living.

Daniel removes many of Petrarch's anecdotes where he is unhappy with the views they imply. Given that life is not to be desired, he removes many of Petrarch's anecdotes about life in society, both drawn from elsewhere and culled from his own experience. For example, Daniel sometimes does not translate sources of quotations, and he preserves stages in Petrarch's arguments as brief illustrations:

neque soli avaritie convenit illud satyricum: *dives qui fieri vult, et cito vult fieri*. Habet hoc comune cupiditas indivisumque cum sororibus suis ira et libidine que, patre conceptuque tartareo edite, confusionem et precipitium et horrorem et naturam proprie originis non dediscunt. (*P*, p. 312)

The observation of the satirist, that whoever wants to become rich wants to do so suddenly, does not apply to avarice alone. This is a trait, which Cupidity shares equally with her sisters, Wrath and Licentiousness, who being begot in hell of an infernal father have not unlearned the confusion and rashness and horror which were the nature of their own origin. (*LoS*, p. 117)

He removes the quotation from Juvenal to translate as follows:[28]

Which is the cause that he whoe desireth to be riche quickly is ever angrie: for noe vice can suffer restraint, because temeritie is joyned to precipitacion. (*LESJH*, p. 333)

Daniel often reworks longer quotations, explanations, and sources.[29] As above, he sometimes abridges—or alters—Petrarch's extended metaphors. In Daniel's Chapter 6, Petrarch's remarks on the *solitarius* at midday (*P*, pp. 312–14; *LoS*, p. 118) are transformed into observations highlighting the solitary man's continual meditation on death:

Nec ita multo post labentem celo diem seque simul collabentem humi cogitans, tetramque caliginem illabentem terris previdens, superni luminis poscit auxilium. Et seu

---

[28] *Juvenal and Persius*, ed. and trans. by Susannah Morton Braund (Cambridge, MA: Harvard University Press, 2004), Satire XIV. 176.

[29] Examples of this treatment in Book I include the following: in Chapter 10 Daniel removes Petrarch's explanation of the consequences of being employed by other men, quoting Virgil (3rd Tractate, Chapter 1, *P*, p. 318; *LoS*, p. 123); in Chapter 14 Daniel also removes a long quotation of Quintilian's advice (4th Tractate, Chapter 3, *P*, p. 336; *LoS*, p. 136); in Chapter 15 he loses the reference to Terence's *Adelphi* (4th Tractate, Chapter 2, *P*, pp. 332–34; *LoS*, p. 134); in Chapter 19 explanation of a quotation from Seneca is removed, though the quotation, and its consequences for the Christian, remain (4th Tractate, Chapter 8, *P*, p. 350; *LoS*, p. 146); in Chapter 23 an anecdote about the need for company even in study and Petrarch's consequent refusal to exclude studious friends from solitude are removed along with anecdotes on Tiberius and Servilius Vatia (5th Tractate, Chapter 4, pp. 374–78; *LoS*, pp. 163–65); in Chapter 24 a second quotation from Virgil is cut as well as Petrarch's analysis of it (5th Tractate, Chapter 5, *P*, p. 378; *LoS*, p. 166); in Chapter 26 Daniel preserves a quotation from Seneca but omits Petrarch's discussion of it—and its contrast with a real solitary man (6th Tractate, Chapter 2, *P*, p. 386; *LoS*, pp. 171–72)—and heavily paraphrases Petrarch's discussion of how Quintilian's advice to imitate is used (6th Tractate, Chapter 2, *P*, pp. 386–88; *LoS*, pp. 172–73).

ne mens suorum criminum pressa ponderibus celo exulet, cum lacrimis precatur, seu fidei puram lucem, seu mentis aduste refrigerium, abstersionem sordide, elise sustentaculum, litigiose pacem flagitat, matutinoque laudum carmini vespertinas preces et laudes de inexhausto pietatis fonte continuat. (P, pp. 312–14)

And so, soon after, as he contemplates the sinking of the sun and imagines himself also declining towards the ground, anticipating descent of black darkness upon the earth, he supplicates the aid of the supernal light. And whether he begs with tears that his spirit may not be exiled from heaven for the weight of its offences or that he may be granted the pure light of faith, that his burning passions may be cooled, his vile thoughts cleansed, his wavering mind supported and its contentions pacified, he still prolongs his morning chants with evening prayers and praises from the inexhaustible fount of his piety. (LoS, p. 118)

There is no clock for Daniel's solitary man:

Contrariwise the solitarie man doth all thinges with deliberacion, never forgettinge such circumstances as appertaine to everie accion, and *cheifely he liveth prepared for Death*: ever hopeing from the fountaine of Gods inexhausted mercie, to be comforted. (LESJH, p. 333, emphasis added)

Petrarch's delight in solitude is shed in favour of a solitary life lived in the full awareness of the imperfect nature of this world.[30] Daniel's treatise does not delight in showing the sins of city life—or even the pleasure of company—but rather touches upon these in order to focus on the honest, austere, and solitary alternative.

Moreover, Daniel removes all of Petrarch's topical references, which further shapes the moral bent of the treatise. He concentrates the reader's attention on the central question of how to live, without digressions which remain specific to Petrarch's time.[31] His treatment of Book I, 6th Tractate, Chapter 3 illustrates this reduction. He keeps Petrarch's final general invective, but he

---

[30] Daniel's cuts to this line of reasoning include: between Chapters 17 and 18, a chapter on the life celestial on earth, that praises the inner nature of the life of solitude, engaged in a battle for Christ, which does not fit with Daniel's view that anything like heaven can be reached on earth (4th Tractate, Chapter 6, P, pp. 342–46; LoS, pp. 140–43); in Chapter 18, Petrarch's praise of the freedom of the ethereal city and of the short time it takes to reach the city of God (4th Tractate, Chapter 7, P, p. 346; LoS, pp. 143–44); and in Chapter 30, Petrarch's discussion of a real solitary man (6th Tractate, Chapter 5, P, p. 398; LoS, pp. 180–81). Abridgements to this effect include the following: in Chapter 18 Daniel abridges Petrarch's list of reflections once in heaven (4th Tractate, Chapter 7, P, pp. 346–48; LoS, p. 144); in the same chapter he removes the passages on the angel's gaze and the person so mad as to abandon himself in the presence of a friend of Christ (4th Tractate, Chapter 8, P, pp. 350–52; LoS, pp. 146–47); in Chapter 20 Petrarch's list of each season's pleasures is summarized (4th Tractate, Chapter 9, P, p. 354; LoS, p. 149); and in Chapter 23 Petrarch's discussion of fair-weather friends is reduced to a pithy remark (5th Tractate, Chapter 4, P, p. 372; LoS, p. 162).

[31] His principal cuts to this end include: in Chapter 10, a comparison of contemporary Italians to the bitter Cretans (3rd Tractate, Chapter 1, P, p. 320; LoS, p. 124); in Chapter 21, a passage on the ancients' perverse belief in gods (4th Tractate, Chapter 10, P, p. 358; LoS, pp. 151–52); in Chapter 27, a discussion of the folly of youth copying the old (6th Tractate, Chapter 2, P, p. 390; LoS, pp. 174–75) and Petrarch's lament for the declining morals of Italy (6th Tractate, Chapter 3,

removes Petrarch's specific voice and extensive discussion of contemporary Italy:

> Private and solitarie life is free from such follies. Let us therefore exclayming saye, whether will you goe? What madnes maketh you so inclyned to change? Why treade you not the steppes of youre Forefathers? Why doe you ymitate the manners of your enemies, whom heretofore you subdued by armes, and nowe are conquered by theire vices? Retorne to the customes of your Auncestors, and laye aside those of strangers. Endevor to live honestly and contented with comelines. So shall you affecte one thinge and doe ever according to discretion and reason. *Ratio dux fida sophorum*. (*LESJH*, p. 353)

Petrarch's Italian nationalism could therefore now apply to any nation, including the English reader's own. *The Prayse of Private Life* presents a universally applicable moral guide, and Daniel thus invites reflection upon how these general principles might apply to a reader's own life.

At the same time, Daniel pares down the diversity of figures within Petrarch's Book II in order to present a classical perspective on solitude: this tradition forms the best part of Daniel's selection of historical solitary figures. In his Book II Petrarch retells saints' lives and those of contemporary religious men, as well as those of classical and biblical figures, to present an 'encyclopaedia of solitude'.[32] He highlights the diversity of reasons, both spiritual and worldly, for entering a solitary life and its many—usually positive—consequences. However, in *The Prayse of Private Life* Daniel removes many of these lives. Fifteen out of Book II's eighteen chapters are about classical statesmen and philosophers who used solitude as a place to write the works for which they would be remembered. Thinking about the afterlife is crucial to Daniel's idea of solitude. Although he abridges Petrarch's description of his desire to write for posterity, Daniel does highlight this idea through Book II's classical figures:

> [. . .] scribendo nostri memoriam posteris relinquere, atque ita dierum fugam sistere et hoc brevissimum vite tempus extendere. (*P*, p. 568)
>
> [. . .] through reflection and writing to leave our remembrance to posterity, and so

---

pp. 390-94; *LoS*, pp. 175-77); and in Chapter 32, Petrarch's lament for his youth, when governors issued a proclamation to abstain from crime when they entered provinces (6th Tractate, Chapter 6, *P*, p. 400; *LoS*, p. 181). In Book II these include: a rebuke that kings and princes have not entered the Holy Land to defend the Catholic faith (4th Tractate, Chapters 2 to 4, *P*, pp. 484-94; *LoS*, pp. 240-45); a comparison of Roman with present virtue (*P*, p. 494; *LoS*, pp. 246-47); a comparison of Mohammed and European princes (4th Tractate, Chapter 6, *P*, pp. 494-98; *LoS*, pp. 247-49); a denunciation of Catholic princes for neglecting their special concerns (4th Tractate, Chapter 7, *P*, p. 498; *LoS*, pp. 249-50); why not every country deserves to be fought for (4th Tractate, Chapter 8, *P*, pp. 498-502; *LoS*, pp. 250-52); and some contemporary non-Christian examples of solitude (6th Tractate, *P*, pp. 510-24; *LoS*, pp. 259-67).

[32] Maggi, 'You Will Be my Solitude', p. 187.

arrest the flight of the days and extend the all too brief duration of our life. (*LoS*, p. 301)

He abridges this in Book II, Chapter 15 to a simple description of why some people might try to 'write any thinge to be lefte unto Posteritie' (*LESJH*, pp. 375–76). Here, Daniel leaves the reasons why someone might do this obscure; his real response to Petrarch's argument here is found throughout his *Musophilus* (e.g. ll. 148–94).[33] In his introductory epistle to John Florio's translation of Montaigne's *Essais*, he equally shows his ambivalence towards writing for posterity: the overproduction of books is to be condemned, but some books are still worth reading.[34] The reader may draw upon this gallery of exemplary, solitary classical figures; solitude takes on a specifically classical, and even Stoic, heritage, which is particularly used by writers and those in the public eye.

The classical traditions of solitude are present too in *De vita solitaria*, but there, only twelve out of fifty-two chapters are about classical lives. Given the modern estimate that five folios are missing from the centre of the manuscript, Daniel probably used Petrarch's Book II, 2nd Tractate (*P*, pp. 418–30; *LoS*, pp. 195–202) as the basis for his Chapter 2, which lacks its opening few lines.[35] In both Petrarch and Daniel, this chapter describes the lives of Old Testament figures. I suggest that Daniel added a new introductory chapter, because he summarizes some of the lives Petrarch mentions earlier in his 1st, 2nd, and 3rd Tractates (*P*, pp. 406–80; *LoS*, pp. 187–236) as follows:

To these mighte wee add the Solytarie lives of *Elias, Hieremias, St. Augustine, St. Jerome, St. Barnard* and others. (*LESJH*, p. 365)

This introductory chapter to Book II, was probably roughly five to six hundred words long, occupying two folios.[36] In Ford's transcript, Book I's final sentence begins 'to conclude' and finishes with a *sententia*, consonant with his other chapters; it is unlikely that it continued further. Frustratingly, then, we can guess that Daniel did not copy Petrarch, but because of this loss, we do not know how he introduced his new Book II.

Daniel does retain some sense of the variety of Petrarch's lives, as he does in the example given above, by listing a number of modern solitary figures at the end of Book II, Chapter 13:

The memory of these noble Captaynes doth also occasion me to thinke of divers great

---

[33] Samuel Daniel, *Poems and 'A Defence of Ryme'*, ed. by Arthur Colby Sprague (Cambridge, MA: Harvard University Press, 1930).

[34] 'To my deere friend M. *John Florio*, concerning *his translation of* Montaigne', in Michel de Montaigne, *The Essays*, trans. by John Florio (London: Blount, 1603), available in facsimile (Menston: Scolar Press, 1969).

[35] Pitcher, 'Margaret, Countess of Cumberland's *Praise of Private Life*', pp. 121–22.

[36] Ibid., p. 121.

princes, whoe lothed with worldly delightes, and tyred in affayres of this life, retyred to Solytude: as Ramirus Kinge of Aragon, Verecundus Kinge of Spayne, Ludovicus, Kinge of Naples, Guglielmus Kinge of Pictes, Carolus magnus the sonne of Carolus Martellus, Lotharius and Lodovicus Kinges of Fraunce, Batilda a Quene of France, Amurat Kinge of Turkye, with many other Princes and great Personages of whome writers have at large discoursed. (*LESJH*, p. 374)

Nevertheless, this list gives so little information that it implies that these lives are not as useful to the reader as those he does translate: Homer, Seneca, Cicero, Demosthenes, Julius Caesar, Augustus Caesar, Diocletian, Numa, Romulus, and the Scipios. A possible model for this new, classical Book II, Plutarch's *Lives*, was available in Thomas North's English translation through four early modern editions (1575, 1579, 1595, 1603).[37] We know that Lady Anne Clifford, Lady Cumberland's formidably bright daughter and Daniel's pupil, had read it, because it is one of the books in her portrait, *The Great Picture*. On the wall in the left-hand panel hangs a portrait of Samuel Daniel, whom she associated with her own youthful learning. Lady Anne's mother— no less bright than her daughter—had most likely read Plutarch too. Daniel might have reworked *De vita solitaria* to present it in a form that his patron could readily understand: five of the lives Daniel presents are in Plutarch, and the others are all classical statesmen or writers, or both, who could be plausibly read in this context. Classical writers constitute Daniel's principal fund of exemplars, and Lady Cumberland knew them well in translated form; their importance in Daniel's thought—particularly in shaping this treatise for his patron—cannot be overestimated.

The Prayse of Private Life was not the only text that Daniel produced for Lady Cumberland. An extended conceit marks his *Epistle to the Lady Margaret, Countess of Cumberland*, written in 1603, comparing strength of character with that of a castle:

> He that of such a height hath built his minde,
> And rear'd the dwelling of his thoughts so strong
> [. . .]
> What a faire seate hath he from whence hee may
> The boundlesse wastes, and weilds of man suruay.
> (ll. 1–2, 10–11)

Later, Daniel describes the 'region of [her] selfe' 'that hath secur'd within brasen walls | Of a cleere conscience' (ll. 79–80), 'brasen' referring to the strength of brass. This image is suggestive for Lady Cumberland, who was embroiled in lawsuits and separated from her husband in 1600.[38] In Book I, Chapter 16 of *The Prayse of Private Life*, translated for the same person, Daniel

---

[37] Plutarch, *Lives*, trans. by John Dryden and rev. by A. H. Clough, 3 vols (London: Home Library, 1864), I, p. xxvi.

[38] Spence, 'Clifford, Margaret', in *ODNB*.

enlarges upon the image of Petrarch's 'arx munita' (*P*, pp. 338–40) ('fortified citadel' (*LoS*, pp. 137–39)), to give 'so that livinge securely, he inhabiteth a Castle inexpugnable' (*LESJH*, p. 341). 'Inexpugnable' has two meanings: first, it refers literally to a fortress which cannot be taken, and second, it refers figuratively to a person 'in reference to his principles or disposition: that cannot be overthrown or overcome'.[39] This phrase shows Daniel drawing on his earlier work for *The Prayse of Private Life*, perhaps as a form of shorthand for the same patron.

Daniel's version limits Petrarch's light-humoured life writing to fashion an ascetic solitude, drawing principally on classical models. Perhaps he recasts *De vita solitaria* in this way to emphasize Petrarch's role in rediscovering classical texts, or because he does not think the classical, biblical, and early Church traditions can be so easily reconciled. His presentation of the manuscript to the puritan Lady Cumberland is most appropriate: new evidence that she is Daniel's dedicatee illuminates his aims in translating.[40] Although the treatise does fit with Daniel's interest in Petrarch's work, witnessed in his *Defence of Ryme* and his *Delia* sonnets, the consonance between Daniel's text, combining Christianity with Stoic philosophy, and Lady Cumberland's outlook strongly suggests that he translated this treatise with her in mind. Her mother died when she was two; she separated from her husband, and both her sons died aged five; only her youngest child, Lady Anne Clifford, survived into adulthood.[41] In her Great Books, which are now lost but preserved in copies, Lady Anne remarked that her mother took the death of Robert, her second child, 'with an inexpressible deal of sorrow'.[42] Later, around the time of composition of *The Prayse of Private Life*, Lady Anne notes that her mother was consumed with 'doubt and fear' that her daughter would be disinherited. She therefore contested her husband's will, in which he left his estates to his brother, Francis Clifford.[43] It is clear that Lady Cumberland was unhappy at many times in her life, and sought solace in religion.

Lady Anne's observations suggest that Daniel's translation of Petrarch was very well judged. First, she claims that her mother did not know any other languages, and so was eager to read in translation.[44] Daniel's focus upon the best way to endure this life, and his strong sense of its ephemerality, is apt for the 'truly religious, devout and conscientious' Lady Cumberland, who was 'a contemner of riches', and who loved the 'country life [. . .] seasoned with the

[39] 'inexpugnable, *adj*', in *OED Online* (Oxford: Oxford University Press, 2004) <http://www.oed.com/> [accessed 12 August 2013].
[40] Pitcher, 'Margaret, Countess of Cumberland's *Prayse of Private Life*', pp. 138–40.
[41] Spence, *ODNB*; Clifford, *Lives*, p. 22.
[42] Clifford, *Lives*, p. 22.
[43] Ibid., p. 19; Spence, 'Clifford, Francis, fourth earl of Cumberland (1559–1641)', and 'Clifford, Margaret', in *ODNB*.
[44] Clifford, *Lives*, p. 19.

grounds of goodness and religion'.[45] This description is evidence that Daniel's emphasis on the most ascetic moments in *De vita solitaria*, which concentrate on eschewing wealth and the trappings of city life, to focus afresh on eternal life, was well suited for his pious patron, whose life was scarred by loss and litigation and who preferred to live in the countryside. We know that Lady Anne had read 'my lady's book in the praise of a solitary life', from her diary entry for 17 March 1619; it is perhaps worth speculating that it was in her mind when she described her mother's outlook.[46]

The Character of 'The Prayse of Private Life'

Close analysis of three chapters sheds further light on the character of Daniel's translation and his particular interest in *De vita solitaria*. I would like to examine three chapters which show Daniel's translation practices clearly: Book I, Chapter 5, which demonstrates his preoccupation with the moral implications of Petrarch's treatise; Book I, Chapter 28, which Daniel writes in the style of Petrarch's early Book I; and Book II, Chapter 7, which highlights the importance of abstaining from worldly pleasures.

Daniel largely translates the *occupatus*'s and the *solitarius*'s days in Book I closely. Nevertheless, he removes digressions and underlines Petrarch's moral implications.[47] In his Book I, Chapter 5, he amplifies Petrarch's stressful opening:

Turbant illum familiaris exercitus, hostesque collaterales, et ruina mensarum, et hominum vasorumque collisio; et ebriorium iocis tecta mugiunt, et querimoniis famescentum. (*P*, p. 310)

The busy man is distraught by the army of his hangers-on, hostile neighbours, the disorder of the tables, and the clatter of men and dishes. The roof groans with drunken jests and the complaints of hunger. (*LoS*, p. 115)

Petrarch's long Latin sentences allow him to jumble together guests arriving, dishes colliding, and tables being ruined. Daniel partly orders this chaos by breaking the sentence and putting some detail in apposition:

Dynner beinge done, the busied man is troubled by a multytude of *familiars, Sutors and Servantes, some frends and some Foes*. *Then* is he offended with *fallinge down of plate*, breakinge of Tables, or *some other part of his furniture*: or haply disturbed by crynge out of some drunkard. (*LESJH*, p. 332, emphasis added)

[45] Ibid.
[46] Lady Anne Clifford, *The Memoir of 1603 and the Diary of 1616–1619*, ed. by Katherine Acheson (Peterborough, ON: Broadview, 2007), p. 163. See Pitcher, 'Margaret, Countess of Cumberland's *Prayse of Private Life*', p. 134, on Lady Anne's reading and the relation between 'private' and 'solitary'.
[47] See also Wyatt's analysis of Chapter 4, 'Other Petrarchs in Early Modern England', pp. 212–15.

Piling up the clauses is important to portraying the *occupatus*'s hectic life. By introducing superficial chronological order, Daniel catches the hurried Latin well. The complaints of hunger are lost, but Daniel increases the chaos through a second tripartite list, adding 'or some other part of his furniture'. The imprecise panic of these details compensates for the pandemonium of Petrarch's sentence.

As he sometimes does elsewhere, Daniel preserves the content but not the sources of his quotations:

[...] *ut verbo utar Ambrosii*, non coquinam sed carnificinam dicas. (*P*, p. 310, emphasis added)

[...] to use the expression of Ambrose, one might call it a slaughter-house rather than a kitchen. (*LoS*, p. 116)

He omits Petrarch's reference to Ambrose, the early Church Father, but keeps his image:

So may the dyninge place be most truely called a slaughter house, then a Hall of civill metinge. (*LESJH*, p. 332)

He also sheds Petrarch's digression on 'prandium, quasi parandium', which leads to an ironic conceit of the dining hall as battleground:

Et licet, ut maioribus placet, a parando prandium, quasi parandium, dictum sit, quod bellatores ad prelium paret, non parari tamen aliquid, sed fieri, vereque prelium ibi gestum putes esse, non prandium. Ita dux saucius ac tremens, ita mero percussi omnes nutantesque abeunt; mensa pro acie fuerit, pro blando et fallaci hoste voluptas, cubilia pro sepulchris, conscientia pro inferno. (*P*, p. 310)

It may be, as the ancients say, that this early meal got its name because it was eaten by the warriors in preparation for battle; in this case, however, it was not a preparation but a complete action. Indeed one might imagine a genuine battle there instead of a meal. The chieftain is wounded and tottering, and the whole army, overcome with drink, goes staggering away. The table is the line of battle, pleasure is the smooth and treacherous enemy, the couches are the tombs, and conscience takes the place of hell. (*LoS*, p. 116)

Daniel suggests instead that the revellers may feel pangs of remorse when they leave lunch:

The Compaine thus filled with aboundance of meate, and Drinke, or *loathed* with sight or sente of a fowle Howse, they departe to their Chambers, bearing about them a surcharged Stomacke, and *perhapps a troubled conscience also*. (*LESJH*, p. 332, emphasis added)

For Daniel, the possible troubled conscience is the dinner's most important consequence. He replaces *De vita solitaria*'s hyperbole with a narrative of the meal's aftermath, which ends in disgust—perhaps even on the part of the busy men themselves—at such decadence. At this juncture, Daniel turns to the *solitarius*.

Daniel draws out the moral cast of the solitary life throughout his translation. For instance, Petrarch describes the *solitarius*'s dwelling as an index of his character:

[. . .] angelorum aula conviviis quam hominum aptior, *odor colorque optimus*, index morum testisque modestie. (*P*, p. 310, emphasis added)

[. . .] his house is better suited for the feasts of angels than of men. Its sweet odour and colour are the best index of his manners and witness of refinement. (*LoS*, p. 116)

By contrast, Daniel examines those *mores* in relation to the *solitarius*'s person. Petrarch's epithets for the house are transferred to the *solitarius*'s body:

Far otherwise is yt with the solitarie Man who beinge a companion more meete for Angells then riotouse Men, appeareth with a *sweete breath* and *good complexion*. (*LESJH*, p. 332, emphasis added)

He adds details to Petrarch's description of the solitary man's house that focus on the *solitarius*'s temper: 'his conversation sober'. The rest of his description of the *solitarius* is translated closely. Daniel removes its end, however, 'conscientia paradisus' ('conscience is a paradise'), perhaps because it parallels the end of Petrarch's earlier conceit, which Daniel also removes: 'conscientia pro inferno' ('conscience takes the place of hell'). Daniel makes the *solitarius* even more perfect by omitting Petrarch's final caveat that 'et necessariam quietem et honesta solatia nichil aut modicum perit' ('no time, or else only a moderate amount of the day, goes for needful repose and innocent recreation'). He intensifies the contrast by emphasizing the *solitarius*'s morality.

Finally, Daniel adds a new English ending and takes part of a *sententia* from Seneca's *De vita beata*: 'contentus amicusque rebus suis'.[48] He thus places the passage explicitly in relation to Senecan thought:

Content he is with his owne, and *more doth not desire. Contentus rebus suis, certissime divitiae*. (*LESJH*, p. 333, emphasis added [Latin italic in the original])

This new emphasis on freedom from desire—and even hope—contributes to Daniel's line of reasoning that all life, not just town life, must be endured.

When Daniel imitates Petrarch's sequence of the daily routine of the *occupatus* and the *solitarius* (*P*, pp. 298–319; *LoS*, pp. 107–20), he aims his satire at worldly mutability. Book I, Chapter 28 (*LESJH*, pp. 353–54) reads as if it were translated from Petrarch. It shares most with Book I, Chapter 5 because

---

[48] 'Reconciled to his circumstances': Seneca, *De vita beata*, 6. 2, in *Moral Essays*, trans. by John W. Basore, 3 vols (Cambridge, MA: Harvard University Press, 1932), II, 114.

it is about the practice of visiting and dining. Daniel imitates the speech of the busy man's world in his prose, as well as explaining the origins of a proverb, paralleling the digression on Ambrose that he removes from Book 1, Chapter 5. He hints at a completely solitary life here, perhaps satirizing Petrarch's comradely solitude.

In this passage the world is changeable. 'Distemper' permeates the unsatisfying life of the *occupatus*. Daniel warns explicitly of the effects of hosting lunches, which 'do worke a contrarie effecte and are the cause eyther of unkinde conceite or quarrel'; Petrarch only hints at the negative effects of such events. Both host and visitor are dissatisfied, as in Chapter 5, when the party leaves the meal with 'perhapps a troubled conscience'.

However, dissatisfaction is only a symptom of deceit:

Theise externall demonstracions of kindnes, hapely well intended, causeth an unkinde evente. (*LESJH*, p. 354)

Daniel extends this reasoning to 'convitacion and Feastes'. Again, he emphasizes the displeasure everyone feels in *De vita solitaria*, omitting Petrarch's description of the event itself, in his 1st Tractate, Chapter 4:

For rarely or never are all the geastes well pleased, or the Ost that did convite them, well satisfied: the one because they like not their cheare, companie, or places and the other feareth to receive no hartie thankes. For one thinketh he was faintly wellcomed, an other he was placed beneath his inferior. One sayth the Oast never saluted him, an other he never druncke to him, an other he sate not at ease, and other he liked not the meate, an other dispraiseth the Coockerie, an other findes faulte with the Wyne, some had not theire fill, some were sicke of over muche eating, and finally neyther the Oste honored as he aspected, not the guestes well pleased. (*LESJH*, p. 354)

His list, using the 'hic ... hic ...' construction, conveys the sound of moaning gossip, where everyone chips in.[49] Polyglossic dialogue is put into prose.

By contrast, the *solitarius* in this passage really is alone. The *solitarius* 'seeketh no bodie, and shooneth occasion to be sought, unlesse urgent occasion do so require. For idle visitacions are true markes of flatterie' (*LESJH*, p. 354). In this way, Daniel suggests that being alone is essential for avoiding over-indulgence and its more serious corollary, spiritual malaise arising from

---

[49] McClure highlights this passage's similarity to Harington's Epigrams 116 and 137, both entitled 'Against Feasting' (*LESJH*, p. 430, note to cap. 28). However, Harington's 'tis to see thee so mad | To spoile the skies of Fowles, the seas of fishes | The land of beastes' (*LESJH*, p. 193) in 116 and 'forty diuers dishes | Of Sallets, and of flesh & fowles and fishes, | With which (God knowes) I little am delighted' (*LESJH*, pp. 200–01) in 137, owe much more, for example, to Petrarch's 1st Tractate, Chapter 3 (*P*, pp. 304–10; *LoS*, pp. 113–15): 'fere horribiles, pisces incogniti, volucres inaudite' (*P*, p. 306) ('horrible beasts, unknown fishes, unheard-of birds' (*LoS*, p. 113)). However, this chapter is not strong evidence for Harington's authorship. As in Petrarch, Harington's solitude is sociable; for example, in his Epigram 116: 'sweet discourse, meane fare; & then beleeue me, | To make to thee like cheere, shall neuer grieue me' (*LESJH*, p. 193).

socializing. This argument is a development from *De vita solitaria*. Chapter 28 reiterates Daniel's generalizing translation of 'omniumque quibus humanum corpus subiacet securus' (*P*, p. 310) ('safe from all the ills to which the human frame is subject' (*LoS*, p. 116)) in his Chapter 5. 'Securely unto himselfe' (*LESJH*, p. 354) indicates a greater need to be alone in body and spirit, consonant with Daniel's wider reworking of the treatise.

However, he still reproduces Petrarch's chapter structure, and so discusses how the solitary man would spend his time. Daniel discusses the *solitarius*'s companions rather than his diet, unlike Petrarch, because 'as for feastes the solitarie man frequenteth none' (*LESJH*, p. 354). The *solitarius* restrains his desires for material goods and company:

> [the solitarie man] seeketh noe companions superior to himself, or baser then are fitt for his qualitie, whereby he is not combered with complementes, nor reputed of abject mynde. He *desireth* nothinge, nor *needeth* any bodie. *Contentus suo, nihil sperat nec timet*. (*LESJH*, p. 354, emphasis added [Latin italic in the original])

Here, the solitary man might well be alone, in contrast to Petrarch's sociable *solitarius*, whose 'solitude is simply a more devious way of pursuing the ambitions he once castigated in the *occupati*', as Augustinus comments in Petrarch's *Secretum*.[50] The *solitarius* is unlikely to find his equals, as Daniel omits all references to Petrarch's dedicatee and friend. 'Contentus suo' comes to mean 'satisfied with one's own company'. In these two chapters Daniel develops *De vita solitaria* excitingly. He writes Petrarchan humour in his satirical dialogue, but replaces Petrarch's dinner-table battle with hung-over disgust.

Book II, Chapter 7 (*LESJH*, pp. 369–70) is a translation of Petrarch's Book II, 8th Tractate, Chapter 3 (*P*, pp. 540–41; *LoS*, pp. 279–80). Daniel's life of Demosthenes demonstrates his enthusiasm for concentration on the afterlife. He found English precedent for his translation in Roger Baynes's *The Praise of Solitarinesse*:

> Farther, marke also what *Quintilian* reporteth of *Demosthenes*, the greatest *Orator* among the *Grecians*: That fervente lover of *Solitarinesse*, used to walke (sayeth he) along the coast of the sea, that so he might acquainte his eares with the roaring of the water, to the ende therby to embolden him selfe, the better to endure the daily noyse and murmure of hys *auditorie*: this also (saith he) is that *Demosthenes*, well knowen to the world to have painefully lerned, and that in Deserts, that excellent arte of *oratorie*, which after else where he practised abroad in divers notable Cities.[51]

We cannot be sure whether Daniel read Baynes; he does follow his translation for this section of *De vita solitaria* to some extent, but he excludes Baynes's

---

[50] Jennifer Petrie, 'Petrarch *Solitarius*', in *Petrarch in Britain*, ed. by McLaughlin and Panizza, pp. 29–38 (p. 34).

[51] *The Praise of Solitarinesse*, p. 80.

remark that Demosthenes grew up in the desert before travelling widely. Both omit Petrarch's remarks illustrating Demosthenes' vanity and comic greed. However, Daniel might have decided to rework Baynes's translation anyway, because it presents solitude as preparation for public life.

Daniel's solitary men are serious and virtuous, whereas Petrarch's examples vary in the extent of their solitary living. For Petrarch, solitude is 'an ideal project denied by reality'.[52] This contradictory feel pervades *De vita solitaria*. A succinct example is Petrarch's Demosthenes, an *occupatus* who occasionally visits the countryside:

est ille 'leviculus', quod Cicero idem ait, qui delectaretur illo muliercularum susurro, ut fit, a tergo insibilantium: 'Hic est ille Demosthenes'. (*P*, p. 540)

Demosthenes was besides rather vain, as Cicero himself points out, deriving great pleasure from hearing old women whispering at his back, 'That is the great Demosthenes'. (*LoS*, p. 279)

Both Baynes and Daniel remove Cicero's anecdote, related by Petrarch, about Demosthenes' shallow, slightly vain humour. Daniel also removes Petrarch's source, simply noting that Demosthenes is 'sometymes pleased with Womans daliance' (*LESJH*, p. 369). Demosthenes' flirtations with admiration are curtailed. In Petrarch and Baynes, Demosthenes practises in solitude for political life:

In litore, in quo se maximo cum sono fluctus illideret, meditans consuescebat contionum fremitus non expavescere. (*P*, p. 540)

He used to accustom himself, by studying on the seashore, where the breakers dashed, with the loudest noise, not to be disconcerted at the uproar of public assemblies. (*LoS*, p. 279)

Daniel presents a reflective Demosthenes:

[. . .] he used to meditate at the Sea-side, when the waves did roare most lowde. (*LESJH*, p. 369)

Daniel plays down solitude's direct utility for public life, clear in Petrarch and Baynes.

Daniel's Demosthenes voices a view of solitude consonant with his contemplation. Petrarch's amusingly self-regarding quipster becomes a 'wearie' character free from worldly desire.

Demosthenem constat, quod in *Noctibus Athicis* scriptum est, precium quoque silentii pepigisse. (*P*, p. 540)

It is well known, as appears from the *Attic Nights*, that Demosthenes put a price even on his silence. (*LoS*, p. 280)

---

[52] Maggi, 'You Will Be my Solitude', p. 184.

He removes the source of Demosthenes' quip, the *Attic Nights*, and alters his meaning:

> He used to saye that *wearie* he was of pleadinge for profitt, neyther did he desire any thinge whereof he myght repent. Hee would never boast of worldly wealth, but *labor to doe all in hope of eternitie*. (*LESJH*, p. 369, emphasis added)

Daniel gives Demosthenes part of Petrarch's later moral exhortation: 'omnia ad salutem viteque legem temporalis et *eterne spem*' (*P*, 540, emphasis added) ('all things should tend to salvation, to the law of life on earth and the hope of the life to come' (*LoS*, p. 280)). Demosthenes' attempt to extinguish desire and his focus on eternity encapsulate Daniel's solitude.

Conclusion

Daniel's version of Petrarch's *De vita solitaria* principally encourages the reader to retreat from the world in order to endure life on earth; he thus reworks Petrarch's often varied lines of argument, including his delight in study and in select company. His *Prayse of Private Life* is a mark of the high regard in which he held Petrarch's Latin, and his awareness of Petrarch's mixed literary fortunes, which he remarks upon in his *Defence of Ryme*:

> [Petrarch's] great Volumes written in Moral Philosophie, shew his infinite reading, and most happy power of disposition: his twelue Æclogues, his *Affrica* containing nine Bookes of the last Punicke warre, with his three Bookes of Epistles in Latine verse, shew all the transformations of wit and inuention, that a Spirite naturally borne to the inheritance of Poetrie & iudiciall knowledge could express: All which notwithstanding wrought him not that glory & fame with his owne Nation, as did his Poems in Italian.[53]

In translating one of Petrarch's Latin treatises into English for a puritan reader, Lady Cumberland, Daniel develops neo-Stoic lines of thought, most recently filtered into English by his patron John Florio when he translated Montaigne; Daniel therefore focuses his version around Senecan *sententiae*. *The Prayse of Private Life* is keen with the awareness that life is fleeting; in writing for his devout and sometimes isolated patron, Daniel creates a moral guide which exhorts the reader to leave off the material desires that prevent him or her from accepting and recognizing the ephemerality of the human condition.

KING'S COLLEGE LONDON   JESSICA STOLL

[53] *A Defence of Ryme*, in *Poems and 'A Defence of Ryme'*, p. 141, ll. 419-29.

THE COURTESAN AND THE BED: SUCCESSFUL TRICKING IN MIDDLETON'S *A MAD WORLD, MY MASTERS*

> Carry yourselves but probably.
> (THOMAS MIDDLETON)[1]

At the exact centre of Middleton's play *A Mad World, my Masters* (III. 2 in modern scenically divided editions), and as the opening to the most explicitly articulated sex un-scene on the Jacobean stage,[2] we are confronted with the following stage direction:

Viols, gallipots, plate, and an hourglass by her. The courtesan on a bed for her counterfeit fit. To her, Master Penitent Brothel, like a doctor of physic. (III. 2. 0)

The bed dominates the stage physically and metaphorically in this scene (as the Globe production of 1998 realized). It is central to the scene and its humour, as well as being the centre-point of the play. The physical presence of the bed is a visible and tangible realization and representation of something crucial to the theatrical effect and meaning of the play. The bed is occupied and used by the courtesan in the same way as Volpone occupies his bed in the opening scene of Jonson's *Volpone*, a play probably performed in 1606, after the first performance of *A Mad World* in late 1605.[3] Middleton's preoccupation with the bed here, and its material signifying in a debate about theatricality, may well have inspired Jonson. Middleton uses the bed in an overtly challenging representation: most obviously his bed is actively occupied by a woman, and explicitly by a kept woman, the courtesan.[4] During the scene's action the cour-

---

[1] Thomas Middleton, *A Mad World, my Masters*, I. 1. 87, ed. by Peter Saccio, annotated by Celia Daileader, in *Thomas Middleton: The Collected Works*, ed. by Gary Taylor and John Lavagnino (Oxford: Clarendon Press, 2007), pp. 414–51 (p. 419).

[2] The term 'un-scene' was invented by Celia Daileader in *Eroticism on the Renaissance Stage: Transcendence, Desire and the Limits of the Visible* (Cambridge: Cambridge University Press, 1998), p. 102. In 'Off-Stage Sex and Female Desire' (pp. 23–50) she discusses this scene as a key example of sex as un-scene.

[3] The 1616 folio of *The Works of Benjamin Jonson* (London: William Stansby, 1616) states that *Volpone* was acted 'in the yeere 1605', a dating that extends to late March 1606 in the Old Style calendar. The reference to porpoises in London (*Volpone*, ed. by Brian Parker and David Bevington (Manchester: Manchester University Press, 1999), II. 1. 4–7) dates its first performance after 19 January 1606, when porpoises were reported in the Thames (ibid., p. 24). Celia Daileader also argues that Middleton's sickroom preceded Jonson's representation in *Volpone*. See 'The Courtesan Revisited: Thomas Middleton, Pietro Aretino, and Sex-Phobic Criticism', in *Italian Culture in the Drama of Shakespeare and his Contemporaries: Rewriting, Remaking, Refashioning*, ed. by Michele Marrapodi (Aldershot: Ashgate, 2007), pp. 223–38 (p. 236).

[4] Valerie Wayne's Introduction to *A Trick to Catch the Old One*, in *Thomas Middleton: The Collected Works* (pp. 375–76), argues that the role and term 'courtesan' in England generally referred to a woman who was 'kept' by a single man, and would therefore not be seen as a 'whore',

tesan feigns illness in order to act as instrumental bawd: since she is ill she 'legimately' receives men in her bedchamber, and thus engineers a meeting between Mistress Harebrain and her lover Sir Penitent Brothel, who dresses as her doctor. Their sexual encounter occurs offstage, but on-scene action continues. The courtesan holds court in her bed, manufacturing the sounds and actions of illness to disguise, complement, and excuse the sounds and actions of supposed off-stage sex. Here the courtesan achieves a remarkable piece of theatrical performance, for her on-stage and off-stage audiences. The bed itself metonymizes both her body (along with the expression of sexuality) and her stage: a double metonymy that evokes the contemporary anti-theatrical discourse associating the stage with whores and sexual excess.[5] However, here that association is a hilarious conjunction of the workings of a female trickster, in which her friends gain their desires (albeit off-stage), her audience is captivated, and she receives money from suitors to pay for her fictitious doctor.[6] Although the courtesan is described as a kept woman (Sir Bounteous visits her on that assumption in this scene), and her mother delineates her daughter's career as a series of sequential sales of her maidenhead (1. 1. 162), the staging of the trick here plays out more generally Jacobean misogynist fears that any woman, even when under the protection of a man, will work her sexuality.[7] The representational and narrative axes here converge, linking the bed, the courtesan, theatrical space, and the female trickster at the literal heart of the play. How can a consideration of the play's use of space, the stage property of beds, and femininity enable ways of interpreting both the discourses surrounding theatricality in the play and the courtesan herself?

Before looking in detail at Middleton's play, I want to examine some broader dramatic, cultural, visual, and literary references to and practices with beds,

and that the courtesan in *A Mad World, my Masters* is an example of a woman who is successively kept by a single man, despite her mother's boast that her maidenhead has been sold fifteen times (1. 1. 162). This article acknowledges Wayne's (and Middleton's) distinctions of status between different sex workers: however, both the courtesan and her mother are explicit about their place in the economies of selling sex and cheating men.

[5] See Ann Jennalie Cook, '"Bargains of Incontinency": Bawdy Behaviour in the Playhouses', *Shakespeare Studies*, 10 (1977), 271–90; Ruth Karras, 'The Regulation of Brothels in Later Medieval England', *Signs*, 14 (1989), 399–433; Joseph Lenz, 'Base Trade: Theatre as Prostitution', *ELH*, 60 (1993), 833–55; Stephen Mullaney, *The Place of the Stage: Licence, Play and Power in the Renaissance* (Chicago: University of Chicago Press, 1988), Chapter 1; and Wallace Shug, 'Prostitution in Shakespeare's London', *Shakespeare Studies*, 10 (1977), 291–313.

[6] Middleton uses the semantic field of 'trick' to trope the connections between knavery, usury, and sexual conduct throughout this play, as well as in the title of his play of the same year, *A Trick to Catch the Old One*.

[7] Daileader, *Eroticism on the Renaissance Stage*, Herbert Heller, *Penitent Brothellers: Grace, Sexuality and Genre in Thomas Middleton's City Comedies* (Newark: University of Delaware Press, 2000), pp. 52–58, and Peter Saccio, 'Introduction' to *A Mad World, my Masters*, in *Thomas Middleton: The Collected Works*, pp. 414–16, all comment on the 'brilliance' of this scene, but Heller and Saccio place it within a tradition of moralized representation of whores, and Daileader focuses on the off-stage sex.

and use these observations to help locate Middleton's theatrical framing of the bed. Discourses about femininity, identity, and theatricality recur in all these different referential fields. As Sasha Roberts shows, textual references to beds, and compound words formed from 'bed', abound in drama between 1590 and 1625:[8] there are at least 350 references to 'bed' within Shakespeare's plays alone, used to describe and symbolize a range of attitudes towards marriage, chastity, and adultery—and hence to sexuality—as well as to death. Celia Daileader has catalogued erotic activity in the extant plays of 1591–1621: of 216 plays there are only ten in which there is none.[9] Alan Dessen and Leslie Thomson's cataloguing of stage directions is another useful resource for assessing how beds are used as stage properties: proxy suggestions of sexuality and sexual activity to be found particularly in plays performed after *Othello*'s first performance in 1604.[10] These figures suggest a shared cultural and theatrical obsession with sex, sexuality, and beds. What is perhaps strange in this context is that we do not 'see' sex on stage.[11]

E. K. Chambers suggests that the new architectural design of the Globe in 1599 prompted bedroom furniture, and in particular the bed, to move from the alcove to the middle of the stage.[12] We can see this in stage directions before 1600: in *2 Tamburlaine*, Act II scene 4 opens, '*the arras is drawn and Zenocrate lies in her bed of state, Tamburlaine sitting by her, three physicians about her bed, tempering potions*'.[13] In *Sappho and Phao* (performed at court in 1584),[14] a play which stages sexuality, narcissism, and desire in ways which prefigure some of the misprisions of *A Midsummer Night's Dream*, a bed appears on stage for much of five sequential scenes, in which Sappho's obsessive love for Phao, a beautiful young man, is played out. The stage directions assume that the bed is in an alcove ('*She falleth asleep. The Curtains drawn*' (III. 3. 37)). Sappho's impossible desire for Phao has rendered her so ill that she has retreated to bed. The women around her discuss how unlucky it is to talk of marriage in a sick-room, and the conjunction of sexual desire, bed, and illness literally stages the Petrarchan discourses of impossible desires through the body of a powerful queen—a complicated reversal of masculine lovesickness

---

[8] Sasha Roberts, '"Let me the curtains draw": The Dramatic and Symbolic Properties of the Bed in Shakespearean Tragedy', in *Staged Properties in Early Modern Drama*, ed. by Jonathon Gil Harris and Natasha Korda (Cambridge: Cambridge University Press, 2002), pp. 153–76.
[9] Daileader, *Eroticism on the Renaissance Stage*, Appendix I.
[10] Alan Dessen and Leslie Thomson, *A Dictionary of Stage Directions in English Drama, 1580–1642* (Cambridge: Cambridge University Press, 1999), pp. 24–25.
[11] The starting-point for Daileader's *Eroticism*, and her examination of the theatrical titillation generated by the relegation of physical sex to off-stage action.
[12] E. K. Chambers, *The Elizabethan Stage*, 4 vols (Oxford: Clarendon Press, 1923), III, 111.
[13] *The Plays of Christopher Marlowe*, ed. by Roma Gill (Oxford: Oxford University Press, 1971).
[14] Lohn Lyly, *Campaspe; Sappho and Phao*, ed. by G. K. Hunter and David Bevington (Manchester: Manchester University Press, 1991), p. 190.

for Elizabeth played out in other literary and aesthetic modes.[15] In subsequent scenes Phao visits Sappho in the bedchamber ('*the curtains are drawn back*' (III. 4. 38)), both characters (unknowingly but impossibly in love with each other) talk at cross purposes about a cure for Sappho's illness, Venus and Cupid visit Sappho, and Sappho agonizes about vivid dreams from her bed (IV. 3). However, despite the visual and narrative metonymizing of bed and sexuality, the dialogue and plot insist that the bed and sexual desire itself are a place of illness: recovery and continuation of life occur when Sappho's lovesickness is cured and she abandons the bed (albeit through Venus's jealousy). There is no evidence that Lyly's play was performed after its court premiere in 1584, as his rather static spectacle-oriented drama was supplanted by the faster-paced drama of the public stages in the 1590s. However, his play in its extended juxtaposition of stage property, sexual desire, and illness tantalizingly implies comic connotations which Middleton knowingly makes explicit, and Lyly's work remained popular in both the 1590s and 1600s.[16] In George Peele's *Edward I* (1591?), stage directions show the King entering Queen Elinor's tent where '*she is discovered in bed* [. . .] *and the Queen dandles his young son*'.[17] The bedroom scene provides a glimpse (once curtains are parted) of an intimate domestic scene, which is crucially also a public occasion representing the monarch's assurance of his genealogical and political succession. The bed is visually and politically central to the monarch's power. In the anonymous *The Wars of Cyrus* (published in 1594), a play which anatomizes masculine martial and imperial power, one of the scenes which configure Araspas as a traitor is his failed attempted seduction of Panthea while she sleeps in her bed ('*Enter Araspas and a magitian to Panthea asleep*').[18] Panthea's virtue is such that even asleep and under the influence of magic, she can withstand illicit sexual advances. Her bed is a place of female virtue, and illicit male invasion and voyeurism: a visual and narrative motif translated later into *Cymbeline*.

Middleton's play is closer in flavour, time, and location to Chapman's *Sir Gyles Goosecappe*, Marston's *What You Will* and *Antonio's Revenge*, and to his own *A Trick to Catch the Old One*, all played originally by one of the

[15] For an excellent and nuanced discussion of such discourses see Adrian Louis Montrose, 'Shaping Fantasies: Figurations of Gender and Power in Elizabethan Culture', in *Representing the English Renaissance*, ed. by Stephen Greenblatt (Berkeley: University of California Press, 1988), pp. 31–64; and Philippa Berry, *Of Chastity and Power: Elizabethan Literature and the Unmarried Queen* (London: Routledge, 1994), pp. 115–36, who discusses *Sappho and Phao*'s figuration of female power, although she does not consider how the bed-scenes provide an imaginative and visual expression of that power.

[16] See G. K. Hunter, 'Lyly, John (1554–1606)', in *Oxford Dictionary of National Biography* (Oxford: Oxford University Press, 2004); see also the list of Lyly's publications and reissues in *The English Short Title Catalogue* <http://estc.bl.uk> [accessed 22 July 2013].

[17] George Peele, *Edward I*, sc. 10 in *The Dramatic Works of George Peele*, ed. by Frank Hook and John Yoklavich (New Haven and London: Yale University Press, 1961), pp. 72–170 (p. 124).

[18] Anon., *The Wars of Cyrus* (London: Wiliam Blackall, 1594), fol. D2^r.

boys' companies between 1601 and 1605 and pre-dating *A Mad World, my Masters*.[19] Each of these plays includes a bed scene. In *Sir Giles Goosecap* Clarence pretends that he is confined to his bed, sick with love ('*draws the curtains and sits within them*'),[20] and is visited by Eugenia, who agrees to marry him because of their shared love of books and knowledge. It is then clear that she hides in the chamber, perhaps behind the curtains of the bed (although she could have gone off stage), to trick her uncle into believing that she has refused Clarence. Chapman's bed as stage property shares resonances with Middleton's use of it in *A Mad World, my Masters*: it is the location for a trick which has sexual connotations, and the bed's occupant feigns sickness to enable the trick to work. It is possible that Chapman's use of the bed provided Middleton with a suggestion for both the courtesan's trick and the on-stage but 'un-scene' nuances of sexual conduct which the bed invokes. Chapman's play is typical of many of the boys' companies' minor plays and those of the Poets' War[21] in its extended riffs on learning, poetry, and philosophy, as well as its loose plot. Unlike the best of those plays, it lacks a self-conscious playfulness about its own representational strategies, including the stage properties. But perhaps Middleton's sense of how a debate about anti-theatricality might use the bed on stage was generated by *Sir Gyles Goosecappe*.

Marston uses the bed to locate a satire on gallant behaviour: in *What You Will* Laverdue is seen in his chamber 'sitting on his bed apparelling himself',[22] a visual and narrational trope replicated in many later Restoration comedies. In *Antonio's Revenge* the bed appears as backdrop and night-time setting for Antonio's revenge-driven murderous spree. The two plots of Middleton's *A Trick to Catch the Old One* are remarkably similar to those of *A Mad World, my Masters*: a young impoverished gallant seeks to trick an old uncle out of his wealth; and a courtesan uses wit and theatrical devices to win a respectable marriage. In *A Trick to Catch the Old One* these two plots are fused, while in *A Mad World, my Masters* the courtesan's trickery trumps the gallant's plot. In *A Trick to Catch the Old One* the stage property of the bed frames Dampit,

---

[19] For a recent discussion of playing conditions and typical meta-theatricality of the boys' companies see Mary Bly, 'The Boy Companies 1599–1613', in *The Oxford Handbook of Early Modern Theatre*, ed. by Richard Dutton (Oxford: Oxford University Press, 2009), pp. 136–52.

[20] *Sir Gyles Goosecappe* (London: John Windet, 1606), v. 1. fol. I2^v. It was published anonymously, and its title-page states it was acted by 'the children of the chapel', dating it to the period just before 1603 (the company closed in that year). Attributed now to George Chapman: see T. M. Parrott, 'The Authorship of *Sir Gyles Goosecappe*', *Modern Philology*, 4 (1906), 25–37; and '*Sir Giles Goosecap, Knight*: George Chapman, *Poetaster*, and the Children of the Chapel', *Medieval and Renaissance Drama in England*, 25 (2012), 42–61.

[21] For the most recent discussion of the literary in-fighting at the turn of the century see James Bednarz, *Shakespeare and the Poets' War* (New York: Columbia University Press, 2001).

[22] Marston, *What You Will*, II. 1. o, in *Old Plays: Being a Continuation of Dodsley's Collection, with Notes, Critical and Explanatory*, ed. by Charles Wentworth, 6 vols (London: Rodwell and Martin, 1816), II, 198–290 (p. 217).

the drunken and melancholy usurer, in Act IV scene 5. The bed scene in this play is compellingly memorable and comic: the initial stage direction reads '*Dampit the usurer in his bed, Audrey spinning by*'.[23] At various points the play implies that Audrey shares Dampit's bed, but here the bedchamber is a place of business transactions: usury and sex are thus explicitly linked to the ailing, drunken, defecating body (Dampit describes his chamber pot as a suitable weapon). Gulf draws explicit attention to Dampit's descent into a kind of hell: 'Is this the end of cut-throat usury, brothel and blasphemy? Now thou mayst see what race a usurer runs' (fol. H1ʳ). Bed is a visual symbol of Dampit's Faustian pact: his illness and confinement are proxy markers of his sin. In this play, then, the subplot enacts the anti-theatricalists' connection between 'usury, brothel and blasphemy', but only as comic exaggeration. The visual and thematic intersection of anti-theatrical discourses through the bed is hinted at here, and arguably provides Middleton with a premiss for his next play, *A Mad World, my Masters*. It is striking that all these dramatic examples of the bed as stage property in comedies associate the bed with the melancholic humour and characteristics of men and women suffering an excess of black bile: lovesickness, drunkenness, and melancholy send them to their beds. Dampit's very name suggests the humour-based connotations for his melancholic character. By associating the bed with illness (albeit sexual melancholy), the connotations of sexual activity are displaced from the bed itself on stage. Nevertheless, a frisson of the bed as a place of such activities functions as a continual unconscious to the actual action of melancholic lovesickness viewed on stage.

On stage, when we see beds where sex may have occurred, or may be about to occur, death often eventually ensues (*Edward II*, *Othello*, or *Romeo and Juliet*), one notable exception being *Sir Gyles Goosecappe*. Beds appear as explicit stage properties in only six of Shakespeare's plays: *The Taming of the Shrew* (I. 2); *2 Henry IV* (IV. 5); *2 Henry VI* (III. 2); *Cymbeline* (II. 2); *Romeo and Juliet* (IV. 3); and *Othello* (V. 2). The bed is a place for death, except in *The Taming of the Shrew* and *Cymbeline*. While Shakespeare's Jacobean contemporaries (particularly after about 1608–09) use the bed as stage property or stage furniture in more diverse social contexts,[24] *Othello*'s literal and figurative bed continues to haunt textual and visual representations of marital infidelity and cuckoldry throughout the seventeenth century. The bed of comedy, however—whether of marital harmony and fertility, of the substitutive bed-trick, or of potential adultery, which figures widely in Shakespeare's plots—appears as a physi-

---

[23] Thomas Middleton, *A Trick to Catch the Old One* (London: George Eld, 1608), fol. G3ʳ. Further references will be given in the text. The recent Oxford editor of the play adds editorial stage directions, rendering the original published stage directions opaque: references here are to the original quarto publication.

[24] The topic of an article currently being researched by the author.

cal stage property only in *The Taming of the Shrew* (1594?) and *Cymbeline* (1609).

In *The Taming of the Shrew* (Induction 1 and Induction 2) the Lord instructs servants to put Sly to bed and awaken him with the temptations of dress and food, which we see enacted at the beginning of Induction 2, with the bed on stage. The bed symbolizes pleasures of all kinds within the story's frame once Sly awakes: he is offered wealth, ease, endless food and drink, postponed sexual pleasure, and finally, a wondrous theatrical performance, which is the subsequent story of Kate and Petruchio—the 'real' play as we know it. The bed, owned by a lord and loaned out as part of an elaborate aristocratic joke to the drunken Sly (promised pleasures only to be denied them), though marginal to the action is central to the complex fictions of the play. The bed as stage property is emblematically the place of both fantasy and disappointment: a physical symbol and metonym for Sly's (and Kate's, Petruchio's, and the audience's) own theatrical and sexualized desires and failings.[25] In the later *Cymbeline* the bed is the symbolic and physical place where chaste married love is physically invaded. Giacomo's voyeuristic masculine gaze is explicitly voiced by his textual stroking of Innogen's sleeping and passive body: a discourse forged visually in the sixteenth century in paintings such as as Giorgione's *Sleeping Venus* and Titian's *Venus of Urbino*.

In both Shakespearian comedies where beds are central stage properties and integral to the dramatic heart of the plays, a double theatrical discourse is suggestively invoked: of a dangerous theatricality closely allied to the playing out of sexual fantasies (the literalization of Stubbes's fantastic fears)[26] which is often combined with the displaced misogyny concomitant with the rationalization of that fantasy through an account of femininity as temptation.[27] Theatricality and performance are demonstrated to be paradoxically a source of both pleasure and deceit, and the bed is a stage and space for the physical and metaphorical exploration of this paradox. All these referential fields reappear, and are re-examined, in Middleton's *A Mad World, my Masters*.

Jonson's *Volpone* uses a bed to anchor Volpone physically to the stage. The bed simultaneously frees him to enable a virtuoso performance and traps him within a stage(d) identity which comes to limit his physical desires and social

---

[25] Lena Cowen Orlin, 'The Performance of Things in *The Taming of the Shrew*', *Yearbook of English Studies*, 23 (1993), 167–88, shows how an audience's attention to the status of material objects within the play enables a reading of the play as a critique of proto-capitalist materialism. She does not talk about the bed as stage property/stage furniture.

[26] Philip Stubbes, *The Anatomy of Abuses* (first published in 1583, and reprinted in 1585 and 1595), is the foundational text of anti-theatricality in Elizabethan England: Stubbes claimed that simply by watching actors (men) dressed as women, the audience would be simultaneously sexually aroused and (paradoxically) turned into women.

[27] See Laura Levine, *Men in Women's Clothing: Anti-Theatricality and Effeminisation 1579–1642* (Cambridge: Cambridge University Press, 1994), pp. 1–10, where she discusses the typically Janus-like construction of supposed anti-theatrical discourse.

status. *Volpone*'s critical and dramatic history has been partly defined by its ambiguous handling of anti-theatricality,[28] although academic critics have not focused that discourse on the bed as stage property.[29] Middleton's bed as stage property and stage signifier concretizes and problematizes anti-theatrical discourses prior to this now more well-known articulation of the problematic in Jonson's work. Both plays use the bed to focalize themes of theatricality and deception: but Middleton adds the staple of seductive femininity and sexuality through both plot and character. The bed as stage furniture is simultaneously a visual, dramatic, and narrational symbol: the static icon or object for a contemplative reflection on the dangers of theatricality as well as the spatial locus for a dramatic narrative which explores the dynamic pleasures of theatrical play.[30]

Middleton places a bed in the central scene of *A Chaste Maid in Cheapside* (first performed seven years later than *A Mad World, my Masters*) to celebrate a recognizable ritual of early modern England: childbirth.[31] The staging of Mrs Allwit's lying-in ceremony in a solely female world of bawdy festive drinking and eating, where the fecundity of the female body is arguably both celebrated and mocked, is central to the discourses of the play.[32] Middleton uses the bed both symbolically and actually as the space from which the rest of the play's examination of sexuality emanates. Mrs Allwit's husband willingly prostitutes her in order to relieve himself of the supposed burden of her sexual demands, in exchange for which her lover foots the bill for the upkeep of his children and household. Cuckoldry (supposedly the great anxiety of masculine identity and selfhood)[33] proves the paradoxically necessary resolution to the problem of masculinity in an urban, proto-capitalist society. The bed and a woman are central to this paradox. Here, however, Mrs Allwit, albeit confined by childbirth to her bed and bedchamber, has invited her gossips to

---

[28] Jonas Barish, *The Anti-Theatrical Prejudice* (Berkeley: University of California Press, 1981), Chapters 4 and 5 ('Puritans and Proteans', pp. 80–131; 'Jonson and the Loathed Stage', pp. 132–54).

[29] Productions of *Volpone* quite clearly intuit this (e.g. Marcus Warchus's 1995 production at the National Theatre in London).

[30] See Andrew Sofer, *The Stage Life of Props* (Ann Arbor: University of Michigan Press, 2008), pp. viii–xi, who argues for a refiguring of stage props as integral to dramatic meaning: in particular the bloody handkerchief and the skull in early modern drama, as icons of sensationalism to both draw in audiences and demystify the sacral nature of objects on stage. Arthur Kinney, *Shakespeare's Webs: Networks of Meaning in Renaissance Drama* (London and New York: Routledge, 2004), examines the physical, symbolic, and narrative connotations and resonances of mirrors, books, clocks, and maps as stage properties in Shakespeare's plays.

[31] Middleton, *A Chaste Maid in Cheapside*, III. 2, in *Thomas Middleton: The Collected Works*, pp. 912–58 (p. 932).

[32] See Gail Kern Paster, *The Body Embarrassed: Drama and the Disciplines of Shame in Early Modern England* (New York: Cornell University Press, 1993), pp. 23–64. Paster focuses solely on the scene as one where the leakiness of women's bodies is anatomized.

[33] See Mark Breitenberg, *Anxious Masculinity in Early Modern England* (Cambridge: Cambridge University Press, 1996), pp. 5–30.

share and celebrate the birth and identity of the child, explicitly said to be like the mother, not the father. While the joke here is that the gossips cannot see Mr Allwit's features in the child because he is not the father, at the same time identity is positively located in the domestic space and in the name of the mother. The bed is thus the located point at which both masculinity and femininity, maternity and paternity are acknowledged.

The bed was one of the most physically substantial of stage properties owned by theatre companies in the early seventeenth century. It is one of the items listed in Henslowe's diary and inventory of stage properties in 1598,[34] along with a canopy, which could have been used to construct curtains for the stage bed. More interior scenes of the period are set in bedrooms than in any other room,[35] and beds were among the most commonly used stage properties at the Red Bull Theatre between 1605 and 1625.[36] Such a stage property could not have been either too heavy or too elaborate, in order to facilitate ease of movement on and off stage. Nevertheless, any scene which required a bed would tend to be long, to justify the expense, time, and effort in getting it on and off stage. The physical requirements attendant upon a large piece of stage furniture may to some extent direct its thematic dominance.

In Elizabethan and Jacobean contemporary social and cultural practice, the bed and the bedroom themselves represented significant physical and geographical theatre. The bed was the place of birth, of the mother's lying-in, of marital consummation, of illicit sexual encounters, both consensual and forced, of illness, and of death. It was a place simultaneously public and private: key rites of passage, such as birth, marital consummation, and death, were events where family members, and professional outsiders such as midwives and priests, would attend the individual's bed. In wealthier households the bed was curtained, practically to ensure warmth, but also to create another room within the chamber. Many accounts of illicit sexual encounters (given by witnesses in court hearings) describe how a servant might overhear such acts because they slept in a truckle bed in the same room.[37] The common practice of visiting the bride and bridegroom in their bed prior to the consummation of their marriage was frequently recorded, and the monarch's bedchamber was also a place of semi-formal public reception: contemporary gossip reported that Queen Elizabeth received the Duc D'Alençon in her

---

[34] *Henslowe's Diary*, ed. by R. A. Foakes, 2nd edn (Cambridge: Cambridge University Press, 2002). This represents an account ledger detailing payments in and out of Henslowe's theatre company between 1592 and 1609, discovered among his papers at Dulwich College in 1790.

[35] Chambers, III, 65. See also Roberts.

[36] George Fullmer Reynolds, *The Staging of Elizabethan Plays at the Red Bull Theater, 1605-1625* (New York: Modern Language Association of America; London: Oxford University Press, 1940).

[37] See Laura Gowing, *Common Bodies: Women, Touch and Power in Seventeenth-Century England* (New Haven: Yale University Press, 2003), pp. 66-71, 105.

bedroom.[38] The bed and the bedroom as a wholly private space, a place for experiences not open to the public view, was an emergent concept in the period. The post-childbirth lying-in ceremony was generally a six-week-long event, with mother and child cloistered in the birthing bed and room, attended by women friends and relatives, and visited occasionally by male family members. Aristocratic women in particular (but not solely) spent huge amounts of money on furnishings and food as part of this celebration: Anna of Denmark (James I's wife) spent £15,593 on her lying-in after the birth of Princess Mary in 1605—a sum four times what an individual and lavish court masque cost.[39] This custom, and the subsequent ceremony of 'churching' the woman and child,[40] transposed the childbirth bed and bedchamber to symbolic seedbed of the family and commonwealth. These practices and ceremonies placed a woman and her fertility as symbolically central to family and social life and culture.

The bed was often the most expensive piece of furniture purchased and owned by a family: passed on down the generations, and one of the most frequently mentioned items in wills.[41] The main family bed was usually passed on to the eldest son (or possible future grandson if there was no son). However, where land passed automatically to an elder son, courts often nominated the moveables (including beds) to pass onto the younger children, and where widows inherited or passed on furniture, they often passed their beds and furnishings to female heirs.[42] The bed in its public legal manifestation was then a cultural and familial symbol of identity, contested by both men and women. Amy Louise Erickson cites a yeoman's will from 1616 which bequeathed his best featherbed to his wife, on condition that she relinquished her dower to

---

[38] See the Spanish Ambassador's reports home in Martin Hume, *The Courtships of Queen Elizabeth: A History of the Various Negotiations for her Marriage* (London: Fisher Unwin, 1898), pp. 228, 265–66.

[39] Leeds Barroll, *Anna of Denmark, Queen of England: A Cultural Biography* (Philadelphia: University of Pennsylvania Press, 2001), p. 104.

[40] See David Cressy, 'Purification, Thanksgiving and the Churching of Women in Post-Reformation England', *Past and Present*, 141 (1993), 106–46.

[41] See F. G. Emmison, *Elizabethan Life: Home, Work and Land*, Essex Record Office Publications, 69 (Chelmsford: Essex County Council, 1976), pp. 12–16; and Tom Arkell, 'Household Goods from Probate Inventories', in *West Penwith at the Time of Charles II*, ed. by H. Beaufort-Murphy (Penzance: Penwith Local History Group, 1998). For additional discussion of willed property and inventories see *When Death Us Do Part: Understanding and Interpreting the Probate Records of Early Modern England*, ed. by Tom Arkell and others (Oxford: Leopard's Head Press, 2000); and Amy Louise Erickson, *Women and Property in Early Modern England* (New York: Routledge, 1993), pp. 66, 110.

[42] Erickson, pp. 72–33, 178. See also Lloyd Davis, 'Women's Wills in Early Modern England', in *Women, Property and the Letters of the Law in Early Modern England*, ed. by Margaret Ferguson and others (Toronto: University of Toronto Press, 2004), pp. 219–36, on the specificity of bequests, as well as on how the writing of a testament gave voice and agency to women often characterized as politically and legally powerless.

his son.⁴³ The 'great bed of Ware' was a contemporary tourist destination, and an iconic representation of fashionable wood-turning, carving, and material furnishings.⁴⁴

For many women of the period, beds were shared (for all classes), or temporary (particularly for the servant classes), being brought out at night within a mistress's or master's chamber. Thus they were places not of permanence, security, or privacy, but of potential danger as well as comfort. Many narratives in court accounts describe such dangers and the 'duties' of servants to submit to masters and mistresses.⁴⁵ Anne Clifford's diary delineates how (for an aristocratic woman) beds had social and personal familial significances. She distinguishes between different beds by key events associated with them (the 'green cloth of gold bed where the child was born', 15 April 1617).⁴⁶ She describes her beds as places for sharing intimacies with Lady Arbella Stuart, Frances Bourchier, and Mary Carey, as well as her children when they are small; a place where her husband came when they were cohabiting (but she often rejects these beds when sleeping alone), and a place to receive guests in her old age when ill. For Anne Clifford, and perhaps for many women like her, the bed was a place of sensual power, of memories and experience: a place to retreat to when worried; a place where women had a measure of autonomy.⁴⁷

Joke books and popular images figure the bed as the centre of marital encounters (sexual and otherwise). Richard Brathwaite's *Ar't Asleep Husband? A Bolster Lecture*—a genre known by mid-century as a 'Curtain Lecture'— represented the scolding woman rebuking her husband.⁴⁸ In this popular comic textual and visual narration, the bed is a space where women act out of place: the bed as metaphor and metonym for the inverted sexual hierarchy feared by Jacobean and Caroline misogyny. The 'Curtain' lectures shared the misogynistic impulse of the populist 'skimmington' of shaming women who transgressed the norms for gender behaviour and expression.⁴⁹ The bed in

---

⁴³ Erickson, p. 66.

⁴⁴ See Annie Carlano and Bobbie Sumberg, *Sleeping Around: The Bed from Antiquity to Now* (Santa Fe: Museum of International Folk Art, 2006), p. 47.

⁴⁵ See Laura Gowing, *Domestic Dangers: Women, Words and Sex in Early Modern London* (Oxford: Oxford University Press, 1998), pp. 71, 258-62; and *Common Bodies*, pp. 66-71, 105; and on lying-in practices, pp. 172-88.

⁴⁶ *The Diaries of Lady Anne Clifford*, ed. by D. J. H. Clifford (Stroud: Sutton, 2003), pp. 19-89 (p. 57).

⁴⁷ See Gowing, *Common Bodies*, pp. 66-68.

⁴⁸ Richard Brathwaite, *Ar't Asleep Husband? A Bolster Lecture* (London: Richard Best, 1640). 'Curtain Lecture' denoted a private 'lecture' to a husband by a wife. For a recent discussion of this genre and its attendant cultural resonances see Michael McKeon, *The Secret History of Domesticity: Public, Private, and the Division of Knowledge* (Baltimore: Johns Hopkins University Press, 2005), pp. 242-49.

⁴⁹ See Linda E. Boose, 'Scolding Brides and Bridling Scolds: Taming the Woman's Unruly Member', *Shakespeare Quarterly*, 42 (1991), 179-213; and Martin Ingram, 'Ridings, Rough Music

these lectures simultaneously represented the domain and power of transgressive women and mocked them as social outcasts.

Public visual representations of beds available to the early seventeenth-century English audience usually symbolized death or sleep.[50] Private or semi-private images of beds could be much more explicitly erotic, and included Aretino's images, which were available to coterie audiences, privately circulated.[51] John Donne's *Songs and Sonnets* circulated among the same audiences as attended the coterie children's theatres (*A Mad World, my Masters* was first performed in 1605 by the Children of Paul's), and documented an emergent private sensibility of the bed. In Elegy 19 ('To His Mistress Going to Bed') the bed and the body are female spaces colonized by the male lover.[52] In 'The Sun Rising' the bed is a metonym for the kingdom owned by every man, and for his female lover. Human experience, defined in terms of sexual relations, is reduced to the domestic geography of the bed ('This bed thy centre is, these walls thy sphere')[53] and simultaneously, symbolically, the world. Private and public coincide. The domestic physical bed, representing conjoined heterosexual lovers as an ideal Platonic fusion and the idealized Protestant example of connubial love, nevertheless betrays a masculine hegemony of image-making and identity.[54]

Anti-theatrical polemicists continually argued that acting effeminates both actor and viewer, but the explicit image linking theatre and bed did not appear until Prynne crystallized it in *Histrio-Mastix* in 1633:

O [. . .] that thou couldest in that sublime watch-tower insinuate thine eyes into these players secretes; or set open the closed doors of their bedchambers and bring all their innermost hidden cells unto the conscience of thine eyes.[55]

The physical staging of this fear using the bed as stage property was arguably first displayed comically in the marginal induction to *A Taming of the Shrew* and then in *Sir Gyles Goosecappe*, but Middleton's *A Mad World, my Masters*

and "the Reform of Popular Culture" in Early Modern England', *Past and Present*, 105 (1984), 79–113.

[50] See Diane Wolfthal, *In and out of the Marital Bed: Seeing Sex in Renaissance Europe* (New Haven and London: Yale University Press, 2010), pp. 13–23.

[51] See Daileader, 'The Courtesan Revisited'; and Wolfthal, Chapter 2.

[52] John Donne, *Complete Poetry and Selected Prose*, ed. by John Hayward (London: Nonesuch Press, 1978), p. 96.

[53] Donne, p. 6, l. 30.

[54] See Helen Carr, 'Donne's Masculine Persuasive Force', in *Jacobean Poetry and Prose: Rhetoric, Representation and the Popular Imagination*, ed. by Clive Bloom (Basingstoke: Macmillan, 1988), pp. 96–118.

[55] William Prynne, *Histrio-Mastix* (London: Michael Spark, 1633), p. 135. The anti-theatricalists most notoriously included Stephen Gosson and Philip Stubbes: William Prynne is a relatively late if encyclopedic chronicler. See Levine, *Men in Women's Clothing*; and Stephen Orgel, *Impersonations: The Performance of Gender in Shakespeare's England* (Cambridge: Cambridge University Press, 1996).

uses the property as its central iconic and thematic axis. The analogy of performance, theatrical space, sex, and bed as a conjoined discourse to debate the anti-theatrical prejudice is not confined to Act III scene 2. The courtesan explicitly makes the connections for us when she is watching the mock play *The Slip*, in Act V:

O'my troth, an I were not married, I could find in my heart to fall in love with that player now and send for him to a supper. I know some i'th'town that have done as much, and there took such a good conceit of their parts into the two-penny room that the actors have been found i'th'morning in a less compass than their stage. (V. 2. 33–40)

Public performance invokes sexual desire in an audience, a retreat to a 'two-penny room', and a morning-after discovery in space of 'less compass than their stage': in other words, a bed. This explicit invocation of the anti-theatricalists' greatest fear about the conjunction of whores, theatres, audiences, and bedrooms foregrounds the conjunction of the bed and women in Middleton's play. Discourses and geographies of the bed represent it as a potentially contested space: an object usually publicly owned, debated, and painted by men. However, it is also occupied and recorded by women at key moments in their life histories, albeit in texts that have been hidden from literary history.[56] It is therefore a liminal space between male and female, masculine and feminine, sexuality and other life experiences, public and private.[57]

Let us now return to the courtesan in her bed. The courtesan literally occupies one of the central places of her trade: the bed in her chamber. The courtesan's experience as viewed by the audience is an almost exact inversion of legal testimonies which recount sounds of sexual activity coming from behind bed curtains.[58] Instead, the courtesan is the proxy theatrical embodiment and mouthpiece of (absent) sexual activity, while simultaneously reclining on her sickbed. Visually and aurally, our attention is on the courtesan's performance: simultaneously we are voyeuristically envisaging both the off-stage sex and all other possible sexual encounters performed on the very bed and with the body before our eyes.[59] Contemporary discourses about courtesans and

[56] See e.g. the recuperative work of Laura Gowing in *Common Bodies* and the diaries collected in *Her Own Life: Autobiographical Writings by Seventeenth-Century Englishwomen*, ed. by Hilary Hinds (London: Routledge, 1989).

[57] Contemporary gender and sexual discourses linked masculinity and femininity with outside and inside spaces respectively—and female identity with liminal spaces such as doorsteps and windows. See Laura Gowing, '"The Freedom of the Streets": Women and Social Space 1560–1640', in *Londinopolis, c. 1500–1750: Essays in the Cultural and Social History of Early Modern London*, ed. by Paul Griffiths and Mark Jenner (Manchester: Manchester University Press, 2000), pp. 130–53.

[58] See Gowing, *Common Bodies*, pp. 60–71.

[59] Daileader, *Eroticism*, pp. 21–50, focuses on the eroticism of off-stage sex, not the physical spaces and events on stage. In 'The Courtesan Revisited' she argues that Middleton's source for

prostitutes associated sickness (particularly the pox) directly with the whore. Middleton uses that association as a convenient, self-conscious theatrical fiction, comically deconstructed in the enactment of sex and illness, and scripted, stage-managed, and directed by the courtesan. In the same way that the bed is a metonym for the stage, theatrical production, and illusion, the courtesan is effective playwright, director, and chief actor. The courtesan's enactments (sex, illness, and theatre) share a focus on the physical body and engage us in a debate and encounter with female sexuality and the female body. Her 'occupation' (her ownership of the space and her serial accumulation of male protectors) symbolizes her function in the play and the performed and generative status of a female trickster. Middleton's comic women represent autonomous, urban women striving to construct and create identities both within and in contradistinction to the dominant patriarchal discourses.[60]

A Mad World, my Masters features two other physical beds. The first is Sir Bounteous's guest bed, sumptuously offered and described to Follywit (as Lord Owemuch):

A hard down bed i'faith, my lord, and poor cambric sheets, and a cloth o'tissue canopy. The curtains indeed were wrought in Venice with the story of the prodigal child in silk and gold, only the swine are left out, my lord, for spoiling the curtains. (II. 2. 4–8)

Sir Bounteous's bed is an object and space for the display of conspicuous consumption (the Venetian gold and silk curtains, cambric sheets, and tissue canopy), functioning simultaneously as an emblem of the host's festive generosity and foolish lack of self-knowledge. This same bed as both representational emblem of identity and dramatic performative space for the tricking of Sir Bounteous is literally performed when it appears on stage in Act II scene 6. Sir Bounteous enters the bedroom to 'alert' Follywit to the fact that he has been robbed, and 'discovers' him tied to the bed. Follywit's

the courtesan's sickness plot is Aretino's *Ragionamenti* and that critics branding Middleton as 'anti-women' are simply replicating populist myths about Puritan attitudes to sex and sexuality.

[60] Jean Howard, *Theatre of a City: The Places of London Comedy* (Philadelphia: University of Pennsylvania Press, 2007), pp. 114–61, locates the early Jacobean plays in which courtesans and whores feature within the shifting economic and social changes of early proto-capitalism: she takes a liberal view of the representation of women and whores on stage in Middleton's *Chaste Maid* and *Honest Whore*, but she omits *A Mad World, my Masters*. Kelly Stage, 'The Roaring Girl's London Spaces', *Studies in English Literature*, 49 (2009), 417–36, changes the debate about Middleton and Dekker's *The Roaring Girl*, arguing that Moll's interventions in social practices and structures through spatial control of the physical stage and its metonymic city offer up a new version of femininity as performance. See also Farah Karim-Cooper, 'Disguise and Identity in the Plays of Middleton', in *Thomas Middleton in Context*, ed. by Suzanne Gossett (Cambridge: Cambridge University Press, 2011), pp. 279–86. These arguments, and that pursued here, acknowledge the conceptual complexities raised by Jonathon Dollimore, 'Shakespeare Understudies: The Sodomite, the Prostitute, the Transvestite and their Critics', in *Political Shakespeares*, ed. by Dollimore, 2nd edn (Manchester: Manchester University Press, 1994), pp. 139–52, and explore the cultural and social representations of courtesans and women without necessarily reinforcing a cultural model of the representation of low life as carnivalesque enjoyment for the purposes of containment.

own performance from the bed authenticates the 'robbery' of his grandfather and proleptically foreshadows the courtesan's bed as emblem of identity and performance a mere two scenes later. The aristocratic bed is put into bathetic comic circulation as a satiric object of grandiose ambition, brought to low humour through visual and narrational action. This stage property is used to embody the physical actualization of the complexities of the whole theatrical experience, an insight achieved through the fusion of bathetic physical with intellectual comedy.

The scene in Penitent Brothel's chamber does not explicitly mention a bed, although the place and time (his chamber at night, *'enter in his chamber out of his study'* (IV. 1. 0)) imply its presence. In the play's narrative his chamber becomes a place of fantastical sexual encounters, private reading, and soul-searching: a masculine space invaded by a sexualized woman. Beds (actual and implied) in the play therefore signal sexual and theatrical temptation, self-fashioning, and key moments of articulation of identity. The play uses different rooms and chambers to signal different classes and genders, supplementing and sharpening the audience's insights into how the bed works as stage property: diegetic space helps invoke mimetic space and narrational symbolism. Sir Bounteous's welcome to Follywit ('Your honour is most *spatiously* welcome' (II. 1. 99, my emphasis)) proclaims a gentry-based festive and spatial generosity over the rural and architectural spaces of his country home: 'Tomorrow your lordship shall see my cocks, my fishponds, my champaign grounds. I keep *chambers* in my house can show your lordship some pleasure' (II. 2. 17–20, my emphasis). This vision of the gentry's spatial freedom contrasts with the articulations of spatial ownership by the play's middling sort and outsiders, such as the Harebrains and the courtesan. The play has very few outdoor spaces as locations: two are indubitably outdoors (I. 1 and IV. 5 are on the street). The city and its people are differentially represented through these two streets and a variety of chambers.[61] While domestic settings are emphasized, many of them are liminal: they are both public and private, allowing movement of people between places and identities. Rooms and their status (locked/open) are linked to identity and power (for example, home, closet, kitchen, chamber). The 'locked' houses and rooms (and their smaller versions, chests) are all broken into by subterfuge (Harebrain's house by the courtesan; Sir Bounteous's house, chamber, and casket by Follywit; and Penitent Brothel's by a succubus). Metonymically, closed

[61] Other explicit interior scenes or references to actions in rooms are: THE BEDROOM SCENES of II. 2, II. 6, and III. 2; MR HAREBRAIN'S HOUSE, which is frequently locked (III. 1, 4. 4); 'A FRIEND'S HOUSE' (III. 3. 79), where Follywit borrows women's clothes from behind a hanging space (logically, another intimate chamber); THE KITCHEN ('nothing comes into th'kitchen but comes through my hands' (IV. 3. 15); THE CLOSET (III. 3; IV. 3), which is the place of Sir Bounteous's (il)licit sexual assignations; Penitent Brothel's 'STUDY' and 'CHAMBER' (IV. 1); SIR BOUNTEOUS'S HALL (V. 1).

private rooms (chamber, closet, bedroom)—the fantasy of bourgeois, aristocratic, and masculine impermeability—are rendered comically untenable by the cumulative theatrical tricks of Follywit, the courtesan, and a succubus. 'Respectable' (middling sort) femininity is linked to small interior rooms by the men (Harebrain's locked house and chamber) and sexualized femininity to street, bedchamber, and closet. Masculine identity is expressed by freedom over all locations.

The courtesan's access to different spaces differentiates her from all other characters except Follywit: she works the street, the bedroom, the squire's country house, the merchant's home, and Mr Harebrain's doorway. This freedom immediately marks her as potentially unchaste: yet the play's structure does not demonize her, as some other Jacobean city comedies and contemporary discourse often would.[62] Her freedom of action across these differing spaces contrasts the spatial constraints on Mistress Harebrain. Mr Harebrain parodically embodies the masculinist discourse of Dod and Cleaver's *A Godly Form of Household Government for the Ordering of Families* (1598). This delineates the binary spatial, discursive, and economic functions of men and women: 'The dutie of the husband is to get goods and of the wife to gather them together. The dutie of the husband is to travel abroad to seek living, and the wive's dutie is to keep home.'[63] The courtesan's successful comic disturbance of these spatial and ideological binaries through her access to and disruption of divergent settings marks both her theatricality and her displacement of and from gender norms. Her physical access to the variety of spatial locations on the stage is equally figured through dialogue and action. When we first meet her, she describes herself in spatial terms:

[Sir Bounteous Progress]'s my keeper indeed, but there's many a piece of venison stolen that my keeper wots not on; there's no park kept so warily but loses flesh one time or another, no woman kept so privately, but may watch advantage to make the best of her pleasure. And in common reason one keeper cannot be so enough for so proud a park as a woman. (I. 1. 144–50)

She simultaneously acknowledges the conventional discourse of femininity as owned parkland and declares her ability to define her own pleasure from within that discourse.[64] *A Mad World, my Masters* has no other woman in the main plot.[65] The figuration of the courtesan through both spatial and material theatricality playfully and forcefully displays Middleton's dramaturgical

---

[62] See Peter Stallybrass, 'Patriarchal Territories: The Body Enclosed', in *Rewriting the Renaissance: The Discourse of Sexual Difference in Early Modern Europe*, ed. by Margaret W. Ferguson and others (Chicago: University of Chicago Press, 1984), pp. 123–42; and Anne M. Haselkorn, *Prostitution in Elizabethan and Jacobean Comedy* (Troy, NY: Whitston, 1983), pp. 1–32, 83–94.

[63] John Dod and Robert Cleaver, *A Godly Form of Household Government for the Ordering of Families* (London: Elliot Court's Press, 1598), fol. M4ᵛ.

[64] Stallybrass, pp. 128–29.

[65] *Feme sole* was the term used to denote a single woman under the law, who had the legal

examination of the intersecting discourses of theatricality, performance, and gender.

In Jonson's *Volpone* the eponymous hero's theatrical expertise and virtuosity eventually become tainted by sexual violence and greed. In Jonson, theatricality is moralized as anti-social.[66] Middleton figures the complexity of this debate and its connection to gender in the opening scene. The courtesan's mother rhapsodizes about the external conduct required in her new proto-capitalist world, and proleptically narrates the courtesan's story:

> 'Tis nothing but a politic conveyance,
> A sincere carriage, a religious eyebrow
> That throws their charms over the worldlings' senses;
> And when thou spi'st a fool that truly pities
> The false springs of thine eyes,
> And honourably dotes upon thy love,
> If he be rich, set him by for a husband.
> (I. 1. 173-79)

The courtesan argues that women excel at such trickery when she advises Mistress Harebrain about how women should match their external behaviour to what men expect, so that they can achieve their own desires privately: *"Tis our best art* to dissemble well. | Put but these notes in use, that I'll direct you' (I. 2. 82-83, my emphasis). She provides the theatrical setting, script ('notes'), and direction for the consummation of those desires, and Penitent exclaims triumphantly, 'women's wit [is] ever at full moon' (III. 2. 176). Penitent's aphoristic couplet at the end of that central scene reminds us that plotting and women, theatricality and feminine wiles are inextricably and effectively linked: 'When plots are e'en past hope and hang their head | Set with a woman's hand, they thrive and spread' (III. 2. 267-68). The courtesan takes on as many identities through her dress and characterization as Follywit does: her most successful cross-dressing, as a gentlewoman for Follywit in Act IV scene 5, creates the illusion of modesty and wealth which entraps her future husband.[67] The courtesan is the self-conscious director and actor par excellence, a fact celebrated in her frank conversation with Penitent in Act II scene 5:

all the world knows women are soon down; we can be sick when we have a mind to't, catch an ague with the wind of our fans, surfeit upon the rump of a lark, and bestow

right to own property and make contracts in her name, and the designation could include widows who had these rights. A *Feme covert*, or married woman, did not have these rights.

[66] Barish, *The Anti-Theatrical Prejudice*.

[67] Richard Levin, 'The Economics and Erotics of Cross-Class Dressing in Early Modern (Formerly Renaissance) English Drama', *Journal of Theatre and Drama*, 3 (1997), 93-101, argues that cross-class dressing may be one of the underexamined aspects of identity-shifting during this period.

ten pound in physic upon't; we're likest ourselves when we're down. 'Tis the easiest art and cunning for our sect to counterfeit sick, that are always full of fits when we are well. (II. 5. 31–36)

Follywit recognizes the associations between femininity, fashioning, and identity when he describes his own theatrically charged cross-dressing: 'thou shalt see a woman quickly made up here' (III. 3. 96). More radically, in dressing as a woman he claims how easy it is to switch outward gender: 'We are all male to th'middle, mankind from the beaver to th'bum. 'Tis an Amazonian time— you shall have women shortly tread their husbands' (III. 3. 117–18). He thus invokes two contemporary commonplaces about gender identity: that fundamentally both men's and women's bodies are the same,[68] and the anxiety that women were increasingly seen to be dominant.[69] Simultaneously joking about such attitudes as he dresses as a courtesan, his character embodies physically the anti-theatricalists' fear that by acting he will become effeminized and literally a woman. The plot itself then delightfully enacts this doubly through Follywit's subsequent story: not only does he voluntarily dress as a woman (albeit to trick his uncle out of his jewels), but he is 'effeminized' by falling for the courtesan, believing her to be a modest virgin. Follywit's story plays out the literal truths of the anti-theatricalists' case: femininity weakens his abilities. However, Middleton complicates this narrative trajectory. The courtesan's own self-conscious femininity produces greater success than Follywit's tricks in the social world of early seventeenth-century London.[70] Constructed, self-conscious, theatrical femininity is more powerful and more effective than masculinity, a message that is not overturned by the play's resolution. In other plays which examine the anti-theatrical premiss (such as *Volpone*, for example), successful theatricality is moralized and punished. A close reading of the structure of Act IV, the crux of Middleton's developing argument about morality and femininity, shows how the play juxtaposes a set of complex ideas about early modern identity, theatricality, and gender.

Throughout the play theatrical notions of provisional and improvisational identity ('carry yourselves but probably' (I. 1. 87)) as social practice are opposed to absolute notions about identity, and these coalesce through a variety

---

[68] See Thomas Laqueur, *Making Sex: Body and Gender from the Greeks to Freud* (Cambridge, MA: Harvard University Press, 1990), for the classic statement of this hypothesis. Although it has been much challenged and amended, the basic premiss remains unchallenged: that physiologically, women's and men's bodies differed only in that some female genitals were inside the body, whereas men's were outside. As Paster shows (pp. 1–22), it was humoral theory that generated 'real' sexual difference.

[69] See David Underdown, 'The Taming of the Scold: The Enforcement of Patriarchal Authority in Early Modern England', in *Order and Disorder in Early Modern England*, ed. by A. Fletcher and J. Stephenson (Cambridge: Cambridge University Press, 1985), pp. 116–36; Levine, *Men in Women's Clothing*; Natalie Davies, 'Women on Top', in *Society and Culture in Early Modern France* (Stanford: Stanford University Press, 1975), pp. 124–51.

[70] See Karim-Cooper, 'Disguise and Identity', pp. 281–82.

of encounters in Act IV. These should be experienced as contiguous and interrelated, since the Penitent Brothel scene is frequently cited as 'proof' that Middleton's argument is anti-feminist,[71] but often considered in isolation from the surrounding scenes. More crucially, these scenes are used to link such sentiments to an account of Middleton as a puritan anti-theatricalist. The scenes successively are: the encounter of Penitent with the succubus; Gunwater's description to Sir Bounteous of the disguised Follywit as courtesan; the encounter of Follywit as courtesan with Gunwater; Sir Bounteous's outburst when he believes that 'the courtesan' has tricked him; Penitent Brothel's conversion of and confession to the Harebrains; and finally the encounter between Follywit and the courtesan. These scenes share a range of discursive foci on femininity: from the theological and physiological to the theatrical. Thus in Act IV scene 1 Penitent Brothel berates his sensual sins after his theological reading and before encountering the succubus, in the form of Mistress Harebrain:

> To dote on weakness, slime, corruption, woman?
> What is she, took asunder from her clothes?
> Being ready, she consists of a hundred pieces,
> Much like your German clock.
> (IV. 1. 18–21)

His absolute characterization of woman as material corruption and a mechanical doll participates in the long tradition of misogynist writings on women and women's bodies. This tradition, both theological and social, demonized female sexuality.[72] The succubus appears moments after, an exact theatrical image of the version of femininity Penitent has voiced: a purely sexual temptation to masculine autonomy.[73] In the subsequent Act IV scene 2 Gunwater's description of the 'courtesan''s appearance with a 'linen cloth about her jaw' reminds the audience of femininity as disguise and prostitution's link with illness (IV. 2. 15). In Act IV scene 3 Gunwater insistently pursues Follywit-as-courtesan, and says: 'I have the command of all the house; I can tell you. Nothing comes into th'kitchen but comes through my hands' (IV. 3. 17–18). Follywit as woman is fair game for the manservant, and masculinity demon-

---

[71] See Daileader, 'The Courtesan Revisited', for a trenchant defence of the feminist approach to Middleton. For the classic take on Middleton as an anti-feminist see Fumiko Takase, 'Thomas Middleton's Anti-Feminist Sentiment in *A Mad World, my Masters*', in *Playing with Gender: A Renaissance Pursuit*, ed. by Jean Brink and others (Urbana: University of Illinois Press, 1991), pp. 19–31. Herbert Heller, *Penitent Brothellers: Grace, Sexuality and Genre in Thomas Middleton's City Comedies* (Newark: University of Delaware Press, 2000), argues that the successive 'repentances' at the end of this play suggest a moral outlook on sexual excess (pp. 58–60, 194).

[72] See Diane Henderson, *Half Humankind: Contexts and Texts of the Controversy about Women in England 1560–1640* (Chicago: University of Illinois Press, 1985), pp. 3–46.

[73] A point implicit in Leanore Lieblin's excellent article on the play, 'The Lessons of Feigning in *A Mad World, my Masters*', *Modern Language Studies*, 8 (1977), 23–32.

strated as predatory. Femininity is visualized and verbalized as vulnerable. However, the opposite social and cultural assumption (of rapacious femininity) lies behind Follywit's use of the courtesan disguise ('Who keeps a harlot, tell him this from me; | He needs nor thief, disease nor enemy' (IV. 3. 53–54)), an assumption which appears to give validity to his disguise and theft. Follywit's binary division of women into virgins and whores, his acquiescence in contemporary ideological assumptions about women's appearance and status, is to be the very root of his own comic downfall in the next few scenes. In Act IV scene 4 Sir Bounteous's festive generosity and gullibility slips into the misogyny Follywit has depended upon for his disguise to work: 'a strumpet's love will have a waft i'th'end' (IV. 4. 47). The tricking of Sir Bounteous, unable to tell the difference between a courtesan and his nephew ('methought her breath had much ado to be sweet, like a thing compounded methought of wine, beer and tobacco' (ll. 3–4)), comically displays Follywit's earlier assertion in Act III scene 3 that gender can be successfully performed. Gunwater is robbed of his chain, and Sir Bounteous's chest of its jewels: stage properties which symbolically stand respectively for a phallic masculinity and virginal femininity. Follywit's gender-crossing and its theatrical effects visually disturb and destroy conventional models of gender, as Middleton's stage properties again literalize the disruptive bogeys of anti-theatricalists.

Penitent arrives at the Harebrains' house in Act IV scene 5, and delivers his anti-theatrical and anti-sexual polemic:

> What knows the lecher when he clips his whore
> Whether it be the devil his parts adore?
> They're both so like that, in our natural sense,
> I could discern no change nor difference.
> No marvel then times should so stretch and turn:
> None for religion, all for pleasure burn.
> Hot zeal into hot lust is now transformed,
> Grace into painting, charity into clothes,
> Faith into false hair, and put off as often.
> There's nothing but our virtue knows a mean.
> He that kept open house, now keeps a quean.
> He will keep open still that he commends,
> And there he keeps a table for his friends;
> And she consumes more than her sire could hoard,
> Being more common than his house or board.
>   (IV. 5. 53–67)

Sexualized, unmarried women are here paradigmatically both the image and the source of modern degeneracy: woman is characterized as an open mouth, an open house, an open vagina, a conventional set of associative tropes.[74] In

---

[74] See Stallybrass, 'Patriarchal Territories'.

Act IV's final scene Follywit meets the courtesan in the street, and in asking her mother about her, falls for the sales pitch:

> Those bashful maiden humours take me prisoner. [. . .] Give me a woman as she was made at first, simple of herself, without sophistication, like this wench; I cannot abide them when they have tricks, set speeches, and artful entertainments. You shall have some so impudently aspected they will outcry the forehead of a man, make him blush first and talk him into silence, and this is counted manly in a woman. (IV. 6. 58–68)

Follywit's folly, then, is his assumption that gender identity is absolute and un-theatrical. His fall demonstrates the truth and untruth of Penitent's conversion rhetoric. Woman is his downfall, but equally so is his seeing 'woman' and femininity as either maidenly or manly, appropriate or inappropriate. The juxtaposed scenes of this act generate an incrementally doubled vision of gender: that represented by the men and that by the courtesan. As the courtesan's mother says: 'I | Am persuaded whene'er she has husband | She will e'en be a precedent for all married wives, | How to direct their actions and their lives' (IV. 6. 50–53). The courtesan's story of social-realization is a palimpsest for female performance and self-fashioning.

Courtesans and prostitutes in Elizabethan and Jacobean London excelled (and had to excel) in the arts of dressing and mimicry: Frances Baker, a woman sent to Bridewell for prostitution in 1599, described in her examination how her mistress would require her to change out of her own clothes and into those of a gentlewoman, a silk and velvet dress:

> when any gentleman do come to her house and be desirous of gentlewomen, then she will send for such wenches as she is acquainted withal, and will shift them from top to toe and put on such apparel as she thinketh the frankness of the gentlemen will be unto her.[75]

Contemporary attacks against prostitution included not only the standard warnings against illness and sin, but also references to the fact that prostitutes cross-dressed: that is, dressed to deceive.[76] The Latin for prostitute (*meretrix*) was becoming synonymous with lying: 'meretricious' is first recorded in English by the *OED* in Bacon's *New Atlantis* of 1626. The interpenetration of theatricality and prostitution was a commonplace theme of the anti-theatrical polemicists and preachers,[77] and the close geographic and economic links between theatres and brothels fuelled this prejudice.[78] In Middleton's text, connections between theatricality and the arts of the courtesan are the most

---

[75] Quoted in Gowing, *Common Bodies*, p. 32.
[76] See n. 5 above.
[77] See nn. 26-28 above. Thomas Heywood's *An Apology for Actors* (1612) was explicitly written to counteract their ideas and stereotypes.
[78] See the references in n. 5, and Paul Griffiths, 'The Structure of Prostitution in Elizabethan London', *Continuity and Change*, 8 (1993), 39–63.

successful of all the aesthetic and theatrical modes within the plot, arguably demonstrating the contemporary demonization of both courtesan and theatre. However, the courtesan's final trick succeeds in drawing the two main plots together, achieving her respectable marriage. The final play-within-the-play, *The Slip*, meta-dramatically articulates (from title to content and audience effect) the play's self-conscious attention to slippages of recognition, disguise, and identity. Social success in the world represented on stage is the recognition of the necessity of, and success in, acting. Of course, the courtesan was really a boy actor: so the original audience watched a boy-as-woman-as-courtesan, and it was s/he who was the most effective actor on stage.[79]

Early modern discourses demonize the female body as leaky, rotten, a temptation to men, and inferior to the closed, cold, dry, and rational body of man.[80] When Middleton's courtesan first walks onto the stage, she is described by Penitent Brothel as 'the close courtesan' (I. 1. 121). The metaphor hints slyly at her connection to the closet and secret sexual encounters and is echoed when her entry into Sir Bounteous's house is described as 'closely conveyed into his closet' (III. 3. 67). However, the metaphor also suggests a closed body, contained and autonomous.[81] The image of a closed body in a woman was conventionally used to refer to a virgin ('I ne'er beheld a perfect maid till now', says Follywit (IV. 6. 77)), to be opened only by the legitimate attentions of her husband.[82] Despite her performance of a 'leaky' body in Act III scene 2, the paradox of a 'close courtesan' posits the notion that agency may reside in her body. She is described by Follywit as 'an uncertain creature, a quean' (III. 3. 34), a term also used by Penitent Brothel in Act IV scene 4, and pointing to a third state between male and female, beyond maid, wife, or widow.[83] Like Lucio's joke about Mariana in *Measure for Measure* (first performed the year before *A Mad World, my Masters*), 'she may be a punk, for many of them are neither maid, widow, nor wife',[84] the descriptions of

---

[79] Not only the courtesan: the play was first performed by Paul's Boys, so all characters were boys. See Levine, introduction, pp. 1–9; Lisa Jardine, *Still Harping on Daughters: Women and Drama in the Age of Shakespeare* (Basingstoke: Harvester Wheatsheaf, 1983), passim; and for the company for which Middleton wrote see Reavley Gair, *The Children of Paul's: The Story of a Theatre Company 1553–1608* (Cambridge: Cambridge University Press, 1982).

[80] See Ian Maclean, *The Renaissance Notion of Woman: A Study in the Fortunes of Scholasticism and Medical Science in European Intellectual Life* (Cambridge: Cambridge University Press, 1980), pp. 28–34; Paster, pp. 9–22. See also Stallybrass, 'Patriarchal Territories'.

[81] See Middleton's *The Revenger's Tragedy* (1606): 'That woman is all male that none can enter' (II. 1. 110), in *The Complete Works*, pp. 547–93 (p. 560).

[82] See *Enclosure Acts: Sexuality, Property and Culture in Early Modern England*, ed. by Richard Burt and John Archer (Ithaca, NY: Cornell University Press, 1994), building on the work of Stallybrass, 'Patriarchal Territories'.

[83] A notion originating in queer theory, posited by Marjorie Garber in *Vested Interests: Cross Dressing and Cultural Anxiety* (London and New York, Routledge, 1997), Chapter 1, pp. 9–13.

[84] Shakespeare, *Measure for Measure*, V. 1. 177–78, in *The Norton Shakespeare*, ed. by Stephen Greenblatt (New York: Norton, 2008), pp. 2048–2108.

the courtesan as a different kind of being, a body both closed and open,[85] as representing uncertainty and doubleness, refocus our attention on the scene with which we began, and the bed she occupies.

In the bed and on the bed the courtesan appears to be all grotesque body. The carnivalesque encapsulation of her sexualized, vomiting, defecating body is so extreme that it drives her suitors away: Inesse, Possibility, and Sir Bounteous literally retreat from the bodily effluent. However, her repulsive body is actually an effective theatrical and autonomous agent, and the audience is privy to the joke. The gross physicality of the female body is perversely celebrated theatrically as the means through which the most successful plot is delivered. This female body ('one that knows no mean' (I. 1. 111)) and its theatricality, albeit inscribed upon a boy's body, posit the possibility of female agency through 'uncertain'ty' (III. 3. 34). The linguistic punning of key words throughout the play crystallizes the dramatic insight that all appearance is constructed and doubled: Sir Bounteous's 'organs'; the courtesan's 'business' and 'occupation'; the 'tricks' of both Follywit and the courtesan; the 'credit' required by Follywit and used by the courtesan; the 'property' which is land, personality, stage furniture, and sex (I. 1. 32, 94; II. 5. 4; III. 3. 37; IV. 6. 65; V. 2. 305). All these key words have economic, sexual, dramatic, and material meanings with concrete theatrical presence, either as stage properties, stage identities, or as motivations.[86] Linguistic and social identity is fluid in the urban world Middleton represented,[87] and success is represented as the effective self-conscious practice of this knowledge.

Middleton's courtesan celebrates her autonomy through her body's talents, acting on multiple stages. Carnivalesque festivity, represented throughout the play by Sir Bounteous's generosity to strangers, his incontinence, and his final festive reconvening of all the characters, nevertheless fuses most successfully in the courtesan's character and actions, and in her final incorporation into the social body via a marriage she has trickingly engineered. In the actor's representation of femininity, she is both autonomous and socially successful.[88] In Dekker's *2 Honest Whore* Bellafront complains, 'She's that a whore | Loves gallants, fares well' (IV. 1. 58–59),[89] and courtesans are shown

[85] A point that echoes Stallybrass's judgement on Emilia's views at the end of *Othello*, in 'Patriarchal Territories': 'the female grotesque could, indeed, interrogate class and gender hierarchies alike, subverting the enclosed body in the name of a body that is "unfinished, outgrows itself, transgresses its own limits"' (p. 142, quoting Bakhtin, *Rabelais*).

[86] See Douglas Bruster, *Drama and the Market in the Age of Shakespeare* (Cambridge: Cambridge University Press, 1992), Chapter 1, 'Towards a Material Theatre', pp. 1–11.

[87] See Karim-Cooper 'Disguise and Identity'; and Susan Wells, 'Jacobean City Comedy and the Ideology of the City', *ELH*, 48 (1981), 37–60.

[88] Susan Wells argues that some city comedy provides recuperative models of an urban festivity in which the greedy accumulation of other comedies is translated into a celebration of 'play'.

[89] Thomas Dekker, *2 Honest Whore*, in *The Dramatic Works of Thomas Dekker*, ed. by Fredson Bowers, 4 vols (Cambridge: Cambridge University Press, 1955), II, 133–218 (p. 183).

to be both in need of moral reform and socially marginal in the correction house of Bridewell. In *A Mad World, my Masters* the courtesan raises more unstable possibilities. Unlike plays which end in an unequivocal celebration of emergent bourgeois ideologies of contained and closed women, of the fixed binary construction of woman as virgin/wife or whore, or of the misogynist representation of women as leaky inferiors,[90] Middleton's festive ending is in contradistinction to the rigid binaries of the anti-theatricalists. He radically offers up a third sex and a gentle satire on how Jacobean masculinity displaced sin onto female sexuality. The woman's bed and bedroom become the centre of productive sexuality, albeit within a patriarchal economy. Stephen Orgel's argument about *The Roaring Girl* ('[it] enacts the dangerous possibility [. . .]: that women might not be objects but subjects, not the other, but the self')[91] applies to Middleton's courtesan. The bed as central stage property coalesces, figures forth, and symbolizes the worst fears of the anti-theatricalists, and transforms them into a comic serenade to provisional, urban female identity. The playing out of material beds in Jacobean comedy, and their resonances in later seventeenth-century comedy, are a rich resource for debating the intersections of gender, identity, and theatricality in early modern drama.

UNIVERSITY OF BRIGHTON   KATE AUGHTERSON

[90] See Pier Paolo Frassinelli, 'Realism, Desire and Reification in Thomas Middleton's *A Chaste Maid in Cheapside*', *Early Modern Literary Studies*, 8 (2003) <http://extra.shu.ac.uk/emls/08-3/fraschas.htm> [accessed 22 July 2013].

[91] Orgel, p. 153.

'THE SENSES OF PRIMITIVE MAN': JOSEPH CONRAD, W. H. R. RIVERS, AND REPRESENTING THE OTHER IN 'THE END OF THE TETHER'

Conrad's relationship with anthropology has been a recurrent topic in Conrad studies ever since Richard Curle identified *The Malay Archipelago* (1869), by the English naturalist Alfred Russel Wallace, as Conrad's 'favourite bedside book'.[1] This article explores Conrad's neglected 1902 Malay tale 'The End of the Tether', and an unspoken confluence between its stress on the visual in the representation of non-Europeans and the contemporary anthropology of W. H. R. Rivers. Rivers is today perhaps better known as a pioneer of experimental psychology and for his work with the British war poet Siegfried Sassoon at the Craiglockhart Hospital for Officers, as enshrined in Pat Barker's *Regeneration* trilogy (1991–95) and Sassoon's fictional memoir *The Complete Memoirs of George Sherston* (1937). Yet Rivers also played a fundamental role in the establishment of social anthropology as an academic discipline in Britain,[2] and his investigations into the visual capacities of 'primitive' cultures were both current and influential when 'The End of the Tether' was first published. Rivers's ideas about primitive vision were developed during the Cambridge Anthropological Expedition to the Torres Strait in 1898, and his researches into the visual capacities of local peoples drawn from the region— situated between 'New Guinea [. . .] and the whole of the solid Australian continent', as Conrad puts it in his late essay 'Geography and Some Explorers' (1924)[3]—constitute the bulk of Volume II of the *Reports of the Cambridge Anthropological Expedition to the Torres Straits*, published in 1901. This article

---

A version of this article was presented at the 37th Annual International Conference of the Joseph Conrad Society (UK), London, 2011. I would like to thank Patricia Pye for bringing the syllabus of Rivers's Royal Institution lectures to my attention and Robert Hampson for his comments on an earlier draft. I am also indebted to Jane Harrison and Katherine Doyle of the Royal Institution of Great Britain archive collections.

[1] Richard Curle, 'Joseph Conrad: Ten Years After', *Virginia Quarterly Review*, 10 (1934), 420–35 (p. 431). Too numerous to enumerate here, such studies include considerations of the influence on Conrad's Malay fiction of Wallace himself, the influence of Conrad on contemporary pioneers such as his compatriot Bronisław Malinowski, and consonances with more contemporary thinkers such as Claude Lévi-Strauss. On Conrad's debt to Wallace see Amy Houston, 'Conrad and Alfred Russel Wallace', in *Conrad: Intertexts and Appropriations. Essays in Memory of Yves Hervouet*, ed. by Gene M. Moore and others (Amsterdam: Rodopi, 1997), pp. 29–48. On Malinowski's debt to Conrad see James Clifford, *The Predicament of Culture: Twentieth-Century Ethnography, Literature, and Art* (Cambridge, MA: Harvard University Press, 1988), pp. 92–114. For a discussion of Conrad and Lévi-Strauss see Tony Tanner, '"Gnawed Bones" and "Artless Tales": Eating and Narrative in Conrad', in *Joseph Conrad: A Commemoration*, ed. by Norman Sherry (London: Macmillan, 1976), pp. 17–36.

[2] See Ian Langham, *The Building of British Social Anthropology: W. H. R. Rivers and his Cambridge Disciples in the Development of Kinship Studies, 1898–1931* (Dordrecht: Reidel, 1981).

[3] Joseph Conrad, 'Geography and Some Explorers', in *Last Essays*, ed. by Harold Ray Stevens and J. H. Stape (Cambridge: Cambridge University Press, 2010), pp. 3–17 (p. 16). Unless otherwise

also examines a series of lectures preceding this publication, entitled 'The Senses of Primitive Man', in which Rivers's theories of primitive vision were circulated and publicized in the early part of 1900, having first considered some of the contemporary ethnographic contexts in which Conrad's early Malay fiction, and 'The End of the Tether' in particular, took shape.

Whalley, Frazer, Cambridge, and the East

'The End of the Tether' focuses on an English skipper called Whalley trading in Eastern waters during the high colonial era. Whalley originally came out East 'with his head full of a plan for opening a new trade with a distant part of the Archipelago',[4] and, as local lore confirms, has succeeded in doing so:

Captain Whalley, Henry Whalley, otherwise Dare-devil Harry—Whalley, of the *Condor*, a famous clipper in her day [. . .] had made famous passages, had been the pioneer of new routes and new trades [. . .] had steered across the unsurveyed tracts of the South-Seas and had seen the sun rise on uncharted islands. (pp. 130–31)

The 'Admiralty Charts' and the '*General Directory*, vol. ii. p. 410', where can be found the co-ordinates of 'Whalley Island', 'Condor Reef', and 'a description of the "Molotu or Whalley Passage"' (p. 131), suggest Whalley's success has also been officially recognized. Whalley has not just opened up parts of the Malay Archipelago to Europe's cartographic gaze (a project dating back to 'that day, four hundred years ago' when the region was 'first beheld by Western eyes from the deck of a high-pooped caravel' (p. 182)), but also to the colonial and economic penetration that follows from this—'a flood of new ships, new men, new methods of trade' (p. 131). Whalley's East has also become, partly thanks to his endeavours, a place of tourism and sightseeing: 'the periodical invasions of tourists from some passenger steamer in the harbour flitted through [. . .] like relays of migratory shades condemned to speed headlong round the earth without leaving a trace' (p. 142). The central irony of the story is that having helped shrink the globe for European commerce and cultural consumption, Whalley finds that his own world is also contracting: 'The old ship was his last friend; he was not afraid of her; he knew every inch of her deck; but at her too he hardly dared to look, for fear of finding he could see less than the day before' (p. 225); Whalley, as the narrative reveals in a carefully extended piece of 'delayed decoding', is going blind.[5] The professional implications of

---

noted, all references to Conrad's works are to the Cambridge Edition published by Cambridge University Press (1990–).

[4] Joseph Conrad, 'The End of the Tether', in *'Youth', 'Heart of Darkness', 'The End of the Tether'*, ed. by Owen Knowles (2010), pp. 129–251 (p. 148). Further references are given after quotations in the text.

[5] Of course, Whalley's world is contracting for reasons other than blindness; his role as an early

this are made clear in Whalley's disclosure to his friend and fellow pioneer Mr van Wyk: 'A ship's unseaworthy when her captain can't see' (p. 223). For Conrad—a former seaman who, as letters suggest, also suffered from unspecified eye trouble—these words must have held a particularly melancholic force. In underlining that a professional seaman must also be a seeing man, 'The End of the Tether' is at one level a meditation on the life of a professional mariner, the career Conrad abandoned in order to take up writing.[6]

'The End of the Tether' also reflects a deepening engagement between Conrad's fiction and anthropology. Whalley arguably has not just made some of the remoter parts of the East available to European colonial and economic influence, but also to European cultural interest and scientific enquiry. This includes the newly professionalized discipline of anthropology, which, like Conrad's lifelong 'passion' geography, partly relied for its conceptual coherence on the idea of the disinterested gaze,[7] and which, as one of what Bernard Smith calls 'the sciences of visible nature',[8] like those acts of cartographic revelation bearing his name ('Whalley Passage', 'Whalley Island'), offers an ironic counterpoint to the darkness now enveloping Whalley. The story's engagement with anthropology is signalled from the opening sentence in the strange name of Whalley's ship: 'For a long time after the course of the steamer *Sofala* had been altered for the land, the low swampy coast had retained its appearance of a mere smudge of darkness beyond a belt of glitter' (p. 129). As if to point up its apparent importance, this name is later the crux of a confused transaction between Whalley and the sampan pilot tasked with transporting him to his final command: '"Sofala", articulated Captain Whalley from above; and the Chinaman, a new emigrant probably, stared upwards with a tense attention as if waiting to see the queer word fall visibly from the white man's lips' (p. 166). The eponymous first tale in Conrad's

---

pioneer in Eastern waters has since been eclipsed by the 'piercing of the Isthmus of Suez' and by the advent and spread of steam power and telegraphy: 'in a world that was able to count its disengorged tonnage twice over every day and in which lean charters were snapped up by cable three months in advance, there [was] hardly any room to exist' (pp. 131, 137). For a discussion of the revelation of Whalley's blindness through Conrad's revisions to the manuscript see *'Youth', 'Heart of Darkness', 'The End of the Tether'*, p. 289. For 'delayed decoding' see Ian Watt, *Conrad in the Nineteenth Century* (Berkeley: University of California Press, 1981), p. 175.

[6] In a letter to George Blackwood of 28 January 1902 Conrad pointedly refers to the story's '[v]ery personal' subject-matter (see *The Collected Letters of Joseph Conrad*, II: *1898–1902*, ed. by Frederick R. Karl and Laurence Davies (Cambridge: Cambridge University Press, 1986), p. 376).

[7] On this reliance in geography see Gearoid Ó Tuathail, *Critical Geopolitics: The Politics of Writing Global Space* (London: Routledge, 1996), p. 57. On the centrality of the disinterested gaze in the construction of ethnographic authority see James Clifford, pp. 21–54. Conrad's fascination with geography features in 'Geography and Some Explorers' (1924) and *A Personal Record* (1912), and, indirectly, in 'Heart of Darkness' (1899), in Marlow's 'passion for maps' (*'Youth', 'Heart of Darkness', 'The End of the Tether'*, pp. 43–126 (p. 48)).

[8] Bernard Smith, *European Vision and the South Pacific* (New Haven: Yale University Press, 1985), p. viii. The other 'sciences of visible nature' identified by Smith are geology, botany, and zoology.

1902 collection *Youth*, which 'The End of the Tether' brings to a close, finds its narrator Marlow similarly dwelling on the '[q]ueer name' of another steamer: '*Judea*, London'.[9] Christopher GoGwilt has argued that through the juxtaposition of these 'categories of East and West' ('Judea' and 'London'), 'Youth' suggests 'a European identity constructed on a mythic and historical identification with an ancient Eastern past'.[10] The name of the *Sofala*, meanwhile, appears to gesture towards an ancient, pre-colonial African past.

As several critics have suggested, the name of Whalley's command almost certainly derives from the ancient city of Sofala, located in present-day Mozambique, whose rituals of kingship are discussed in Sir James Frazer's influential work of anthropology, *The Golden Bough*.[11] Whalley's physical deterioration and subsequent suicide roughly mirror a practice of the kings of ancient Sofala, for whom it was a custom, according to Frazer, to take their own lives 'when any disaster or natural physical defect'—such as blindness—'fell upon them'.[12] Originally published in 1890, the second edition of *The Golden Bough* was heavily previewed, and later reviewed, in the *Fortnightly Review*—a publication that Conrad, according to H. G. Wells, read regularly—during the winter of 1900,[13] little more than a year before Conrad began work on 'The End of the Tether'.[14] Conrad may also have been acquainted with Frazer's work via his friendships with Edmund Gosse and Sidney Colvin, who during the mid-1880s had been contemporaries of Frazer at Trinity College, Cambridge: Gosse when giving his Clark lectures in 1885, Colvin when helping to plan Frazer's translation of Pausanias in 1884.[15] In his Preface to *The Golden Bough* Frazer refers to these and other networks of academe when pointing to Malaya and 'the Dutch East Indies'—the setting for much of Conrad's early fiction, including 'The End of the Tether'—as 'a very important field to the ethnologist'.[16] Indeed, just as Cambridge would become the centre of British social anthropology over the turn of the twentieth century, so the East to which Frazer refers

---

[9] Joseph Conrad, 'Youth', in '*Youth*', '*Heart of Darkness*', '*The End of the Tether*', pp. 11–39 (p. 12).
[10] Christopher GoGwilt, *The Invention of the West: Joseph Conrad and the Double-Mapping of Europe and Empire* (Stanford, CA: Stanford University Press, 1995), p. 23.
[11] See Robert Hampson, 'Frazer, Conrad and the "Truth of Primitive Passion"', in *Sir James Frazer and the Literary Imagination: Essays in Affinity and Influence*, ed. by Robert Fraser (London: Macmillan, 1990), pp. 172–91.
[12] James George Frazer, *The Golden Bough: A Study in Comparative Religion* (London: Macmillan, 1890), p. 272.
[13] See Hampson, 'Frazer, Conrad and the "Truth of Primitive Passion"', p. 172. Conrad subsequently placed the essays 'Autocracy and War' (1905) and 'The Crime of Partition' (1919) in the magazine. Conrad and Wells were at the time near neighbours in Kent; their friendship is clearly detectable in Conrad's early works, and underlined by his 1907 dedication to Wells in *The Secret Agent: A Simple Tale*, ed. by Bruce Harkness and S. W. Reid (1990), p. 2.
[14] See Rosalind Walls Smith, 'Dates of Composition of Conrad's Works', *Conradiana*, 11 (1979), 63–90 (p. 69); and Owen Knowles, *A Conrad Chronology* (London: Macmillan, 1989), pp. 45–48.
[15] See Hampson, 'Frazer, Conrad and the "Truth of Primitive Passion"', p. 174.
[16] Frazer, p. xi.

would become central to anthropology's establishment and self-definition, providing the scene, source, and substance of much of its fieldwork.[17] Frazer's allusion to the East as the future crucible for anthropology also carries a particular resonance in relation to his own work. As Langham notes, Frazer had asked his contemporary Alfred Haddon to collect information about totemism during Haddon's first expedition to the Torres Strait in 1888, and considered, before declining, the opportunity to join Haddon—along with C. G. Seligman, Sidney Ray, Anthony Wilkin, and W. H. R. Rivers—on another expedition there in 1898.[18] It was during this second expedition that Rivers conducted the fieldwork that later provided the substance of his lectures on 'The Senses of Primitive Man' in 1900, and of his volume for the *Reports of the Cambridge Anthropological Expedition to the Torres Straits* in 1901.

Wallace, Clifford, and the 'real Malay'

The first page of 'The End of the Tether' also carries the beginnings of a sustained representation of the *Sofala*'s serang (or 'boatswain'): 'an elderly, alert, little Malay, with very dark skin', known to Whalley from his previous command the *Fair Maid* (p. 172). The description of the serang's character (his 'childlike impulsiveness' (p. 163)) and physiognomy ('a face of the Chinese type' (p. 173)) broadly reflects Conrad's reading of A. R. Wallace, and the racial taxonomies laid out in *The Malay Archipelago*. Part travelogue, part natural history, part ethnographic study, Wallace's 1869 work is one of the 'dull, wise books', as Conrad put it elsewhere,[19] that played a key role in the construction and authentication of Conrad's represented Eastern world—here, by helping to delineate Conrad's representation of the various non-European peoples inhabiting that world. Rivers's engagement in the *Reports* with the work of other gentleman explorers and independent travellers, including Aimé Bonpland and Alexander von Humboldt (whose work in Ecuador during the 1850s yields '[p]erhaps the most frequently quoted instance of extraordinary visual acuity in a non-civilized race'), Julius Brenchley (whose 1873 narrative *Jottings during the Cruise of H.M.S. Curaçoa* 'noted that the men of San Christoval in the Solomon Islands had "eyes like lynxes"'), and A. J. Duffield (who during the 1880s had reported on the 'remarkable' 'keenness of sight of the natives of New Ireland'),[20] demonstrates

[17] See Anita Herle and Sandra Rouse, 'Introduction: Cambridge and the Torres Strait', in *Cambridge and the Torres Strait: Centenary Essays on the 1898 Anthropological Expedition*, ed. by Anita Herle and Sandra Rouse (Cambridge: Cambridge University Press, 1998), pp. 1–22.

[18] Langham, pp. 64–66.

[19] *The Collected Letters of Joseph Conrad*, II, 130 (Letter to William Blackwood, 13 December 1898).

[20] W. H. R. Rivers, *Reports of the Cambridge Anthropological Expedition to Torres Straits*, II/1: *Physiology and Psychology* (Cambridge: Cambridge University Press, 1901), pp. 1–140 (p. 19).

a similar reliance on 'dull, wise books'. This underlines that the practice of direct observation in the field which anthropology regularized was always already filtered through particular reading practices at 'home'. Whereas his co-pioneer Bronisław Malinowski claimed that 'scientific ethnography had begun only recently with professionals [such as] himself', Rivers's reliance on 'dull, wise books' also underlines that 'anthropology derived much of its ethnographic tradition from the work of naturalists, missionaries, and independent travellers of the previous three centuries', including Wallace's.[21]

In *The Malay Archipelago* Wallace, who like Conrad's Marlow had possessed since his early training as a surveyor in the Welsh hills 'a passion for maps',[22] maps what he perceives are the region's principal racial and ethnic boundaries.[23] He draws a line dividing 'the Archipelago into two portions', 'an Indo-Malayan and [an] Austro-Malayan region'.[24] This cartographic division reflects his belief that '[t]wo very strongly contrasted races inhabit the Archipelago': 'the Papuans' to the east, 'whose headquarters are New Guinea and several of the adjacent islands', and 'the Malays, occupying almost exclusively the larger western half of it'. According to Wallace, the Malay 'is undoubtedly the most [*sic*] important' of the two races, because 'it is the one which is the most civilized, which has come into contact with Europeans, and which alone has any place in history'. Wallace then divides this 'Indo-Malay' region into 'four great, and a few minor semi-civilized tribes, and a number of others who may be termed savages'. The 'semi-civilized Malays' 'inhabit chiefly Ternate, Tidore, Batchian, and Amboyna', while the 'savage Malays' comprise 'the Dyaks of Borneo; the Battaks and other wild tribes of Sumatra; the Jakuns of the Malay Peninsula; the aborigines of Northern Celebes, of the Sula island, and of part of Bouru'. The four 'great' tribes, meanwhile, inhabit the Malay Peninsula and the coastal regions of Borneo and Sumatra (home to 'the Malay proper'); Java, Madura, Bali, and parts of Lombock and Sumatra (home to 'the Javanese'); Celebes and Sumbawa (home to 'the Bugis'); and the Philippine Islands (home to 'the Tagalas'). These, Wallace concludes, are '[w]hat may be called the *true Malay* races'.[25]

The idea of 'the true Malay' resurfaces in contemporary notices of Conrad's early Malay fiction. In one of the first general assessments of Conrad's writing,

---

[21] Joa Pau Rubiés, 'Travel Writing and Ethnography', in *The Cambridge Companion to Travel Writing*, ed. by Peter Hulme and Tim Youngs (Cambridge: Cambridge University Press, 2002), pp. 242–60 (p. 251).

[22] Conrad, 'Heart of Darkness', p. 48.

[23] On Wallace's background as a surveyor see Felix Driver, *Geography Militant: Cultures of Exploration and Empire* (Oxford: Blackwell, 2000), p. 39.

[24] Alfred Russel Wallace, *The Malay Archipelago: The Land of the Orang-Utan, and the Bird of Paradise. A Narrative of Travel, with Sketches of Man and Nature*, II (London: Macmillan, 1869), pp. 278–79.

[25] Ibid., pp. 270–71 (emphasis added).

an 1898 review of *Tales of Unrest*, Hugh Clifford concluded that 'Mr Conrad's Malays are [. . .] very vividly described, very powerfully drawn, *but not Malays*'.[26] Clifford's charge, one anchored in and authorized by his years of experience as a colonial official in Malaya (Clifford was the British Resident in Pahang at the time), was that Conrad had failed to capture the 'real' Malay. Referring to Conrad's debut novel *Almayer's Folly* (1895), Clifford offered that 'a real' Nina Almayer would not go back to native ways, and that 'a real' Babalatchi would never dare to yawn and scratch himself in the royal presence. Shortly before Clifford's review appeared, Conrad had given a largely positive review of Clifford's second volume of stories deriving from his experiences in Malaya, *Studies in Brown Humanity* (1898), in the 23 April 1898 issue of the *Academy*. Conrad wrote approvingly that 'this book is only truth', 'truth unadorned, simple and straightforward'—thus bestowing on Clifford the very kind of representational authority subsequently denied him by Clifford's review.[27]

Conrad himself appears to relinquish any claims to such authority, both privately and publicly. In a letter of 13 December 1898 to his publisher William Blackwood Conrad drily counters Clifford's charge by claiming he had not intentionally 'set up as an authority on Malaysia',[28] and reiterates this claim in the Author's Note to his 1912 memoir *A Personal Record*, which contains a recollection of his first meeting with Clifford:

he ended by telling me with the uncompromising yet kindly firmness of a man accustomed to speak unpalatable truths even to Oriental potentates [. . .] that as a matter of fact I didn't know anything about Malays. I was perfectly aware of this. I have never pretended to any such knowledge, and I was moved [. . .] to retort: 'Of course I don't know anything about Malays. If I knew only one hundredth part of what you [. . .] know of Malays I would make everybody sit up.'[29]

As far as other critics were concerned, however, what Conrad knew of Malays was considerable. Despite Clifford's grumble, Conrad's 'Malay' fiction frequently *was* seen not just as an accurate representation, but a precise transcription, of the ethnic and cultural realities of 'the East'. Typifying this response, another contemporary review of *Tales of Unrest* 'crowned' the collection as one of the better books of 1898 for its perceived 'geo-graphing'

---
[26] Hugh Clifford, 'Mr. Conrad at Home and Abroad', *Singapore Free Press*, 30 August 1898, p. 142 (emphasis added).
[27] Joseph Conrad, 'An Observer in Malaya', in *Notes on Life and Letters*, ed. by J. H. Stape (2002), pp. 50–52 (pp. 51–52).
[28] *The Collected Letters of Joseph Conrad*, II, 129–30.
[29] Joseph Conrad, *A Personal Record*, ed. by Zdzisław Najder and J. H. Stape (2008), p. 4. Conrad is recalling the occasion of Clifford's first visit to his home at Pent Farm, Kent, in mid-August 1899. The two subsequently became firm friends, with Conrad dedicating his commercial breakthrough *Chance* (1913–14) to Clifford (who, having helped secure its American serialization in the *New York Herald*, played a key part in the novel's popular success). For a discussion of their relationship see Linda Dryden, 'Conrad and Hugh Clifford: An "Irreproachable Player on the Flute" and "A Ruler of Men"', *The Conradian*, 23.1 (Spring 1998), 51–73.

of Malaya, 'the real transference to paper of something of the very heart of the country, the nation, described'.[30]

That Conrad resurrects in his Note the memory of Clifford's denunciation some twenty years after its appearance ('in the year '98, I think, of the last century'[31]) might seem odd given that Conrad, a keen follower of the critical fortunes of his works, could not have been unaware of this alternative, consensual view of his Malay fiction—a view that after all had seen him, not Clifford (then a fellow contributor at *Blackwood's Magazine*), heralded as the future 'Kipling of the Malay archipelago'.[32] Yet Conrad was also never one to let some criticisms drop, as is evidenced elsewhere in the Note, which alludes to the misreading of his life and works through the prism of 'Sclavonism' by Edward Garnett and H. L. Mencken; and to the popular, but for Conrad equally unfounded, 'impression of my having exercised a choice between the two languages, French and English', attributed to 'an article written by Sir Hugh Clifford'.[33] Conrad's assertion that he had 'never *pretended*' to any knowledge 'about Malays', with its discernibly ironic inflection, perhaps suggests that an equally sceptical view regarding the authority and authenticity of contemporary European representations of Malay indigeneity—whether Clifford's or his own—obtained.

Whether emphasizing the authenticity or otherwise of Conrad's represented Malay worlds, at one level the very idea of the 'real' Malay was a fiction produced by colonial discourse. As Robert Hampson underscores, the 'notion of a "Malay race" (*bangsa Melaya*) was developed in the nineteenth century through contact with European categorization'.[34] It is nothing if not apt, therefore, that Clifford should decry Conrad for failing to portray Malay indigeneity, given that the idea of the 'real' Malay issued from the racial imagination of British colonial administrators in the Malay Archipelago such as Clifford, and a textual tradition of 'writing Malaysia' begun by antecedents such as William Marsden, Sir Stamford Raffles, and James 'Rajah' Brooke (a model for the figure of 'Tuan' Jim in Conrad's 1900 novel *Lord Jim*), and continued by Clifford's contemporary in British Malaya, later Conrad's acquaintance, Sir Frank Swettenham, Governor of the British Straits Settlement and author of *The Real Malay* (1900), the very title of which

---

[30] Unsigned article, 'Our Awards for 1898: The "Crowned" Books. Mr. Joseph Conrad and "Tales of Unrest"', *Academy*, 14 January 1899, pp. 65–67; repr. in *Conrad: The Critical Heritage*, ed. by Norman Sherry (London: Macmillan, 1973), pp. 109–10 (p. 110).

[31] Conrad, *A Personal Record*, p. 3.

[32] *Conrad: The Critical Heritage*, p. 61.

[33] Conrad, *A Personal Record*, pp. 5, 3. For the article in question see Hugh Clifford, 'The Genius of Mr Conrad', *North American Review*, June 1904, pp. 847–48.

[34] Robert Hampson, *Cross-Cultural Encounters in Joseph Conrad's Malay Fiction* (Basingstoke: Palgrave, 2000), p. 13.

crystallizes this pretension to representational authority.[35] In his Introduction to Volume II of the *Reports of the Cambridge Anthropological Expedition to the Torres Straits* Rivers mentions that '[t]he natives were told [. . .] that their performances would all be described in a big book so that everyone would read about them'. This suggests the extent to which—exaggeration aside—this volume, and by extension the *Reports* as a whole, was promoted as belonging to a similarly authoritative textual project on Australasia.[36]

The 'Salvage' Paradigm

Whalley's early navigations in the Archipelago were conducted under the protection of the colony's 'Queen's ship', 'the *Dido*' (p. 148), revealing that the realization of Whalley's commercial plans to 'open new trade' in the Archipelago partly rest upon the exercise of British colonial, and in particular naval, power. Like the *Sofala*, the name of the colony's 'Queen's ship' is particularly freighted. The *Dido* was associated with Captain Henry Keppel, under whose command she was engaged in the suppression of piracy in British North Borneo during the mid-1840s, and Keppel's 1846 narrative *The Expedition to Borneo of H.M.S. Dido for the Suppression of Piracy* is another of the 'dull, wise books' upon which Conrad drew when constructing his fictional Malay worlds. Accompanying Keppel's narrative are several maps, including a plan of the 'Forts & Villages of Patusan' (after which Conrad named the fictional Malay community represented in *Lord Jim*). According to the map's legend, Patusan was 'stormed & taken by the boats of H.M.S. Dido [. . .] Aug^t.1844'. These maps, as another legend reveals, were 'taken on Board the Boats of H.M.S. Dido when employed destroying the nests of Pirates'.[37] As Hampson points out, Patusan, like these other piratical geographies recorded by Keppel, was therefore mapped 'at the moment of its destruction'.[38] 'The End of the Tether' suggests that Whalley, a representative of the post-Enlightenment projects of imperial exploration and mapping that

[35] As J. de V. Allen points out, 'Swettenham's accounts of "the real Malay" or "the Peninsular Chinaman" were regarded as positive contributions to scholarship' at the time (J. de V. Allen, 'Two Imperialists: A Study of Sir Frank Swettenham and Sir Hugh Clifford', *Journal of the Malaysian Branch of the Royal Asiatic Society*, 37.1 (1964), 41–73 (p. 45)). For a discussion of Clifford and Malaya see Robert Hampson, 'Hugh Clifford in Malaya', in *Writing, Travel, and Empire: In the Margins of Anthropology*, ed. by Peter Hulme and Russell McDougall (London: I. B. Tauris, 2007), pp. 147–68. According to Clifford, Swettenham and Conrad met in 1903 at a Wellington Club luncheon (Hugh Clifford, 'Joseph Conrad: Some Scattered Memories', *Bookman's Journal and Print Collector*, 11 (October 1924), 3–6 (p. 5)).

[36] Rivers, *Reports*, p. 3.

[37] Henry Keppel, *The Expedition to Borneo of H.M.S. Dido for the Suppression of Piracy: With Extracts from the Journal of James Brooke, Esq. of Sarāwak*, II (London: Chapman and Hall, 1846), pp. 90–91, 48–49.

[38] Robert Hampson, 'Conrad's Heterotopic Fiction: Composite Maps, Superimposed Sites, and Impossible Spaces', in *Conrad in the Twenty-First Century: Contemporary Approaches and*

Conrad in *Last Essays* (1926) famously labels 'Geography militant',[39] has made his name through a similar interplay of cartography and violence:

> His fame remained writ, not very large but plain enough, on the Admiralty charts. [...] On that dangerous coral formation the celebrated clipper [the *Condor*] had hung stranded for three days, her captain and crew throwing her cargo overboard with one hand and with the other, as it were, keeping off her a flotilla of savage war-canoes. (p. 131)

As another set of inscriptive and knowledge-gathering practices, anthropology shared with geography a problematic interdependence with the 'militant' kinds of colonial expansion typified here by Keppel and Whalley. This interdependence is indirectly underlined by Rivers in the *Reports*: 'We found [...] that an enthusiastic native [...] had announced that if [the other islanders] told lies Queen Victoria would send a man-of-war to punish them.'[40] By threatening the existence of the other, anthropology's 'object' of study (here literally), such expansion gave the new discipline its discursive framework and impetus. As James Clifford explains: 'Ethnography's disappearing object is [...] a rhetorical construct legitimating a representational practice: "salvage" ethnography in its widest sense. The other is lost, in disintegrating time and space, but saved in the text.'[41] Such a conceptual manœuvre can be seen to colour some of the contemporary literature on which Conrad relied heavily for his Malay material. Hugh Clifford comments on the disappearance of Malay culture in the 1927 Preface to *In Court and Kampung* (1897), and Wallace's *The Malay Archipelago* sounds a concluding note of concern for ethnography's 'disappearing object': 'the more numerous Malay race seems well adapted to survive', 'even when his country and government have passed into the hands of Europeans'; however, 'if the tide of colonization should be turned to New Guinea, there can be little doubt of the early extinction of the Papuan race', 'who [...] must disappear before the white man as surely as do the wolf and the tiger'.[42] The representation of the other in 'The End of the Tether' as either a phantasmagorical presence ('the elusive shadow[s] of [...] native craft' (p. 130)) or one that, like van Wyk's neighbouring melancholic sultan on Batu Beru, is obsessed with the dispersing effects of European expansion on his own culture ('[h]e [...] hoped he would die before the white men were ready to take his country from him' (p. 207)), is keyed to this 'salvage' paradigm and integral to the story's engagement with contemporary anthropological thought.

Perspectives, ed. by Carola M. Kaplan and others (London: Routledge, 2005), pp. 121–55 (p. 121). Patusan's (or 'Patusen's') destruction is confirmed in the text that appears alongside the map: 'The town was very extensive; and after being well looted, made a glorious blaze' (Keppel, p. 90).

[39] Conrad, 'Geography and Some Explorers', p. 6.
[40] Rivers, *Reports*, p. 4.
[41] Cited in GoGwilt, p. 70.
[42] Wallace, p. 282.

'Primitive Vision'

This engagement also marks Conrad's 'adjectival insistence upon inexpressible and incomprehensible mystery', as F. R. Leavis memorably anatomized Conrad's prose.[43] This 'adjectival insistence' dramatizes a non-European view of Europeans in 'The End of the Tether', as in this misattribution of profound meaning to the profoundly meaningless, drunken, ravings of the *Sofala*'s white engineer:

> the solitary lascar [on] night duty in harbour, perhaps a youth fresh from a forest village, would stand motionless in the shadows of the deck listening to the endless drunken gabble. His heart would be thumping with breathless awe of white men; the arbitrary and obstinate men who pursue inflexibly their incomprehensible purposes—beings with weird intonation in the voice, moved by unaccountable feelings, actuated by inscrutable motives. (p. 170)

A similarly uncomprehending 'native' view of Europeans is filtered through the viewpoint of the *Sofala*'s Malay serang: 'He had swept the decks of ships, had tended their helms, had minded their stores, had risen at last to be a serang; and his placid mind had remained [. . .] incapable of penetrating the simplest motives of those he served' (p. 172). As the *Sofala*'s English mate Sterne later remarks—having given himself over to an almost zoological contemplation of the serang's relationship with Whalley ('they [. . .] recall[ed] to the mind an old whale attended by a little pilot-fish' (pp. 191, 187))—such things are 'beyond [their] apprehension. They aren't capable of finding out anything about us [Europeans]' (p. 229). Thus the European project of ethnography referenced in Conrad's story, of knowing the other by inscribing him within what Derek Gregory calls 'an emergent grid of intellectual authority in Europe',[44] is set against a corresponding inability of the other to know, or even understand, Europeans.

How the narrative describes the serang's visual grasp of the world around him is, in this ethnographic context, particularly salient:

> The record of the visual world fell through his eyes upon his unspeculating mind as on a sensitised plate through the lens of a camera. His knowledge was absolute and precise, nevertheless, had he been asked his opinion, and especially if questioned in the downright, alarming manner of white men, he would have displayed the hesitation of ignorance. (p. 172)

Stephen Donovan observes that this conflation of the uncomprehending glance with the technical processes of photography is one of several instances throughout his fiction where Conrad's negative opinion of 'the camera's

---

[43] F. R. Leavis, *The Great Tradition: George Eliot, Henry James, Joseph Conrad* (London: Chatto and Windus, 1948), p. 180.

[44] Derek Gregory, *Geographical Imaginations* (Oxford: Blackwell, 1994), p. 23.

inadequacy' is manifested.[45] Donovan argues that by 'casually elid[ing] photography with "blind" faith in sensory experience in an orientalizing portrait of the serang helmsman', 'The End of the Tether' 'indicate[s] that Conrad saw photography as defined by undiscriminating inclusiveness and relentless equivalence'—as being, in effect, 'a mere footprint of the visual'.[46] Donovan's reading foregrounds a broader comment upon photography, to which Conrad's 'orientalizing portrait' merely seems incidental. Yet from another angle, Conrad's use of photography is as much a comment on the processes through which the serang is orientalized as on the medium itself. On a local level, Conrad's representation of the *Sofala*'s serang chimes with Sterne's assumption that such visual acuity among Malays 'could not in any way' be connected to 'superior knowledge' (p. 188). More broadly, this representation is also calibrated to ideas about 'primitive' vision then being constructed, circulated, and consolidated in contemporary anthropological thought.

In December 1899, its centennial year, the Royal Institution advertised a course of three lectures running between 18 January and 1 February 1900 on 'The Senses of Primitive Man', to be delivered by Rivers, recently returned from Haddon's second expedition to Australasia. Recalling Smith's characterization of anthropology's emergence over the turn of the twentieth century as a 'science of visible nature', in Rivers's case the visual not only provided the method and the medium, but also the principal object, of measurement. Indeed, despite the promise of inclusiveness indicated in the title, this series of lectures (like Rivers's fieldwork) focuses mainly on the visual realm, as the *Reports* elaborate: 'The subjects [. . .] investigated, included visual acuity and sensibility to light difference; colour vision, including testing for colour-blindness, colour nomenclature, the thresholds for different colours, after-images, contrast, and the colour vision of the peripheral retina; binocular vision; line-dividing; visual illusions.'[47] The first of these lectures, entitled 'Acuteness of Vision', is especially germane to Conrad's vision-centred representation of the other in 'The End of the Tether'.

The anthropological 'material' for this keynote lecture derives, as the syllabus announces, from fieldwork conducted in 'the Torres Straits and New Guinea'. Rivers's address therefore derives from fieldwork conducted in a part of the world with which Whalley, either in his 'Dare-devil' past as 'the pioneer of new routes' 'between Australia and China' (p. 131), or during more recent visits to his daughter in Melbourne from his base in Singapore, has at some point had contact. This was, of course, also a region with which Conrad was familiar from his years as a seaman. During the voyage from Sydney to Mauritius in early August 1888, Conrad, then captain of the *Otago*, charted a passage

---

[45] Stephen Donovan, *Joseph Conrad and Popular Culture* (Basingstoke: Palgrave, 2005), p. 28.
[46] Ibid.
[47] Rivers, *Reports*, pp. 1–2.

through the less-travelled Torres Strait, a feat described in 'Geography and Some Explorers'. In this essay Conrad stresses that, although its 'true contours were first laid down on the map by James Cook', this 'region [. . .] even in my time remained very imperfectly charted and still remote from the knowledge of men'.[48] This sketchy presence of the Torres Strait within what Conrad calls 'the geography triumphant of our day',[49] when there remained in the world few uncharted spaces, no doubt appealed to the organizers of the Cambridge expedition, because it represented 'the privileged field for the anthropologist', the possibility of 'the pure, uncontaminated tribe'.[50] This is confirmed by Rivers's description in the *Reports* of the inhabitants of Murray Island:

The people were [. . .] sufficiently near their primitive condition to be thoroughly interesting. There is no doubt that thirty years ago they were in a completely savage state, absolutely untouched by civilization. Owing to its inaccessibility, Murray Island has been much less affected by outside influences than the other islands in the Torres Straits.[51]

While pointing up the transformative effects on the East of European colonialism and capitalism, 'The End of the Tether' also underlines that there are spaces relatively untouched by such encroachments—'out of men's knowledge' (p. 169)—as a description of native life not dissimilar to Rivers's in the *Reports* makes clear:

their lives ran out silently; the homes where they were born went to rest and died—flimsy sheds of rushes and coarse grass eked out with a few ragged mats—were hidden out of sight from the open sea. No glow of their household fires ever kindled for a seaman a red spark upon the blind night of the group. (p. 184)

Conrad elsewhere suggests that New Guinea, another of the main sites visited by the Cambridge expedition, was as unknown to Europeans as the Torres Strait which cut past its southernmost edge. In 'Freya of the Seven Isles' (1912), for instance, the narrator recalls a legend concerning the eponymous heroine's father, who, like Whalley a one-time pioneer of European expansion in the East, 'had been known to stroll up to a village

[48] Conrad, 'Geography and Some Explorers', pp. 28, 26.
[49] Ibid., p. 9. Conrad's celebration of a 'triumphant' geography echoes the sentiment of Halford J. Mackinder's hugely influential paper 'The Geographical Pivot of History', delivered to the Royal Geographical Society on 25 January 1904. Mackinder also gave a course of Thursday afternoon lectures at the Royal Institution on the geography of East Africa—immediately after the RI lectures given by Rivers—in March and April 1900.
[50] Rubiés, p. 259.
[51] Rivers, *Reports*, pp. 2–3. As Jan B. Deręgowski notes: 'Sir Francis Galton had just published his Isochronic Passage Chart which clearly showed that only the most remote parts of the world such as the central region of South America, Africa, Australia and the frozen Canadian north required in excess of forty days of travel from London. Remote populations were becoming accessible and, simultaneously and inevitably, increasingly subject to alien influences and therefore to dilution or even to the loss of their characteristics' (Deręgowski, 'W. H. R. Rivers (1864–1922): The Founder of Research in Cross-Cultural Perception', *Perception*, 27 (1998), 1389–1406 (p. 1394)).

of cannibals in New Guinea in a quiet, fearless manner [...] on some matter of barter that did not amount perhaps to fifty pounds in the end'.[52] In *The Malay Archipelago* Wallace records visiting '[t]he whole of the great island of New Guinea' and the surrounding islands of 'Ké and Aru', 'Mysol, Salwatty, and Waigion', but makes no mention of cannibalistic practices.[53] Wallace also records finding 'no trace of any other tribes inhabiting the interior of New Guinea'.[54] This is a revealing absence: as Derek Gregory underlines, 'colonial imaginaries typically let monsters loose in the far-away',[55] a deployment that less reflects European knowledge of that 'far-away' than an absence of knowledge. Rather than reflecting the reality of cultural practices on the ground, in other words, the assertion of anthropophagy in 'Freya of the Seven Isles' instead reflects a European knowledge gap about New Guinea ('the greatest *terra incognita* that still remains for the naturalist to explore', as Wallace puts it),[56] and a corresponding need to fill that gap.

A similar correlation between empire and contemporary knowledge practices marks Rivers's lectures on 'Primitive Man'. By pointing up an apparent need 'for exact investigation' into a '[g]eneral belief in the great acuteness' of the visual sense in 'savage races', Rivers's lectures promote science as a legitimating frame for the spread of empire.[57] Indeed, the Royal Institution lectures given either side of Rivers's own likewise suggest the production and contemplation of scientific knowledge fitted to a wider imperial purpose. These include one by the pre-eminent British imperial geographer Halford J. Mackinder on the geography of East Africa, and others on 'Steam Power [and] High-Speed Navigation', 'Wireless Telegraphy', and 'Malaria and Mosquitos'. If Rivers's lectures promote science as a legitimating frame for the spread of empire, these other RI lectures gesture to the technical and medical knowledges mobilized in support of that spread.[58] Moreover, Rivers's lectures, like the fieldwork on which they are based, can also be seen as retrospectively affirming the racial legitimation on which imperial expansion was, in part, based. A key supposition underpinning Rivers's

[52] Joseph Conrad, 'Freya of the Seven Isles', in *'Twixt Land and Sea*, ed. by Jacques Berthoud and others (2008), pp. 121–89 (p. 124).
[53] Wallace, p. 277.
[54] Ibid.
[55] Derek Gregory, *The Colonial Present: Afghanistan, Palestine, and Iraq* (Oxford: Blackwell, 2004), pp. 45–46.
[56] Wallace, p. 263.
[57] London, Royal Institution archive collections, MS GB 4 p. 231, leaflet numbered 425, p. 1 of 2. This syllabus details the three lectures given by Rivers at the Royal Institution on the afternoons of 18 and 25 January and 1 February 1900. Because records were not kept of the afternoon lectures at the RI (unlike the evening or more famous Christmas lectures), the syllabus is the only surviving record of Rivers's RI lectures. The material cited is in the process of being properly catalogued within the RI archive collections.
[58] RI archive, 'Lecture Arrangements before Easter', MS GB 4 p. 231, leaflet numbered 422, p. 3 of 4.

research is that the 'acuteness of [the visual] sense' is a hindrance to 'high mental development' among the 'savage races'.⁵⁹ Such theorizations were based, in part, on a simple experiment using string figures (or 'cat's cradles'), which Rivers believed evidenced a highly developed pictorial imagination. According to Rivers, however, good sight was not conducive to insight, but rather the sign of its absence. 'The End of the Tether', roughly contemporaneous with the 'scientific' views circulated in these lectures, draws a similar line between the visual acuity and 'ignorance' of Malays, as we have seen.⁶⁰

Rivers's fieldwork on primitive vision, though conducted far from Europe itself, remained tethered to and mediated by European conceptual categories and European ways of seeing. This has a bearing on the story's represented seafaring context. The *Sofala* charts a 'monotonous huckster's round, up and down the Straits': 'Malacca to begin with, in at daylight and out at dusk, to cross over with a rigid phosphorescent wake this highway of the Far East', before 'steaming through [a] maze of [. . .] small islands up to a large native town at the end of the beat'; 'the old round of 1600 miles and thirty days' (p. 130). Whalley's stock of local knowledge of this part of the Strait (here the Malacca rather than the Torres Strait) is therefore considerable: he 'knew its order and its sights and its people' (p. 130). The 'sights' of the Straits here serve a navigational purpose, corresponding to places to be seen and steered by. 'Sights', in other words, mark a category into which local sailorly knowledge of the Straits is condensed. In its presentation of the visually 'alert' Malay, 'The End of the Tether' hints at a parallel narrative, whereby 'sight' also provides ethnographers like Rivers with an index by which to measure, and moreover affirm, Western preconceptions about an underlying order of races. Whalley's conception of the underlying 'order' of the Straits region and 'its sights and its people' has, in this context, a broader scientific reference and resonance.

The second of Rivers's lectures focuses on the topic of 'Primitive Colour Vision'. As before, the lecture centres on a marked binary opposition of 'savage' and 'civilized'. Providing the measure of 'civilization' are '[t]he views of [W. E.] Gladstone',⁶¹ whose *Studies on Homer and the Homeric Age* (1858) had suggested that the small colour vocabulary of the ancient Greeks was comparable to the modern-day Dani of Papua New Guinea, and that a study of such peoples would, in turn, highlight a perceived depth of colour vocabulary in modern Western societies.⁶² Rivers seems to back up the views of this armchair ethnography by positing that the comparatively small

---

⁵⁹ Ibid.
⁶⁰ This connection between a highly developed visual imagination and low mental development can also be felt in Conrad's 1907 novel *The Secret Agent*, in Stevie's scrawled concatenations.
⁶¹ RI archive, MS GB 4 p. 231, leaflet 425, p. 2 of 2.
⁶² William Ewart Gladstone, *Studies on Homer and the Homeric Age* (Oxford: Oxford University Press, 1858). See also Gladstone, 'The Colour-Sense', *Nineteenth Century*, 2 (1877), 366–88.

'colour vocabulary [. . .] among existing primitive races'—for whom 'native' peoples from in and around the Torres Strait and New Guinea again provide the cross-section—offers linguistic evidence of a '[d]eficiency in colour sense'.[63] As Langham glosses: 'Upon discovering [. . .] that the islanders had trouble in distinguishing blue from black, and that their colour vocabulary included no word for "blue"', Rivers determined 'that a "primitive confusion" was involved'.[64] Rivers's first lecture posits that 'savages' might see better than Westerners, but without any corresponding cognitive facility. In this second lecture, which posits that 'savages' have little linguistic capacity for representing colour, the argument that vision is indexical of race, and of racial 'inferiority' in particular, is apparently sealed. A similar conceptual sleight of hand can be found in the *Reports*, where Rivers, acknowledging the existence of 'native' systems of representation and classification, concludes that these supply evidence of the absence, rather than the substance, of any corresponding intellectual capacity: '[n]early every detail of landscape and seascape has its special name and nearly every species which the zoologist or botanist would recognize as distinct was also differentiated by the native and had its distinctive name'; however, '[m]inute distinctions of this sort are only possible if the attention is predominantly devoted to objects of sense, and I think there can be little doubt that such exclusive attention is a distinct hindrance to higher mental development'.[65] In this way, the other is kept as an object of classification and representation, rather than a classifying subject.

A stress on the visual acuity of Malays can also be found in Conrad's other Malay-set works, notably the early parts of *The Rescue* (1920), the belated prequel to Conrad's second novel *An Outcast of the Islands* (1896). In Chapter 1 the Malay helmsman of the *Lightning* highlights the presence of another vessel, unseen by any of the Europeans on board, to a fellow crewman:

'I am Sali, and my eyes are better than the bewitched brass thing that pulls out to a great length', said the pertinacious helmsman. 'There was a boat, just clear of the easternmost island. There was a boat, and they in her could see the ship on the light of the west—unless they are blind men lost on the sea. I have seen her.'[66]

This passage bears a striking similarity to some of the anecdotal evidence compiled by Rivers in the *Reports*:

Travellers have repeatedly called attention to the way in which savages are able to distinguish birds among the thick foliage of trees, and the quickness of the natives of

---

[63] RI archive, MS GB 4 p. 231, leaflet 425, p. 2 of 2.
[64] Langham, p. 74. See also W. H. R. Rivers, 'Primitive Colour Vision', *Popular Science Monthly*, 59 (1901), 44–58.
[65] Rivers, *Reports*, p. 45.
[66] Joseph Conrad, *The Rescue* (Harmondsworth: Penguin, 1950), p. 25.

Torres Straits in this respect was very striking. *Their power of distinguishing boats at a distance was also remarkable.*[67]

Although *The Rescue* was not completed until 1919 or published until 1920, the passage belongs to a section of the novel written between 1896 and late 1902. In other words, it belongs to a similar period and derives—as this echo of Sterne's view of the 'native' seaman's 'far-reaching eye' (p. 188) underlines—from much the same imaginative vein as 'The End of the Tether', to which Conrad put the finishing touches in early November 1902 shortly before laying aside 'The Rescuer' (as it was then known) in late December.[68]

Conclusion

'The End of the Tether' was serialized between July and December 1902 in *Blackwood's Magazine*, a bellicosely imperialist publication that, as Conrad elsewhere points out, found its way into every 'club and mess room and man-of-war' in the British Empire,[69] and certainly would have been circulated in Singapore, at that time the capital of the British Straits Settlement, where the story is partly set.[70] Conrad's idea of addressing an imperial audience carries an obvious resonance in relation to more celebrated works such as 'Heart of Darkness'—which immediately precedes 'The End of the Tether' in Conrad's *Youth*, and whose multiple and varied interrogations of the imperial project constitute one of the more thoroughly mapped terrains of modern criticism.[71] Conrad's idea of addressing an imperial audience is also interesting given that contemporary pioneers in the new discipline of anthropology, one of the scientific projects underwriting empire—most notably Conrad's compatriot and fellow exile Bronisław Malinowski, who acknowledged Conrad's influence on his own work—comprised part of this audience.[72] The intriguing intertextuality with Rivers's ideas of primitive

[67] Rivers, *Reports*, pp. 42–43 (emphasis added).

[68] The manuscript of the text quoted shows little revision, and can be attributed with some confidence to this earlier phase of composition (London, British Library, MS 4787, p. 54 of 598). For a detailed commentary on the composition dates of *The Rescue* see Thomas Moser, '"The Rescuer" Manuscript: A Key to Conrad's Development—and Decline', *Harvard Library Bulletin*, 10 (Autumn 1956), 325–55. See also Knowles, *A Conrad Chronology*, p. 48.

[69] *The Collected Letters of Joseph Conrad*, IV: *1903–1907*, ed. by Frederick R. Karl and Laurence Davies (Cambridge: Cambridge University Press, 1991), p. 506 (Letter to J. B. Pinker, November 1911).

[70] Though unnamed in published versions of the story, the 'Eastern port' is clearly identifiable as Singapore. See Norman Sherry, *Conrad's Eastern World* (Cambridge: Cambridge University Press, 1966), pp. 171–94.

[71] For a discussion of 'Heart of Darkness' as a touchstone of contemporary critical practices, see the 'Reading Biscuits, Reading Gaol' section of Val Cunningham, *In the Reading Gaol: Postmodernity, Texts, and History* (Oxford: Blackwell, 1994).

[72] See James Clifford.

vision in 'The End of the Tether', as well as its borrowings from Wallace and Frazer, indicates that this relationship also ran the other way.

Conrad's representation of the other in 'The End of the Tether' and 'The Rescuer' does not just reflect the singular viewpoint of Rivers, but a view that quickly became the consensus. Rivers's work on vision was highly and widely regarded by his contemporaries, as is underlined by an appreciation issued following his death in 1922 by Charles S. Myers, who accompanied Rivers on the Torres Strait expedition: 'Rivers's work on vision is still regarded as the most accurate and careful account of the whole subject in the English language. [. . .] His psychological investigations among the Torres Straits islanders [. . .] will ever stand as models of precise, methodological observations in the field of ethnological psychology.'[73] A former student of Rivers at Cambridge as well as a later professional peer, Myers might justifiably be suspected of over-praise. Yet, as Langham has noted: 'From about 1906 until 1930, eight years after his death, Rivers's work was probably the most-talked about in academic anthropology. Long before Malinowski's influence was felt, Rivers was hailed as the apostle of the new approach to fieldwork, and as the greatest ethnographer who had ever lived.'[74] Given his access to and interest in periodicals such as the *Fortnightly Review*, which excerpted and reviewed contemporary works of anthropology including Frazer's, Conrad could not have been unaware of this gathering apotheosis.

Conrad's portrait of the other in 'The End of the Tether', in particular the stress on visual acuity and perception integral to his representation of Malay indigeneity, certainly corresponds to a then growing academic consensus, and Rivers's investigations into the visual capacities of 'primitive' cultures were current and influential when 'The End of the Tether' was drafted and first published, having begun to circulate in the early part of 1900 (even if, as Langham suggests, they did not become academic orthodoxy until roughly four years after the publication of the book edition of *Youth* in 1902). The currency and influence of Rivers's theories of visual perception, which grew out of fieldwork conducted in parts of the world that Conrad knew from his sea years, and which can be felt in the pages of 'The End of the Tether', suggest that Rivers might usefully, albeit tentatively, be placed alongside more familiar names such as Wallace and Frazer, or Clifford and Swettenham, as having helped shape the construction of Conrad's fictional Malay world.

ROYAL HOLLOWAY, UNIVERSITY OF LONDON   ANDREW PURSSELL

[73] C. S. Myers, 'The Influence of the Late W. H. R. Rivers', in W. H. R. Rivers, *'Psychology and Politics' and Other Essays* (London: Kegan Paul, Trench, Trubner, 1923), pp. 149–81 (pp. 154–59).
[74] Langham, p. 50. For a more recent appraisal see Deręgowski.

MEDITERRANEAN MEDIATIONS: LANGUAGE AND CULTURAL (EX)CHANGE IN BNF, MS FR. 19152

The version of *Floire et Blancheflor* attested only in Paris, Bibliothèque nationale de France (BnF), MS fr. 19152, fols 193ʳ–205ᵛ, has enjoyed little of the critical attention lavished on its more popular relation, the 'aristocratic' strain contained in three codices, also held at the Bibliothèque nationale de France.[1] Critics differentiate the two forms by audience: the aristocratic strain on the one hand, and the 'popular' version on the other.[2] Alternatively, they are sorted by genre, with the aristocratic strain called a *conte oriental* or *roman idyllique*, and the popular a *roman d'aventures*.[3] Jean-Luc Leclanche considers the *roman* to be an early offshoot of the French variant of the *conte*.[4] Regardless of its exact temporal provenance, the *roman* is distinct from the *conte* in language, plot, and style. While the *conte* has been linked repeatedly to Mediterranean, specifically Arabic, literature,[5] the *roman* has evaded such celebrity, going largely unremarked upon. Yet the strain of *Floire et Blancheflor* found in BnF, MS fr. 19152 displays a deep anxiety about its own Mediterranean themes and tropes, attempting to disavow or displace them into a new framework. The scope and source of this tension come into focus, however, only when the *roman* is read in concert with the entire codex.

Viewed as a sustained literary project rather than an atomistic collection of texts, the codex emerges as a document fundamentally underwritten by the

---

[1] Paris, Bibliothèque nationale de France, MSS fr. 375, fr. 1447, and fr. 12562. For works considering the aristocratic strain see e.g. Patricia E. Grieve, '*Floire and Blancheflor*' and the European Romance (Cambridge: Cambridge University Press, 1997); Norris J. Lacy, 'The Flowering (and Misreading) of Romance: *Floire et Blancheflor*', *South Central Review*, 9 (1992), 19–26; Huguette Legros, *La Rose et le Lys: étude littéraire du 'Conte de Floire et Blancheflor'*, Senefiance, 31 (Aix-en Provence: CUERMA, 1992); Megan Moore. 'Boundaries and Byzantines in the Old French *Floire et Blancheflor*', *Dalhousie French Studies*, 79 (2007), 3–20.

[2] The aristocratic vs. popular distinction is widely used. One of the earliest sources is Édélestan Du Méril, *Floire et Blancheflor: poèmes du XIIIᵉ siècle, publiés d'après les manuscrits avec une introduction, des notes et un glossaire* (Paris: Jannet, 1856). Modern usage was established in Jean-Luc Leclanche, *Contribution à l'étude de la transmission des plus anciennes œuvres françaises: un cas privilégié. 'Floire et Blancheflor'*, 2 vols (Lille: Service de reproduction des thèses, Université de Lille III, 1980).

[3] For a discussion of the *roman* vs. *conte* distinction see *Le Conte de Floire et Blanchefleur*, ed. and trans. by Jean-Luc Leclanche (Paris: Champion, 2003); Marla Segol, *Religious Conversion, History and Genre in 'Floire et Blancheflor', 'Aucassin et Nicolette', and 'Flamenca'* (Saarbrücken: Lambert, 2011); Marion Vuagnoux-Uhlig, *Le Couple en herbe: 'Galeran de Bretagne' et 'L'Escoufle' à la lumière du roman idyllique médiéval*, Publications romanes et françaises, 245 (Geneva: Droz, 2009).

[4] Leclanche, *Contribution à l'étude de la transmission des plus anciennes œuvres françaises*, pp. 80–82.

[5] Virtually every source since the late 1800s references *Floire et Blancheflor*'s 'Eastern' origins in one way or another. For a summary of the existing work see Grieve, '*Floire et Blancheflor*' and the European Romance, pp. 15–20, and Cynthia Robinson, *Medieval Andalusian Courtly Culture in the Mediterranean: 'Ḥadīth Bayāḍ wa Riyāḍ'* (London: Routledge, 2007), Chapter 4, 'Wandering in Babylon: The *Ḥadīth Bayāḍ wa Riyāḍ* and the *roman idyllique*', pp. 171–212.

relationship between an increasingly vernacularized French literary culture and its Mediterranean others at the end of the thirteenth century. Through the arrangement of its contents, BnF, MS fr. 19152 participates in what Sharon Kinoshita calls the 'active, even aggressive reformulations of both literary form and political vision' which take place during a 'period of rapid transformation in Latin Europe's relations to its external others'.[6] Faced with such 'rapid transformation', BnF, MS fr. 19152 struggles to create an illusion of 'French' linguistic and literary wholeness. To do so, the codex imagines and positions itself against a monolithic Mediterranean other, that is at turns Latin or Arabic, Saracen or Jewish. This double textual illusion defies the historical reality, where a rich dialectal and cultural variance between regions was the norm, and where no governing concept of 'French' culture was yet available.

To present the mirage of a unified 'French' literary culture, BnF, MS fr. 19152 uses its lengthy initial and final texts as a frame narrative, enclosing a selection of shorter *fabliaux* and religious texts between them. This frame narrative opposes two didactic texts (Marie de France's *Fables* (fols 15^r–24^v) and the *Châtoiement d'un père à son fils* (fols 1^r–15^r)) with three romances: *Partonopeus de Blois* (fols 124^r–174^v), *Blancandin* (fols 174^v–193^r), and *Floire et Blancheflor*.

While previous critics have largely focused on the *fabliaux*,[7] the present essay centres on the role of the frame narrative, particularly *Floire et Blancheflor*, in the codex. I first consider the frame as an overarching structure which defines the codex's relationship to 'Frenchness' and textual authority, and then move to an extended close reading of key passages in *Floire et Blancheflor* which add further nuance to the manuscript's complicated relationship to vernacular literariness and authority.

By the end of the thirteenth century manuscript production in northern France was not only surviving but thriving.[8] As such, those responsible for compiling BnF, MS fr. 19152 were probably not severely constrained in their choice of exempla, particularly as the codex was most likely produced for a wealthy aristocratic or bourgeois patron. This textual availability, combined with the single hand of the manuscript, provides a firm basis for reading the codex as a sustained literary project.[9]

---

[6] Sharon Kinoshita, *Medieval Boundaries: Rethinking Difference in Old French Literature* (Philadelphia: University of Pennsylvania Press, 2006), p. 236.

[7] Tracy Adams, 'The Cunningly Intelligent Characters of BN f fr 19152', *MLN*, 120 (2005), 896–924; Keith Busby, *Codex and Context: Reading Old French Narrative Verse in Manuscript*, 2 vols (Amsterdam: Rodopi, 2002), I, 450–51.

[8] Richard H. Rouse and Mary A. Rouse, *Manuscripts and their Makers: Commercial Book Producers in Medieval Paris, 1200–1500*, 2 vols (Turnhout: Harvey Miller, 2000), pp. 10–24.

[9] Despite the manuscript's legibility, the scribe makes frequent transcription errors. As Margaret Pelan notes, 'le copiste, s'il a une belle écriture, est souvent négligent', in *Floire et Blancheflor: seconde version*, ed. and trans. by Margaret Pelan (Paris: Éditions Ophrys, 1975), p. 11.

Moreover, the scribe's dialect suggests an engagement with the broader textual culture of central and north-eastern France, rather than a deep involvement with one centre of literary production in particular. Scholars cannot agree on the scribal dialect. E. Faral first commented on the scribe's tendency to insert elements from different dialectal regions in 1934.[10] Keith Busby localizes his dialect to the Aube or Haute-Marne, T. B. W. Reid to south-west Champagne, and Margaret Pelan to Picardy. Franklin Sweetser, in turn, labels the language *francien*.[11] Certainly, the codex was produced in what is now northern France, towards the end of the thirteenth century, or perhaps in the very early fourteenth. The copyist, for his part, hailed from north central or north-east France. This lack of dialectal specificity only strengthens the impression of a generalized 'vernacular' which the manuscript's contents in turn convey.

Tracy Adams and Keith Busby have dealt with the manuscript holistically,[12] but neither addresses the version of *Floire et Blancheflor* found in BnF, MS fr. 19152, nor do they pay much attention to the frame. Both, however, argue forcefully for reading the codex as a coherent whole.

Working from the recent critical literature on miscellany in French vernacular codices,[13] Adams suggests that we should read BnF, MS fr. 19152 as a book 'controlled by an ideology initiated in the set of framed tales with which the manuscript begins' (p. 898). Her analysis argues that the didactic texts which open the anthology—the *Châtoiement* and the *Fables*—set the tone for a particular species of moral instruction, one of 'cunning intelligence' or *mētis*, which is then exemplified by the *fabliaux* (p. 896). Despite her detailed analysis of the first half of the frame, Adams is less intrigued by the final romances: *Partonopeus*, *Floire et Blancheflor*, and *Blancandin*. She first notes, 'the manuscript ends with three long romances' (p. 902), and later comments, 'It would belabor the point to consider how the heroes and heroines of the other courtly *lais* and of the romances with which the manuscript closes exemplify shows of cunning intelligence' (p. 920). On the contrary, I argue

---

[10] E. Faral, *Le Manuscrit 19152 du Fonds français de la Bibliothèque nationale: reproduction phototypique publiée avec une introduction* (Paris: Droz, 1934), pp. 11–12.

[11] Busby, *Codex and Context*, pp. 528–29; Pelan, *Floire et Blancheflor*, p. 11; T. B. W. Reid, *Twelve Fabliaux* (Manchester: Manchester University Press, 1958), p. xv; *Blancardin et l'Orgueilleuse d'amour: roman d'aventure du XIIIe siècle*, ed. by Franklin P. Sweetser (Geneva: Droz, 1964), cited in 'Manuscript G', *Partonopeus de Blois: An Electronic Edition*, ed. by Penny Eley and others (Sheffield: HriOnline, 2005) <http://www.hrionline.ac.uk/partonopeus/Gmanuscriptnotes.htm>.

[12] Adams, 'The Cunningly Intelligent Characters of BN f fr 19152'; Busby, *Codex and Context*, I, 450–51.

[13] Sylvia Huot, *From Song to Book: The Poetics of Writing in Old French Lyric and Lyrical Narrative Poetry* (Ithaca, NY: Cornell University Press, 1987); Steven Nichols, '"Art" and "Nature": Looking for (Medieval) Principles of Order in Occitan Chansonnier N (Morgan 819)', in *The Whole Book: Cultural Perspectives on the Medieval Miscellany*, ed. by Stephen Nichols and Siegfried Wenzel (Ann Arbor: University of Michigan Press, 1996), pp. 83–123.

that only through careful consideration of both the initial and the final halves of the frame does the larger structuring of the codex become clear.

Busby attempts to do just that, beginning, like Adams, with the reasonable assumption that the didactic opening texts provide a controlling ideology for the entire work:

> This [opening] sets a serious tone for the whole manuscript and suggests that the group of two dozen *fabliaux* which follows, as well as providing a stark contrast with the opening sequence, could indeed be read with a view to the morals with which they usually conclude [. . .]. The theme of education qualifies these [final three romances] as *Bildungsromane*, and links them to each other and to the didactic pieces and the fabliaux. (pp. 450–51)

Busby takes the *fabliaux* seriously, as didactic texts rather than (or perhaps in addition to) mere farce. This aligns the *fabliaux* with the shorter religious texts interspersed between them, such as the *XV Signes*, as well as the opening, didactic texts.

While Busby makes a strong case for reading BnF, MS fr. 19152 as structured by 'the theme of education', one might continue by asking what, in fact, this education is geared towards. Adams's analysis offers a partial answer: the manuscript 'offers instruction in a particular kind of intelligence' which eschews black and white morality in favour of a practical cunning (p. 904). Building on Adams's and Busby's work, I broaden Adams's reading of *mētis* to suggest that BnF, MS fr. 19152 educates the reader in a specific vision of 'Frenchness', and that the practical cunning which Adams traces across 'high' and 'low' literary genres represents one aspect of that literary and cultural acculturation, under the aegis of the manuscript's relationship to literary authority.

The frame sets up that relationship with its opposition of didactic and romance texts, troubling the easy distinction between genres at the same time as it blurs the distinction between 'legitimate' literary authorities and the broader category of the foreign. The terms 'frame' and 'frame narrative' generally apply to a narrative structure within an individual text. In this article I use these terms to indicate the overarching structure within the codex formed by its initial and final texts, and view it as providing a powerful way to read the manuscript as an anthology loosely structured around the narrative set up within its frame. That narrative takes us from texts with an explicit moral *telos* to the decidedly murkier literary universe of romance. While the didactic texts are forced to confront the spectre of a specific author or set of authorities, the romances struggle to negotiate their place in the literary reclamation of *translatio studii*.

The *Châtoiement d'un père à son fils* is the first of these didactic texts. The *Châtoiement* is one of two French verse translations of the *Disciplina clericalis*, a Latin text written by Petrus Alfonsi, a *converso* of al-Andalus, and later of Aragon, England, and France.[14] The *Disciplina* draws its inspiration from a plethora of Arabic and Hebrew sources, rewoven into thirty-four short, didactic stories presented as a framed dialogue between teacher and student. There is no one, easily identifiable source for this text composed, to quote its author,

partim ex prouerbiis philosophorum et suis castigacionibus, partim ex prouerbiis et castigacionibus arabicis et fabulis et uersibus, partim ex animalium et uolucrum similitudinibus.[15]

in part of the proverbs and admonitions of the philosophers, in part of the proverbs, admonitions, fables, and verses of the Arabs, and in part of likenesses drawn from the world of animals and birds.

Folklorists have identified pieces of these 'proverbs and admonitions' as having been drawn from the Talmud, al-Mas'ūdī's *Murūj al-dahab*, the *Kalīla wa-Dimnah* cycle, the *Kitāb al-Sindibād*, and the *Alf Layla wa-Layla*.[16] Still, as Lourdes María Álvarez notes, any attempt to outline Alfonsi's sources definitively is 'a fruitless task: the "chain" of transmission is more like a web or tapestry of versions'.[17] Even before the Old French translation, the *Disciplina* is overdetermined, weaving together multiple textual traditions under a single rubric. As the first text of BnF, MS fr. 19152, the *Châtoiement* offers a *mise en scène* for the structure of the codex as a whole: first, in that like BnF, MS fr. 19152, it is a series of short texts held together by a frame narrative. Second, the *Châtoiement* pulls together multiple sources, in multiple languages, to create a coherent whole, while at the same time effacing the narrative specificity and linguistic origin of those sources.

The translation of the *Disciplina* attested in BnF, MS fr. 19152 retains the patchwork source material while disavowing its origin. There are two French verse strains of the *Châtoiement*, A and B, dating from the thirteenth century, and two later prose versions. In total, seventeen manuscripts are extant, of which three are prose and fourteen verse. BnF, MS fr. 19152 contains the second verse strain, B. It is slightly more complete than A, with thirty-two of thirty-four tales present. Both A and B elide the Arabic influences on the *Châtoiement*; B, however, does not even mention Alfonsi as the original author, cutting the translator's prologue entirely in order to begin with the following lines:

[14] For an overview of Alfonsi's life and work see John Victor Tolan, *Petrus Alfonsi and his Medieval Readers* (Gainsville: University Press of Florida, 1993).

[15] *La Discipline de clergie: introduction, texte latin et traduction nouvelle*, ed. and trans. by Jacqueline Genot-Bismuth (Paris: Éditions de Paris, 2001), p. 200. English translations from Latin and Old French are my own. Free translations are sometimes preferred over literal ones to capture better the spirit of the texts.

[16] Tolan, *Petrus Alfonsi*, p. 80.

[17] Lourdes María Álvarez, 'Petrus Alfonsi', in *Literature of al-Andalus*, ed. by María Rosa Menocal and others (Cambridge: Cambridge University Press, 2000), pp. 288–91 (p. 288).

> Li perres son fill chastioit,
> Sen et savoir li aprenoit:
> Beaux filz, dit il, a moi t'entent:
> Ne laisse pas coler au vent
> Ce que ton perre te dira!
> (ll. 1–5, fol. 1ʳ)[18]

The father counselled his son; knowledge and wisdom he taught him. 'Good son', he said, 'Listen to me: do not fritter away what your father will tell you!'

The father's desire to teach 'sen et savoir' is foregrounded here, emphasizing the primary function of the *Châtoiement* as wisdom literature, but losing the authority, preserved in A, of a well-known author and scholar. Yet, unlike A, B does not change place names or the identity of characters to make them appear more familiar to the reader. For example, A's translator changes the names of nearly all the text's many foxes to Renart, and in doing so instantly regrounds the tale in the network of European Renart stories. In refraining from this kind of adaptive move, B preserves a thematized exoticism which is also highlighted in the romances, allowing the reader to take pleasure in the textualized 'Orient' while effacing the identity of its Andalusian Jewish author.

In addition, the first tale preserves the origin of the narrator in B and loses it in A, so that B reads as follows:

> Un preudons estoit en Arabie,
> Si avoit a non Lucanable.
> Il estoit du siecle molt saige
> Et si estoit de grant aaige.
> (ll. 106–09, fol. 1ᵛ)

There was a worthy man in Arabia; his name was Lucan. He was very worldly wise, and was also very wizened.

In A, the 'preudons' is introduced in the following way: 'Uns sages hons jadis estoit | Qui a fil sovant disoit [. . .]' ('Once, in ancient times, there was a wise man who often said to his son [. . .]').[19] The A strain removes 'Arabie' entirely, but keeps the lengthy translator's prologue and clearly attributes the text to Alfonsi at its very beginning. In BnF, MS fr. 19152, then, we find a versified strain of the *Châtoiement*, one which stresses the text's foreign setting while simultaneously erasing the reality of its Jewish-Andalusian author, Arabic authorities, and Latin language, replacing it with a vernacular polyglot that implicitly performs and works out the mediation between Self and Other, Frank and Saracen, which the final three romances explicitly thematize.

---

[18] *Étude et édition des traductions françaises médiévales de la 'Disciplina clericalis' de Pierre Alphonse*, ed. by Yasmina Foehr-Janssens and others (Geneva: Université de Genève, 2006) <http://www.unige.ch/lettres/mela/recherche/disciplina.html> [accessed 4 March 2012]. All subsequent quotations from the French manuscripts of the *Disciplina* come from this edition.

[19] Paris, Bibliothèque nationale de France, MS fr. 12581, ll. 115–16.

Moving from the *Châtoiement* to the *Fables*, Adams discusses the possible Arabic origins of Marie's text at length, drawing on Saher Amer's monograph *Ésope au féminin*,[20] to argue that the collection 'derives from Arabic tradition as opposed to the Latin tradition of Aesop's fables'.[21] Amer suggests *Kalīla wa-Dimnah*'s extensive manuscript tradition as a potential source for the *Fables*.[22] While I agree with Amer that *Kalīla wa-Dimnah* probably had some effect on the *Fables*, a complete consideration of Marie's sources is beyond the scope of the present article. For BnF, MS fr. 19152 the salient issue is that, like the *Châtoiement*, the *Fables* draw on multiple forms of authority, blurring the lines between what is Latin and what is Arabic, and then re-create and transmit that knowledge in the vernacular.

Further, the strain of the *Fables* found in BnF, MS fr. 19152 has never been edited, due to its relatively short length (sixty-six tales) and textual errata. However, as Bernadette Masters points out, these 'errors' assume that the scribal goal was always to produce as faithful a copy as possible. In her careful linguistic analysis of the fables preserved in BnF, MS fr. 19152 Masters shows that the scribe introduces creative changes which highlight his role as 'story-teller [. . .] achieving his end by using his writing implements, written language, and his power to distort the traditional tale'.[23] This active scribal intervention foreshadows the claims of *Partonopeus*'s narrator later in the codex. Where the *Fables* shrug off not only their potential Arabic and Latin heritage, but also that of their immediate exemplar, *Partonopeus* continues this working-out of difference at the level of language in its introduction.

Here, the narrator justifies his use of vernacular at length (ll. 63–133). In the middle of his introduction he claims:

> Cil clerc dient ce nest pas sens
> Descrire estoire dencians
> Quant ge nes escrif en latin
> Et que gi pert mon tens enfin
> Cil le perdent qui ne font rien.
> (ll. 77–81)[24]

These clerks say that it makes no sense to write the history of the ancients when I am not writing them in Latin, and that I am ultimately wasting my time. Those who waste their time [however] are those who do nothing.

---

[20] Sahar Amer, *Ésope au féminin: Marie de France et la politique de l'interculturalité* (Amsterdam: Rodopi, 1999), p. 243.

[21] Adams, 'The Cunningly Intelligent Characters of BN f fr 19152', pp. 909–10.

[22] Amer, *Ésope au féminin*, p. 243.

[23] Bernadette Masters, 'Li lox, lililions, and their compaig: Exemplary Error in the Fables of BN MS, f. fr 19152', *Parergon*, 13.2 (1996), 203–22 (p. 209).

[24] All quotations are from the edited transcription of BnF, MS fr. 19152 found in '*Partonopeus de Blois*': *An Electronic Edition*, ed. by Penny Eley and others (Sheffield: HriOnline, 2005) <http://www.hrionline.ac.uk/partonopeus> [accessed 1 March 2012].

'Sens' and 'dencians' are paired here, with the imagined clerks declaring that history contains meaning, 'sense', only when written in Latin. Our narrator retorts that, on the contrary, doing 'nothing' is the true waste of time. *Perdre* retained the sense of 'to lose one's way' in Old French, giving the couplet the sense of not only wasting or losing time, but of being lost outside or within one's own time, '*mon* tens'. In this way, those who insist upon Latin are figured as permanently behind the times, excluded from the avant-garde represented in '*mon* tens'.

Further, the narrator does not specify *which* language clerks believe is such a waste of time. Instead, it is the undifferentiated mass of not-Latin which threatens to unmoor the 'history of the ancients' from the historical and temporal anchor of the Latinate tradition. Like the translator of the *Châtoiement*, *Partonopeus*'s narrator scrubs the proper name of any specific authority from his text, claiming only that he found his material in 'li livre grieu et li latin' (l. 133: 'Greek and Latin books'). As the narrator stakes a claim to the authority of these texts, while simultaneously 'losing' or forgetting them, he reinscribes the nascent Anglo-Norman literature of the 1150s[25] in a lineage which lays claim to Latin material while disavowing its language.

When this twelfth-century passage is read in the early fourteenth-century context of BnF, MS fr. 19152, the narrator brings the reader or listener back to the *Châtoiement* and its expurgation of Alfonsi's name. Further, the pairing of 'sens' with 'dencians' recalls the opening of the *Châtoiement*, where the father claims to teach his son 'sen et savoir' (ll. 1–2). By placing these two texts at either end of the frame narrative, enclosing no fewer than twenty-three *fabliaux*, BnF, MS fr. 19152 demands that its reader question the construction of meaningful knowledge, and the relationship of that knowledge to hierarchy and authority. In the *Châtoiement* this authority is represented by the father, and overlaid by the absent present of Alfonsi which haunts the text. In *Partonopeus* the weight of the clerkly tradition carries that same filial authority.

Hence both texts make way for a new kind of vernacular creativity which must forget or actively erase its parentage in order to proceed forward. This thematization of forgetting occurs at diverse levels in the tales. In *Partonopeus*, as in *Floire et Blancheflor*, scenes of education do this allegorical work. Partonopeus de Blois is thirteen years old when he becomes lost while boar-hunting in the Ardennes. Separated from the group, he boards a mysterious boat ('nef') which leads to an amazing castle. In this castle he meets Mélior, the conveniently Catholic Empress of Byzantium, who wishes

---

[25] The earliest extant example of *Partonopeus* is probably Vatican City, MS Vat. Pal. Lat. 1971: see Brian Woledge and Ian Short, 'Liste provisoire de manuscrits du XII siècle contenant des texts en langue française', *Romania*, 102 (1981), 1–17. Busby and Nixon agree that the text is Anglo-Norman in origin: Busby, *Codex and Context*, p. 496; Terry Nixon, '*Amadas et Idoine* and *Erec et Enide*: Reuniting Membra Disjecta from Early Old Manuscripts', *Viator*, 18 (1987), 227–51.

to marry him. She insists that for them to be together, he must not look upon her for the two years until their marriage.[26] When he asks permission to return to France, Mélior tells him that his father has been killed and his country invaded by Saracens. She grants his request, but first insists on instructing him in the ways of effective and honourable knighthood.[27]

This 'lecon', as Mélior calls it, draws on none of Mélior's extensive education in what Bruckner calls 'the entire encyclopedia of twelfth-century learning'.[28] Mélior is not only educated, she is brilliant, surpassing her tutors by the time she turns fifteen, and using her knowledge to appear as an invisible fairy creature to Partonopeus:

> Maistres oi de grant escienz
> Par foiees plus de·ii·c·
> Diex me dona grace daprandre
> Et descriture bien entendre
> Les ·vii· arzz toz premierement
> Apris et soi parfitement
> [. . .]
> Ainz queusse ·xv· anz passez
> Oi toz mes maistre sormontez.
> (ll. 4562–4567, 4580–4581)

I had masters of great wisdom, over time more than two hundred. God gave me the grace to learn and to understand writing well. The seven arts first I learnt and knew [them] perfectly. [. . .] Before fifteen years had passed I had surpassed all of my masters [in knowledge].

Mélior excels at the twin pair of 'aprandre' and 'entendre', of learning and comprehension. Specifically, she understands writing 'escriture' and learns the seven liberal arts 'les ·vii· arzz', entering into a position of learned authority paralleling *Partonopeus*'s narrator, who, having read and understood his 'livre grieu et li latin', chooses to educate the reader in a different idiom altogether. For Mélior passes on none of her learning to her young lover. Instead, she emphasizes chivalric and religious norms[29] which enable him to succeed as a young lord of France who must retake his country from Saracen invaders and defeat a litany of 'Oriental' figures in a three-day tournament for Mélior's hand, represented by such diverse and interchangeable signifiers as Sultan, Saracen,

---

[26] The basic premiss draws on both the Cupid and Psyche narrative and the Matter of Britain. Further, one immediately hears clear echoes of Marie de France's *lai, Guigemar*, linking *Partonopeus* back to the *Fables* through the *lais*.

[27] For an excellent treatment of Mélior's pedagogical role in the Middle English *Partonopeus* see Amy N. Vines, 'A Woman's "Crafte": Melior as Lover, Teacher, and Patron in the Middle English *Partonope of Blois*', *Modern Philology*, 105 (2007), 245–70.

[28] Matilda Bruckner, *Shaping Romance: Interpretation, Truth, and Closure in Twelfth-Century French Fictions* (Philadelphia: University of Pennsylvania Press, 1993), p. 123.

[29] Namely, how to attract and keep good knights (give them gifts and clothing), and when to praise God (frequently), ll. 1919–47 (fol. 131ʳ).

Pagan, Persian, Almerian, Byzantine, and Syrian (ll. 6990–7185). In this way, Mélior's deep textual engagement with the Latin tradition of liberal arts gives way to the 'lecon' the romance endeavours to teach: to be French is to engage in the French language, and to engage in that language is to vanquish all others.

Unlike the narrator of *Partonopeus*'s prologue, *Floire et Blancheflor*'s narrator never deals directly with the weight of the Latin 'estoire dencians'. Rather, the way in which the *roman d'aventures* displaces, alters, or deletes elements from its sister story, the *conte oriental*, underscores for a final time the codex's complex relationship to literariness and authority.

Leclanche, in his 2003 edition of *Floire et Blancheflor*, argues that the *roman* is a 'negative' of the *conte*, replacing the clerkly hero with a courtly one and enacting the iconic thirteenth-century debate between *clerc* and *chevalier*.[30] Yet, Leclanche himself has discussed the porosity of plot and detail between the narratives: the scene where Floire throws himself into the lion pit, for example, migrates wholesale from the *roman* to the version in BnF, MS fr. 375, itself compiled in late thirteenth-century Arras. Even as the text struggles, and largely succeeds, in becoming a *roman d'aventures*, it fails, falling back into the pattern of the *conte*: the description of the golden cup is cut short, but the cup remains. A battle scene on the road to Babylon is added, but the road, and the bourgeois families that Floire stays with on his journey, remain.

Moreover, Floire never takes up arms against the Emir of Babylon, failing to enact the 'conversion by the sword' which the chivalric topos demands. This violence is instead diverted into the battle with Jonas de Handres, in which Floire fights *for* the Saracen king. Thus, the *roman* stands between the clerical idea of 'conversion by ideas' and the chivalric 'conversion by the sword'. As such, it mirrors the frame of the larger codex, which, in its efforts to erase or efface its classical and Arabic heritage, can never fully expel their influence. Nowhere is this so clear as in the changes the *roman* makes to *Floire et Blancheflor*'s pedagogical scene.

In BnF, MSS fr. 1447 and fr. 375, the main representatives of the aristocratic strain, the children are educated together, leading to this passage:

> es les vos andeus a l'escole
> molt delivre orent la parole
> cascuns d'aus deus tant aprendoit
> pour l'autre que merveille estoit
> [. . .]
> Livres lisoient paienors
> u ooient parler d'amors
> en çou forment se delitoient
> es engiens d'amor qu'il trovoient

---

[30] *Le Conte de Floire et Blancheflor*, ed. and trans. by Leclanche, p. xxv. All quotations from the *conte* are from this edition, unless otherwise indicated.

> [. . .]
> Ensamle lisent et aprendent
> a la joie d'amor entendent.
> (ll. 215-18, 227-30, 235-36)

There they were, both of them at school. They spoke to each other there with great ease, each one from the other learning so much that it seemed a marvel. [. . .] They read pagan books, wherein they heard talk of love, taking a great delight in the instruments of love that they found there. [. . .] Together they read and learnt, gaining great knowledge of the joys of love.

Floire and Blancheflor *heard* ('ooient') of love from their books, and *learnt each one from the other* ('cascuns d'aus deus'). 'Ooient' is not merely a rhetorical flourish on the part of the scribe, but a literal description of the scene: the children read aloud, teaching each other through that reading. This dialogic act of reading aloud to each other thus becomes a pedagogical performance, one shot through with the possibility of danger from both foreign books ('livres lisoient paienors') and forbidden carnal love: Blancheflor is both a slave and a Christian, and thus doubly unfit to marry Floire.

Reading this passage, Roberta Krueger observes that the *conte* is 'more than a love story', and 'inscribes the activities of reading, writing, storytelling and interpretation as critical'.[31] But Krueger dismisses the *roman* as lacking in 'literariness', and as failing to 'invite the audience to reflect on its own role as reader' (p. 66). On the contrary, the *roman* is hyperaware of the power of reading, and manipulates scenes from the version of *Floire et Blancheflor* predating both the *conte* and the *roman* in order to create a specific political and cultural effect when the *roman* is read as the final text in BnF, MS fr. 19152.

Foreign books become mixed up with foreign bodies in both the *roman* and the *conte*, and the status of 'pagan' texts vacillates uneasily between foreign invader and reclaimed cultural patrimony. For example, while the texts in BnF, MS fr. 375 are simply 'livres [. . .] paienors', in BnF, MS fr. 1447 the children specifically read Ovid. In Boccaccio's *Il filocolo* Ovid plays an even greater role, his writings serving as the children's 'holy book' and standing alongside Dante as one of the two writers admired by the narrator. Patricia Grieve argues that the tension between the Christian figure of Dante and the classical one of Ovid never approaches a 'graceful merging', but is rather a 'jarring shift in the text' and a kind of 'radical discontinuity' between Christianity and its pagan, literary others (pp. 176-77). For Grieve, *Il filocolo* grapples with 'the ongoing dilemma of how to deal with ancient literature in a requisite contemporary Christian framework' (p. 176). I argue that Grieve's observations extend to the narrative tradition of *Floire et Blancheflor* in French as well, rather than being particular to the *Filocolo*. Historically,

---

[31] '*Floire et Blancheflor*'s Literary Subtext', *Romance Notes*, 24 (1983-84), 65-70 (p. 66).

critics of *Floire and Blancheflor* fall into one of three camps: those who think the romance is Byzantine in origin, those who think it is Arabic, and those who dismiss both of the first two camps, arguing for a purely French text. This critical confusion over influence and authority mirrors back the fraught status of language within the *conte*'s pedagogical scene.

In *Floire et Blancheflor* the textual instability over what the children read, and if they read it at all, reflects the 'ongoing dilemma' of integrating classical and Arabic texts into the European tradition, and the false binary separating 'good' pagan influences from 'bad' ones. Within BnF, MS fr. 19152, this binary overlays another: a mythic, unified 'French' language and literature in need of a monolithic, exoticized Other against which to define itself. In *Floire et Blancheflor* these two structuring principles drive the generic shift away from the *conte* towards the martial world of the *roman*.

The *roman* handles this collapse into binary oppositions through erasure: rather than name a particular text or author, the narrator never allows Floire and Blancheflor to read together at all. This deletion is unique in the French, Spanish, Italian,[32] and English manuscript traditions of the narrative. As soon as the possibility of this literary, pedagogical engagement with 'foreign' texts arises, the pagan king orders Floire to leave for sixty days for school, separating him from Blancheflor:

> A l'escole velt [l]'envoier
> Por dessevrer icel amor
> Qu'il avoit a Blanceflor.[33]

He wished to send him to school in order to sever this love which he had for Blancheflor.

Sending Floire away creates both a geographic and an educational gap between the children, working to 'dessevrer' their love. To 'dessevrer' something can simply mean to cut off or extinguish it; however, when said of the soul, it indicates the separation of body and soul, unified during life on earth, after death. When said of a married woman, it indicates living apart or separation from one's spouse. The king's desire to leave Blancheflor out of the pedagogical scene, then, speaks to his desire to completely destroy their connection to each other, to the point of death. Indeed, the king views only Blancheflor's death as a suitable substitute for sending Floire away to school, highlighting the joint risk and power of allowing the couple to be taught together.

Floire reluctantly agrees, but soon returns to beg for Blancheflor's inclusion in his schooling, pleading for his teacher to intercede with the king on his behalf:

[32] As the *roman* is traditionally seen as the source of the Italian texts, this is even more surprising.

[33] *Floire et Blancheflor: seconde version*, ed. and trans. by Pelan, ll. 267–69. All future quotations from the *roman* are from this edition.

> Ambedui sont venuz au roi
> Dist li maistres: Entendez moi
> Ge vos veuil demander un don
> Ne vos en venra se bien non
> Faites amener la meschine
> Qui sert es chanbres la roïne
> Aprenrai la por amor Dé.
> (ll. 317-23)

Both of them went together to the king. The teacher said, 'Hear me, I wish to ask you for a gift. Nothing but good will come to you on its account. Order the young lady who works in the queen's chambers to come. I will teach her, for the love of God.'

The king initially appears to agree, claiming that he will send Blancheflor within four days; yet, as soon as Floire leaves his presence, the king begins to plot Blancheflor's execution. In the *conte*, the queen successfully intercedes on Blancheflor's behalf, persuading the king to 'merely' sell Blancheflor into slavery. Here, however, the king first tries to poison her (l. 341), then sends men to kill her (l. 452), then attempts to have her executed before the court on trumped-up charges (l. 503). The queen unsuccessfully attempts to intercede after the second attempt, and it is only as a last resort that the king, unable to rid himself of Blancheflor, sells her to slavers. In this way, the primary scene of scandalous reading shifts from the sublimated danger of writing and reading in the *conte* to the blatant violence of seigniorial murder. At first glance, the reader might assume that the resistance to the children's love is provoked by Blancheflor's Christianity and low status. However, the text never gives an explicit reason for the king's objections, and, even in the *conte*, the decision to kill or sell Blancheflor always comes just at the moment the children have become fully literate. Literacy becomes mixed up with carnal knowledge here, just as books become mixed up with bodies.

By the end of five years of schooling in the *conte*, the couple can 'bien [...] parler latin | et bien escrire en parkemin' (ll. 267-68: 'speak well in Latin and write well on parchment'). Such education, even among the elite, was rare both in romance and in reality;[34] for a young couple, specifically a young woman, to learn to this extent in a beautiful palace surrounded by gardens evokes the Edenic trope of dangerous knowledge. Thus the pedagogical scene ties sexual transgression to reading, and reading to sexual transgression.

While we are primed to view this transgression as miscegenation, Megan Moore astutely comments that while Floire-as-Muslim-Arab is strongly implied, it is never directly stated within the narrative (pp. 4-5). Instead, I argue that this connection between the carnal and the textual operates at the level of intertextuality, figured as incest.

---

[34] See *A History of Reading in the West*, ed. by Guglielmo Cavallo and Roger Chartier, trans. by Lydia Cochrane (Cambridge: Polity Press, 1999), pp. 120-48, especially pp. 120-31.

Such incest is both sexual and textual; Floire's and Blancheflor's forbidden physical intimacy mirrors the intertextual congress which the text and, in turn, the codex programmatically seek (and fail) to expel. Both the *conte* and the *roman* begin with raids on Christian convoys: Floire's father raids the pilgrimage road to Santiago de Compostela, capturing Blancheflor's mother and only later discovering her pregnancy. All versions of the text insist that Blancheflor's mother was pregnant by a Christian man before her capture, but only the *roman* gives him a name and rank: Henri, the Duke of Olenois.[35] But despite bothering to give him such a specific identity, the narrator seems to forget his existence, leaving us with a queen and her noble servant, both bearing children on the same day who look nearly identical. Even that birthday, 'pasques florie' (fol. 193^v), confounds any effort to disentangle the strands of 'Christian' and 'pagan': it may signify either Palm Sunday, or Eastertide, or a 'Saracen' (probably fictitious) flower holiday.[36] Through such convenient coincidences, the possibility of sexual mixing between half-brother and half-sister, as well as Christian and pagan, troubles the narrative.

The uncanny resemblance of the two children, their identical birthdays, their twinned names, and the too eager willingness of the king to have Blancheflor killed in order to avoid sexual congress between the couple all suggest the possibility of incest within both the idyll of the *conte* and the harsher world of the *roman*.[37] In the linguistic and literal relationship between master/slave and Christian/pagan, the potential for incestuous violence is always already present.[38] Thus, the king's repeated failed attempts to rid himself of Blancheflor in the *roman* should not be read merely as a monarch's desire to prevent his son from falling into an undesirable marriage or even an undesirable, incestuous marriage. By coding miscegenation as incest, *Floire et Blancheflor* articulates the literary process of *translatio studii* as both something foreign and something entirely too close to home. Instead, we may read the deletion of the pedagogical scene and the king's actions as the narrative's failed attempt to expel the trace of cultural exchange and learning from its very core. But because that exchange is essential to its narrative make-up or blueprint, the 'livres [. . .] paienoors' assimilated within the whole, the attempt to expel its trace is doomed to fail from the start.

---

[35] In BnF, MS fr. 1447 the pregnant woman's spouse is a dead knight, and her father is bringing her to Compostela. In BnF, MS fr. 375, she is a merchant's daughter, pregnant with her lover's child.

[36] Grieve, *'Floire and Blancheflor' and the European Romance*, pp. 95–96.

[37] For example, when Floire lodges with a bourgeois family on the road, they comment, 'el vos resanle, en moie foi | bien pöes estre d'un eage | si vos resanle du visage' (ll. 1294–96: 'By my faith, she looks just like you! You must be about the same age, and your faces look just alike').

[38] It is critical to note that this clean distinction between Christian and pagan, even Christian and Muslim, in the text reflects an imagined community rather than the historical reality. See in particular Christopher MacEvitt, *Rough Tolerance* (Philadelphia: University of Pennsylvania Press, 2008).

At the moment when Floire and Blancheflor are revealed as fully literate in the *conte*, the narrator relates:

> bien sorent parler latin
> et bien escrire en parkemin
> et conseillier oiant la gent
> en latin, que nus nes entent.
> (ll. 267-270)

They knew how to speak Latin well and to write well on parchment and to speak with each other, when they heard people coming, in Latin, such that no one understood them.

Latin is at once foreign, incomprehensible to anyone who might hear the children speak it, and intimate, a secret language between lovers or siblings. The children do not write on wax tablets, but on 'parkemin', skin scraped clean and prepared for the intrusion of Latin letters. The image of the blank parchment, forming a rhyming pair with 'latin', allegorizes Latin as letters written on the body, on the 'corpus' of vernacular literature. As with actual parchment, when BnF, MS fr. 19152 scrapes away the pedagogical scene, we are left with a palimpsest, a textual residue of this foundational scene in the form of Galerïen's three attempts to kill Blancheflor.

The importance of writing 'en parkemin' in the pedagogical scene captures its dual nature: Floire et Blancheflor enact a literary transgression when they read together, but also a physical one, as textuality here cannot separate from corporality. Corporality functions first at the level of bodies exchanged across porous geographic borders in both al-Andalus and Capetian France: as much of the historical work of recent years has shown, intermarriage, conversion, and geographic displacement were simply a fact of medieval life, and the clean lines between one ethno-religious group and another muddled and inconsistent.[39] I do not invoke the potentially problematic notion of *convivencia* here, but simply underscore that the degree of cultural and physical exchange across Europe was great, particularly in the Iberian peninsula, where the majority of the romance takes place. In choosing to end the codex with *Floire et Blancheflor*, the compiler of BnF, MS fr. 19152 thus symbolically finishes his book with an act of closure towards this literary heritage and rapid cultural (ex)change.

---

[39] See Elisabeth van Houts, 'Intermarriage in Eleventh-Century England', in *Normandy and its Neighbours, 900-1250: Essays for David Bates*, ed. by D. Crouch and K. Thompson (Turnhout: Brepols, 2011), pp. 237-70. For al-Andalus and Spain see S. Barton, 'Marriage across Frontiers: Sexual Mixing, Power and Identity in Medieval Iberia', *Journal of Medieval Iberian Studies*, 3 (2011), 1-25; Louise Mirrer, *Women, Jews and Muslims in the Texts of Reconquest Castile* (Ann Arbor: University of Michigan Press, 1996); Jessica A. Coope, *The Martyrs of Cordoba: Community and Family Conflict in an Age of Mass Conversion* (Lincoln: University of Nebraksa Press, 1995); David Nirenberg, 'Conversion, Sex and Segregation: Jews and Christians in Medieval Spain', *American Historical Review*, 107 (2002) 1065-93; MacEvitt, *Rough Tolerance*.

Second, corporality acts at the level of text written on parchment, handwritten on the (dead) body and physically carried from one location to another. The claim of an unbroken textual lineage reaching back to Rome rested on a particular linearity which drew the chain of transmission straight from Greece, to Troy, to Rome, and finally France. This was a valuable political belief, allowing Capetian France under Philippe le Bel to lay claim to a massive trove of literary, scientific, and philosophical knowledge. Such credence requires a kind of conscious forgetting, a purposeful erasure of non-linearity and the messy, often horizontal routes of human transmission that brought the classical texts to France, often through Arabic via al-Andalus.[40] In the *roman*'s refusal of the pedagogical moment, we may read in turn the contamination of this *muthos* with the contemporary reality, and thus with the fertile, incestuous intertextuality operating across Europe at the end of the thirteenth century. This peripatetic movement of bodies and texts underlies the pilgrimage road in *Floire et Blancheflor*, and the road Floire must follow to Babylon.

At the root of the rhetoric surrounding foreign textuality in both *Floire et Blancheflor* and BnF, MS fr. 19152 lies this embedded corporality: a distinct relationship between self and other, where the immediacy of the other is felt on or under one's own skin, carried within the self. A resonant echo of this relation arises in Levinas's description of 'avoir-l'autre-dans-sa-peau'.[41] Within this unsettling image lies a particularly useful way of visualizing how BnF, MS fr. 19152 treats 'foreign' texts as both inside itself and outside itself, and as profoundly embodied in both the skin of the page and the bodies of the men and women who copied, carried, and exchanged such texts. Our codex is keenly aware of that presence of the other which is felt 'comme une peau s'expose à ce qui la blesse, comme une joue offerte à celui qui frappe'.[42] In the excision of the pedagogical scene lurks the allegorized refusal of that radical vulnerability to the other, the three attempts to kill Blancheflor accreting around its absence like scar tissue on a wound.

At the beginning of this article I argued that Busby and Adams are correct in suggesting that BnF, MS fr. 19152 attempts to educate the reader, but

---

[40] In the twelfth and thirteenth centuries the immense translation activity between Latin, Hebrew, and Arabic taking place in Toledo brought classical, Hebrew, and Arabic texts into Latin Europe. Following this period of intense cultural and intellectual exchange, the late thirteenth and fourteenth centuries saw Arabic philosophy increasingly censored and banned. Of course, the very existence of items in the historical record condemning these books meant that they were highly popular and impossible to expel from learned culture. See e.g. Roland Hissette, *Enquête sur les 219 articles condamnés à Paris le 7 mars 1277*, Philosophes médiévaux, 22 (Paris: Louvain, 1977); Maria Rosa Menocal, *The Arabic Role in Medieval Literary History* (Philadelphia: University of Pennsylvania Press, 1990); Charles Burnett, 'The Coherence of the Arabic–Latin Translation Program in Toledo in the Twelfth Century', *Science in Context*, 14 (2001), 249–88.

[41] Emmanuel Levinas, *Autrement qu'être ou au-delà de l'essence* (The Hague: Martinus Nijhoff, 1974), p. 180.

[42] Ibid.

questioned the objective of that 'theme of education'.⁴³ The choice and placement of the five texts making up the narrative frame refuse the presence of that diverse, intertextual other, instructing us in how to read a universal 'French' vernacular, constructed against an equally mythic foreign other. This opposition constantly cracks and crumbles around its own edges, as the codex seeks to expel thematic, authorial, and descriptive elements which are integral to its own literary identity. In doing so, both halves of the frame turn away from the Latin and Arabic authorities that created them: Alfonsi becomes a nameless 'wise man of Arabia', *Partonopeus*'s narrator explicitly disavows Latin, and *Floire et Blancheflor* frantically attempts to renegotiate its thematic relationship to foreign learning and difference.

Ultimately, the codex stages the education of the reader in a particular vision of what it meant to read in Old French at the beginning of the fourteenth century. Under Philippe le Bel Parisian manuscript culture grew exponentially, and vernacular manuscripts gained immense traction over the course of the century. Vernacular French literature had, over the course of the past two centuries, become part of the cultural discourse of the elite, edging out reading knowledge of Latin among the aristocracy. Still, as Busby notes, the presence of macaronic manuscripts across the century indicates that the overall picture was more complex than simple illiteracy in Latin (p. 53). BnF, MS fr. 19152 centres on one thread of this complex linguistic picture: the desire to position the multiple vernaculars of Old French literature as a whole entity, one which arises from the ashes of Greek and Latin *sui generis*, and denies its cultural and textual entanglement with the early medieval Byzantine⁴⁴ and Arabic literary cultures responsible for the transmission of much of the classical Latin and Greek material. Read liberally, even the scribe's tendency to insert multiple dialectal elements into his work becomes part of this totalizing literary project. Yet this process can never fully erase the complicated and rich itineraries of medieval literary texts across cultural and linguistic boundaries. They remain as an absent present, allowing us to envision the processes of erasure, exchange, and appropriation active between French literature and its Others, be they Greek, Latin, Hebrew, or Arabic, over the course of the twelfth and thirteenth centuries.

NEW YORK UNIVERSITY						T. S. MENDOLA

[43] Busby, *Codex and Context*, pp. 450–51.
[44] While I have focused largely on the routes of Arabic literary transmission in this essay, the importance of Byzantine manuscripts in preserving and transmitting classical texts cannot be ignored.

GALDÓS, SHAKESPEARE, AND WHAT TO MAKE OF *TORMENTO*

This article seeks to shed light on two key areas of recent Galdós studies: firstly, the question of how to interpret his 1884 novel *Tormento*; secondly, the range and depth of his literary debts to Shakespeare. Of these, the former has seen the most significant disagreements: *Tormento*'s critics are far from reaching a consensus over a novel that remains an elusive gem in the midst of the author's 'Naturalist' period. That Galdós read Shakespeare avidly and drew inspiration from him is not in dispute.[1] He wrote most prominently of his admiration for the bard in his memoirs and in the accounts of his European travels. Not the least of these was his 1889 pilgrimage to Stratford, written up as 'La casa de Shakespeare', and in which he paid homage to the historic birthplace.[2] According to his memoirs, many of the destinations he visited on trips around Europe in the 1870s and 1880s—Denmark, Scotland, Venice, Verona—were more real to him as settings for *Hamlet*, *Macbeth*, *Othello*, and *Romeo and Juliet* than as backdrops to contemporary life. He comments wistfully that 'En mis correrías, las personas y cosas imaginarias me seducían más que las reales'.[3] Nicholas Round and James Whiston have produced model studies of how Shakespearian influence shaped *El amigo Manso* and *Lo prohibido* respectively, but a comprehensive picture of how and why Galdós alluded to Shakespeare in his fiction is yet to emerge.[4] This article therefore contributes to the formation of that picture and contends that *Tormento* displays an unobtrusive but decisive indebtedness to Shakespeare's *Othello*, a play Galdós regarded as 'el drama más maravilloso que han compuesto los

---

I would like to express my gratitude to Eric Southworth, who was kind enough to read a draft of this article and whose insights both on it and on Galdós more widely I have found invaluable.

[1] Among the first to make such a claim was his contemporary Emilia Pardo Bazán, who took it for granted that *El abuelo* was a free adaptation of *King Lear*. See her *La obra periodística completa en 'La Nación' de Buenos Aires (1879-1921)*, ed. by Juliana Sinovas Maté, 2 vols (A Coruña: Diputación Provincial de A Coruña, [n.d.]), I, 189-92 (pp. 191-92). A useful overview of Galdós's allusions to Shakespeare is provided by Hope K. Goodale, 'Allusions to Shakespeare in Galdós', *Hispanic Review*, 39 (1971), 249-60. A further article on the use of a quotation from *Richard III* to provide the title of one of the Episodios Nacionales is William H. Shoemaker, 'Galdós' La de los tristes destinos and its Shakespearean Connections', *Modern Language Notes*, 71 (1956), 114-19. For a discussion of the possible links between Galdós's *Electra* and *The Tempest*, see José Manuel González, *Shakespeare y la generación del 98: relación y trasiego literario* (Madrid: Biblioteca Nueva, 1998), pp. 132-38.

[2] For an account of the history of mass tourism to Stratford in the Victorian period see Julia Thomas, *Shakespeare's Shrine: The Bard's Birthplace and the Invention of Stratford-upon-Avon* (Philadelphia: University of Pennsylvania Press, 2012).

[3] Benito Pérez Galdós, *Recuerdos y memorias* (Madrid: Giner, 1975), p. 258.

[4] Nicholas Round, 'Máximo Manso: Love's Fool', *Hispanic Research Journal*, 11 (2010), 82-93; James Whiston, 'Heroes and Villains in Galdós: *Lo prohibido* and *Macbeth*', *Anales galdosianos*, 27-28 (1992-93), 77-92.

hombres'.[5] It further argues that once readers apprehend the full resonances of this intertextual link, a richer understanding of the novel emerges.

Tormento has provoked divergent interpretations despite at first appearing to tell a straightforward story. Amparo Sánchez Calderón, a vulnerable, orphaned young woman, commits to a relationship with the stupefyingly wealthy Agustín Caballero, he a middle-aged *indiano* newly returned to the old country after thirty years in Central America. Quite how vulnerable Amparo is until she meets Caballero we can judge both from the trilogy of novels in which she features and from external contextual evidence. When she first appeared in *El doctor Centeno*, she had been at the mercy of Pedro Polo, the priest and teacher who seduced her and later offered her a home after her father's death. As Geoffrey Ribbans has pointed out, several factors coalesce to paint their relationship as a rather grubby piece of opportunism on Polo's part. They include the fact that he has taken holy orders, is her mother's cousin, and is twenty-five years her senior: 'Not only has he broken the supportive role he might have been expected to play (and ruined himself to such an extent that he is [in] need of support), but he has involved her in socially dishonourable conduct which threatens to destroy her matrimonial prospects.'[6] When we see her in *Tormento*, her actions are driven to a significant extent by the need to avoid social and financial ruin; the latter in particular since she and her sister Refugio are endeavouring to make a living as seamstresses. As Refugio points out, all they are earning is '[m]iseria y más miseria', not helped by Amparo's inability to escape the imposed servitude of her despotic relative, Rosalía de Bringas.[7] The latter fills Amparo's day with a ceaseless round of errands, shopping, cooking, and child care while her only pay is whatever meagre sum her husband can scrape together from the remnants of the weekly budget. Research undertaken by Geraldine Scanlon indicates that Refugio's verdict is anything but an exaggeration. According to Scanlon's sources, a seamstress in the period in which *Tormento* is set (1867–68) could expect to earn for six weeks' work enough money to survive on the breadline for all of eight days.[8]

The novel would appear, then, to present a happy outcome for Amparo: a tale of misfortune overcome and adversity avoided. But critics have been far from unanimous in endorsing such a view. Peter Bly, Lou Charnon-Deutsch, Eamonn Rodgers, and Rodney Rodríguez are those most vociferously op-

---

[5] Benito Pérez Galdós, *Prosa crítica*, ed. by José-Carlos Mainer and Juan Carlos Ara Torralba (Madrid: Espasa, 2004), p. 789.

[6] Geoffrey Ribbans, '"Amparando/Desamparando a Amparo": Some Reflections on *El doctor Centeno* and *Tormento*', *Revista Canadiense de Estudios Hispánicos*, 17 (1993), 495–524 (p. 502).

[7] Benito Pérez Galdós, *Tormento*, ed. by Teresa Barjau and Joaquim Parellada (Barcelona: Crítica, 2007), p. 236. All subsequent references to the novel are to this edition and appear in brackets in the text.

[8] Geraldine Scanlon, *La polémica feminista en la España contemporánea 1868–1974* (Madrid: Akal, 1986), pp. 83–85.

posed to it.⁹ For Rodgers and Rodríguez in particular, *Tormento* represents a study in female duplicity and cunning, with Amparo cast in the role of ruthless ensnarer of the unworldly Caballero. Charnon-Deutsch sums her up with 'she is a hypocrite in her dealings with Refugio, her abandon of Polo is cruel and her secrecy with Caballero a betrayal. It must be accepted that morally Amparo is as ill as her decrepit apartment'.¹⁰ On the other side of the argument stand Elizabeth Amann and Ribbans, who see no such picture of Amparo emerging. According to the former, the novel is an updated version of the rags-to-riches fairy tale, one that owes much to Zola's *Au bonheur des dames* (1883).¹¹ My own views coincide most closely with those of Ribbans. His article '"Amparando/Desamparando a Amparo": Some Reflections on *El doctor Centeno* and *Tormento*' offers an object lesson in meticulous scholarship and balanced moral judgement. In it he concludes that Galdós's criticism focuses not on the novel's heroine but on individual characters and a society 'which provides no sort of protection for its most fragile members and indeed arbitrarily condemns women for errors essentially not of their making'.¹² James Whiston, meanwhile, has taken a middle road and called it 'perhaps [Galdós's] most "slippery" novel', which, in view of the divergence on either side, may not be far from the mark.¹³

Debate on the novel's characterization hinges on how one views Amparo's ineffectual attempts to make a clean breast of her past dishonour and tell Caballero the truth before he finds out for himself. Is she a prevaricator faced with an impossible choice or a chancer on the make? Likewise, it hinges on whether or not we believe that Amparo made herself attractive to Caballero in calculated fashion or that she had simply been in the right place at the right time. Those who have examined the novel's manuscript are agreed that the ambiguity of the final version is far from accidental.¹⁴ Galdós appears to

⁹ Peter Bly, 'From Disorder to Order: the Pattern of *Arreglar* References in Galdós's *Tormento* and *La de Bringas*', *Neophilologus*, 68 (1978), 392–405; Lou Charnon-Deutsch, 'Inhabited Space in Galdós's *Tormento*', *Anales galdosianos*, 10 (1975), 35–43; Eamonn Rodgers, *From Enlightenment to Realism: The Novels of Galdós 1870–1887* (Dublin: [n. pub.], 1987), pp. 95–112; Rodney T. Rodríguez, 'The Reader's Role in *Tormento*: A Reconstruction of the Amparo–Pedro Polo Affair', *Anales galdosianos*, 24 (1989), 69–78.
¹⁰ Charnon-Deutsch, 'Inhabited Space in Galdós's *Tormento*', p. 40.
¹¹ Elizabeth Amann, 'From *Magasin* to Magazine: *Au bonheur des dames* and Galdós's *Tormento*', *Revista Canadiense de Estudios Hispánicos*, 28 (2003), 455–77. See also Rodolfo Cardona, 'Note on Zola and Galdós: 1883–1887', *Revista Canadiense de Estudios Hispánicos*, 32 (2008), 475–88.
¹² Ribbans, '"Amparando/Desamparando a Amparo"', p. 518.
¹³ James Whiston, *The Practice of Realism: Change and Creativity in the Manuscript of Galdós's 'Fortunata y Jacinta'* (Lewisburg: Bucknell University Press, 2004), p. 159.
¹⁴ Michael A. Schnepf writes that examination of the *Tormento* manuscript reveals considerable changes to the relationship between characters and the ways in which they are presented. Not the least of these is the removal of the suspicions the Bringas couple have of Amparo's moral fibre. Others include the suggestion that until recently Amparo had made the journey to Polo's home 'con más o menos gusto' and the decision to place the fallen priest in the novel's background

have taken considerable pains to ensure a finely balanced uncertainty over precisely these points: '[las] supresiones suelen tener como fin sugerir antes que afirmar, insinuar o dejar en el aire mejor que dar plena constancia de los hechos'.[15] While the novel's manuscript will not be the subject of discussion here, the amendments made to the text at the proof stage will be commented on in detail since in several instances they offer telling evidence of Galdós's careful nuancing of his material.[16] Detailed commentary on *Tormento*'s proofs has, to my knowledge, been thus far absent from the bibliography of Galdós studies. This article will therefore be the first to offer a reading of the novel supported by such archival evidence.

Ordinarily, we would expect *Tormento*'s denouement to resolve any remaining ambiguities of interpretation. Were the reader being encouraged to take the kind of condemnatory line Rodríguez and Rodgers have advocated, Galdós could have drawn on plenty of literary precedents in the then contemporary novel for the reckoning meted out against the adulterous female. And yet, *Tormento* leaves us with an outcome that is on the face of it far happier than the fate of Anna Karenina, say, but still oddly unsatisfactory from the point of view of conventional morality. While both orphaned sisters appear to have secured their financial future, neither has done so with her honour intact: Refugio has taken to prostitution and Amparo will be Caballero's unmarried concubine in their new life together in Bordeaux. That she should consent to live in sin would have left her no better than her sister according to the conventional wisdom of Galdós's time. In spite of which, from the information he decided to supply in the trilogy's concluding volume, *La de Bringas*, neither sister is suffering for her sins. Rather the contrary: Amparo's relationship with Caballero in Bordeaux is happy and stable, so stable in fact that the couple offer to play host to the Bringas family for a holiday in the late summer of 1868; and, even more importantly for the denouement of the later novel, Refugio's business is thriving, she having attracted a wealthy clientele up to and including Manuel Pez and the novel's narrator. Her apparent fate stands in contrast to Isidora Rufete, for example, whose descent into the life of a streetwalker is charted so unflinchingly in *La desheredada* (1881) and whom we meet years later (both in narrative time and in the composition

---

where he can better perform the role of the 'haunting "sombra negra" which continually disturbs Amparo's thoughts'. See his 'The Manuscript of Galdós's *Tormento*', *Anales galdosianos*, 26 (1991), 43–49. See also Teresa Barjau and Joaquim Parellada, 'La génesis de *Tormento* a partir de los manuscritos', *Isidora: Revista de estudios galdosianos*, 9 (2009), 49–64.

[15] Teresa Barjau and Joaquim Parellada, 'Prólogo', in the cited edition of *Tormento*, p. 32.

[16] My researches on the manuscript of *Tormento* were facilitated enormously by the staff of the Casa-Museo Pérez Galdós in Las Palmas de Gran Canaria. I would like to thank in particular Ana Isabel Mendoza de Benito and Francisco David Valido Perdomo, who could not have been more helpful or welcoming.

of the novel) as the lover of an impoverished dying artist in the pages of *Torquemada en la hoguera* (1889).[17]

Looked at as a whole, the trilogy would seem to offer a steer towards how we should understand this most equivocal of conclusions to *Tormento*. The climactic scene of *La de Bringas* is, as Whiston has observed, one of the most unsettling come-uppances in nineteenth-century fiction.[18] It sees a frantic Rosalía running out of time to pay off the merciless Torquemada and turning in desperation to Refugio. The latter seizes the opportunity to avenge the many slights she has suffered at the hands of her condescending one-time protector and makes Rosalía act as her servant, scrabble round the floor for her discarded clothes, help to dress her, and put up her hair. Refugio eventually gives her the money, only to tell her in the next breath that the well-connected woman who has been her partner in plundering the family's coffers has called her that most hated of all things, 'una cursi', behind her back. Rosalía has earned her come-uppance for the sadistic joy she had taken in the revelation of Amparo's past dishonour, for the effort she had made to rub salt in the wound and steal clothing from the future bride's trousseau.

If such is the fate of the priggish, hypocritical woman who had been so quick to cast the first stone at Amparo, Galdós can hardly be said to be endorsing that response to his earlier heroine. There is a direct link of poetic justice, with one sister avenging the other, which would suggest a considerable degree of planning on the novelist's part. Moreover, the narrator of *La de Bringas* draws the same explicit link of cause and effect between the taste for finery Rosalía gained while stealing from Amparo and her own later downfall:

Aquel bendito Agustín había sido, generosamente y sin pensarlo, el corruptor de su prima; había sido la serpiente de buena fe que le metió en la cabeza las más peligrosas vanidades que pueden ahuecar el cerebro de una mujer. Los regalitos fueron la fruta cuya dulzura le quitó la inocencia, y por culpa de ellos un ángel con espada de raso me la echó de aquel Paraíso en que su Bringas la tenía tan sujeta.[19]

La de Bringas ends with the revelation that Rosalía has herself taken to selling sex to keep her in the manner to which she has grown accustomed. That interpretation of the conclusion of *La de Bringas* would also chime with what critics have taken to be a wider representative aspect to the Bringas household as standing for the parasitic, nepotistic, and morally bankrupt Spain presided over by Isabel II prior to the Revolution of 1868.[20] And yet, that obvious

[17] Rhian Davies suggests that the action of *Torquemada en la hoguera* takes place 'probablemente en febrero de 1883'. See 'Estudio de *Torquemada en la hoguera* (2): *Torquemada en la hoguera* en el contexto del siglo diecinueve' <http://www.hrionline.ac.uk/galdos/>.

[18] Whiston, *The Practice of Realism*, p. 153.

[19] Benito Pérez Galdós, *La de Bringas*, ed. by Alda Blanco and Carlos Blanco Aguinaga, 4th edn (Madrid: Cátedra, 1994), pp. 92–93.

[20] See e.g. Peter Bly, *Galdós's Novel of the Historical Imagination* (Liverpool: Cairns, 1983),

shape to this trilogy of Galdós's novels has not stopped Charnon-Deutsch, Rodríguez, or Rodgers from painting him as the crude moralizer he clearly is not.

The role assigned to Rosalía across *Tormento* and *La de Bringas* suggests that Galdós either set out with, or improvised, a pleasing overall shape to his trilogy such that the reader could develop a sense of a character's evolution over time and in response to changing fortunes. If Amparo's most significant oppressor gets her due in *La de Bringas*, another reason for suggesting that Galdós's sympathies lie strongly with the former is the role played by Felipe Centeno in her would-be suicide. He is another character whose trajectory we trace from one novel to the next, in his case from *Marianela* (1878) and *El doctor Centeno* to *Tormento*. He is also the innocent observer of the only glimpses we get of the affair between Amparo and Pedro Polo both before it begins and during its course. The first indication we have is at a dinner in Madrid's Observatory during which Felipe can hear but not see the guests, among whom are Polo and Amparo. The confused succession of sounds overheard by the young lad, newly arrived in Madrid, is presented in the staccato rhythm of the prose:

Risas y más risas, apremios, protestar, carcajadas; mucho de *No, por Dios*; repetición incesante del *Vamos, Amparo, esta copita*; luego otra vez: *Ay, no, no, don Pedro, por Dios*. Y después: *Jesús, qué melindrosa... Pero usted me quiere emborrachar... vamos... así, valiente... ¡Ay, cómo pica!*[21]

The reader has not yet been introduced to these characters and might easily miss the detail in passing, especially as Felipe is a naive witness to the scene and does not later put two and two together. (The knowledge that Polo's attentions towards Amparo include what are clearly efforts to ply her with drink calls into serious question Rodríguez's baseless assertion that Amparo is the instigator of their affair.)[22] That Felipe might draw more substantial inferences from that early exchange is confirmed when he innocently tells one of his street-urchin friends that he has overheard Polo making love to Amparo: 'Una noche estaba en la sala de don Pedro: entré yo, y oí que don Pedro le decía que había bajado del Cielo... ella, ella. Yo la llamo *La Emperadora*.'[23] While under Polo's 'care', Felipe has developed an adolescent crush on her, one that is only reinforced when she tries to intercede on his behalf following his expulsion from the priest's appalling school. She even gives him

pp. 61–75; Jo Labanyi, *Gender and Modernization in the Spanish Realist Novel* (Oxford: Oxford University Press, 2000), pp. 139–64.

[21] Benito Pérez Galdós, *El doctor Centeno*, ed. by José Carlos Mainer (Madrid: Biblioteca Nueva, 2002), p. 114.

[22] Rodríguez, 'The Reader's Role in *Tormento*', pp. 73–74. See also Ribbans, '"Amparando/Desamparando a Amparo"', p. 502.

[23] *El doctor Centeno*, p. 182.

the money that tides him over until he is able to meet up once more with Miquis and become his servant. It is the death of his master at the conclusion of the novel that throws him once more onto Madrid's scrapheap, his future far from certain. At the start of *Tormento*, set three years after the action of *El doctor Centeno*, it is with surprise and delight that we learn that he has secured a position as servant to Caballero, a man to whom Felipe applies the admiring epithet 'Capitalista' with solemn reverence (p. 135).

As several critics have observed, the first chapter of *Tormento* in fact picks up where the finale of its predecessor had left off, with both scenes taking the form of a meeting between José Ido del Sagrario and Felipe Centeno written up in dramatic dialogue.[24] The former has now established himself as the *folletinista* he was threatening to become at the end of the earlier novel whereas Felipe has landed on his feet, having found employment with Caballero. His role will bring him once again into contact with Amparo, as the quietly besotted witness to her rise and fall from grace. In this he strongly resembles Flaubert's Justin, the apothecary's assistant who for so long worships Emma Bovary from afar and unlocks for her the attic room where Homais keeps his poisons, giving her access to the arsenic that will eventually kill her. The scene in which Amparo attempts suicide looks like a deliberate ironic reprise of Flaubert, with Felipe dispatched to the pharmacy to procure the potassium cyanide with which Amparo wants to end it all. Fortunately for her, Felipe has more wit than his literary ancestor and substitutes nothing more deadly than 'tintura de guayaco', a remedy for toothache, for the would-be lethal dose (p. 425). As Julian Barnes has said of the role played by Justin in *Madame Bovary*, he is 'an echo of her, that perfectly placed bit of kindling which makes Emma's story blaze the brighter. To change the metaphor: if Madame Bovary were a mansion, Justin would be the handle to the back door; but great architects have the design of door-furniture in mind even as they lay out the west wing.'[25] If we take up Barnes's figurative language, that sense of meticulous architectural planning here extends not only through a single novel but across the first two volumes of the Galdosian trilogy. That impression is further reinforced when we consider what Scanlon has highlighted as the interest in education as practical enquiry and scientific exploration that underpins Felipe's maturation in the trilogy's first instalment.[26] *El doctor Centeno* had traced the rapid dampening of whatever hopes Felipe's determined tread at the conclusion of *Marianela* might have sparked. Instead, his naive

---

[24] See e.g. Peter Bly, *The Wisdom of Eccentric Old Men: A Study of Type and Secondary Characters in Galdós's Social Novels, 1870–1897* (Montreal and London: McGill-Queen's University Press, 2004), pp. 96–97; Ribbans, '"Amparando/Desamparando a Amparo"', p. 503.

[25] Julian Barnes, 'Justin: A Small Major Character', in *Something to Declare* (London: Picador, 2002), pp. 289–302 (p. 302).

[26] Geraldine Scanlon, '*El doctor Centeno*: A Study in Obsolescent Values', *Bulletin of Hispanic Studies*, 55 (1978), 245–53, passim.

ambitions come up against the brick wall of Polo's insistence on rote learning and the systematic belittling of his charges. But those same tentative hopes for his future are rekindled, once he has left Polo's stifling tutelage, in the oddly touching scene where he dissects Rosa Ido's dead dog, the better to understand the tuberculosis that is killing his master. His actions point to a growing capacity to marry his lively curiosity with practical methodology, a proof that some vestige of his enquiring mind has survived the humiliations Polo inflicted. In *Tormento* it is that same scientific intuition that persuades him, once the pharmacist has warned him that Amparo has ordered poison, to prepare a draught that is innocuous in content but cloudy in appearance, such that it gives a sufficiently convincing imitation for her to drink it off rather than demand he return with the real thing: Felipe is after all a subordinate who must follow orders, but he has learnt that disobedience may in fact be the way to serve his mistress's best interests. Scrutiny of the novel's proofs reveals that Galdós was intent on emphasizing precisely this sense of Felipe's canny subterfuge. The initial draft of Felipe's speech explaining what he had added to the water she thought was her poison had read: 'Polvos de arroz... y lo puse todo en un frasco vacío que había en su cuarto, de cuando al señor le dolieron las muelas.' The final version became instead this more scientifically detailed and impressive explanation: 'Le eché un poco de tintura de guayaco... de la que trajo doña Marta cuando le dolieron las muelas.' The fact that he has retained the name of the medicine enhances the sense that this is a boy with a mind as well as a heart.

Hence, as *Tormento* opens we cannot help but feel that Amparo and Felipe complement one another in their exposure to a world far more difficult to navigate than either could have imagined. Nevertheless, the sequel to *El doctor Centeno* will take great pains to make that picture still more variegated, not so much in the characterization of Felipe, who remains peripheral to the action, as in that of Amparo. As so often, Leopoldo Alas was more than alive to what Galdós was attempting, and realized that it hinged crucially on the portrayal of complex personalities in equally complex situations. Alas's review of the novel asserted that 'nos hace penetrar otra vez, y con buen pie, en esos *interiores ahumados* de que habla Marcelino Menéndez en su notable prólogo a las *Obras completas* de Pereda'.[27] He went on to praise the fact that Galdós was for the first time allowing the contemporary Spanish novel to delve into a woman's psyche:

> en general, la mujer está poco estudiada en nuestra literatura contemporánea; se la trata en abstracto, se la pinta ángel o culebra, pero se la separa de su ambiente, de su olor, de sus trapos, de sus ensueños, de sus veleidades, de sus caídas, de sus errores,

---

[27] Leopoldo Alas, *Obras completas*, ed. by Jean-François Botrel and others, 12 vols (Oviedo: Nobel, 2002–09), IV: *Crítica (Primera parte)*, ed. by Laureano Bonet (2003), p. 518.

de sus caprichos; les sucede a esas mujeres lo que a los personajes de nuestro teatro: llevan un nombre, pero no pueden llevar dignamente un apellido.[28]

Certainly, Rodgers would have it that Amparo is far more 'culebra' than 'ángel', and it is worth dwelling at some length on his arguments since they constitute the most trenchant denunciation of her character yet written. According to Rodgers, *Tormento* 'seriously calls in question the whole "ideology" of bourgeois society', an argument he rests on the belief that Amparo is the focus of opprobrium for her flagrant pursuit of self-interest and economic motive over a more authentic future with her former lover Pedro Polo.[29] I would suggest that such an argument is, at best, misconceived. To be sympathetically disposed towards Polo, readers of *Tormento*'s predecessor *El doctor Centeno* would have had to ignore the fact that the teacher-priest had so conscientiously set out to destroy any vestige of self-worth in Felipe Centeno at precisely the moment when that quality was at its most fragile in the young pupil. Their reservations would only have been reinforced by the volatile, bullying, and sexually predatory behaviour he displays towards Amparo in the later novel. While Rodgers would have it that 'in repudiating him [Amparo] may well be turning her back on something very genuine', a more sensitive or attentive reader of *Tormento* might suggest that the man who tries to coerce her into sex via threats and imprisonment is not necessarily recommending himself as a future life partner.[30]

What is most frustrating about Rodgers's reading of *Tormento* is that it appears to be inflected with an undercurrent of gender bias. Thus while Amparo is continually upbraided for selfishness in wanting to secure her financial future: 'The truth of the matter is that repentance is a convenient religious cliché behind which self-interest can hide, and the same is true of the way in which she thinks of her assisting Polo as an "act of charity"',[31] Polo, by contrast and despite all his flaws, acquires tragic status: 'One of the most tragic ironies in the novel is that Don Pedro only achieves his wish to go abroad at the price of stifling the real self he has been struggling to discover.'[32] The apparent mismatch of gender roles is implicit in the following suggestion that Amparo has no right to think of a future as anything other than an appendage to the man who dishonoured her:

Not for nothing does Polo visibly revive in this episode, progressing in a matter of minutes from indolence and depression to greater cheerfulness and vitality. It is Amparo's presence which works this miracle, but she is too wrapped-up in her own concerns to see how necessary she is to Polo's well-being, or to realise that if she were

[28] Alas, *Crítica*, p. 519.
[29] Rodgers, *From Enlightenment to Realism*, p. 97.
[30] Ibid., p. 98.
[31] Ibid., p. 105.
[32] Ibid., p. 107.

to join him in his quest for a more purposeful and authentic existence, there would be a greater prospect of this quest succeeding.³³

The suggestion that Amparo's greatest hopes for the future are at the side of a fallen priest who was also her known seducer is not only at odds with contemporary attitudes—which would have repudiated the couple every bit as much as if not more than an unmarried Amparo and Caballero—but also misguided because of the rebarbative personality of Polo himself. An important piece of evidence in this connection, one not considered by Rodgers, is the substantial and telling passage Galdós inserted at the proof stage in the scene between Marcelina and Caballero in what would become Chapter 36 of the finished text. There, Marcelina describes her brother's future prospects in a climate more suited to his expansive ambitions. In the original proofs the passage read: 'Pues allí, en aquella isla de Zamboanga, mi hermano convertirá herejes y hará grandes méritos. Y mienten los que le suponen mal natural; pues si no le hubieran sorbido los sesos otro gallo le cantara.' Having made slight adjustments to the word order of the first sentence quoted here, the author then inserted after the full stop the following substantial passage:

> No es esto decir que confíe absolutamente en la salvación, pues como la cabra tira al monte, el vicio tira siempre... á lo que tira. ¡Oh! ¡qué esfuerzos tuvimos que hacer á última hora. Si hubiera V. visto...! ¡Qué hombrazo! En la estación nos decía que allá sera un Nabucodonosor con sotana. Que sea lo que quiera con tal que no vuelva á las andadas, ni parezca más por acá... Y no crea V... ¡tengo un susto...! Se me figura que de Barcelona ó de Marsella se nos vuelve á Madrid y se me entra por la puerta cuando menos lo espere... V. no le conoce bien.

This addition to the text could scarcely be more crucial to our understanding of his character or the wider issue of how to interpret the novel. Not least because Marcelina's speech indicates she has come to question her previously unshakeable belief that Amparo was to blame for her brother's disgrace: 'pues como la cabra tira al monte, el vicio tira siempre...'. Were this to be the case, it would also explain her ultimate decision to burn the love letters the pair have exchanged instead of handing them over to Caballero. If even the unpleasantly puritanical Marcelina can come to question Amparo's blameworthiness, why should we reinvest it with interpretative authority? More important still, however, is Marcelina's anxiety that her brother should quit Spain for good. While it may not speak highly of her familial loyalty, it does beg the question, if Polo's own flesh and blood cannot wait to be shot of him, why should Amparo shoulder such a heavy burden alone?

Her attitude towards her former lover resembles that of many young people who have been the victims of sexually coercive or unequal relationships when too innocent to recognize them for what they were. Hence, when he reminds

---
³³ Ibid., p. 106.

her: 'Tu boca preciosa, ¿qué me dijo? ¿No lo recuerdas? Yo sí. ¿Para qué lo dijiste?' (p. 365), he is alluding to what remains to him an enjoyable and sexually fulfilled episode but which for her is redolent only of shame and self-reproach. Rodgers sees nothing to condemn—or at least nothing worth commenting on—in Polo's imprisonment of her against her will, his sexual threats, or his manipulative subjugation of her. Instead he sees 'something appalling about the ease with which she can fall back on sentimental images drawn from the world of fiction in order to assuage her guilty feelings about continuing to conceal her secret from Agustín'.[34]

An aspect of *Tormento*, however, which has attracted no mention from its critics but may yet shed light on what we are to make of this tangled affair is its allusiveness to Shakespeare's *Othello*. Galdós had already used that play as a fleeting intertext in *La desheredada*, to add belated gravitas to the suffering of José de Relimpio, the love-struck old Don Juan whose years of service to Isidora Rufete are as faithful as they are ineffectual. The novel intertwines their trajectories and ends with their parallel decline, hers into the social suicide of prostitution, his into alcoholism and death. Bly has commented in detail on the pathos Galdós extracts from his deterioration, pathos that comes from the nobility of his sacrifice and increasing self-awareness faced with a future he knows to be hopeless.[35] A character who when first introduced elicits the remarks 'Era el hombre mejor del mundo. Era un hombre que no servía para nada' is forced to watch on as Isidora takes up with a succession of cads whose exploitation of her is always sexual and usually also financial.[36] Isidora forbids him to intervene in her life on pain of severing all ties and so he mutely observes the rabble of ne'er-do-wells who inexorably work her ruin. It is in one such scene, Chapter 12 of Part II of the novel, that we find him in dialogue with Joaquín, the lothario and cause of her initial dishonour, while the two of them await her arrival home. During their conversation, a letter arrives stuffed with money, a gift from Isidora to clear yet another of Joaquín's debts. While Joaquín goes through a show of moral scruples at accepting money from a woman who lives from hand to mouth, Relimpio soliloquizes in unexpectedly Shakespearian terms: 'DON JOSÉ. (*Aparte y tétricamente, coincidiendo en sus expresiones sin sospecharlo, con Otelo.*) ¡Oh! Flor graciosa y bella, ¿por qué has nacido?'.[37] He evokes one of the Moor's laments at the necessity of ridding the world of the woman he both loves and despises:

> O thou weed,
> Who art so lovely fair and smell'st so sweet

---

[34] Ibid., p. 107.
[35] Bly, *The Wisdom of Eccentric Old Men*, pp. 61–72.
[36] Benito Pérez Galdós, *La desheredada*, ed. by Germán Gullón, 3rd edn (Madrid: Cátedra, 2004), p. 177.
[37] *La desheredada*, p. 425.

>   That the sense aches at thee, would thou hadst
>   ne'er been born!
>   (IV. 2. 76–79).[38]

Joaquín asks him where Isidora has got the money from, to which Relimpio replies 'No lo sé... (*Aparte, lleno siempre de espíritu shakespeariano.*) ¡Estúpido!, ¿cómo quieres que te lo diga? No me atreveré a decirlo ni aun a vosotras, ¡oh castas estrellas!'[39] Again, he adapts Othello's apparent revulsion at the avenger's task, not wishing to bring into public sight the fact that Isidora has in all probability earned the money for Joaquín by sleeping with yet another of her wealthy lovers. Relimpio's adoption of this borrowed rhetoric, even when he does not know he has borrowed it, forms part of the narrator's strategy in reminding us that this most unlikely of tragic heroes may yet be capable of 'unexpected heights of noble altruism'.[40]

In *Tormento*, allusion to *Othello* comes explicitly in Chapter 35 when Rosalía says to the distraught and confused Caballero: 'Ya le [referring to Amparo] dije que no eres un Otelo y que no te dará tan fuerte' (p. 414). He has just learnt of Amparo's dishonour and sought Bringas's advice on what to do next. Rosalía is playing a Machiavellian game at this stage of proceedings, doing her best to keep the couple apart by advising each of them separately to stay at home and wait for the other to call. In the meantime she is also syphoning off linen from Amparo's trousseau and taking delight in the disgrace of her upstart former servant. But if Caballero is no Othello, neither is she a Iago. She is far from having mastered what Harold Bloom called 'the arts of disinformation, disorientation, and derangement', and her plans to scupper their union fail ignominiously.[41] Although it is not for want of trying. Her speech to Caballero could be taken at its conciliatory face value but could equally be interpreted as a form of goading, pricking Caballero's sense of honour by reminding him of the archetypal jealous husband of Western drama. Perhaps she hopes that her words will call to mind the obligations of the cuckold who must cleanse his honour with blood in the 'finest' traditions of the Renaissance stage.[42]

I have argued elsewhere that a crucial step on the road towards Amparo's unmasking as Polo's lover and her ultimate dishonour owes an implicit debt to

---

[38] William Shakespeare, *Othello*, ed. by E. A. J. Honigmann (London: Arden, 1999). Subsequent quotations will refer to this edition.
[39] *La desheredada*, p. 425.
[40] Bly, *The Wisdom of Eccentric Old Men*, p. 68.
[41] Harold Bloom, *Shakespeare: The Invention of the Human* (London: Fourth Estate, 1999), p. 436.
[42] It is also worth mentioning that the Spanish penal code in this period looked leniently on husbands who punished their adulterous wives. A man who caught his wife in flagrante with another man and killed or wounded her could expect only to spend a maximum of six years exiled from his local community. If he inflicted less serious injuries he could expect no punishment at all. See Scanlon, *La polémica feminista*, p. 131.

just such dramatic precedent.[43] When Amparo finally manages to escape from Polo's flat following his imprisonment of her in Chapter 30, she leaves behind one of her gloves, an object seized upon by his puritanical sister Marcelina as she scours the rooms for evidence of the mysterious visitor. In her anxiety to flee Polo's coercive demands for sex, she has left behind, to use Othello's phrase, 'ocular proof' (III. 3. 363) of her former association with the fallen priest. Just as Desdemona's stolen handkerchief provides all the confirmation her husband needs of her guilt, Marcelina takes the glove as confirmation of her most prurient fears, and Amparo's reputation is as good as ruined.

However, that evocation of a familiar dramatic trope takes its place alongside Rosalía's explicit allusion to Shakespeare, and both begin to resonate beyond their immediate context. The harder we listen, the more we realize that *Othello* echoes further and further through Galdós's novel. In consoling or goading Caballero, Rosalía plays on another of the dominant characteristics shared by Shakespeare's Moor and the wealthy *indiano*: their nagging sense of themselves as outsiders. Othello's reasons for such insecurity centre on his age, ethnicity, sexual prowess, and status as a paid mercenary on the fringes of a wealthy society, while Caballero's mirror them in important respects. He too has spent prolonged periods in the company of uncivilized peoples—the traders, natives, and outlaws of the Central American border country where he made his fortune; he too has sought comfort and stability in an unfamiliar urban environment; like Othello, he is significantly older than his bride (forty-five to her twenty-something); like Othello, he is doing his best to negotiate the intrigue and double-dealing of a moneyed culture where appearances count for far more than moral rectitude. And while he shares the ethnic background of his peers in Madrid, Caballero does stand out from the crowd due to his physical appearance. The harsh sun of the tropics has left a permanent tinge to the colour of his skin: 'color de América, tinte de fiebre y fatiga en las ardientes humedades del golfo mejicano [. . .] una hermosura tostada al sol' (p. 173). Alan E. Smith's scrutiny of the *Tormento* manuscript held in the Biblioteca Nacional revealed an intriguing note Galdós had evidently written to himself on the reverse of one of its pages: 'ojo al nombre de la ciudad BROWNSVILLE'.[44] That place name, referred to three times by Caballero as one of the backwaters he inhabited during his thirty years in Central America, might well be a pun on the skin colour he has acquired as a result. Rosalía especially, but the narrator too, often refer to him with the words 'salvaje' and 'bruto'. The former even imagines a day when her husband would be out of the picture and she might marry Caballero instead,

[43] Gareth Wood, 'The Illustrated *La Regenta*: An Inexplicable Neglect and a Debate that Never Happened', *Bulletin of Hispanic Studies*, 87 (2010), 773–99 (pp. 794–95).
[44] Alan E. Smith, 'Catálogo de los manuscritos de Benito Pérez Galdós en la Biblioteca Nacional de España', *Anales galdosianos*, 20 (1985), 143–56 (p. 153).

a union she couches in terms of taming a wild animal: 'Pero al año y medio, o a los dos años, me casaría con este animal... Yo le desbastaría, yo le afinaría' (p. 183). The predicament both Caballero and Othello face, therefore, is that the cities they inhabit tolerate them as accepted outsiders because they bring indisputable benefits to the community: Othello offers security through his military prowess, Caballero brings much-coveted capital.

In his comments on *Othello*, prompted by a visit to Venice, Galdós astutely observes that it is a drama steeped in a sense of place:

> Sólo el primer acto de este drama único pasa en Venecia, los cuatro restantes pasan en Chipre; pero siendo esta isla entonces colonia de la República y siendo de venecianos de pura raza todos los personajes. Venecia es el escenario de aquella acción conmovedora y profundamente humana.[45]

He had noted how much the setting, the wealthy city-state, feeds Othello's insecurities. It is the latter on which Iago draws so expertly in the 'temptation scene' when describing the ways of Venetian women:

> I know our country disposition well—
> In Venice they do let God see the pranks
> They dare not show their husbands.
> (III. 3. 204–06)

Caballero will be presented as no less of a fish out of water in decadent pre-revolutionary Madrid. When he is first introduced, the narrator comments on his lack of social graces, one that is conspicuous enough to attract the mirth of his fellow citizens:

> Había hecho sonreír con trivial malicia a muchas personas; era torpe para saludar, e incapaz de sostener una conversación sobre motivos ligeros y agradables. En medio de las expansiones de alegría, se mantenía seriote y taciturno. Si no ignoraba las fórmulas elementales del vivir social, era lego en otras muchas de segundo orden, que son producto del refinamiento de costumbres y de las continuas innovaciones suntuarias. (p. 174)

Galdós has noted—anticipating Thorstein Veblen by fifteen years—that one of the leisure class's most salient features is its devotion of considerable time and energy to the development of elaborate and pointless niceties of courtesy.[46] Caballero would have it that his time in Central America has been formative in positive ways, that it has taught him self-reliance and perspicacity in

---

[45] *Prosa crítica*, p. 789.

[46] 'Witness the masterful presence of the high-minded gentleman or lady, which testifies to so much of dominance and independence of economic circumstances, and which at the same time appeals with such convincing force to our sense of what is right and gracious. It is among this highest leisure class, who have no superiors and few peers, that decorum finds its fullest and maturest expression; and it is this highest class also that gives decorum that definitive formulation which serves as a canon of conduct for the classes beneath' (Thorstein Veblen, *Conspicuous Consumption: Unproductive Consumption of Goods is Honourable* (London: Penguin, 2005), p. 30).

discerning others' motives. This conviction underlies his claim in that same chapter where he first appears that years spent away from the society of his fellow men have saved him from the 'disgusto de ver lo que llamamos una persona' (p. 175). Again like his Shakespearian counterpart, time spent in largely male company, reliant on his mettle to see him through tight spots, has proved as much a blessing as a curse. Where Othello can command respect with 'one massive and menacingly monosyllabic line'—'Keep up your bright swords, for the dew will rust them' (I. 2. 59)—his prowess in matters military does not guard him against fears that he is too old, too uncouth, and too foreign to keep his bride from straying.[47] Thus it is that Iago can dupe his commander with the imputation of aberrance on Desdemona's part in having chosen so unlikely a husband:

> Not to affect many proposed matches
> Of her own clime, complexion and degree,
> Whereto we see, in all things, nature tends—
> Foh! one may smell in such a will most rank,
> Foul disproportion, thoughts unnatural.
> (III. 3. 233–37)

Rosalía meanwhile, and at least in this regard like Iago before her, knows exactly how to twist the knife in the still bleeding wound:

Y di una cosa: al fijarte en ella para hacerla tu mujer, ¿nos consultaste a nosotros sobre punto tan delicado, como parecía natural? Nada de eso. Allá tú lo arreglaste solo, y cuando nos percatamos de ello ya lo tenías muy bien guisado y comido. (p. 413)

Her condescension, her knowingness after the event, are intended to fulfil the same purpose as Iago's temptation of his master: to bend Caballero to her will, to convince him that in future he cannot take a single step without her blessing. Once in Iago's power Othello becomes an angel of vengeance on a scale at which his puppeteer can only wonder, much as Rosalía hopes that a pliant Caballero will fulfil her dreams of finery beyond imagining.[48] To her chagrin, rather than sink to his knees and swear a hellish blood pact at her side, Caballero retires to consider his next move in measured fashion, eventually deciding to treat Amparo's lack of candour with compassionate tolerance. Rosalía's only consolation, meanwhile, is to feign moral outrage at their decision to remain unmarried while the real source of her wrath is to be found in the fact that Caballero has slipped through her controlling grasp.

[47] Bloom, *Shakespeare*, p. 434.
[48] Confirmation of this can be found in the final passage of Chapter 37, where Rosalía claps her hands in delight at the thought that Caballero is theirs at last. She embarks on an extended reverie, imagining all the fabric she can buy with his money at her disposal: 'veía montones de rasos, terciopelos, sedas, encajes, pieles, joyas sin fin, colores y gracias mil, los sombreros más elegantes, las últimas novedades parisienses, todo muy bien lucido en teatros, paseos, tertulias' (p. 432).

Nevertheless, her rebuke to Caballero over his rapid engagement does remind us that his courtship has resembled Othello's in disrupting ordinary social protocol. By eloping with Desdemona, Othello acknowledges at its inception the transgressive quality of his relationship with her. Caballero's courtship of an orphaned girl has similarly ridden roughshod over convention. Rosalía may be alluding to the Bringas' position *in loco parentis* to the young woman when she rebukes Caballero for not asking their blessing. Julian Pitt-Rivers's description of Spanish courtship customs, albeit far from contemporary with Galdós, acts as an important reminder that betrothals were preceded by a visit from the *novio* to the prospective father-in-law to seek permission.[49] Caballero's mother would also have been expected to visit Amparo's mother before a formal announcement was made. Caballero is unlikely to have made such visits because he is shrewd enough to know that the Bringas family value Amparo more for her cheap service than for her personal qualities. He will later tell her that 'esto es peor que servir' (p. 296), alluding to her position in the Bringas home.

In fact, Rosalía's allusion to Caballero's courtship of Amparo, coming as it does hard on the heels of her reference to Othello, evokes further significant resonances with Shakespeare's play. Her claim that 'tú lo arreglaste solo' is tinged with dramatic irony when we recall his tortured efforts to say anything at all on their first evening alone together:

En el cerebro del tímido surgió bullicioso tumulto de ideas; palabras mil acudieron atropelladas a sus secos labios. Iba a decir admirables y vehementes cosas: sí, las diría... Ó las decía, o estallaba como una bomba. Pero los nervios se le encabritaron; aquel maldito freno que su ser íntimo ponía fatalmente a su palabra, le apretó de súbito con soberana fuerza, y de sus labios, como espuma que salpica de los del epiléptico, salpicaron estas dos palabras: «Vaya, vaya». (p. 201)

He had taken trouble to dispatch the Bringas clan to the theatre so that he might find Amparo alone in their home. In other words, he has emulated his literary antecedent by engineering a 'pliant hour' in which to do his wooing:

                             This to hear
     Would Desdemona seriously incline.
     But still the house affairs would draw her hence,
     Which ever as she could with haste dispatch,
     She'd come again, and with a greedy ear
     Devour up my discourse; which I observing
     Took once a pliant hour and found good means
     To draw from her a prayer of earnest heart
     That I would all my pilgrimage dilate,

---

[49] Julian Pitt-Rivers, *The People of the Sierra*, 2nd edn (London: University of Chicago Press, 1971), p. 95.

> Whereof by parcels she had something heard
> But not intentively.
>
> (I. 3. 146–56)

And yet, though he has the confidence to set the scene as he would like, when the moment arrives, he suffers an attack of stage fright. Amparo it is who comes to his rescue by asking him about his time in Central America: 'Habrá usted pasado muchos trabajos y también grandes sustos, porque yo he oído que hay allá culebras venenosas y otros animaluchos, tigres, elefantes...' (p. 200). It is as if she were artlessly feeding him the line to get them back on the track of re-creating Shakespeare's scene, though she no more knows this than he does. The most heavily annotated copy of *Othello* in Galdós's personal library displays on its title-page an illustration of precisely this moment in the play: Othello as seducer through the power of his oratory.[50] Galdós is alluding to Othello's courtship account since both his own and Shakespeare's creation woo their brides with the tales of derring-do and exotic hardship that come to be associated with them. In fact, Galdós extracts humour from the gap between the literary antecedent Caballero does not know he is trying to emulate and his faltering efforts to reproduce what Wilson Knight called 'the *Othello* music':[51] 'Vaya, vaya' is after all a far cry from Othello's 'travailous history' and polysyllabic evocation of the 'Anthropophagi'. It is left to Amparo to do the running, which she does guilelessly enough: 'Leopardos, dragones o no sé qué, y, sobre todo, unas serpientes de muchas varas que se enroscan y aprietan, aprietan... Jesús, ¡qué horror!' (p. 200). We shall return to her reference to the boa constrictor shortly.

In the meantime we should note that Galdós took care at the proof stage to strip this scene of the signs of calculation on Amparo's part that had persisted from an earlier draft. There, the final words of the speech just quoted were followed by a separate paragraph which read 'Amparo se cubrió la cara con sus manos'. Galdós drew a line through the sentence and left an instruction to the typesetter to run her previous speech together with the following one, which is how the final version reads. What he is removing is a piece of self-consciously theatrical behaviour, the kind that could be seen as Amparo playing up to the role of the weak female awed by the all-conquering male. But nor is Amparo a complete ingénue. She realizes that Caballero's discomfort in her presence is caused by something more than his customary shyness, and the narrator

---

[50] *Œuvres complètes de Shakespeare*, trans. by Émile Montégut, 3 vols (Paris: Hachette, 1867), vol. III. Stephen Miller is the critic who has done most to make readers of Galdós aware of the latter's considerable talents as a painter and illustrator. Evidence of such a developed sensitivity to the plastic arts argues strongly in favour of his being far from immune to the illustrations in the books he owned.

[51] G. Wilson Knight, 'The *Othello* Music', in *The Wheel of Fire* (London: Routledge, 2001), pp. 109–35.

draws attention to the fact: 'Amparo, con su penetración natural, comprendió que Agustín tenía dentro algo más que aquel *vaya, vaya* tan frío, tan incoloro, tan insulso' (p. 201). At the proof stage that sentence originally had begun 'Amparo, por admirable instinto y penetración natural', with 'por admirable instinto y' deleted and replaced by 'con su'. Again, the change seems designed to remove any impression that Amparo is stalking her prey in calculated fashion, that reference to 'instinto' perhaps too suggestive of the predatory motives and behaviour of a lower-class chancer. Galdós evidently wanted their courtship to proceed with the fits and starts of daring and awkwardness that the final version displays, with two naturally reticent people stumbling their way towards a not quite mutual understanding.

By denying Caballero what F. R. Leavis regarded as the Moor's self-conscious oratorical flair, Galdós presents him as the less demonstrative person he wishes him to be but at the same time loses none of the important resonances of the scene.[52] Both wooers gain the sense that they are valued to some extent as an exotic novelty; the precise extent will importantly vary depending on how robust their own self-image remains: when their confidence is high, such exotic travels are a badge of honour setting them apart from cosseted companions; when confidence is low, their travels just set them apart. Galdós's scene also begs the same questions in the reader's mind as its Shakespearian precedent. How much is Othello/Caballero attracted to Desdemona/Amparo because she projects back to him the cherished self-image of a grizzled man of action? Can a relationship based on such an image of masculinity survive the sedate rhythms of domesticity? How much space is there in such a tangle for a realistic appraisal of Desdemona's/Amparo's true qualities and personality? As so many readers and audiences of *Othello* will have been tempted to ask, how well did the Moor really know Desdemona before their marriage? Our image of her will be shaped significantly by how we react to her in the moments when she is on stage without him, her responses to Iago's sexual banter in II. 1 being a prominent example. Certainly, her artless pursuit of Cassio's case in III. 4 suggests an inability to read situations sensitively or gauge her husband's mood accurately.

Where Caballero is concerned, Galdós supplies the speech Caballero has rehearsed in his mind, ready to be unfurled as he proposes to her. But what characterizes the sections of it pertaining to Amparo is, above all, a self-deceiving, even hubristic, claim to absolute knowledge of someone who is a comparative stranger:

Figurábame que poseía yo todos sus secretos y que ninguna particularidad de su vida me era desconocida. No sé por qué su semblante y sus ojos eran su alma, su historia,

[52] F. R. Leavis, 'Diabolic Intellect and the Noble Moor', in *The Common Pursuit* (London: Chatto & Windus, 1952), pp. 136–59.

y tenían una diafanidad admirable y como milagrosa. Cosa rara, ¿verdad? Todo lo que de ella necesitaba yo saber, lo sabía sólo con mirarla. Sospechas de engaño, de doblez, de mentira... ¡oh! nada de esto cabía en mí viéndola. (p. 207)

His words give every indication that he has replaced the real Amparo with an idealized distillation of her that retains only tenuous links with the woman herself. Caballero believes that she can fulfil the high expectations he has of returning to his homeland and founding the model of a respectable, God-fearing family. With so much invested in his cherished image of her, he inadvertently backs Amparo into a corner and makes the honest unburdening of her past all but impossible. Such romanticized visions will come up hard against reality when news of her dishonour eventually reaches him.

And yet Caballero is, as Rosalía observes, not Othello. His reaction to the rumours of Amparo's sexual past oscillates between confusion and rage. The revelations challenge him to reassess his place in what now feels even more like an adopted environment—'sin poder guardar las formas de la buena educación, por ser el hombre más perteneciente a la Naturaleza que a la Sociedad, en la cual se hallaba como cosa prestada' (p. 422)—but it is to his great credit that he sees the fault in the environment rather than the individual:

Bruto, desgraciado salvaje, que no debías haber salido de tus bosques, júrate que si te dice la verdad la perdonarás... Sí que la perdonaré... me da la gana de perdonarla, señora Sociedad... Si es culpable y está arrepentida, la perdonaré, señora Sociedad de mil demonios, y me la paso a usted por las narices. (p. 423)[53]

Instead of revelling in his righteous anger, Caballero abjures the imposed beliefs he imagined would underpin his life in Spain. The interior monologue in which his thoughts are delivered is worth quoting at length as it is where the heart of Caballero's decision to forgive yet not marry Amparo is to be found:

¿No reparas, tonto, que estás haciendo todo lo contrario de lo que pensaste al inaugurar tu vida europea? Recréate, hombre sin mundo, en tu contradicción horrible, y no la llames desafuero, sino ley; porque la vida te la impone, y no hacemos nosotros la vida, sino la vida quien nos hace... Y a ti, ¿qué te importa el *qué dirán* de que has sido esclavo? Te criaste en la anarquía, y a ella, por sino fatal, tienes que volver. Se acabó el artificio. ¿Qué te importa a ti el orden de las sociedades, la Religión, ni nada de eso? Quisiste ser el más ordenado de los ciudadanos, y fue todo mentira. Quisiste ser ortodoxo: mentira también, porque no tienes fe. Quisiste tener por esposa a la misma virtud; mentira, mentira, mentira. Sal ahora por el ancho camino de tu instinto, y encomiéndate al Dios libre y grande de las circunstancias. No te fíes de la majestad convencional de los principios, y arrodíllate delante del resplandeciente altar de los hechos... Si esto es desatino, que lo sea. (p. 440)

As both a passage of prose and a depiction of a man's unsparing self-scrutiny,

[53] See also pp. 428–29.

this is writing of exceptional force. Caballero will cease trying to go through the 'strait gate' of others' expectations and will instead follow the 'ancho camino' of his instincts; the biblical antithesis seems implicit here since his is a 'Dios libre y grande de las circunstancias'. In seeking to match his expectations to an imposed convention he has learnt not only that happiness lies elsewhere but also that the convention itself is tainted by association with the people who impose it while flouting its rules with impunity. The narrator of the novel had hinted earlier that the values Caballero was pursuing were too high-minded for their own good. In the courtship scene, the wealthy *indiano* comes upon Amparo reading the Bible alone in the light of a lamp. A more touching sight could hardly be conceived, nor one better suited to tug at the heartstrings of a man seeking the simple comforts of hearth and home with a virtuous wife at his side. So far, so predictable, but if we read closely we notice that Amparo has not composed the scene with womanly cunning. Instead she is just tired at the end of her day's work, has not managed to find a single other book in the house save for a dictionary, and is doing little more than looking at the pictures in an illustrated edition of the Good Book (pp. 197–98).

Nor is Caballero immune from the debunking. His reflections on Amparo's guilt force him to acknowledge that his pursuit of her has been fuelled by flames of lust as well as more high-minded ideals: 'La manzana que cogí parecióme buena. Ábrese y la veo dañada. ¡Me da más rabia cuando pienso que la parte que aún conserva sana ha de ser para otro…!' (p. 434). That objectification of her in the image of an apple, steeped as it is in the Christian iconography of the Fall, perfectly encapsulates Caballero's self-deception by using the very same Christian frame of reference with which he had sought to hide part of his true motives from himself. Othello too will learn the hard way that he can lie to himself about his sexual identity:

> Vouch with me, heaven, I therefore beg it not
> To please the palate of my appetite,
> Nor to comply with heat, the young affects
> In me defunct.
>
> (I. 3. 262–65)

The fact that Caballero's motives for forgiving Amparo are a mixture of daring generosity and basic lust acts as a reminder of the complexity of his Shakespearian antecedent. It is also a reminder to Galdós's audience that the Manichaeism around which society feigns to build its moral codes almost never gives an adequate account of what Alas had called 'interiores ahumados'—real people in complex situations.

Caballero may lack the graces of high society but he shares the view of his creator that those same conventions more often than not serve to mask a world that is shallow, parasitic, and immoral. The narrator comments when he is first introduced that 'parecía muy fuera de lugar en una capital burocrática donde hay personas que han hecho brillantes carreras por saber hacerse el lazo de la corbata' (p. 174), where the joke is on that nepotistic, unproductive city rather than the man who stands aloof from it. Textual changes made at the proof stage to one of the passages in which Caballero submits his own behaviour to unsparing scrutiny reveal the author's anxiety to emphasize this sense of social critique. Those lines had originally read: 'Me voy, huyendo de ella [Amparo] y de esta sombra mía, de este yo falsificado y postizo que quería amoldarse a las formas de la civilización.' The amended version replaced that final clause with 'que quiso amoldarse a la viciosa cultura de por acá', where the change of verbal tense from the open-ended imperfect to the finite preterite emphasizes his clean break with such beliefs; the change from an unquestioning faith in Madrid's civilized values to an awareness of its deep flaws could not be clearer.

In Chapter 37 Bringas rails against the destruction and anarchy the impending revolution will bring, his outburst prompted, not uncharacteristically, by nothing more epoch-making than the theft of his coat. Caballero's terse replies punctuate each prognostication of disaster in a simple refrain: 'Me alegro' (pp. 430–31). The Spain presided over by Isabel II was indeed a society crying out for top-down reform, as Caballero has belatedly come to realize. Like a sensible man, he quits the country before the Revolution of 1868, and wants no part in its institutions or conventions, up to and including its Church, hence his decision not to marry Amparo. In Diane Urey's words:

For Agustín and Amparo there is now no longer any need, any sense/meaning/signified to be achieved in their identity with or difference from the terms society imposes upon them [. . .] They have elected to live within the anarchy of difference, in the space between these terms and their signified social values—sin/virtue, honour/dishonour, clean/dirty.[54]

Part of the conventionality of that society is to react with outrage at the revelation that an unmarried woman has a sexual past. Ribbans suggests that the 'whole import of [*Tormento*] is to show that Galdós did not share this view'.[55] As Frank Kermode has observed, a voyeuristic disgust at sex characterizes Iago's language in *Othello*, one that serves up a succession of degrading visions of Desdemona defiling the marital bed:[56] 'Would you, the supervisor, grossly gape on? | Behold her topped?' (III. 3. 398–99). While that linguistic trope has no direct equivalent in *Tormento*, there is in the opprobrium of women like Marcelina and Rosalía a misogynistic moral standard against

[54] Diane F. Urey, 'Repetition, Discontinuity and Silence in Galdós's *Tormento*', *Anales galdosianos*, 20 (1985), 47–62 (pp. 61–62).
[55] Ribbans, '"Amparando/Desamparando a Amparo"', p. 507.
[56] Frank Kermode, *Shakespeare's Language* (London: Penguin, 2001), p. 167.

which the novel appears to fight. One way it does so is by running the action alongside Ido del Sagrario's *folletín* account of the lives of Amparo and Refugio. When Ido learns of Amparo's disgrace he reaches the conventional conclusion: that her only future lies in a convent. However, as Ribbans points out: 'this is surely not a situation which should be accepted, by contemporaries or later readers, with any satisfaction; and it makes natural and morally justifiable whatever strategy of survival such a woman may adopt'.[57] As a number of critics have observed, Galdós uses Ido's *folletín* to ridicule both sentimental serialized fiction and the mindless moral certainties it peddles. Not for Ido and his ilk is Caballero's 'resplandeciente altar de los hechos'.[58] The action of the novel highlights that one 'hecho' the world needs to address less hysterically is the possibility that a woman might marry when no longer a virgin. Galdós's personal library features at least five editions of *Othello* published before 1884, all but one of which follow the Folio text in including Emilia's speech on the right of women to a sexual life independent of the whims of their erring husbands.[59] Among those editions, that which is most closely contemporaneous with the writing of *Tormento*, Menéndez Pelayo's 1881 prose translation, includes Emilia's words:[60]

> Say that they slack their duties
> And pour our treasures into foreign laps;
> Or else break out in peevish jealousies,
> Throwing restraint upon us; or say they strike us,
> Or scant our former having in despite,
> Why, we have galls: and though we have some grace
> Yet have we some revenge. Let husbands know
> Their wives have sense like them: they see, and smell,
> And have their palates both for sweet and sour
> As husbands have.
> (v. 1. 86–95)

And it is not in the badlands of Central America that Amparo finds a realization of her fear of the boa constrictor but in the arms of Pedro Polo during one of his overbearing attempts to persuade her to resume their affair: 'Si me dices que quieres a ese pelele más que a mí... ahora mismo, ahora mismo, ¿ves? te voy apretando, apretando hasta ahogarte. Te arranco el último suspiro y me lo bebo' (p. 370). Does the 'civilized' world with which Caballero's past

---

[57] Ribbans, '"Amparando/Desamparando a Amparo"', p. 505.
[58] On this subject see also David Cluff, 'The Structure and Meaning of Galdós's *Tormento*', *Reflexión*, 3–4 (1974–75), 159–67 (p. 165).
[59] The reason for the deliberate imprecision used here—'at least five editions'—is that he owned several copies of Shakespeare which lack publication dates.
[60] See Sebastián de la Nuez, *Biblioteca y archivo de la Casa Museo Pérez Galdós* (Madrid: Cabildo Insular de Gran Canaria, 1990), p. 122. Menéndez Pelayo's translation is listed as item number 958 in the inventory of Galdós's library.

life so heavily contrasts really uphold more enlightened values? the narrator appears to be asking. Should Amparo be at the mercy of a man like Polo just because to admit to their coercive and unequal relationship would mean social suicide? Or as Chad C. Wright has put it:

> In [Galdós's] novelistic world, everything seems to develop in reverse; one is tainted by contact with so-called civilization instead of being bettered by it; the very priest who should protect virtue and exemplify it seduces the heroine; the wife who boasts of her virtue in the novel begins a downward moral spiralling which results in adultery and prostitution in *La de Bringas*.[61]

Othello likewise challenges any suggestion that uncivilized 'otherness' is to be found only outside the confines of its sophisticated urban setting: 'The Venetian state is, in fact, less imperilled by the Other—the Turkish barbarian against whom Othello is engaged to fight, or indeed by the Moor himself— than it is by its own kind, a super-subtle Venetian whose evil is the more invidious for being homegrown.'[62]

As we have seen, the single explicit mention of *Othello* in Galdós's novel is to the Shakespearian hero as shorthand for a set of behaviours and reactions to adultery. Rosalía reads Shakespeare as Ido del Sagrario hopes his customers will read his *folletín*: on the lookout for archetypes, easy categories in which to slot characters, and by extension human beings. It is not uncommon in Spanish literature of this period to find characters like Iago or Othello used in this synecdochic fashion, standing as malevolence or jealousy personified, as they do in Pedro Antonio de Alarcón's *El escándalo* (1875).[63] Indeed, Leopoldo Alas did much the same when writing his prologue to Emilia Pardo Bazán's *La cuestión palpitante* (1883), praising its author for a display of sound judgement that stood her alongside Portia from *The Merchant of Venice*.[64] By contrast, Juan Valera had drawn attention precisely to the irreducibility of Shakespearian characters to mere archetype in a prologue to an edition of the plays published in 1870, an edition Galdós also owned:

> Eminentes han existido algunos que, en mi sentir, sólo han logrado personificar las virtudes o los vicios, producir tipos o símbolos con habla y figura humanas: el hipócrita, el avaro o el misántropo; pero la fuerza creadora para no limitarse a la abstracción, a la generalización, a un concepto destilado y extraido [sic] de lo real por medio del discurso, y vestido luego de cuerpo por la fantasía, y sí para producir individuos

[61] Chad C. Wright, '"La eterna mascarada hispanomatritense": Clothing and Society in *Tormento*', *Anales galdosianos*, 20 (1985), 25–35 (pp. 34–35).
[62] Catherine Bates, 'Shakespeare' Tragedies of Love', in *The Cambridge Companion to Shakespearean Tragedy*, ed. by Claire McEachern (Cambridge: Cambridge University Press, 2003), pp. 182–203 (p. 195).
[63] Pedro Antonio de Alarcón, *El escándalo*, ed. by Juan Bautista Montes (Madrid: Cátedra, 1986), pp. 255, 283.
[64] Leopoldo Alas, 'Prólogo a *La cuestión palpitante*', in *Obras completas*, XI: *Varia*, ed. by Leonardo Romero Tobar (2006), pp. 1037–45 (p. 1039).

verdaderos, definidos, determinados, complejos en su carácter y condiciones, como son todas las criaturas humanas, y con más vida y más perfecta vida que la vida que da [la] naturaleza: este don, este arte, pocos le han tenido como Shakespeare.[65]

As I have shown, Galdós's exploration of the resonances of *Othello* are likewise more sustained than Rosalía's invocation of the archetype. In fact, I would go so far as to suggest that Galdós's energies in this novel—as in so much of his fiction—are directed towards exploding facile categories of value and interpretation; he is at pains to show how noxious they are to real thought. Caballero does not cleave to his self-image so long that he destroys his chance to be happy at Amparo's side. His behaviour moves beyond archetype, instead embracing the positive implications of Iago's maxim that ''tis in ourselves that we are thus or thus' (I. 3. 320). He displays a readiness to adapt, learn, and forgive that is as surprising as it is joyous.

This break with an imposed artistic identity sends our thoughts back to Ido, his *folletín*, and the conventional expectations of a society in which artistic mirrors face individuals at every turn. Galdós appears to observe in *Tormento* the difficulty of leading an authentic life against such a backdrop. Even at the crisis of her life when she has fled to Caballero's home to kill herself, Amparo is oddly conscious of acting like someone from a novel: 'En la preocupación del suicidio no dejó de ocurrírsele la semejanza de todo aquello con pasos de novela o teatro, y de este modo se enfriaba momentáneamente su entusiasmo homicida' (p. 409). That death scene is marked by the ironic juxtaposition of Amparo's despair with the cabinet of twittering mechanical birds whose squawks offset what ought to be the solemn tone of the young woman's final moments. They are an example of what Walter Benjamin would later theorize as the artistic object stripped of its aura by mass production.[66] Just as Amparo's action is tainted by association with a tawdry litany of melodramatic deaths in sentimental novels, so the mechanical birds bear only faint resemblance to the real objects they are intended to represent. It is not until after the crisis has passed and the truth lies between her and Caballero that an alternative and truer glimpse of the (natural) world might be had. It occurs on the sunny day when Caballero finally tracks her down and she makes her confession of all that occurred between her and Polo. As a prelude

[65] Juan Valera, 'Prólogo', in *Obras de Shakespeare*, trans. by Jaime Clark, 5 vols (Madrid: Medina y Navarro, [n.d.]), I: *Otelo, Mucho ruido para nada* (1870?), pp. 9–26 (p. 20). Although these editons were published undated, Ricardo Rupprt y Ujaravi asserts that they were published between 1870 and 1876. See his *Shakespeare en España: traducciones, imitaciones e influencias de las obras de Shakespeare en la literatura española* (Madrid: Tip. de la Rev. de Archivos, Bibl. y Museos, 1920), p. 104.

[66] Walter Benjamin, 'The Work of Art in the Age of its Technological Reproducibility', in *'The Work of Art in the Age of its Technological Reproducibility' and Other Writings on Media*, ed. by Michael W. Jennings and others (London: Harvard University Press, 2008), pp. 19–55.

to that scene, we see Amparo reclining in an armchair looking out of the window: 'Por los vidrios de la estrecha ventana miraba los gorriones que en el tejado hacían mil monerías, y luego volaban en grupos, perdiéndose en el cielo azul' (p. 438). The detail seems to tell us what the action will confirm: these characters have moved beyond the artifice of imposed values and fictional archetypes to embrace something more vital. Art and existence shorn of their self-conscious artifice are maddeningly effective and maddeningly elusive routes to authenticity, Galdós appears to conclude. The paradox from his point of view is that his art, to reach the same conclusions, must steep itself in an elaborate structure involving Ido's novel within a novel, a complex cast of characters, and a plot that slow-burns over three volumes of his trilogy. It is not surprising that the narrator of *Tormento* comments so fervently on the cabinet of South American curios in Caballero's study and the wonderfully simple pleasure their primitive form gives:

Nada existe más bonito que estas creaciones de un arte no aprendido, en el cual la imitación de la Naturaleza llega a extremos increíbles, demostrando la aptitud observadora del indio y la habilidad de sus dedos para dar espíritu a la forma. Sólo en el arte japonés encontramos algo de valor semejante a la paciencia y gusto de los escultores aztecas. (p. 302)

UNIVERSITY COLLEGE LONDON   GARETH J. WOOD

MEDIEVAL HUMOUR? WOLFRAM'S *PARZIVAL* AND THE CONCEPT OF THE COMIC IN MIDDLE HIGH GERMAN ROMANCES

Modern Theory of Humour

Humour is a ubiquitous, well-established phenomenon of our times.[1] This makes it tempting to apply the concept of humour in its current everyday meaning to texts that were written well before the modern idea of humour was developed. In the following, I propose to argue that modern concepts of humour are not helpful when it comes to interpreting medieval texts, and that going back to ideas concerning the production and use of laughter established in classical rhetoric is better suited to identifying the significance of the obvious comic elements in medieval literature. Following a brief discussion of the development of modern Western concepts of humour, I will outline the importance that rhetoric attributes to laughter, wit, and ironic modes of speaking. Attention will then focus on one of the most prominent Middle High German romances, Wolfram von Eschenbach's *Parzival*, as a prime example of pre-modern poetic uses of laughter and the comic as distinct from humour.

The development of modern concepts of humour began in the sixteenth century, when humour detached itself from the medieval idea of the four temperaments and gradually came to signify 'peculiar forms of mental variation from the norm',[2] which were derided in comedy. Over the centuries, a threefold approach to the phenomenon evolved: while Thomas Hobbes understood humour as a feeling of superiority and Francis Hutcheson established the idea of incongruity as a source of humour, the 'release of pent-up nervous energy' formed the basis of a relief theory formulated by Herbert Spencer.[3] Today, a mixed approach combining elements of all three major theoretical strands is predominant; and often the theoretical complexity recedes when humour is understood simply as a source of 'amused laughter'[4] of any kind.

Parts of this article were presented as a paper at LMU Munich in May 2010. For a fuller elaboration of the research on which the following discussion is based and a comprehensive bibliography see Stefan Seeber, *Poetik des Lachens: Untersuchungen zum mittelhochdeutschen Roman um 1200*, MTU, 140 (Berlin: de Gruyter, 2010).

[1] 'Humour is a pervasive feature of human life. We find it everywhere' (Noël Carroll, 'Humour', in *The Oxford Handbook of Aesthetics*, ed. by Jerrold Levinson (Oxford: Oxford University Press, 2003), pp. 344–65 (p. 344)).

[2] Stuart M. Tave, *The Amiable Humorist: A Study in the Comic Theory and Criticism of the Eighteenth and Early Nineteenth Centuries* (Chicago: University of Chicago Press, 1960), p. 91.

[3] See Simon Critchley, *On Humour*, Thinking in Action (London: Routledge, 2002), p. 3.

[4] Carroll, 'Humour', p. 346. For a distinction between amused laughter and amusement which does not necessarily have to result in laughter, see Dolf Zillman and Joanne R. Cantor, 'A Disposition Theory of Humour and Mirth', in *Humour and Laughter: Theory, Research and Applications*, ed. by Antony J. Chapman and Hugh C. Foot (London: Wiley, 1976), pp. 93–116.

Between the sixteenth and twenty-first centuries, numerous different points of view emerged that were informed by a wide range of philosophies and aesthetic approaches in Europe.[5] The German approach to humour initially derived from the English tradition, but soon a distinctive idea of humour as *Weltanschauung* developed which diverged significantly from the English roots. One of the most influential humour theories of this kind was established by Jean Paul in his *Vorschule der Ästhetik*,[6] first published in 1804 and reprinted with major additions in 1813. Jean Paul has rightly been called the founding father of a German aesthetics of humour.[7] His impact on German Studies and especially on Wolfram scholarship is still tangible today, and it is therefore worth dwelling on his concept of humour[8] before proceeding to the special case of *Parzival* as a text displaying humour.

Jean Paul's 'Vorschule der Ästhetik' and Humour as 'Weltanschauung'

In Chapters VI to VIII of his work, Jean Paul develops a tripartite theory distinguishing between the ridiculous, the comic, and humour. Humour as a philosophy of life (*Weltanschauung*) encompasses ridicule and comedy; it forms the pinnacle of Jean Paul's aesthetic hicrarchy of the three concepts. For Jean Paul, the ridiculous points to the mistake or inappropriate behaviour that provokes laughter based on superior insight. This laughter is without bitterness or hints of satirical derision, and is instead distinguished by harmless pleasure.[9] Comic perception is seen as an aestheticizing process (VI, § 30, p. 122) that raises the ridiculous elements to the next level of the tripartite hierarchy. At the highest level, when humour is at work, the focus shifts from the ridiculous object that attracts laughter and that can be aestheticized—humour is solely concerned with the beholder, not with the object. It is a 'completely internalized experi-

---

[5] See Erhard Schüttpelz, 'Humor', in *Historisches Wörterbuch der Rhetorik*, ed. by Gert Ueding and others, 10 vols (Tübingen: Niemeyer; Berlin: de Gruyter, 1992–2012), IV (1998), cols 86–98 (col. 87).

[6] Jean Paul, *Vorschule der Ästhetik. Kleine Nachschule zur ästhetischen Vorschule*, ed. and comm. by Norbert Miller, afterword by Walter Höllerer (Munich: Hanser, 1974). I cite Jean Paul's text by giving chapter numbers, paragraphs, and page numbers in parentheses after quotations. Use of italicization follows Miller's edition. For an English translation see *Horn of Oberon: Jean Paul Richter's 'School for Aesthetics'*, trans. by Margaret R. Hale (Detroit: Wayne State University Press, 1973).

[7] Wolfgang Preisendanz, 'Humor', in *Historisches Wörterbuch der Philosophie*, ed. by Joachim Ritter and Karlfried Gründer, 11 vols (Basel: Schwabe, 1971–), III (1974), cols 1232–34 (col. 1233).

[8] For a detailed analysis see Otto Mann, 'Die kulturgeschichtlichen Grundlagen des Jean Paulschen Humors', *DVjs*, 8 (1930), 660–79, and the introduction to the English edition: Margaret R. Hale, 'Introduction', in *Horn of Oberon*, pp. xvii–lx, esp. pp. xxvi–xxxv.

[9] See Jean Paul, *Vorschule*, VI, § 28, p. 114: 'Man erlaube mir der Kürze wegen, daß ich in der künftigen Untersuchung die drei Bestandteile des Lächerlichen als eines sinnlich angeschaueten unendlichen Unverstandes bloß so nenne, wie folgt: den Widerspruch, worin das Bestreben oder Sein des lächerlichen Wesens mit dem sinnlich angeschaueten Verhältnis steht, nenn' ich den *objektiven* Kontrast; dieses Verhältnis den *sinnlichen*; und den Widerspruch beider, den wir ihm durch das Leihen unserer Seele und Ansicht als den zweiten aufbürden, nenn' ich den *subjektiven* Kontrast.'

ence' of the humorist, who 'perceives within himself a split between the finite and the infinite'.[10] This is why humour destroys 'nicht das Einzelne, sondern das Endliche durch den Kontrast mit der Idee' (VII, § 31, p. 125).

This refers to three main conceptual principles of Jean Paul's approach: firstly the strong emphasis on the self, i.e. the identity of the individual; secondly the relationship of individual and eternity; and thirdly the concept of the sublime. Humour in the *Vorschule der Ästhetik* is characterized by the humorist's 'Humorous Subjectivity', which is the cause of a specific view of the world and its follies: 'Folglich setz' ich mich selber in diesen Zwiespalt [. . .] und zerteile mein Ich in den endlichen und unendlichen Faktor und lasse aus jenem diesen kommen. Da lacht der Mensch, denn er sagt: "Unmöglich! Es ist viel zu toll!" Gewiß!' (VII, § 34, p. 132). This constellation of a paradox is put in a nutshell in Jean Paul's comparison between a humorist and the 'Vogel Merops, welcher zwar dem Himmel den Schwanz zukehrt, aber doch in dieser Richtung in den Himmel auffliegt' (VII, § 33, p. 128). On the basis of this use of paradox, humour in Jean Paul's view is equivalent to the 'umgekehrte[s] Erhabene[s]' (VII, § 32, p. 125).[11] As the inverted sublime, it is endowed with annihilating powers that destroy established patterns and understandings of the world and replace them with uplifting and soul-warming laughter (VII, § 32, p. 128) that comes with a reconciliatory view of the world's folly.

This, in Jean Paul's view, distinguishes the humorous perspective from the medieval theological idea of the connection between finite and infinite factors.[12] In Jean Paul's opinion, humour is nothing less than a privileged relationship between the individual, the world, and eternity, permitting the humorist to perceive himself as a part of a world full of folly while at the same time looking at the world from a higher point of view.

Humour as 'Weltanschauung' in Wolfram's 'Parzival'

Jean Paul confined his concept to a Romantic idea of humour, and also called it 'das romantische Komische' (VII, § 31, p. 125). His idea explicitly refrains from including pre-modern texts. But this limitation did not discourage modern readers of Wolfram's *Parzival* from applying Jean Paul's ideas to the medieval romance. It is now widely accepted that Wolfram can be seen as a humorist avant la lettre, and that his *Parzival* can be read as a humorous text. First attempts of this kind were made as early as 1878 and 1879, when Christian Starck and Karl Kant undertook to elucidate the profile of Wolfram

[10] Hale, 'Introduction', pp. xxxii and xxxiii.
[11] On Jean Paul's concept of the sublime see Hale, 'Introduction', p. xxvii.
[12] See Jean Paul, *Vorschule der Ästhetik*, VII, § 33, p. 120: 'Wenn der Mensch, wie die alte Theologie tat, aus der überirdischen Welt auf die irdische herunterschauet: so zieht diese klein und eitel dahin; wenn er mit der kleinen, wie der Humor thut, die unendliche ausmisset und verknüpft: so entsteht jenes Lachen, worin noch ein Schmerz und eine Größe ist.'

the humorist.¹³ But it was not until Max Wehrli published his seminal article on 'Wolframs Humor' (1950) that this reading of *Parzival* became canonical; Wehrli's text is still considered a forward-looking approach to Wolfram's romance,¹⁴ and its influence is far-reaching. This justifies a closer look at his interpretation, especially with regard to his methodology.

Wehrli's main concern is to connect Wolfram's writing with Jean Paul's concept of the tripartite hierarchy of the ridiculous, the comic, and humour, and to establish Wolfram as one of the earliest masters of poetic humour in European literature.¹⁵ Wehrli's reading of Wolfram is based on an analysis of the 'Blutstropfenszene',¹⁶ for which he postulates a humorous structure that embraces the inherent comic arrangements. This structure, in Wehrli's opinion, is expressed in the spiritual and emotive meaning of the text. It results in a humorous totality of narration that is grounded in the narrator's subjectivity and imbues the narrative style.¹⁷

The consequences are significant and far-reaching: If we accept Wehrli's reading of *Parzival*, Wolfram's subjectivity makes up for the notorious lack of coherence, and the author's genius connects the antagonistic elements of the text. This unifies a story that at first sight oscillates between the poles of comedy and transcendence, sanctity and the profane, the foolishness of the young boy and the hero as the chosen saviour.¹⁸ It also permits contradictions to be reconciled—between the narrator and the narrated, between the various digressions, and between the diverging motivations of the characters' actions. In addition, it seemingly helps to give the end of the work—which indeed has some 'nasty sting[s]'¹⁹ in its positive utopia—a comprehensive and placatory meaning in the form of a humorous master plan. This explains why Wehrli's interpretation has proved so influential since its first publication and why the idea of *Parzival* as a humorous romance retains such prominence.²⁰ In recent

---

¹³ Christian Starck, *Die Darstellungsmittel des Wolframschen Humors* (Schwerin: Bärensprung, 1879); Karl Kant, *Scherz und Humor in Wolframs von Eschenbach Dichtungen* (Heilbronn: Henninger, 1878).

¹⁴ According to Joachim Bumke, it is 'in die Zukunft weisend' (Joachim Bumke, *Wolfram von Eschenbach*, 8th edn (Stuttgart: Metzler, 2004), p. v).

¹⁵ Max Wehrli, 'Wolframs Humor' (1950), repr. in *Wolfram von Eschenbach*, ed. by Heinz Rupp, Wege der Forschung, 57 (Darmstadt: WBG, 1966), pp. 104–24 (p. 104).

¹⁶ See Joachim Bumke, *Blutstropfen im Schnee: Über Wahrnehmung und Erkenntnis im 'Parzival' Wolframs von Eschenbach*, Hermeae, 94 (Tübingen: Niemeyer, 2001), esp. p. 4 with regard to the comic contrast between the Arthurian court and the cognitive process of Parzival.

¹⁷ See Max Wehrli, 'Wolfram von Eschenbach: Erzählstil und Sinn seines *Parzival*', *Der Deutschunterricht*, 6 (1954), 17–40 (p. 26).

¹⁸ Klaus Ridder, 'Narrheit und Heiligkeit: Komik im *Parzival* Wolframs von Eschenbach', *Wolfram-Studien*, 17 (2002), 136–56 (pp. 138–39).

¹⁹ Annette Volfing, '"Welt ir nu hoeren fürbaz?" On the Function of the Loherangrin-Episode in Wolfram von Eschenbach's *Parzival* (P 824,1–826,30)', *Beiträge zur deutschen Sprache und Literatur*, 126 (2004), 65–84 (p. 65).

²⁰ See e.g. Rainer Madsen, *Die Gestaltung des Humors in den Werken Wolframs von Eschenbach:*

years, however, a shift of focus has directed attention to the importance of laughter in the text, not only from a semantic point of view,[21] but also with regard to narrative patterns which the laughter might allude to. This opens the field for new questions—and for an approach to the topic that draws on rhetoric.[22]

A Different Approach: The Rhetoric of Laughter

Wehrli's interpretation satisfies the modern reader's need for coherence and for taming a complex text, but it entails difficulties which are both numerous and far-reaching. The humorous structure he posits cannot encompass all irony, mockery, and jest. The narrator's obscene interjections resist humorous interpretation, as does the obvious ridiculing of the baptism in Book XVI. The dramatic events that precede Parzival's accession to the grail throne also call into question the humorous, conciliatory, soft-focus lens of Wehrli's interpretation. I will return to these issues later and use Book XVI as an example to elucidate the poetics of laughter (rather than humour) in Wolfram's *Parzival*.

Before presenting my reading of the romance, I propose to outline the theoretical basis of this approach to the work. I intend to use the rhetorical theory of *ridiculum*, of comedy, and of laughter which had a high profile throughout the Middle Ages and was accessible in the Latin discourse on rhetoric as well as in poetical treatises.[23] In particular, the widely used *Rhetorica ad Herennium*, composed around 80 BC and until the Renaissance attributed to Cicero[24] provides an extensive theory of laughter and its use, as well as foregrounding phenomena such as *urbanitas* and irony. In addition, Cicero's *De oratore* (55 BC) and Quintilian's *Institutio oratoria* (c. AD 95) served as sources of advice on how to induce and utilize laughter.

From its beginnings, the Latin theoretical tradition listed incongruity and

Untersuchungen zum 'Parzival' und 'Willehalm' (doctoral thesis, University of Bochum, 1970). For a detailed appreciation of Wehrli's influence see Seeber, *Poetik des Lachens*, pp. 132–35.

[21] For a semantics of laughter see Waltraud Fritsch-Rössler, 'Lachen und Schlagen: Reden als Kulturtechnik in Wolframs *Parzival*', in *Verstehen durch Vernunft: Festschrift für Werner Hoffmann*, ed. by Burkhardt Krause, Philologica Germanica, 19 (Vienna: Fassbaender, 1997), pp. 75–98, and Madsen, *Humor*. For an analysis concerned especially with comic narrative patterns see Sebastian Coxon, 'Der Ritter und die Fährmannstochter: Zum schwankhaften Erzählen in Wolframs *Parzival*', *Wolfram-Studien*, 17 (2002), 114–35.

[22] See Gert Ueding: 'Rhetorik des Lächerlichen', in *Semiotik, Rhetorik und Soziologie des Lachens: Vergleichende Studien zum Funktionswandel des Lachens vom Mittelalter zur Gegenwart*, ed. by Lothar Fietz and others (Tübingen: Niemeyer, 1996), pp. 21–36. Ralf-Henning Steinmetz, 'Komik in mittelalterlicher Literatur: Überlegungen zu einem methodischen Problem am Beispiel des *Helmbrecht*', *Germanisch-Romanische Monatsschrift*, n.s. 49 (1999), 255–73.

[23] See Steinmetz, 'Komik', p. 262. For a general overview see Joachim Suchomski, *'Delectatio' und 'Utilitas': Ein Beitrag zum Verständnis mittelalterlicher komischer Literatur*, Bibliotheca Germanica, 18 (Bern and Munich: Francke, 1975).

[24] See James J. Murphy, *Rhetoric in the Middle Ages: A History of Rhetorical Theory from Saint Augustine to the Renaissance* (Berkeley and London: University of California Press, 1974).

superiority as causes of laughter—this makes the rhetoric of laughter (at least to a certain extent) a predecessor of a modern aesthetics of humour.[25] Derision of minor mistakes and flaws as well as of corporal deformities and ugliness is known to Cicero's *De oratore* as laughter induced by superiority.[26] Incongruity is captured in the concept of *dissimulatio*, which Cicero explains in part by referring to the incongruity between outer and inner appearance, or between the expectation and what is actually presented.[27] The idea that laughter may induce light relief is not common in classical rhetoric as the treatises focus less on the psyche of the listener than on the attentiveness that can be achieved by evoking laughter.

The *Rhetorica ad Herennium* gives a wide range of examples to elucidate what may be used to provoke laughter:

Si defessi erunt audiendo, ab aliqua re quae risum movere possit ab apologo, fabula veri simili, imitatione depravata, inversione, ambiguo, suspicione, inrisione, stultitia, exsuperatione, collectione, litterarum mutatione, praeter expectationem, similitudine, novitate, historia, versu, ab alicuius interpellatione aut adrisione. (I. 10)

If the hearers have been fatigued by listening, we shall open with something that may provoke laughter—a fable, a plausible fiction, a caricature, an ironical inversion of the meaning of a word, an ambiguity, innuendo, banter, a naivety, an exaggeration, a recapitulation, a pun, an unexpected turn, a comparison, a novel tale, a historical anecdote, a verse, or a challenge or a smile of approbation directed at someone.[28]

This list draws on common rhetorical principles and makes it clear that the rhetorical theory of laughter is informed by the principles of general rhetoric and uses well-established techniques designed to make the audience laugh. Quintilian's *Institutio* in addition identifies various modes of provoking laughter which range from harmless or gallant wit to what Quintilian calls *salsum* (salted, sharp wit).[29] It is evident, then, that there is wide-ranging and far-reaching interest in the subject from the beginning of the rhetorical tradition, and that laughter is, from the start, accepted as one of the major means of influencing the audience.

Central to this rhetoric of laughter is the idea of *urbanitas*, which points to the sophistication that comes with life in the city (i.e. Rome). The concept

---

[25] D. J. Monro, 'Art. Humor', in *Encyclopedia of Philosophy*, ed. by Donald M. Borchert and others, 2nd edn, 10 vols (Detroit: Thomson Gale, 2006), IV (2006), 514–18 (p. 514).

[26] Cicero, *De oratore*, II, 237 and 239, trans. by E. W. Sutton and H. Rackham, with an introduction by H. Rackham, Loeb Classical Library, 348, 2 vols (Cambridge, MA: Harvard University Press; London: Heinemann, 1979), I, 374–75.

[27] For the differing ancient definitions of irony see Cicero, *De oratore*, II, 269 and 284, and Quintilian, *Institutio oratoria*, IX. 2. 44–53, in *The Orator's Education*, IV: *Books 9–10*, ed. and trans. by Donald A. Russell, Loeb Classical Library, 126 (Cambridge, MA, and London: Harvard University Press, 2001), pp. 58–65.

[28] [Cicero], *Rhetorica ad Herennium*, , trans. by Harry Caplan, Loeb Classical Library, 403 (Cambridge, MA, and London: Harvard University Press, 1954), pp. 18–21.

[29] Quintilian, *Institutio oratoria*, IX. 3. 17–27.

of *urbanitas* as a Ciceronian[30] framework encompasses the persuasive and ethical functions of laughter: ethically, it requires the *vir bonus* as a performer, someone whose refinement is manifested outwardly in 'a sophisticated humor and a careful manner of speaking'.[31] While this conversational ideal does not necessarily entail humour and laughter,[32] the connection between *urbanitas* and *facetia* is nevertheless striking.[33] It shows the urbane rhetorician to be a witty and entertaining person who responds appropriately (i.e. according to *decorum*)[34] to the conversation and is of high ethical standing. This idea is handed down from antiquity to the Middle Ages and the Renaissance,[35] defining courtly behaviour in general but also finding expression in the ideal of the *vir facetus*.[36] Accordingly, *urbanitas* and *facetia* (i.e. moderate jesting without agitating the listener) are prominent in medieval discourse. This makes them invaluable keys to an analysis that seeks to elucidate the function of laughter and comic elements in the texts of the time without involving the concepts of subjectivity and infinity that are so central to Romantic theories of humour.

The Importance of Laughter and Comedy in Wolfram's 'Parzival'

Before turning to the prominent finale that has been used to justify the humorous reading of *Parzival*,[37] I should like at least to touch upon some aspects which allow a more complete overall picture of the text to come into view. The point I wish to make is that Wolfram uses methods of the Latin *ridiculum*, comic aspects, and phenomena such as irony, *facetia*, and *urbanitas* deliberately and as part of an overall structure. His *Parzival* seeks interaction with the audience and relies on the purpose of persuasion as

[30] See Edwin S. Ramage, '*Urbanitas*': *Ancient Sophistication and Refinement* (Oklahoma: University of Oklahoma Press, 1973), pp. 8–49, esp. p. 56 on Cicero's concept. Differences between Cicero and Quintilian are highlighted in id., 'Urbanitas: Cicero and Quintilian, a Contrast in Attitudes', *American Journal of Philology*, 84 (1963), 390–414 (p. 410).
[31] Ramage, *Ancient Sophistication*, p. 56.
[32] Ramage, 'Cicero and Quintilian', p. 404.
[33] Ibid., p. 396.
[34] Cf. I. Rutherford, 'Decorum 1.', in *Historisches Wörterbuch der Rhetorik*, ed. by Gert Ueding and others, 10 vols (Tübingen: Niemeyer; Berlin: de Gruyter, 1992–2012), II (1994), cols 423–34, esp. col. 423 with regard to *decorum* as ethical, rhetorical, and aesthetic appropriateness.
[35] See Thomas Zotz, '*Urbanitas*: Zur Bedeutung und Funktion einer antiken Wertvorstellung innerhalb der höfischen Kultur des hohen Mittelalters', in '*Curialitas*': *Studien zu Grundfragen der höfisch-ritterlichen Kultur*, ed. by Josef Fleckenstein, Veröffentlichungen des Max-Planck-Instituts für Geschichte, 100 (Göttingen: Vandenhoeck & Ruprecht, 1990), pp. 392–451, and Georg Luck, '*Vir Facetus*: A Renaissance Ideal', *Studies in Philology*, 55 (1958), 107–11.
[36] See Gerd Dicke, '*Homo facetus*: Vom Mittelalter eines humanistischen Ideals', in *Humanismus in der deutschen Literatur des Mittelalters und der Frühen Neuzeit. XVIII. Anglo-German Colloquium Hofgeismar 2003*, ed. by Nicola McLelland and others (Tübingen: Niemeyer, 2008), pp. 299–332.
[37] I quote the Middle High German text using Wolfram von Eschenbach, '*Parzival*': *Studienausgabe*, Mittelhochdeutscher Text nach der sechsten Ausgabe von Karl Lachmann, Übersetzung von Peter Knecht, Einführung zum Text von Bernd Schirok (Berlin and New York: de Gruyter, 1998) (abbreviated in the following as 'Pz').

a force to bind the listener to the narrative. Laughter is one of the tools Wolfram uses—among other, more serious tools.

That laughter is a highly significant gesture in the epic[38] is made clear by the prominence of Cunneware's 'prophetic laughter',[39] which does not indicate a somehow ridiculous occasion[40] but acts as a potent symbol and transcends the realm of comedy: laughter here replaces speech and takes over its semantic powers. This special importance of Cunneware's gesture testifies to the high value of laughter in the text and suggests that it is worth analysing laughter in Wolfram's romance in general, not only with regard to an implied humorous structure.

Four aspects of laughter in Wolfram's *Parzival* are central and need to be addressed.[41] They are: the social function of laughter, the use of irony, the importance of the narrator, and finally the influence all these aspects have on the listener or reader. The first point, the social function of laughter and derision, is both a fundamental and a highly prominent feature of the work. It is the basis for the structured use of *ridiculum* in the romance and conveys that the poetic use of laughter is socially relevant to the audience. For example, Parzival's father Gahmuret uses *facetia* to establish himself as a new political leader and king in the realm of his newly won wife Belacane: he plays to the gallery by standing up alone and pretending to be a humble supplicant rather than what he actually is: the most powerful person at court. In doing so, he makes use of *subabsurdum*,[42] the deliberate assumption of a fatuous stance. This stance can easily be seen through—as is shown by the laughter that his remark provokes (Pz 46. 14).

The social power of laughter is also present in derision of characters that cannot or refuse to stand up to it, for example in Kaylet's mockery of Hardiz, who is made the object of debasing laughter in the second book of the text (Pz 90. 7). On many occasions the narrator makes fun of the heroes, especially young Parzival and also Gawan the womanizer, who constantly blunders into trouble.[43] Wolfram thereby undermines the consistency of his own telling,

---

[38] For the classification of laughter as a gesture see Jean-Claude Schmitt, *Die Logik der Gesten im europäischen Mittelalter*, trans. from French by Rolf Schubert and Bodo Schulze (Stuttgart: Klett-Cotta, 1992), p. 258.

[39] Dennis H. Green, 'Advice and Narrative Action: Parzival, Herzeloyde and Gurnemanz', in *From Wolfram and Petrarch to Goethe and Grass: Studies in Literature in Honour of Leonard Forster*, ed. by Dennis H. Green and others, Saecula Spiritalia, 5 (Baden-Baden: Koerner, 1982), pp. 33–81 (p. 67).

[40] For a different opinion see Albrecht Classen, 'Keie in Wolframs von Eschenbach *Parzival*: "Agent Provocateur" oder Angeber?', *Journal of English and Germanic Philology*, 87 (1988), 382–405 (p. 402). My view partly coincides with that of Fritsch-Rössler, 'Lachen und Schlagen', p. 84 and passim.

[41] See the similar approach of Steinmetz, 'Komik', to the *Meier Helmbrecht* epic.

[42] As outlined in Cicero, *De oratore*, II. 289, and Quintilian, *Institutio oratoria*, VI. 3. 99.

[43] See Sonja Emmerling, *Geschlechterbeziehungen in den Gawan-Büchern des 'Parzival'*, Hermaea, n.s. 100 (Tübingen: Niemeyer, 2003).

mocking almost every character, presenting them in an ambiguous light, and at least occasionally making them seem funny. This technique extends to his own persona since he presents himself as the unreliable narrator par excellence. The ridiculous aspect of the description thus becomes a major factor of the narration, for example when Parzival's foolishness becomes a landmark of his first steps in the courtly world. This structured use of the ridiculous gives it significance well beyond pure *delectatio*. The fun provided by the derision of single scenes, episodes, and traits of characters is not an end in itself but is used in a broader context to engage the listener or reader.

Irony (in the sense of rhetorical *dissimulatio*) makes up the second area of a structured poetic use of laughter. The ironic view of Minne that is offered in Book VIII is typical of Wolfram's general use of irony in his *Parzival*. When Gawan encounters Antikonie, the sister of his arch-enemy Vergulaht,[44] he is instantly captivated and sexually attracted to her. Antikonie is, by all standards, portrayed as a lady of easy virtue who responds to Gawan's most unambiguous offer in a strikingly affirmative way. The mocking undertone of their conversation makes it clear that their exchange is a joyous matter until it is interrupted by her brother's men, who sound the alarm. The would-be lovers flee into the castle's tower and fight off the king's troops using a chessboard and its pieces (Pz 408. 20–409. 11). This burlesque action is accompanied by conventionally courtly conversation and the narrator's sympathetic commentary, both of which emphasize the lady's honour and indisputable virtue. The ironic dissimulation uses the clash of profane facts and courtly pretensions which are captured in the equation of Minne-service and hunting, in the courtly vocabulary of description, and in the caricature of the enemy as an uncourtly king.[45] It is finally and most clearly exposed in the comparison of the courtly lady's looks with those of 'an spizze hasen' (Pz 409. 26), which functions as an eye-opener for even the most irony-resistant members of the audience.[46] The ridiculous and the ironic are thereby combined to produce comic effect and provoke laughter, holding up some of the most prominent features of courtly culture and behaviour of the time for scrutiny and ridicule.

In this and many others scenes (e.g. Parzival's unsuspecting misbehaviour at the beginning of his knightly career),[47] the narrator's commentary defines

[44] For a discussion of Vergulaht's inappropriate behaviour see Hans-Joachim Ziegeler: '"der herzoge Liddamus": Bemerkungen zum 8. Buch von Wolframs *Parzival*', in *'Texte zum Sprechen bringen': Philologie und Interpretation. Festschrift für Paul Sappler*, ed. by Christiane Ackermann and Ulrich Barton (Tübingen: Niemeyer, 2009), pp. 107–17; for a discussion of Wolfram's irony see esp. p. 111.

[45] Rüdiger Schnell, 'Vogeljagd und Liebe im 8. Buch von Wolframs *Parzival*', *Beiträge zur Geschichte der deutschen Sprache und Literatur (PBB)*, 96 (1974), 246–69 (pp. 259 and 250).

[46] See Dennis H. Green, 'On Recognising Medieval Irony', in *The Uses of Criticism*, ed. by A. P. Foulkes, Literaturwissenschaftliche Texte: Theorie und Kritik, 3 (Bern: Herbert Lang; Frankfurt a.M.: Peter Lang, 1976), pp. 11–55.

[47] See the extensive descriptions in Madsen, *Humor*, pp. 43–71.

the way the situations are to be understood. His asides, digressions, and occasionally misplaced remarks enrich the narrative by adding a complex array of perspectives to decisive situations. For example, when young Parzival attacks the sleeping beauty Jeschute to steal a kiss, her ring, and a brooch, it is the narrator who gives the situation an erotic undertone. He points out details that Parzival, inexperienced as he is, does not see, for example the 'minne wâfen' (Pz 130. 4) the lady is displaying, especially 'ein munt durchliuhtic rôt' (Pz 130. 5) which shows 'der minne hitze fiur' (Pz 130. 9). During a second encounter between Parzival and Jeschute, which the now grown-up hero uses to apologize, the narrator's stance remains unchanged. He again focuses on Jeschute's 'brüstelîn, als si gedraet solden sîn. diu stuonden blanc hôch sinewel' (Pz 258. 25-27) and her almost naked body. He undermines the sobriety of many other scenes, too, mocking countless serious passages, such as the famine in Pelrapeire, which he compares to his own empty cupboard that leaves him starving (Pz 185. 7).[48] In all cases, the narrator's interventions indicate that no part of the narration is neutral, and no object or character is sacrosanct. He mocks the Grail[49] as well as Parzival's marriage, and even combines Parzival's thoughtfulness in the 'Blutstropfenszene' with the description of the hero's enforcedly very unconventional style of fighting that introduces comic elements into the scene.[50] Again and again the narrator moves into the foreground and obstructs the view of the narrated plot.

Yet the narrator's assessment of the situation is almost invariably challenged at a later point in the narrative, or the laughter he provokes proves to be an inappropriate response to the scene—this induces a feeling of insecurity in the listener or reader, as the narrator obviously cannot be trusted. This is especially true when it comes to the poetic legitimization of his narration, which in other texts of the time is normally given by referring to sources and stating the will to entertain and provide a useful narrative. In *Parzival* the narrator does his very best to destroy the illusions that are associated with a work of fiction.[51] His sources tell him that Gawan had breakfast in the morning (Pz 431. 1-2), in the prologue the text itself is compared to a 'schellec hase' (Pz 1. 19) doubling the wits of 'tumben liuten' (Pz 1. 16), and occasionally the audience is called to account with respect to the truthfulness of the narration: 'sol ich des iemen

---

[48] See Bumke, *Wolfram von Eschenbach*, p. 63. See Madsen, *Humor*, pp. 60-63, for a humorous interpretation of the scene.
[49] Walter Haug, '*Parzival* ohne Illusionen', DVjs, 64 (1990), 199-217 (p. 203).
[50] See Tomas Tomasek, 'Bemerkungen zur Komik und zum "Humor" bei Wolfram von Eschenbach', in *Komik und Sakralität: Aspekte einer ästhetischen Paradoxie in Mittelalter und Früher Neuzeit*, ed. by Anja Grebe and Nikolaus Staubach, Tradition — Reform — Innovation, 9 (Frankfurt a.M.: Peter Lang, 2005), pp. 94-103 (p. 97).
[51] On Wolfram's destructive tendencies see Thomas Rausch, 'Die Destruktion der Fiktion: Beobachtungen zu den poetologischen Passagen in Wolframs von Eschenbach *Parzival*', ZfdPh, 119 (2000), 46-74.

triegen, sô müezt ir mit mir liegen' (Pz 238. 11–12), the narrator tells the audience in the course of his portrayal of the Grail procession. This means that the readers and listeners are complicit with this occasionally obscene and often foolish jester and philanderer manqué who has complete control over the work and, on the other hand, again and again calls into doubt his own competence and ability to fulfil his duty. One may laugh about and indeed with Wolfram and his narrator, but one can never be sure where he will lead the audience.

Even this short look at important features of the narrative indicates that the ridiculous, the ironic, and the comic together with the laughter they provoke are not self-sufficient. In most cases they point to a deeper meaning, they unsettle the listener or reader, and they act as a catalyst that instigates a cognitive process. The comic structures, especially those refined uses of irony which demand attentiveness, convey the meaning of the text. Thus, the structured use of the ridiculous, the comic, and the ironic contributes to an overarching structure not of reconciliation, but of provocation.

Book XVI and the Non-Humorous Poetics of Laughter

Agony is the opening feature of the last book[52] of *Parzival*. The Grail King Anfortas, unable to bear the pain caused by inflammation in his loin, is longing for death (while the reader, of course, knows that help is on the way). At the end of Book XVI Anfortas stands next to his successor, laughing (Pz 815. 1–2) about the heathen Feirefiz's eagerness to get baptized because of his love for the Grailkeeper Repanse. This radical reversal from near-suicidal tragedy to burlesque comedy[53] has contributed centrally to the readings of the final part of the poem as humorous. Spirits are high, laughter seems to come easily, and nothing is taken too seriously; a main feature of Book XVI seems to be hilarity.[54]

Yet the 'parody of true baptism' at the centre of Book XVI is 'blasphemous',[55] and the serious matters hidden beneath the light coating of comedy must be addressed in order to properly assess the final part of the romance. The text shows no sign of contempt for Feirefiz's behaviour—even the otherwise outspoken narrator remains silent, although the baptism is a farce that neglects all Christian values and ideals. Feirefiz is indifferent to the religion he joins; the sacrament of baptism is functionalized as a means of

[52] See Michaela Schmitz, *Der Schluss des 'Parzival' Wolframs von Eschenbach: Kommentar zum 16. Buch* (Berlin: Akademie Verlag, 2012).

[53] Bumke, *Wolfram von Eschenbach*, p. 121.

[54] Sebastian Coxon, 'Laughter and the Process of Civilization in Wolfram von Eschenbach's *Parzival*', in *Un-Civilizing Processes? Excess and Transgression in German Society and Culture. Perspectives Debating with Norbert Elias*, ed. by Mary Fulbrook, German Monitor, 66 (Amsterdam and New York: Rodopi, 2007), pp. 17–38 (p. 34).

[55] Neil Thomas, 'Wolfram von Eschenbach: Modes of Narrative Presentation', in *A Companion to Wolfram's 'Parzival'*, ed. by Will Hasty (Columbia, SC: Camden House, 1999), pp. 124–39 (p. 138).

opening Repanse's arms to Feirefiz, who is instantly able to see the Grail that was previously invisible to his heathen eyes (Pz 818. 20–23). This degrades baptism to a mere mechanism and turns hilarity into a farce that seems to debase the values and ideals promoted throughout the course of the text.

Behind the comic lies the sincerity of a textual composition that has voluntarily gone astray. Many assessments of the earlier narration are revised in this final chapter, not only in a comic way, but also by means of serious questioning. This is the case when Trevrizent talks to Parzival, who according to the hermit has 'ab got erzürnet [. . .] daz sîn endelôse Trinitat iwers willen werhaft worden ist' (Pz 798. 3–5). Trevrizent then abrogates all his earlier teachings as described in Book IX by saying: 'Ich louc durch ableitens list vome grâl, wiez umb in stüende' (Pz 798. 5–6). This seemingly inexplicable behaviour has provoked Joachim Bumke to argue that Trevrizent is 'im Zustand der Verwirrung'.[56]

Even though scholars have not succeeded in working out what the lie told by Trevrizent actually consists of,[57] the uncertainty which his abrogation evokes in the listener or reader is quite obvious. Other than Parzival, who is not interested in Trevrizent's advice but rather wants to get back to his wife (Pz 799. 1–12), we cannot help but add Trevrizent's cryptic statement to the list of unsettling items Book XVI confronts us with. Another significant entry on that list is the outlook offered by the work in its final paragraphs. The volatile Grail decides that asking questions has been counter-productive and forbids all further questioning (Pz 818. 24–819. 8). This decision sets the seal on Loherangrin's fate. He is going to fail in the outside world and will have to return to Munsalvaesche because of his wife's curiosity. While Trevrizent calls past actions into question and Feirefiz's behaviour destroys Munsalvaesche's present order, it is Loherangrin's fate that shows the future failings of the Grail family. The story ends by provoking questions that remain unanswered.

'Urbanitas' as the Key to the Pre-Modern Poetics of Laughter

In giving his narration this final twist, Wolfram does what Jean Paul in his *Vorschule der Ästhetik* calls the belittling of the Great, but he does so without providing a corresponding elevation of the Small (VII, § 32, pp. 125–26). There is no reconciliation, only open endings that expose the text's inconsistencies[58] and open *Parzival* up to the audience's scrutiny. If we define humour according to Jean Paul as the philosophical reflection on man's place in God's creation, based on the firm conviction that everything is as it

---

[56] Joachim Bumke, 'Parzival und Feirefiz — Priester Johannes — Loherangrin: Der offene Schluß des *Parzival* von Wolfram von Eschenbach', *DVjs*, 65 (1991), 236–64 (p. 240).

[57] Bernd Schirok, '"ich louc durch ableitens list": Zu Trevrizents Widerruf und den neutralen Engeln', *ZfdPh*, 106 (1987), 46–72 (p. 51 and passim).

[58] Walter Haug, 'Literaturwissenschaft als Kulturwissenschaft?', *DVjs*, 73 (1999), 69–93 (p. 90).

should be and part of a bigger picture in which the world's folly makes sense, *Parzival* only goes half the way. And if we understand humour, according to Jean Paul, to be the attitude of mind of someone who has reached a certain state of self-awareness (VII, § 34, p. 94), Wolfram's romance again stops short of fulfilling expecations by removing certainty without facilitating insight into the self. Wolfram calls fundamental beliefs into question without giving us answers to the questions he asks.

The decisive point of his art is that he does this in an entertaining and indeed funny way—we do not mind being misled while it happens and only realize later that the epic leaves us empty-handed. It is our task to find answers if we wish to make sense of *Parzival*. Interpretations of the text as humorous constitute one distinctively modern response to this challenge, but a definitive response which fails to grasp the most important point Wolfram makes: that sense is not within his work, but needs to be generated afresh by every listener or reader, without ever being definitive. It is characteristic of Wolfram's poetics that *Parzival* requires the audience to be actively involved: the narrative continually invites criticism and requires double-checking. This involvement brings about intellectual *utilitas*, and one part of this strategy is the systematic use of comic elements to produce *delectation*. Over the course of the narration, one soon realizes that every instance of laughter invites reflection on the topic that provoked it.

The basis for this structured use of laughter in *Parzival* is the rhetorical pattern situated in the tension between *delectatio* and *utilitas*. While Horace in his *Ars poetica* sees the combination of both *delectatio* and *utilitas* as ideal,[59] Wolfram subordinates *delectatio* to *utilitas* and uses it as one of the tools of his art among others. The framework for his concept is not humour, but rather the rhetorical idea of *urbanitas*. This is not to say that *urbanitas* is Wolfram's unquestioned ideal; there are considerable frictions, especially when it comes to the opaque narrator figure that undercuts the persuasive power of urbane comedy and induces new levels of scrutiny for all jokes, puns, and ironic comments. *Parzival* makes use of the persuasive idea of laughter, but subjects it to second thoughts. One never just laughs and gets on with it; instead one is forced to use *delectatio* as a catalyst for making up one's mind about the text. In doing so, the audience cannot rely on the narrator, who gives inconsistent advice—the main point of Wolfram's romance is that not only laughter but meaning itself is problematic, as no proper lesson can be drawn from the text.

Wolfram's concept of *utilitas* which is served by *delectatio* is quite distinct from the classical ideal: the text is concerned with guiding the listener or reader to think about the literary work. The making of sense is—at least

---

[59] Horace, *Ars poetica*, ll. 333–34, in *'Satires', 'Epistles' and 'Ars poetica'*, trans. by H. Rushton Fairclough, Loeb Classical Library, 194 (Cambridge, MA: Harvard University Press; London: Heinemann, 1978), p. 447.

partly—shifted to the audience.[60] As the tale does not lay claim to having a simple meaning, we are compelled to form our own view. This effect is reinforced by the use of the persuasive power of laughter and entertainment in the text, for in most instances when laughter occurs or jokes are cracked, we will find an abrogation, a denial, or a contrasting point afterwards. The comic elements of the poem function as cognitive triggers to induce further thinking. Every statement requires further investigation, and even the simplest forms of *delectatio* point to a deeper meaning which is not meant to be decoded, but serves rather as a basis for creative invention by the reader or listener: this transgression of the text's boundaries is what is new in Wolfram's *Parzival*.[61]

The characteristic use of the ridiculous and of comic elements places the text close to the rhetorical theory of *ridiculum*, but a long way away from humour as Weltanschauung, and an equally long way away from the rather general, undefined idea of humour that prevails today. While the latter concept is too superficial to grasp the text's complex structure, the former idea places a burden on the text which it is not designed to bear. Wolfram does not provide answers, but rather asks questions. He lures the listener or reader out of their shell by using well-known rhetorical strategies of persuasion only to destroy the rhetorical refinement through ineptitude and at times obscenity. In the end he leaves the vital poetic entity of *utilitas* at our disposal. This is what makes *Parzival* special: it is a romance that depicts the ongoing development in the relationship between the listener or reader and the text, a development that transgresses the boundaries of long-established patterns of interaction and reaches out to the audience in a distinctively new way. This is also what makes *Parzival* a classic text, challenging every generation anew.

UNIVERSITY OF FREIBURG   STEFAN SEEBER

[60] In doing so, Wolfram forces the audience to bridge the gaps in his narrative in the way that Iser outlines in his aesthetics of reception: see Wolfgang Iser, *How to Do Theory* (Oxford: Blackwell, 2006), pp. 57–69. But *Parzival* offers more than Iser's theory is able to cover, as it presents its audience with a superficially coherent narrative world and then encourages the listener or reader to question the whole narrative: *Parzival* is not about gaps and negations, but deceiving the audience's expectations.

[61] Susanne Knaeble, *Höfisches Erzählen von Gott: Funktion und narrative Entfaltung des Religiösen in Wolframs Parzival*, Trends in Medieval Philology, 23 (Berlin: de Gruyter, 2012), comes to a similar conclusion after reviewing the religious structures of the text. She sees 'Räume der Auslagerung' and states that *Parzival* inspires a timeless 'Aufforderung zur Auseinandersetzung mit dem erzählerischen Spannungsgefüge' (p. 293).

AFTER THE *FLÂNEUR*: TEMPORALITY AND CONNECTIVITY IN WILHELM GENAZINO'S *BELEBUNG DER TOTEN WINKEL* AND *DAS GLÜCK IN GLÜCKSFERNEN ZEITEN*

For the sociologist Nobert Elias the ability to perceive the passage of time is a socially acquired and complex synthesis, enabling human agents to regulate their behaviour with reference to three interdependent temporal spheres: the natural environment, the social setting, and their individual biographies.[1] Elias, who was writing before the arrival of the digital era, accentuated the social dimension of human temporality. Digital technologies did not yet feature in his thinking as a major instrument that was transforming the relationship between individuals, their worlds, and their temporal horizons. Evidently the ever tighter enmeshing of human worlds with digital media alters the very notion of experience: the ontological difference between lived and virtual experience is diminishing as the digital arena emerges from its status as a simulated order. While this is perhaps most apparent in the financial sector with its split-second transactions, it also holds for everyday culture, where technology transmutes dispositions, habits, and perceptions. John Tomlinson aptly speaks of a new culture of immediacy that is seemingly characterized by the shift from 'effortful speed to an effortless mediated delivery'.[2] Tomlinson further argues that in the digital arena the divide between departure and arrival has now been virtually closed, so that the notion of departure seems redundant.[3] Because the new culture of immediacy promotes instant access, it erodes the expectation of temporal processing. This new era of the 'digital now', where the furthest goal is only a click of the mouse away, not only challenges established notions of delayed gratification but also the very idea of time as a multidimensional concept that integrates past, present, and future into human experience. The philosopher Hermann Lübbe has coined the term 'Gegenwartsschrumpfung', the shrinking of the present, to capture the erosion of experience. He defines the shrinking of the present as a shortening of the time period for which we can assume stability of our living conditions.[4] While for Lübbe the Age of Information has devalued the past, Hans Ulrich Gumbrecht proposes the emergence of an ever burgeoning present which

---

[1] Norbert Elias, *Über die Zeit*, ed. by Michael Schröter (Frankfurt a.M.: Suhrkamp, 1988), pp. xvii and xxiv.
[2] John Tomlinson, *The Culture of Speed: The Coming of Immediacy* (Los Angeles and London: Sage, 2007), p. 81.
[3] Ibid., p. 90.
[4] Hermann Lübbe, 'Gegenwartsschrumpfung', in *Die Beschleunigungsfalle oder der Triumpf der Schildkröte*, ed. by Klaus Backhaus and Holger Bonus, 3rd edn (Stuttgart: Schäffer-Poeschel, 1998), pp. 263–93 (p. 264).

is on the one hand flooded by pasts that we can no longer shake off, and on the other stifled by simultaneities that expose us to directionless movement without future horizons.[5] According to Gumbrecht, the information revolution has undermined the experience of 'real presence' by reducing our encounters with the world to the level of simulacra without any experiential imprints. In his book *Weltbeziehungen im Zeitalter der Beschleunigung* (2012), Hartmut Rosa considers the quest for the good life in the twenty-first century and seeks 'relations of resonance' that would enable human actors to relate to their worlds in meaningful ways.[6] For Rosa the prospect of maintaining reciprocal relations between selves, others, and their human habitats has been unhinged. He contends that in classical modernity the notion of a rational subjectivity still incorporated elements of a Romantic self that bridged the Cartesian gap between reason and feeling, between body and soul. In late modernity, he argues, human creativity has been entirely subjugated to the systemic requirements of accelerated capitalism.[7] In his view human actors in the twenty-first century are reduced to building merely temporary identities from flexible elements that ultimately fragment subjectivity.[8]

Although the spectre of a 'runaway world'[9] chimes with recent global economic history, the approach to the digital present as a disaster narrative demands critical intervention because it rests on a misleading dualism of space and time that obliterates the heterogeneous temporality of subjective experience. Geographers such Yi-Fu Tuan, Nigel Thrift, Jon May, and Doreen Massey have challenged this monolithic story of modernity by reviewing the relationship between time and space. Instead of subscribing to the idea that space in the Age of Information has been eliminated by high-speed technologies, they debate inhabited space, i.e. places as sites of multidimensional temporal practice, stages of cultural, ethnic, and gendered contestation, or as embodied structure of feeling. If place is a 'field of care' brought about by the 'affective bond between people and places', as Tuan suggests, then this also means that places are not only composed of material objects but also of imprints of past attachments, present perceptions, and feelings as

---

[5] Hans Ulrich Gumbrecht, *Unsere breite Gegenwart* (Frankfurt a.M.: Suhrkamp, 2010), pp. 16 and 17; see also id., *Präsenz*, ed. by Jürgen Klein (Frankfurt a.M.: Suhrkamp, 2012).

[6] Hartmut Rosa, *Weltbeziehungen im Zeitalter der Beschleunigung: Umrisse einer neuen Gesellschaftskritik* (Frankfurt a.M.: Suhrkamp, 2012), p. 10; also id., *Beschleunigung: Die Veränderung der Zeitstrukturen in der Moderne* (Frankfurt a.M.: Suhrkamp, 2005).

[7] Rosa, *Weltbeziehungen*, pp. 174 and 248.

[8] Ibid., p. 225.

[9] See Antony Giddens, *Runaway World: How Globalization is Reshaping our Lives* (London: Routledge, 2002). On the temporal effects of globalization see also Zygmunt Bauman, *Globalization: The Human Consequences* (Cambridge: Polity, 1998); id., *Liquid Times: Living in an Age of Uncertainty* (Cambridge: Polity, 2007).

well as future orientations.[10] Nigel Thrift and Jon May aptly speak of 'multi-dimensional networks of TimeSpace' to accentuate the disparate geography of social temporality that complicates any simple linear narrative of modernity as acceleration:

> Thus, the picture that emerges is less that of a singular or uniform social time stretching over a uniform space, than of various (and uneven) networks of time stretching in different and divergent directions across an uneven social field. [. . .] The result is therefore a radical unevenness in the nature and quality of social time itself, with this spatial variation a constitutive part rather than an added dimension of the multiplicity and heterogeneity of social time or what, for precisely these reasons, we prefer to call 'SpaceTime'.[11]

Doreen Massey's book *For Space* also refutes the one-dimensional 'discursive victory of time over space' envisaged by proponents of the inevitable triumph of modernity, who interpret contemporaneous differences as developmental stages on the trajectory of progress.[12] For Massey 'the really serious question which is raised by speed-up, by the communications revolution, and by cyberspace is not whether space will be annihilated but what kinds of multiplicities (patternings of uniqueness) and relations will be co-constructed with these new kinds of spatial configurations'.[13] Space is 'always under construction', she argues. It is 'a simultaneity of stories so far'.[14] This performative notion of multiple, contested, and open spaces not only rewrites the narrative of the Information Age from the perspective of the local production of the global, but it roundly rejects all deterministic interpretations of human subjectivity and agency. For Hartmut Rosa, totalizing and inescapable acceleration forces all subjects in late modernity under its rule.[15] I would argue along with Thrift, May, and Massey that subjectivity at the dawn of the twenty-first century is capable of negotiating varied temporalities in multiple spaces by way of differentiated modes or tactics of social relatedness. While cyberspace and the culture of immediacy do indeed constitute genuinely new arenas of social interaction, these do not necessarily signal the end of social relations, the flattening of time, the erosion of presence, or the end of memory. The

---

[10] Yi-Fu Tuan, *Topophilia: A Study of Environmental Perception, Attitudes and Values* (New York: Columbia University Press, 1990), p. 4.

[11] *TimeSpace: Geographies of Temporality*, ed. by Jon May and Nigel Thrift (London and New York: Routledge, 2001), p. 5. They argue that for most people the experience of acceleration is more intermittent and less dramatic than is commonly acknowledged: 'The picture is less of any simple acceleration in the pace of life or experiences of spatial "collapse" than of a far more complex restructuring in the nature and experience of time and space reaching through the nineteenth and into the early decades of the twentieth century' (p. 10).

[12] Doreen Massey, *For Space* (London: Sage, 2005), p. 71: 'The multiplicities of the spatial have been rendered as merely stages in the temporal queue.'

[13] Ibid., p. 91.

[14] Ibid., p. 9.

[15] Rosa, *Weltbeziehungen*, p. 284.

question then is in what way and how our cultural attachments to the past and the experience of the depth of time are being reconfigured in the era of the digital present. Given the premium placed on instant access and continual innovation, how is cultural identity in the twenty-first century to be understood?

This is precisely the concern of Genazino's poetics lectures *Die Belebung der toten Winkel*, which address the transformation of human experience in the contemporary arena.[16] Genazino approaches his quest for cultural connectivity by elaborating the fundamental difference between the modern figure of the *flâneur*, who emerged in the nineteenth century, and his contemporary successor, the stray city walker. Referring to Walter Benjamin's Baudelaire essays, he argues that the *flâneur*'s enjoyment of modernity's electrifying visual spectacles depended on an urban environment that, in spite of the increased pace of life, could still be assimilated by the receptive individual (*BtW*, p. 95).[17] According to Genazino, Joyce's work stages a subjectivity that manages to derive pleasure from the urban environment by transforming fleeting impressions into moments of quasi-metaphysical vision. The Joycean epiphany thus accentuates the sovereignty of the modern self that is at liberty to mobilize a heightened attention in the service of the subject's own creative imagination (*BtW*, p. 93). But this modern aesthetic of 'Plötzlichkeit', to use Karlheinz Bohrer's term, depended on the ability of individuals to select whether, when, and for how long they should direct their gaze at specific phenomena.[18] As a sovereign subject the *flâneur* commanded modernity's culture of speed by means of two co-dependent cultural techniques which helped to filter modernity's dazzling sensations through two modes of perception, namely attention and distraction. *Fin-de-siècle* discourse discovered attention as a vital cultural strategy that could ward off the danger of too much distraction and ultimately of psychic disintegration. Attention as the ability to focus for a defined period of time on selected external phenomena contained and disciplined the perpetual production of the new as one of modernity's striking features.[19] Distraction as the flipside of attention indicated a tempor-

[16] Wilhelm Genazino, *Die Belebung der toten Winkel: Frankfurter Poetikvorlesungen* (Munich: Hanser, 2006). Henceforth cited in the text as *BtW*.
[17] In line with this, Benjamin writes that the leisurely mode of the *flâneur* is made possible by the arcades which turn the boulevard into an *intérieur* and as such into a sphere of domesticity. See Walter Benjamin, 'Das Paris des Second Empire bei Baudelaire', in *Abhandlungen: Gesammelte Schriften*, ed. by Rolf Tiedemann and Hermann Schweppenhäuser, 7 vols (Frankfurt a.M.: Suhrkamp, 1991), I/2, 539.
[18] Karlheinz Bohrer, *Plötzlichkeit: Zum Augenblick des ästhetischen Scheins* (Frankfurt a.M.: Suhrkamp, 1981).
[19] On the discourse on attention around 1900 see Jonathan Crary, *Suspensions of Perceptions: Attention, Spectacle, and Modern Culture* (Cambridge, MA: MIT Press, 2001); Anne Fuchs, 'Why Smallness Matters: Smallness, Attention and Distraction in Franz Kafka's and Robert Walser's Short

ality of leisure brought about by this wealth of intoxicating external stimuli. The modern subject thus entertained fleeting interests in a rapid succession of visual attractions that, at the point of their appearance, were already destined to be superseded by new excitements and thrills. Georg Simmel's classic essay 'Die Großstädte und das Geistesleben', Siegfried Kracauer's 'Der Kult der Zerstreuung', and, of course, Benjamin's elaborations on the *flâneur* articulate and explore specifically modern strategies of coping with such radically new conditions of perception.[20] The new tempo of life unleashed new aesthetic possibilities that found articulation in modern poetry, short prose, fiction, film, and fine art. In his Frankfurt lectures Genazino argues that the conditions of early modernity were still sufficiently stable to fuse the observing self and the observed object through a temporality of meaningful observation. He agrees with Rosa's diagnosis that late modernity has destroyed the momentary stability of this fourfold constellation of subject, object, time, and mode of seeing (*BtW*, p. 92). The contemporary metropolis is an illegible jungle which has lost the 'strukturiertes, eingängiges Stadtbild' (*BtW*, p. 104) that, according to Genazino, was a central condition of the *flâneur*'s epiphanic connectivity with the urban environment (*BtW*, p. 104). The *flâneur*'s contemporary successor is a stray self who roams the city exposed to the 'Durcheinander der verwischten Bilder' (*BtW*, p. 104):

> Die Figur des Flaneurs hat in der zerstückelten Stadt abgedankt und ist ersetzt worden durch einen moderneren Typus, den des Streuners. Der Streuner ist jemand, der selbst der Ungemütlichkeit noch einen Reiz abgewinnen möchte und dabei oft erfolgreich ist. [. . .] Der Streuner fühlt sich als displaced person, aber er weiß auch, daß es andere Plätze für ihn nicht mehr gibt. Die Identität des Streuners ist genauso beschädigt wie die Gestalt der Metropole selbst. (*BtW*, p. 103)

With its glitzy surfaces and flat projection screens, the contemporary city has—in the eyes of Genazino—morphed into a fake stage set which engenders nothing but 'fake Tagesgefühle, die genauso prekär sind wie die Kulissen der Stadt, denen sie mühsam abgefühlt worden sind' (*BtW*, p. 105). Because the quick succession of rapid images has destroyed the conditions of intimacy, the only option left to the stray self of late modernity is to retreat momentarily into 'die Ordnung seiner Innerlichkeit' (*BtW*, p. 106) or to adopt various tactics of temporal resistance, which I will discuss below. Genazino summarizes the difference between early capitalism and its late version as follows:

Prose', in *Kafka und die kleine Prosa der Moderne/Kafka and Short Modernist Prose*, ed. by Ritchie Robertson and Manfred Engel, Oxford Kafka Studies, 1 (Würzburg: Königshausen & Neumann, 2010), pp. 167–79. Carolin Duttlinger, 'Kafkas Poetik der Aufmerksamkeit von *Betrachtung* bis *Der Bau*', ibid., pp. 79–97.

[20] See Georg Simmel, *Die Großstädte und das Geistesleben* (Frankfurt a.M.: Suhrkamp, 2006); Siegfried Kracauer, 'Der Kult der Zerstreuung' (1926), in *Das Ornament der Masse: Essays* (Frankfurt a.M.: Suhrkamp, 1977), pp. 311–17.

Früher, sagen wir in der prähysterischen Phase des Kapitalismus, richtete sich der Blick der Menschen auf die Dinge. Heute richtet sich der Blick der Dinge auf den Menschen. Niemand entgeht den Übergriffen ihrer Kaufappelle. Die Zudringlichkeit kassiert die betrachtende Distanz, auf die der Flaneur einmal Wert gelegt hatte. Die Penetranz der Waren macht den Flaneur zum Streuner und ist der Grund für die Fluchtförmigkeit seines Umherstreifens. In Umgebungen ohne Diskretion kann es Flaneure deshalb nicht mehr geben. (*BtW*, p. 107)

Philosopher Byung-Chul Han celebrates the emergence of a deterritorialized and disembedded global culture that he envisions as populated by 'hypercultural tourists' who neither long for nor fear the encounter with a 'there'.[21] He claims that the figure of the hypercultural tourist knows no difference between here and there as he 'windows' the world—a term coined in analogy of the ubiquitous computer operating system.[22] For Byung-Chul Han this new state of hyperculturality has the potential to realize freedom if it abandons prevailing notions of fulfilled time and narration in favour of what he calls 'point-time' or 'event-time'.[23] Without past and future horizon, this 'point time' carries no meaning and is thus not burdened by 'gravitation', the term by which Byung-Chul Han captures conventional ideas of narration and history. 'Das Sein', explains Byung-Chul Han, 'zerstreut sich zu einem Hyperraum aus Möglichkeiten und Ereignissen, die, statt zu gravitieren, darin gleichsam nur schwirren.'[24] Evidently Byung-Chul Han's eulogy of hyperculturality completely ignores the negative effects of global capitalism, as manifest in the sharp disjuncture between a mobile extraterritorial elite and 'the ever more localized rest' which, as Zygmunt Bauman argues, is left behind as human debris in largely disenfranchised localities.[25] In contrast to Byung-Chul Han's rather euphoric view, Genazino emphasizes the pathologies of late capitalism: its hysterical phase is characterized by the 'Penetranz der Waren', which has destroyed the contemplative distance between subject and object. While the nineteenth-century *flâneur* still managed to exploit this distance in the pursuit of an epiphanic connectivity, his Genazinean successor inhabits an environment without contemplative distance and discretion. Surrounded by the impoverished trappings of hysterical capitalism, Genazino's figures who wander the city suffer from the enduring consciousness that they are

---

[21] He writes: 'Der hyperkulturelle Tourist ist nicht zu einer Gegenwelt, nicht zu einem Dort unterwegs. Er bewohnt vielmehr einen Raum, der keine Asymmetrie von *Hier* und *Dort* aufweist. Er ist ganz *hier*.' Zygmunt Bauman's critique of globalization, Byung-Chul Han argues, lacks appreciation of the hypercultural tourist: 'Für Bauman ist der Tourist noch ein Pilger, der zerrissen ist zwischen der Sehnsucht nach dem Dort und der Furcht vor diesem. Der hyperkulturelle Tourist dagegen hat weder Sehnsucht noch Furcht' (Byung-Chul Han, *Hyperkulturalität: Kultur und Globalisierung* (Berlin: Merve, 2005), pp. 45 and 47).
[22] Ibid., p. 49.
[23] Ibid., p. 54.
[24] Ibid.
[25] Bauman, *Gobalization*, p. 3.

ridiculously out of place and time. But as Ernst Bloch's famous formulation suggests, history is marked by 'die Gleichzeitigkeit des Ungleichzeitigen'.[26] The apparent defect turns out to be a strategic position: Genazino's figures discover their non-contemporaneity with the contemporary to be a creative resource that allows them to exercise a degree of temporal sovereignty in an era that is otherwise ruled by the hectic just-in-time ideology. In the following I will illustrate such resistance to the prevalent *Zeitgeist* with reference to Genazino's novel *Das Glück in glücksfernen Zeiten*.

Nearly all of Genazino's heroes abhor the drudgery of the world of work as they contend with its alienating effects and find these amplified in the contemporary open-plan office environment, where employees become agents of mutual surveillance. The *Abschaffel* trilogy of the late 1970s—*Abschaffel* (1977), *Die Vernichtung der Sorgen* (1978), and *Falsche Jahre* (1979)—relates the story of a male employee who is the embodiment of the unhappy white-collar worker in the latter part of the twentieth century, and as such a successor of Kafka's Josef K.[27] Aged thirty-one and single, he feels trapped by his job in the open-plan office of a transport company. The boring routine of his working life is only punctuated by office gossip, long and empty Sundays, dissatisfying leisure activities, including casual relationships with women, the occasional visit to a brothel, and far too many cigarettes.

Thirty years later, in *Das Glück in glücksfernen Zeiten* (2009), we encounter Gerhard Warlich, who is the manager of a big laundry company that services hotels in the Frankfurt region.[28] In the opening scene we meet Warlich after work in a street café in Frankfurt, where he observes 'die endlich zur Betrachtung freigegebenen feierabendlichen Goldränder unserer Leistungsgesellschaft' (*GigfZ*, p. 7). This setting bears all the tacky signs of global capitalism: the café's menu of drinks has been printed on the back of the

---

[26] See Ernst Bloch, *Erbschaft dieser Zeit* (Frankfurt a.M.: Suhrkamp, 1962), p. 1: 'Nicht alle sind im selben Jetzt da. Sie sind es nur äußerlich, dadurch daß sie heute zu sehen sind. Damit aber leben sie noch nicht mit den anderen zugleich. Sie tragen vielmehr Früheres mit, das mischt sich ein.' Bloch coined the phrase 'Gleichzeitigkeit des Ungleichzeitigen', but the concept goes back to the late eighteenth century, when European civilization was set as a benchmark for overseas cultures seen as having been left behind. As Reinhart Koselleck argues, a dynamic and qualitative interpretation of time was propelled by global scientific exploration, which drew attention to coexisting cultural levels that were then subjected to chronological ordering by way of cultural comparison (Reinhart Koselleck, '"Neuzeit": Remarks on the Semantics of Modern Concepts of Movement', in id., *Futures Past: On the Semantics of Historical Time* (New York: Columbia University Press, 2004), pp. 236–38). See also Hanns-Georg Brose, 'Das Gleichzeitige ist ungleichzeitig: Über den Umgang mit einer Paradoxie und die Transformation der Zeit', in *Unsichere Zeiten: Herausforderungen gesellschaftlicher Transformationen. Verhandlungen des 34. Kongresses der Deutschen Gesellschaft für Soziologie in Jena 2008*, ed. by Hans-Georg Soeffner and others (Wiesbaden: Springer, 2010), pp. 547–62.

[27] Wilhelm Genazino, *Abschaffel: Roman-Trilogie* (Munich: dtv, 2002).

[28] Wilhelm Genazino, *Das Glück in glücksfernen Zeiten: Roman* (Munich: Hanser, 2009). Henceforth cited in the text as *GigfZ*.

employees' T-shirts, half a dozen Russian immigrants are messing around with a slot machine, and a young couple next to him are slurping their green drinks so loudly that Warlich feels tempted to pay them a fiver to stop their noisy sucking. Warlich himself is self-consciously aware of the consumer slogans on his plastic bags, which he shoves under the table in embarrassment. Reflecting on his desire for change in his life, he then observes a begging trumpeter who, in spite of his poor performance, manages to collect some money (*GigfZ*, p. 9). Overcome by this 'allgemeine Ödnis des Wirklichen' (ibid.), Warlich is desperately in need of a small-scale occurrence that could appease his injured soul.

Although Warlich is a version of Genazino's earlier protagonist, his situation has become much more precarious in the age of neo-liberalism and the erosion of the social securities of the post-war era. In many ways Warlich is the embodiment of the new educated 'Prekariat' facing social and economic decline.[29] He wrote a Ph.D. on Heidegger, in all likelihood on the phenomenology of time, but landed his permanent job because he introduced just-in-time deliveries in the laundry company. Warlich has long abandoned the naive belief that the conventional pathway through the education system can influence one's prospects in life: the alienating reality of the world of work has exposed his academic qualifications as 'Bildungslametta', educational tinsel without use or value (*GigfZ*, p. 45). In his professional life Warlich is not only responsible for further rationalizations, such as the introduction of the one-day laundry service, but also for spying on the delivery men whom his boss suspects of time-wasting. As he follows the company drivers Wrede and Ehrlicher through the outskirts of Frankfurt, he is struck by the drab appearance of these urban edgelands, which bear all the signs of long-term neglect. Disused shopping malls line the streets, sheltering the homeless, the drunk, and other misfits along with Asian discount stalls that flog off tacky wares:

> Die Leute leben zwar, aber sie haben vergessen, wo sie einmal zu Hause waren, so ähnlich wie traurige Tiere im Zoo. Der Blick fällt auf verstopfte Abfallkörbe, nicht weggeräumte, vermoderte Blätter vom Vorjahresherbst, leerstehende Geschäfte, in den Kaufhauseingängen herumliegende Obdachlose und Gestrandete, dazu immer mehr Asiatenbasare, wo es Plastiksandalen, Gummirosen und Strohperücken zu kaufen gibt. (*GigfZ*, p. 41)

The visual and emotional deprivation of this scene accentuates the sharp disjuncture between, on the one hand, Frankfurt's financial centre as a global

---

[29] On this topic see *Exklusion: Die Debatte über die 'Überflüssigen'*, ed. by Heinz Bude and Andreas Willisch (Frankfurt a.M.: Suhrkamp, 2007); Heinz Bude, *Die Ausgeschlossenen: Das Ende vom Traum einer gerechten Gesellschaft* (Munich: dtv, 2010); *Prekariat, Abstieg, Ausgrenzung: Die soziale Frage am Beginn des 21. Jahrhunderts*, ed. by Robert Castel and Klaus Dörre (Frankfurt a.M.: Campus, 2009).

investment hub that proudly showcases its architectural signature buildings and, on the other, its down-at-heel urban fringes, which have swept up the trash of globalization, losing all connection with place as a 'field of care' (Tuan). And yet, this shabby *non-lieu* houses a small oasis, a *Volksgarten* that offers respite to mothers, children, and the elderly. As a communal space, the *Volksgarten* represents a social locality that reanimates the damaged bond between the environment and its inhabitants. However, for Warlich it is a tainted paradise because of his hateful 'Observierungsauftrag' (*GigfZ*, p. 41): in the park's beer garden he then spots the two company drivers, who are enjoying a drink during their working hours. As he considers his unenviable role as a company snoop (*GigfZ*, p. 41), he realizes his systemic enmeshment in existing power structures: 'Diese wachsende Unfreiheit in den Verhältnissen nennt man Verstrickung' (*GigfZ*, p. 41).

In his encounter with a reality that is simultaneously drab and demanding, Genazino's hero pursues five tactics of resistance:[30] melancholy self-absorption, the performance of private rituals, the fabrication of stories, the prolonged gaze, and, finally, a tactical slowness. This ensemble of tactics creates a multilayered temporal ecology that, as I will show below, allows the protagonist either to cultivate a melancholy subjectivity at a remove from the world or to periodically experience 'topophilia', i.e. attachment to local places.[31]

All of Genazino's heroes foster a highly self-conscious mode of melancholy. Their regular retreat into melancholy self-absorption creates a form of Bergsonian *durée* that suspends the 'Zwangsabonnement der Wirklichkeit' (*GigfZ*, p. 10) and as such the obligation to be 'always connectable, available and public'.[32] By indulging in bouts of 'melancholische Verwilderung' (*GigfZ*, p. 23)—a term that possibly alludes to Benjamin's short essay on Robert Walser[33]—Warlich gains access to his innermost self, where all disturbing

---

[30] Michel de Certeau distinguishes between strategy as an operation of institutionalized power and tactics, 'which cannot count on a "proper" (a spatial or institutional localization) [*sic*], nor thus on a borderline distinguishing the other as a visible totality. The place of the tactic belongs to the other. A tactic insinuates itself into the other's place, fragmentarily, without taking it over in its entirety, without being able to keep it at a distance' (Michel de Certeau, *The Practice of Everyday Life*, trans. by Steven Rendall (Berkeley: University of California Press, 1984), p. xix).

[31] See Gaston Bachelard, *The Poetics of Space*, trans. from the French by Maria Jolas (Boston: Beacon Press, 1969), and Tuan, *Topophilia*.

[32] Helga Nowotny, *Time: The Modern and Postmodern Experience* (Cambridge: Polity, 1996), p. 34.

[33] Benjamin's comments on Walser's style resonate with Genazino's poetics of melancholy opposition: 'Denn während wir gewohnt sind, die Rätsel des Stils uns aus mehr oder weniger durchgebildeten, absichtsvollen Kunstwerken entgegentreten zu sehen, stehen wir hier vor einer, zumindest scheinbar, völlig absichtslosen und dennoch anziehenden und bannenden Sprachverwilderung. Vor einem sich Gehenlassen, das alle Formen von Grazie bis zur Bitternis aufweist' (Walter Benjamin, 'Robert Walser', in *Über Robert Walser*, ed. by Katharina Kerr (Frankfurt a.M.: Suhrkamp, 1978), pp. 126–29 (p. 126)).

interaction with the outside world is temporarily suspended. In his depiction of Warlich's melancholy, Genazino clearly plays with the ancient tradition of melancholy as a physiological condition (caused by too much black bile and the influence of the planet Saturn) and as a sign of the genius.[34] However, in Genazino's novel the reactivation of this tradition, which, from antiquity to the present day, provides a rich cultural narrative, is always lined by humour. Warlich is therefore not a creative genius but merely a 'Beinahe-Künstler [...]; ich mache Collagen. Ich zeichne und male. Ich filme, ich schreibe Nonsens-Gedichte, aber nichts davon so richtig [. . .]' (GigfZ, p. 17). And while his periodic spells of 'Verrücktheit' (GigfZ, p. 86) are a further indication of his melancholy inclination, they are divorced from the grand cosmological context of the mad genius. Once he reaches the recesses of his melancholy 'Innenraum', he can wallow in a form of self-pity that is framed by a good dose of self-knowledge:

Dort bedauert mich niemand so kenntnisreich wie ich selber. Die Leisigkeit, mit der ich neben Traudel sitzen bleibe und gleichzeitig verschwinde, wirkt auch auf mich unangenehm. Ich bin in einer Stimmung, in der ich kaum ertrage, daß es abends immer Abend wird und daß die Dunkelheit draußen auch in unsere Wohnung eindringt. (GigfZ, p. 23)

The whimsical expression of selfhood presented here revitalizes a sentimental subjectivity that, in analogy to the Age of *Empfindsamkeit*, links the physiological and emotional spheres through an all-encompassing mood.[35] It comes as no surprise that Warlich understands his hyperconscious melancholy as a mode of refinement which recuperates the purity of a subjectivity that otherwise feels assaulted by the demands of a runaway world: 'Etwas von der Feinheit, die ich zum Leben brauche', reflects Warlich, 'finde ich nur in meiner Melancholie' (GigfZ, p. 63). By tapping into his melancholy disposition, Genazino's hero restores interiority as a basic condition of intimacy. As shown before, in his poetics lectures Genazino describes the contemporary city environment as dominated by reflective surfaces, projection screens, and the rapid sequence of indiscreet images (BtW, p. 105). This new surface reality has eliminated intimacy because—as a spatio-temporal relationship between

[34] See the seminal study by Raymond Klibansky, Erwin Panofsky, and Frith Saxl, *Saturn and Melancholy: Studies in the History of Natural Philosophy, Religion, and Art* (London: Nelson, 1964); *The Nature of Melancholy: From Aristotle to Kristeva*, ed. by Jennifer Radden (Oxford: Oxford University Press, 2002); on melancholy in post-war German fiction see Mary Cosgrove, *Born under Auschwitz: Melancholy Traditions in Postwar German Literature* (Rochester: Camden House, forthcoming).

[35] On *Empfindsamkeit* see Catherine J. Minter, 'Literary *Empfindsamkeit* and Nervous Sensibility in Eighteenth Century Germany', *MLR*, 96 (2001), 1016–28. On the return of 'Stimmung' as a literary category see Hans Ulrich Gumbrecht, *Stimmungen lesen: Über eine verdeckte Wirklichkeit der Literatur* (Munich: Hanser, 2011); see also *Stimmung: Zur Wiederkehr einer ästhetischen Kategorie*, ed. by Anna Katherina Gisbertz (Munich: Fink, 2011).

social actors—intimacy presupposes interiority as well as access to private time or *Eigenzeit*. As Helga Nowotny argues, *Eigenzeit* designates the modern subject's ability to cultivate 'temporal sovereignty' over local time in the face of the commodification and acceleration of time in the public sphere.[36] While the modern era gave rise to what Nowotny calls a specific 'I-time perspective' by polarizing the public time of work and the self's private time of leisure,[37] the digital era complicates the modern quest for *Eigenzeit* by eroding this clear-cut division between the self's public time and private time alongside spaces of intimacy.

The melancholy disposition of the Genazinean protagonist fuels a mode of empty longing following from loss of any vision for a better life. For example, as Warlich happens upon an anarchist demonstration in the financial centre of Frankfurt, he observes wryly that he has lost belief in the possibility of change: 'Dafür dauert das, was hätte verändert werden müssen, schon zu lange an. Trotzdem haben meine Wünsche ihre Nichterfüllung überlebt' (*GigfZ*, p. 98). Ironically, the next day he is sacked without notice because a colleague mistakenly reported him for participating in the demonstration during regular working hours.

The fabrication of stories is the second tactic employed by Warlich in the search for meaning and attachment. In the course of the novel he fantasizes about founding a 'Schule der Besänftigung' which, as he explains to his old friend Gerd Angermann, will at last teach what people really want to know (*GigfZ*, p. 57). Later on we learn that this alternative knowledge should focus on the composition of happiness in environments at a remove from happiness: 'Das ist mein Spezialgebiet. Wir müssen uns das Außerordentliche selber machen, sonst tritt es nicht in die Welt' (*GigfZ*, p. 80). Although this is initially an entirely fabricated story, the project gains momentum when Warlich applies to the City Council for funding, a request that is granted on condition that the School of Appeasement will be a Pop-Academy for young wannabe celebrities.

Such cock-and-bull stories are a regular occurrence: they give metaphoric expression to Warlich's deepening sense of alienation and a crisis of connectivity that he tries to contain with 'borrowed' forms of emotional identification. For example, when he concocts a story about his mother's childhood—he tells his colleague Frau Weiss that she nearly died as a young child in the bombing raids—his fabricated story produces half a false tear in his eye, then a sense of shame, and, finally, a genuine tear in recognition of his own neediness (*GigfZ*, p. 100). Warlich's stories unleash emotional responses in the recipient, including in Warlich himself as he adopts the dual perspective of

---

[36] Nowotny, p. 13.
[37] Ibid.

author and listener when inventing stories about an alternative life. But these fictions also point to an imminent crisis of connectivity which finally erupts when, after many years, he by chance meets his old friend Annette with her teenage son. Instead of shaking her hand when they part, Warlich gives her a slice of stale bread that he had earlier slipped inside the inner pocket of his jacket (*GigfZ*, pp. 127–28). With its biblical connotations, this abject gesture symbolizes a moment of utter exposure and vulnerability. The episode ends with him breaking down sobbing and his admission to a psychiatric hospital.

Warlich's third tactic involves symbolic performances and private rituals that suspend the perceived impoverishment of life. A prime example in this regard is his clothing: he reveals early on that he enjoys wearing an old rag of a vest under an impeccable shirt. This small act of resistance allows him to fantasize about his future as a 'Kleiderkünstler' or 'Verwesungskünstler' who, as he explains, enacts the slow dissolution of life through his sense of dress (*GigfZ*, p. 18). When his girlfriend Traudel asks him to buy new clothes, he acquiesces but quietly hatches a plan to leave his old and worn trousers hanging out on the balcony so that he can observe their slow decay (*GigfZ*, p. 25). He also plans to keep a diary about the dissolution of his trousers and their gradual return to a state of nature. Later on, the memory of his rotting trousers releases a sense of contentment in Warlich because they are weathering away in his place, thus banishing the threat of death (*GigfZ*, p. 44). The trousers are a sort of humorous totem pitched against the commodity fetishism which, according to Marx, regulates social relations in capitalism.[38] Warlich idolizes the loss of exchange value in objects and thus their ability to escape the capitalist circuit of exchange. As curator of his old trousers he symbolically salvages the 'Gleichzeitigkeit des Ungleichzeitigen', the contemporaneity of the non-contemporaneous, by dispensing with capitalist prestige indicators such as price, novelty, and up-to-date design.[39] Every evening he feels comforted by his weathered trousers on the balcony because they represent the passage of time: 'Es ist das Gefühl, das Vergehen der Zeit sei anschaulich geworden. Manchmal denke ich sogar, es handle sich um das Vergehen meiner Zeit' (*GigfZ*, p. 83). For Warlich, his Beuys-like project equips a mass-produced consumer product with symbolic resistance to the *Zeitgeist*; for Traudel it is a sign that he is clearly going over the edge. While the comic nature of this episode may be seen to underline the futility of such acts of 'resistance', which arguably shrink into pathetic gestures with cast-off clothing, it nevertheless communicates the protagonist's desperate search for connectivity with an environment that fetishizes innovation and change. Even though Genazino's protagonists appear as comical heroes of fu-

[38] See Karl Marx, *Das Kapital: Kritik der politischen Ökonomie*, I: *Der Produktionsprozess des Kapitals*, ed. by Institut für Marxismus-Leninismus (Berlin: Dietz, 1977), pp. 85–98.
[39] See above, n. 26.

tility, their seemingly absurd ideas bring to the fore a fundamental emotional need. As Genazino argued in his poetics lectures, in the contemporary city environment the continual onslaught of shrill images leaves nothing to the imagination. Global capitalism and its flashy simulacra in the cityscape have disrupted intimacy and deterritorialized the public sphere and its inhabitants, so that enormous effort is required to retrieve moments of intimacy.

The fourth and perhaps most strategic technique of connecting the fragile self with the city is, however, the practice of the 'prolonged gaze' which recuperates the possibility of experience in face of the continual production of obsolescence. In an essay devoted to this subject, Genazino explains this notion as follows: 'Der gedehnte Blick sieht auch dann noch, wenn es nach allgemeiner Übereinkunft, die schon längst beim nächsten und übernächsten Bild angekommen ist, nichts mehr zu sehen gibt.'[40] Its work consists of a constant transformation of the image, which, by breaking through habitual patterns of perception, rediscovers the enigmatic quality of the perceived object. For Genazino this transformative effect of the prolonged gaze is most evident when social actors are perplexed by the realization that they can no longer make sense of an image. He writes: 'Die Perplexion ist das allmähliche Vertrautwerden mit der uns melancholisch stimmenden Zumutung, daß wir immer nur Splitter und Bruchstücke von etwas verstehen.'[41] While such puzzled perplexity disrupts the ordinariness of everyday life, it also draws attention to the semiotic nature of the relationship between self and object. In this way, the prolonged gaze enables Genazino's protagonists to anchor themselves temporarily in a phenomenological reality. Their perplexing observations are an antidote to the absence of sustained attention in the city environment. Scanning the environment for quirky encounters, Genazino's hero is always on the lookout for unexpected situations that challenge the rationalization of attention, that hallmark of turbo-capitalism. As Georg Franck has argued in two books on the subject, the new digital era is marked by a fundamental shift from the modern economy of exchange towards a new economy of attention where attention itself is a prized good.[42] Of course this does not mean that the ever accelerating circuit of production and consumption is no longer the driver of capitalism. Rather, attention has become a scarce capitalist resource, requiring constant investment and management.

Das Glück in glücksfernen Zeiten adds a new component to the prolonged gaze: here Genazino introduces the notion of the 'Blickkette', which involves more than one social actor. An example occurs at the beginning of the novel

---

[40] Wilhelm Genazino, 'Der gedehnte Blick', in *Der gedehnte Blick* (Frankfurt a.M.: dtv, 2007), pp. 39–61 (p. 42).
[41] Ibid., p. 51.
[42] See Georg Franck, *Ökonomie der Aufmerksamkeit: Ein Entwurf* (Munich: Hanser, 1998); id., *Mentaler Kapitalismus: Eine politische Ökonomie des Geistes* (Munich: Hanser, 2005).

when Warlich discovers a half-eaten piece of cake on the roof of a parked car. As he preoccupies himself with construing various stories about how the owner and his cake might have been separated, a young man arrives on the scene and starts eating the cake. Engaging in further speculation as to whether or not the young man is the rightful cake owner or a possible cake thief, Warlich then realizes that he too is being observed by a fruit vendor who might view him as a potential fruit thief:

> Ich beobachte den Kuchendieb und werde selbst des geplanten Obstdiebstahls beargwöhnt, das heißt ich kann mich in diesen Sekunden als Erfinder einer Blickkette fühlen, die unbekannte Ereignisse miteinander verbindet und mich selber auf unaussprechliche Weise auszeichnet beziehungsweise erhöht beziehungsweise in eine andere Wirklichkeit hineinhebt. (*GigfZ*, p. 13)

The 'Blickkette' between himself, the fruit vendor, and the young man establishes a network of speculative relations and as such a space for imaginary stories that open up both space and time to alternative practice. The 'Blickkette' is a fleeting spatio-temporal constellation that reinstates an extremely fragile cultural connectivity between Warlich and the city environment. As a performance that creates imaginary relations between social actors who do not know each other, it exemplifies Doreen Massey's notion of space as 'a sphere of possibility of the existence of multiplicity'.[43] Furthermore, by equipping a banal observation with such imaginary potential, Warlich re-enacts the *flâneur*'s modern epiphany.

Warlich invests huge hope in such imaginary relations as he takes them as evidence 'daß es hinter der ersten Wirklichkeit eine zweite und eine dritte gibt, an denen ich teilhabe und die ich, so ich Glück habe, irgendwann zu meinem Beruf machen möchte' (*GigfZ*, p. 17). This is of course misleading because it mistakes a particular moment of connectivity for the idea of transcendence. While his ensuing plan to start up his School of Appeasement founders, this humorous episode is exemplary of the subject's longing for happiness in unhappy times. Genazino's humour never belittles his protagonist's various endeavours; rather it accentuates the potential of an eccentric otherness to disrupt habitual modes of perception and patterns of behaviour.

Slowness is the fifth tactic employed by Warlich to protect himself from the culture of speed. As a stigmatized temporality, slowness disrupts an economic performance ideology that aims to close the gap between here and there and now and then in favour of instant delivery. Even though the very idea of slowness is in itself a by-product of a modernity that prioritized an ever faster speed, it can be used tactically to open up a self-conscious space of reflection. And while his strategy of slowing down may look pathetic and defensive, it nevertheless allows Warlich to defy the temporal serfdom of the

[43] Massey, *For Space*, p. 8.

culture of immediacy: 'In der Langsamkeit verarbeite ich, daß ich wenig verstehe und nicht viel Neues kennenlernen möchte. Das Nichtverstehen wird in der Langsamkeit aufbewahrt und die Langsamkeit im Nichtverstehen' (GigfZ, p. 73). By extending the present into a prolonged duration that is divorced from fast-paced activities, slowness strategically disrupts the idea of the right moment, which is an essential part of modern chronopolitics. And so it is that slowness reinstates temporality as a mode of experiencing real presence without any gain or purpose.

The ensemble of Warlich's various tactics aims to rehabilitate the self's *Eigenzeit* by way of a temporal ecology that recovers place as a sphere of possibility. But this recovery requires tremendous performative effort that comes at a price. In the course of the novel Warlich not only loses his job but also his mental health. As a patient of the psychiatric hospital he finally finds an attentive listener in his therapist Dr. Treukirch, who invites Warlich to explore his melancholy disposition. In the protective and slow environment of the clinic Warlich develops a new sense of tranquillity, which is, however, also induced by a cocktail of medication.

Genazino's analysis of the hysterical phase of late capitalism in his poetics lectures resonates with those critics who worry about the erosion of subjectivity in the digital era. Like Rosa, Lübbe, Nowotny, and Gumbrecht, Genazino too considers the transformation of the affective bonds between people and places in an era that embraces what Tomlinson aptly refers to as 'scripts of instant delivery'.[44] Although Genazino is concerned about the conditions of subjectivity in the twenty-first century, he departs from the more dystopian conclusions about the end of human subjectivity. Hartmut Rosa's analysis of late modernity predicts a Spenglerian ending to the modern story of acceleration. In his view, all counter-cultural movements are doomed to failure because they are symptoms of the very condition they attempt to overcome. In contrast, Genazino arrives at a much more measured assessment: as his many essays show, he considers that literature has the capacity to restore interiority and intimacy as essential conditions of cultural connectivity. As a recipient of Genazino's exercises in decelerated particularity, the reader too participates in this programme: reading rescues the precarious conditions of intimacy by suspending the economy of time efficiency; the act of reading mobilizes the play of imagination by immersing the reader in a specifically poetic temporality. While this is perhaps an ontological condition of fiction, there is a further reason why literature can maintain its counter-cultural potential in opposition to the cult of immediacy. The narrative form brings into view the culture of the everyday as a complex web of social interactions, pathways of recognition, and differentiated intensities. As Barbara Adam argues,

[44] Tomlinson, p. 90.

temporality in the human domain inevitably involves 'rhythm with variation, a dynamic structure of framing, timing, synchronization, duration, sequence, tempo and intensity'.[45] In line with this, the Genazinean protagonist traverses uneven temporal geographies in the city that always carry the possibility of disruption. Even though life in the twenty-first century is dominated by the ideology of innovation and immediacy, his heroes manage to experience happiness by taking care of non-consequential moments of connectivity. As Warlich considers the topics of his next therapy session with Dr. Treukirch, he awaits the appearance of a chicken in a courtyard: 'Eine Art Glück durchzittert mich. Offenbar kann ich, trotz allem, immer noch wählen, wie ich in Zukunft leben will' (*GigfZ*, 158).

UNIVERSITY OF WARWICK   ANNE FUCHS

[45] Barbara Adam, *Timewatch: The Social Analysis of Time* (Cambridge: Polity, 1995), p. 17.

EVGENII POPOV: A NEW GOGOL' FOR A NEW RUSSIA?

Evgenii Popov (b. 1946) remains a prolific and socially engaged writer whose work shows both a thematic consistency over the decades and a stylistic and formal innovation bordering on the iconoclastic. He began his literary career very much in the spirit of 'village prose' in his early short stories published in the 1979 samizdat almanac *Metropol'* ('The "baker's dozen"'), and in the collection published in Ann Arbor in 1981 under the title of *Veselie Rusi* (later published in English as *Merry-Making in Old Russia*).[1] Popov has always defined himself within a Russian literary tradition, and his first published works in the Soviet Union in 1976 carried an introduction by his fellow Siberian Vasilii Shukshin, one of the most popular writers of his generation.[2]

Shukshin was Popov's mentor until his death in 1974, and the two share common ground in their depiction of wilful, anarchic male characters at odds with their environment. Shukshin's *chudak* is a hapless, socially disoriented but sympathetic figure whom Popov develops into a much more self-destructive and morally vacant *mudak*, as characterized by Jeremy Morris:

> While the *chudak* was directly concerned with the relationship between self and society within a milieu of civic consciousness, the *mudak* is part of a comprehensive and complex aesthetic and ontological statement by Popov. This is both anti-utopianism, in that it satirizes the possibility of social progress, and utopian, in that it insists on the primacy of art through absurdism and resists the ascription of meaning (and therefore utility) to writing.[3]

The work of Nikolai Gogol' (1809–1852) has been analysed and discussed for decades, and from varying viewpoints. Soviet critics, taking their lead from Belinskii, would lay emphasis on Gogol''s 'social' satire, whereas Westerners delighted in his comic vision and grotesque narratives. In works such as *The Government Inspector* (1836), *The Overcoat* (1842), and the 'poem' *Dead Souls* (1835–52) Gogol' painted a picture of a venal and corrupt government administration indifferent to the lives of ordinary people, with the theme of moral bankruptcy permeating all these works. Gogol' thought of future chapters of *Dead Souls* as pointing to a spiritual regeneration of Russia, though they were never written (or if they were, they were destroyed). Like Gogol', Evgenii Popov lambasts the incongruities and absurdities of life in Russia, though

---

[1] *Metropol'* was edited by Popov and Viktor Erofeev and contained the work of over twenty writers, some of them very eminent, such as Bella Akhmadullina and Vasilii Aksenov. It was published only by Ardis in Ann Arbor in 1979. Evgeny Popov, *Merry-Making in Old Russia*, translated by Robert Porter (London: Harvill Press, 1996).

[2] E. Popov, 'Rasskazy', *Novyi mir*, 1976, no. 4, 164–72 (Shukshin's 'preface' is on p. 164).

[3] Jeremy Morris, 'From *chudak* to *mudak*? Village Prose and the Absurdist Ethics of Evgenii Popov', *MLR*, 99 (2004), 696–710 (p. 703).

unlike Gogol', Popov's anger is mainly provoked by the sufferings of the common man.

Gogol''s work has been celebrated for its gallery of grotesque characters, absurd and seemingly irrelevant digressions, and lacerating satire of legal and bureaucratic institutions. Unlike Popov, he does not generally portray ordinary people (with the exception of Akakii Akakievich in *The Overcoat*) or peasants; rather, the objects of his scorn are venal civil servants, materialistic landowners, and other representatives of the ruling classes. Gogol''s digressions often veer off into the absurd and phantasmagorical, whereas Popov's usually serve to reinforce his own outrage and sense of helplessness at the perceived injustices and social absurdities in the new Russia.

Rather like Venedikt Erofeev and Sergei Dovlatov, writers who similarly did not see eye to eye with the Soviet authorities, Popov's protagonists drink themselves into oblivion because they realize that they cannot do anything to improve their lives. Also like his compatriot Vladimir Sorokin, Popov refuses to acknowledge causality and rationality in post-Soviet society, though he does not go as far as Sorokin's antidote of nihilistic grotesqueness. Popov transforms the world into an absurdist chaos, and resists the writer's marginality in what he consistently refers to as the 'stunted democracy' of the new Russia.[4]

There is a further curious if perhaps fortuitous connection between Popov and Shukshin, as Popov himself has noted. Shukshin's father was arrested by the NKVD in 1933 when he himself was four years old, and, as he subsequently learnt, was shot in 1942. Shukshin never discovered the reason behind his father's arrest, though it may have been connected with 'wrecking' the village technical hardware, a common charge in those years. His mother then changed the family's surname to her own maiden name: Popov. She later remarried. Shukshin bore this surname until he was sixteen years old, when he received his passport and insisted it bore his father's name. His childhood spent with his stepfather lies at the basis of his 1968 cycle of short stories *Iz detskikh let Ivana Popova* (*From the Childhood Years of Ivan Popov*). Ivan Popov was the name of Shukshin's second cousin.[5] Popov, indeed, is Shukshin's ebullient, salacious, and scabrous alter ego.

After Popov began to be published again in his native country during Gorbachev's glasnost, he turned away from the third-person narratives of the socially abrasive short stories published in *Metropol'* and the *Veselie Rusi*

---

[4] David Gillespie, 'Evgenii Popov and the Satire of Collapse: The "I" of the Narrator', in *Uncensored? Reinventing Humor and Satire in Post-Soviet Russia*, ed. by Seth Graham and Olga Mesropova (Bloomington, IN: Slavica, 2008), pp. 27–39.

[5] E. Popov, 'Khorosho, chto vy s nami: k iubileiu Vasiliia Aksenova', *Oktiabr'*, 2007, no. 7, 122–53; V. Shukshin, 'Ia rodom iz derevni…', in Shukshin, *Sobranie sochinenii v shesti tomakh*, I (Moscow, Nadezhda-I, 1998), pp. 5–6, 500–01.

collection, and embraced a first-person narrative which consistently expresses the views, feelings, experiences, and more often than not the moral outrage of the author himself. The hero may be called Ferfichkin, Gdov, or Bezobrazov, but the moral standpoint is always that of Evgenii Anatol'evich Popov (not least because they all share features of Popov's own biography).

Popov's cast of characters in his glasnost period includes many of his own friends, such as Dmitrii Prigov, Viktor Erofeev, and Bella Akhmadulina (in *Dusha patriota*), or Roman Solntsev in later works. His choice of genre self-consciously foregrounds the false solemnity of Soviet official language while simultaneously debunking it, as in his reproduction of press statements, imbued with a knowing sarcasm and often to hilarious effect, in *Prekrasnost' zhizni* (*The Beauty of Life*, 1990). In the early post-Soviet years Popov uses his own 'I' as a position of cultural and moral authority from which to attack the lies and crimes of Russian history, where his stance as a formerly repressed writer comes to take second place to that of an angry, socially committed polemicist. In these first-person narratives he seeks to satirize the 'stunted' democracy ('neokrepshaia demokratiia') post-1991, with particular criticism of the suffering of ordinary people. Both his novels *Podlinnaia istoriia 'zelenykh muzykantov'* (*The Real Story of the 'Green Musicians'*, 1999) and *Master Khaos* (*Master Chaos*, 2002) are prime examples of Popov's self-appointed right to mock, judge, and condemn society's failings by affirming his own moral superiority as a writer, a stance squarely within the classical Russian tradition as demonstrated by Nikolai Gogol' two centuries previously.

Parody, satire, and laughter are never far from the surface of *Prekrasnost' zhizni*, bearing the subheading 'chapters from a novel with a newspaper, which will never be begun or finished', and composed essentially of a mammoth series of newspaper clippings and stories. Not only is the cumulative effect to demonstrate the mendaciousness and false optimism generated by the Soviet media, but also, through retrospective irony and a knowing sarcasm, to show clearly the impoverishment and ultimate corruption of the Russian language. Soviet officialese becomes the medium for peddling lies or at best half-truths, and for wrapping all citizens in a cocoon of illusion. Sorokin, too, castigates the falsity of official discourse, but Popov alleviates his harsh sarcasm with humour and knowing irony.

On the one hand *Prekrasnost' zhizni* is a work of prodigious labour, containing as it does over 400 pages of assorted headlines and quotations from newspapers (some penned by a certain E. Popov!), doggerel verse by 'official' poets such as Sergei Mikhalkov, author of the lines of both the Soviet and post-Soviet national anthems—who, along with Iurii Bondarev, comes in for particularly sarcastic treatment—and stories and anecdotes, all relating to the development of Soviet society from the early 1960s to 1985. Topics covered include the Soviet Union's internal politics, relations with foreign powers, and the country's literary and artistic development. Events reported and discussed in the Soviet media thus include the following: Iurii Gagarin's flight into space in 1961; the Cuban missile crisis of 1962; Khrushchev's removal from power in 1964; the trial of Andrei Siniavskii and Iulii Daniel' in 1966; the 'fraternal assistance' accorded by the Soviet Union and its Warsaw Pact allies to Czechoslovakia in 1968; Solzhenitsyn's expulsion from the USSR in 1974; Feliks Kuznetsov's fulminations against the 'pornographic' *Metropol'* of 1979 (a favourite butt for Popov's sarcasm); the Afghan government's 'request for urgent political, moral and economic assistance, including military aid' in that same year; the Moscow Olympics and the death of Vladimir Vysotskii in 1980; the collapse of the Soviet 'gerontocracy' in the early 1980s, the coming to power of Mikhail Gorbachev, and the beginning of the end of a hated and bankrupt system.

A defining feature of Popov's narrative is that it covers history as it has affected individuals and societies, ignoring such abstractions as international relations, meetings of world leaders, or international agreements, or even the space and arms races. Popov's history is that of a people's suffering and betrayal by successive generations of Russian leaders, history as experienced by the many, let down and exploited by the few.

Of particular curiosity value today are the indulgent references to young and then unknown writers of the 1960s, such as Eduard Topol', Valentin Rasputin, Fridrikh Gorenshtein, and Vladimir Voinovich. Nevertheless, given the time when it was written (1987) and published (1990), life in the Soviet Union was anything but 'splendid', and Popov's novel reads today as a sustained ironic tirade against the falsity and mendacity of the dying Soviet regime.[6]

Literature and the nature of artistic creativity are the subject of much of Popov's work: his 1993 novel *Nakanune nakanune* (*On the Eve of On the Eve*) plays obviously with Turgenev. *Podlinnaia istoriia 'zelenykh muzykantov'* offers a postmodernist wink at the audience and resembles a metafictional exercise in literary one-upmanship. The reference in the title is to a popular children's cartoon based on a fairy tale, and in his own foreword Popov acknowledges that the work is akin to a fairy tale. He takes a children's story and in very adult terms uses it to attack all things Soviet and totalitarian, peeling away the illusion and artifice to expose the 'real story'. Through the prism of his own experience and subjective reflections, the author uses the act of

---

[6] Robert Porter notes that 'when the book was published in 1990 its title could hardly have been more ironic [. . .] official life had itself become a parody of reality' (*Russia's Alternative Prose* (Oxford: Berg, 1994), p. 134). Deming Brown agrees: 'Popov lets his mosaic of historic facts speak for itself, but it is so arranged that the ironies are inescapable: in a culture of mass deceit even good men become subtly corrupted, without realizing it. The ultimate irony of the work is the title itself' (*The Last Years of Soviet Literature: Prose Fiction 1975-1991* (Cambridge: Cambridge University Press, 1993), p. 162).

writing as both a warning and a lament: 'For young people, on the one hand, to be proud of their fathers and, on the other, to avoid their mistakes and sufferings.'⁷

In *Podlinnaia istoriia* the focus is not so much the iniquities of the Soviet regime, although they get their customary lambasting, but the struggles of Ivan Ivanych, a budding writer with more than a hint of Popov in him, to get his work published in the USSR. The work is structured in two parts: the first a purportedly accurate account of Ivan Ivanych's struggles with the censorship and literary bureaucracy, the second, and much longer, a series of footnotes that expand on the text, digress and fulminate, and generally provide a supposed factual background. With this dual structure the work obviously follows in the footsteps of Vladimir Nabokov's *Pale Fire* (1962), which consists of a poem followed by detailed commentary containing all sorts of word games and extratextual literary illusions.⁸ It is an artistic strategy to which Popov returns in his novel *@rbeit* (2012).

Popov's primary text justifies, in suitably ironic terms, Ivan Ivanych's acceptance into the literary brotherhood, his increasing conformity, and eventual descent into mediocrity, thus offering a mirror image of the trajectory of the archetypical Soviet literary career, as well as perhaps an ironically wistful reflection on what Popov himself might have become had he followed what were then the rules of the game.

At first this career follows the classic model of the young dissident writer: expulsion from higher education, work as night watchman, then taken down a peg or two by a world-weary journalist:

> The point is, old man, that essentially you are a greenhouse plant. A mimosa. Do you remember the children's rhyme? A mimosa. After all, in practical terms you have not experienced *anything* in life. You've always had a roof over your head, you've never gone hungry. I am right, aren't I? Not *anything*, not the terrible alcoholism that sucks away your energy every day, nor debauchery, nor horrendous relationships that end with your face getting slapped, hysterics, and vein-cutting... (pp. 41–42)

The commentary, however, subverts this self-serving narrative, and is obviously the work of the sarcastic and unforgiving author himself. The commentary, as with Nabokov's novel, expands the world of its 'literary' space

---

⁷ Evgenii Popov, *Podlinnaia istoriia 'zelenykh muzykantov'* (Moscow: Vagrius, 1999), p. 7.

⁸ In her introductory essay to the first edition of *Pale Fire* in 1962, Mary McCarthy uses terms that can be similarly applied to Popov's novel: 'When the separate parts are assembled, according to the manufacturer's directions, and fitted together with the help of clues and cross-references, which must be hunted down as in a paper-chase, a novel on several levels is revealed, and these "levels" are not the customary "levels of meaning" of modernist criticism but planes in a fictive space, rather like those houses of memory in medieval mnemonic science, where words, facts, and numbers were stored till wanted in various rooms and attics, or like the Houses of astrology into which the heavens are divided' ('A Bolt from the Blue', in Vladimir Nabokov, *Pale Fire* (Harmondsworth: Penguin, 1991), pp. v–xxii (p. v)).

with what is presented as 'truth'. Fiction and fact coexist, and one cannot do without the other. As footnote 142 explains, fact and reality, and the Soviet literary representation of that reality, are not necessarily the same thing: 'Reality was indeed nonsense. Therefore only the ABSURD is entitled to claim the title of SOCIALIST REALISM, because many other works by so-called SOVIET WRITERS are sheer fantasy' (pp. 102–03). Footnote 257 begins with a semi-frivolous literary anecdote, but ends by offering a devastating critique of a society governed by lies and secrecy, complete with a metafictional allusion to one of the key texts of Socialist realism:

The 'intelligentsia' liked to scare girls just as badly as Party officials! There is a novella by Roman Solntsev which has a scene where some 'poets' on a train journey scare the girls by deliberately speaking nonsense, and waving around fake knives covered in red ink for poetic effect. While some scared them, others screwed them.

They shouldn't have been scaring the girls, but bringing to the people the light of anti-Soviet agitation and propaganda. For instance, about the Kyshtym disaster in the Urals, when the red swine allowed a radioactive leak but did not bother to inform the local population, who ate the contaminated fish and poisoned mushrooms and slowly died out.

A relative of mine, Boris Baranov, the husband of my elder sister Natasha and an army officer, did his officer training in the late 1950s and did his 'radioactivity practice' in these parts. The 'zone' there was worse than in Tarkovskii's film *Stalker*. The marsh was divided into two parts by a high dam. One step to the right or left of the dam and you were lethally exposed. Also sprach Zarathustra, that is how the steel was tempered. (p. 149)

Just as the author purports to tell the truth behind the fairy tale of the title, so he sets out to strip away from Soviet society the veneer of respectability, to debunk its pomposity, hypocrisy, and lies, and to highlight the brutality and contempt with which it treated its citizens.[9] Half-literary anecdote and half-political criticism, *Podlinnaia istoriia* progresses within accepted narrative models and ends on a Pasternakian note of hope for the world, including a nod to the 'happy-ever-after' morality of the fairy tale (footnote 885):

True reality, given to us by God, lies not at all in the vanity of this world, but in the good word, in the vague attempt to gain brotherhood, love, and forgiveness, vanquishing the bitterness of one's isolation amid the crowd and thus overcoming death. The earth has long been inhabited and we are all fellow citizens on it, and thus let us stand in dignity

---

[9] Ingunn Lunde argues that Popov's novel above all 'reflects, and reflects on, the language question in post-perestroika Russia': 'Popov's commentary displays a strong dislike of clichés, stereotypes and conventionalisms. He dismantles dead thinking and dead language, dethrones grand subjects, attacking them through derision and satire. He exposes nonsense and meaninglessness, subtly alluding to the relevance and necessity of this critique today' ('Footnotes of a Graphomaniac: The Language Question in Evgenii Popov's *The True Story of "The Green Musicians"*', *Russian Review*, 68 (2009), 70–88 (p. 87)). On the novel's synthesis of style and theme see E. E. Barinova, 'Metatekst v romane E. Popova *Podlinnaia istoriia "zelenykh muzykantov"*', *Filologiia i chelovek* (Barnaul), 2007, no. 2, 102–10.

not before the Lord, who is our good Father and loves us all, but before cold and aloof Chaos, which is undoubtedly hostile to us, as is any lack of clarity in life. Our world is full of secret harmony, and we will gradually dissolve in it, as a corpse dissolves in the graveyard earth, but this will not be a death and an end, because neither death nor the end exists, and we will all be happy—who said that we should be unhappy? And—young people, children, don't be afraid of anything. Be calm. The evil giants have departed and will never return. Everything is in order. Life goes on. Life is eternal. We will all be saved. (pp. 343–44)

It is no surprise that Chaos raises its ugly head in Popov's next novel, and indeed, features in its very title. *Master Khaos* is another exercise in first-person narrative that attempts to describe and analyse the collapse of the Soviet Union and Communist-controlled Eastern Europe. It was first published in the monthly journal *Oktiabr'* in 2002, and appeared in a separate book edition shortly afterwards. It is described by the author as an 'open multiagent literary system with an afterword by an academic' ('otkrytaia mul′tiagentnaia literaturnaia sistema s poslesloviem uchenogo cheloveka'), and this knowing semi-parodic and pseudo-scientific designation fully corresponds to the tongue-in-cheek style and content of the work. *Master Khaos* is a deliriously disorganized trawl through the travails of Russian and Soviet history, with ironic asides and occasionally impassioned polemics against Bolshevik excesses and injustices. It is narrated both in the first person and through the eyes of the fictional cypher Bezobrazov and his views on Russia's post-Soviet 'stunted democracy', a phrase that comes to symbolize the failure of Russia's political establishment to deliver Western-style prosperity or even stability.

Some pages seem totally disconnected from the narrative, such as towards the end of Chapter 1, where just about every country in the world (apart from Scotland and Wales) is placed in alphabetical order, from Australia to Japan. There is no explanation, no linking words or even conjunctions, simply a list. Elsewhere there is the typical criticism of the Bolsheviks, where for Popov politico-economic matters are just as important as the deeply personal:

Bolshevism reduced our society not only to economic, moral, and political disaster, but sexual, too. Instead of the purported rosy-cheeked, broad-shouldered, but moronic builder of Communism, there appeared a screwed-up creature suffering from all the thinkable and unthinkable complexes.[10]

But the Bolshevik 'moron' nevertheless waged sadistic war on the people, as Popov recounts in a single sentence that lasts almost a whole page (this is a reduced extract):

The Chekist Peters, transferred to Moscow, drowned the city in blood, and among his servants there were Chinese and one Negro, whose speciality was to draw out the veins from people's bodies, in Vologda the hatchet-man Kedrov committed many atrocities,

[10] Evgenii Popov, *Master Khaos* (Moscow: MK-Periodika, 2002), p. 129.

in Voronezh people were put into nail-studded barrels which were then rolled down a hill, in Nikolaev people were bricked up in walls, in Orel eyes were poked out or Soviet stars cut into their foreheads or chests, people were thrown into vats of boiling water, joints were broken, skin peeled off, molten tin poured down throats, in Pskov the Chinese sawed 200 captured officers into pieces, in Poltava the Chekist Grishka savagely executed 18 monks by having them impaled on a spike, a method also used by the Chekists of Iamburg, in Blagoveshchensk they drove gramophone needles under people's fingernails, in Omsk they tortured pregnant women, cut open stomachs, and dragged out the intestines.[11]

Popov's history is also told through the soundbites of selected newspaper headlines and clippings, personal anecdote, and occasional satirical aside; it therefore has much in common with *Prekrasnost' zhizni*. The following is a typical example of a potted history of the last twenty years or so of Soviet power:

So it happened that perestroika came and went. The Communists organized a coup, as it happened, and they were tried then released with honour. There was one Chechen war, then another. In Russia there was freedom and McDonalds. Russia was again awash with money, but not for everyone and not for the country, which had learnt to be much smarter in its cap-in-hand begging than under Len'ka Brezhnev. Russia is now a very cheerful place, every day something happens.[12]

Master Khaos is a seemingly random and disorganized collection of thoughts and clippings on Russian and East European political history, but governed by a sharply critical intelligence that all the time laments the human cost. In the 1990s, for instance, the currency becomes devalued and democracy, in the eyes of many Russians, becomes synonymous with banditry and penury, as in fact happened. Political leaders are castigated, and Popov's favourite stylistic device of repetition adds an extra layer of irony to the narrative. The final few pages recount all manner of accidents and natural disasters, but such elemental and seemingly unavoidable chaos is nothing compared to the man-made kind that Russia has suffered under the Bolsheviks.

Literature, its importance to the Russian national psyche, and the nature of artistic creativity become increasingly the subject of much of Popov's work: apart from *Nakanune nakanune*, his collection *Opera nishchikh* (*The Beggars' Opera*, 2006) self-consciously references John Gay's 1728 satirical ballad of that name. Gay's work ridiculed the high and mighty of his day, showing how society is riddled with crime and vice from top to bottom. Popov pointedly shows how greed and corruption are as pernicious and widespread in late twentieth-century Russia as they were in early eighteenth-century England.

Scholars have noted Popov's reliance on literary traditions, be it those of Russian folklore, the Russian classics, or more contemporary trends.

[11] Ibid., pp. 231–32.
[12] Ibid., p. 28.

Alexandre Dumas, Ivan Turgenev, and Boris Pil'niak are all alluded to in the titles of works from the 1990s, and Popov's deliberate mimicry of literary models (the folk tale or Nabokov, for instance) foregrounds the literary paradigm as a means of passing judgement on the 'brave new world' post-1991.

Popov's abandonment of third-person narrative for first-person polemics in *Master Khaos* is indicative of a much more deeply felt concern. In his post-Soviet works, many of which touch on personal issues such as the breakdown of relationships, the author essentially abandons all literary pretence and lays himself bare before the reader. Banality becomes a signifier of dislocation, as in the following reflection: 'I had an urge for some watery Soviet beer in the grimy café "Café" of the stagnation period, when the whole country, worn down by totalitarianism, languished under the yoke of tyranny, waiting only for FREEDOM.'[13] Elsewhere the proliferation of cars is not a signifier of the wealth of the population newly liberated from this tyranny, but the cause of interminable traffic jams on Leningradskii prospekt in Moscow, showing that 'the future is dark, misty, completely undefined' (p. 45).

The work 'Krestovozdvizhenskii: vybrannye mesta iz perepiski Gdova i Khabarova' ('Krestovozdvizhenskii [lit. "he who raises the cross"]: Selected Passages from the Correspondence of Gdov and Khabarov'), published in 2007, is a tour de force of impassioned social commentary, scatological humour, and stream-of-consciousness narrative, whose common themes are the vileness of the recent Soviet past and the moral and material impoverishment of the nation since. Khabarov may be one of Popov's literary alter egos, but here he has another string to his bow: he also represents the ingrained chauvinism and anti-Semitism of the lumpenproletariat, who like their vodka and their *Rodina* but who hate the intelligentsia. He also (like Popov) has nothing but contempt for contemporary culture, beloved of the new 'slobs' (*bydlo*), and the work ends with an assertion of Russia's essence: despite the poverty and the cruelty, the 'eternal themes' of Russia are really thievery, drunkenness, and fornication: the merrymaking of old Russia lives on and thrives today. In a recent celebration of the bicentennial of Gogol''s death, Popov raged against the injustices visited since the writer's death on Russians 'who have perished from the inhuman conditions of life, duped and debauched to the marrows of their bones, and who have destroyed their own beautiful land through feckless projects to transform everything and anything for the sake of acquiring something unknown'. Given the scale of the crimes in Russia today, Chichikov's misdemeanours look like 'innocent horseplay' (*bezvinnaia shalost'*), for which, if he were alive today, 'at worst

---

[13] E. Popov, 'Krestovozdvizhenskii: vybrannye mesta iz perepiski Gdova i Khabarova', *Znamia*, 2007, no. 1, 38–65 (p. 42).

he would receive a suspended sentence and probably escape punishment altogether'.[14]

Popov's heart may be on his sleeve, but his pen remains dipped in poison for those who have let down the Russian people. His literary alter egos Gdov and Bezobrazov are reduced to a bemused helplessness as they ponder the market realities of the new Russia. Popov constructs his satire and parody through an extra-literary space between the reported fact and the words used to report it, a space that alerts the reader to the falseness of authoritarian discourse, and shows how language can be used as a tool for suppression. This, of course, was the favoured medium of satirists under the Soviet regime, Popov included, but Popov's post-Soviet emotive, highly personal discourse attempts to replace the 'truth' of authoritative narrative with the truth of the individual story. If during the Soviet period it was writers and artists who suffered materially for their nonconformism, since the collapse of that regime it is the common man who faces the 'beastly snarl of Capitalism'.[15]

Popov's works since 2000 offer an increasingly grim and ironic account of life for the ordinary Russian since the collapse of the Soviet Union, as well as the customary angry condemnation of the iniquities of Soviet history. Chaos threatens here not only in the subject-matter, the near-collapse of Russia in the 1990s, but also in the language and syntax of the narrative. History may be to blame, but in *Master Khaos* hope can be found in the symbol of Gotland, the Swedish island that has been bypassed by the major cataclysms of twentieth-century history and, more importantly, by Russians.

Popov's satire in *Master Khaos* embraces radical social commentary, and his first-person narrator bemoans the pauperization of the 'new' Russia, where people survive on $20 per month and resort to thievery and crime. As he travels from St Petersburg to Moscow, he compares his own picture of an impoverished nation with that drawn by the radical writer Alexander Radishchev two centuries earlier, self-consciously using a historico-literary framework for ironic comment on the state of his nation.

Language for Popov retains a singular importance, for although it can be used to deceive and betray, it also provides a link with the culture of the past, and the hopes of freedom in the future. He is a master of the Russian sentence, where the use of participles and gerunds produces effects of both linguistic dexterity and political irony. Popov has excelled in compiling whole books of official (Soviet) sayings, slogans, bureaucratic waffle, and journalistic inanities. Even in his shorter pieces long sentences, sometimes a paragraph long, with subordinate and relative clauses and a confusing multitude of gerunds and participles, convey in a stream-of-consciousness narrative historical

[14] 'Gogol': real'nost' voobrazheniia', *Znamia*, 2009, no. 4, 163–77 (pp. 171–72). Chichikov is the 'hero' of Gogol''s *Dead Souls*.
[15] E. Popov, 'Oskal', *Oktiabr'*, 2008, no. 1, 105–14 (p. 106).

events, personalities, more contemporary developments, and the author's own feelings or thoughts. This often deliriously convoluted and exuberant delivery is frequently made up of foreign words (usually English), slang, references to popular culture, and comically distorted officialese of both the Soviet and post-Soviet administrations. Humour, above all, is not forgotten amid the harsh polemical tone.

The short story 'Virtual'naia real'nost'' ('Virtual Reality') begins with Gdov reflecting on the artist Vladimir Boer, his compatriot, who lived

в слободе 3-его Интернационала, на улице Лагерной, где держали коров, население которой хоть и нечетко, но все же делилось на сидевших и сажавших, проживших длинную поучительную жизнь, неоднократно менявшихся местами.[16]

in the settlement of the 3rd International, on Camp Street, where they kept cows, the population of which, though strictly delineated, were divided into those who had been inside and those who had put them there, who had lived long instructive lives and several times had changed places.

Popov uses language as both weapon and instrument, recording and expressing pain, injustice, and the humour required to continue the struggle with everyday reality.

Popov's linguistic dexterity can turn the tables on past and present, as in his 2005 article engagingly entitled 'Russkaia literatura luchshe, chem seks' ('Russian literature is better than sex'):

Previously Soviet propaganda would harp on about the recurrent killings, robberies, thievery, and persecution of the workers, about the drugs trade and rock-'n'-roll dancing. Therefore, Russians were sure that paradise existed over there. In the imagination of many of the Western media in our country today there are recurrent killings, robberies, thievery, and persecution of the workers, drugs are sold, monuments are erected to bandits, and people dance the *kazachok*.[17]

In this article Popov affirms the power of the Russian writer over his political environment, though he accepts it remains a 'mystery' why the Soviet regime not only could not destroy Russian literature, but actually strengthened its greatest exponents: Pasternak, Akhmatova, Bulgakov, Zoshchenko, Maiakovskii, Platonov, Solzhenitsyn, and Sholokhov.

Popov/Khabarov/Gdov can transform the most banal, everyday problem into a symbol of universal chaos. Thus, in the short story 'Starik i skvazhina' ('The Old Man and the Well') Gdov's inability to extract water from the well at his country dacha becomes a metaphor for his (and Popov's) inability to deal with the modern world: 'Even water that looks horrible does not flow from the well, despite my titanic efforts. I cry. But why bother crying, if it's too

[16] Evgenii Popov, 'Virtual'naia real'nost'', in *Opera nishchikh: rasskazy o neponiatnom, besedy, sluchai* (Moscow: Vagrius, 2006), pp. 13–23 (p. 13).

[17] E. Popov, 'Russkaia literatura luchshe, chem seks', *Oktiabr'*, 2005, no. 6, 135–38 (p. 135).

late to cry?'[18] In the short story 'Pritornyi ad' ('Sickly Hell') Khabarov enters a public toilet and sees the words 'fuck off' scribbled on the wall, prompting him to reflect that this 'undoubtedly confirms that the new Russia has moved a long way forwards, at least in the learning of foreign languages'.[19]

There is no doubt, though, that Popov, through his various literary incarnations, expresses the fears and disillusionment of both the intelligentsia and the ordinary people over the dashed hopes of post-Soviet Russia. There is even a nostalgic whimsy for a more innocent past, as in the 2008 short story 'Oskal' ('The Snarl'), the title expressing the ferocity of the new capitalism and its contempt for the ordinary citizen. The writer Gdov, sitting in a restaurant with his friend Khabarov, surrounded by a cornucopia of wines, cheeses, and fish and meat dishes, all of them way beyond the means of the average Russian, notes that 'these days everything, of course, is not the same, [. . .] the beauty of life has been replaced by universal human progress'.[20] Gdov recounts a story from twenty-eight years previously when he was on a bus whose passengers were suddenly seized by a collective sexual mania, leading to the eventual crash of the bus, from which only Gdov emerges unscathed. Being the only one not at the mercy of an animal-like lust, Gdov is set upon by the others just before the crash takes place. His only defence is in his assertion of basic humanity: 'We are after all human beings. We have to abide by certain laws, or progress will stop. [. . .] My dear citizens! I don't want to turn into an animal and lose my human face.'[21] Elsewhere the sexual act is absurd, usually demeaning, and used solely for physical gratification (especially by women).[22]

Post-Soviet Popov remains upbeat, though, on the resourcefulness and durability of his native Siberians, a stance he shares with Shukshin and another Siberian 'patriot' Valentin Rasputin (b. 1937), although it is unlikely that he and the latter share any other political or cultural views. In the sketch 'Sibir'' ('Siberia', coincidentally also the title of a work by Rasputin) he recalls his own youth in Krasnoiarsk, and how he got to know a Hungarian who had spent more than fifteen years in the Gulag, remained in Siberia after his release, and became 'simply a Siberian peasant'. This spurs him on to the reflection that in Siberia 'any peasant can often have a biography worthy of the pen of Alexandre Dumas-*père*, creator of the Count of Monte Cristo'.[23] Siberia is remarkable not so much in its reserves of natural resources as in the

---

[18] Evgenii Popov, 'Starik i skvazhina', in *Opera nishchikh*, pp. 59–84 (p. 83).

[19] Evgenii Popov, 'Pritornyi ad', in *Opera nishchikh*, pp. 94–113 (p. 106).

[20] 'Oskal', p. 106.

[21] Ibid., p. 113.

[22] Sex in public and even in the snow holds a peculiar attraction: see, for instance, the story 'Tainstvennaia krysa, ili Potselui na moroze' ('The Mysterious Rat; or, A Kiss in the Frost'), *Znamia*, 2011, no. 2, 96–103, and Chapter XIII of *@rbeit* (entitled, significantly, '"Vse moe" — skazala Zlata' ('"Everything is mine", said Zlata')).

[23] E. Popov, 'Sibir'', *Oktiabr'*, 2005, no. 12, 68–74 (p. 71).

fact that 'people here can mysteriously turn the minuses of life into pluses' (p. 73). He illustrates the strength of Siberia with the story of a village of Old Believers who had no electricity, did not drink, prospered by selling various local foodstuffs to tourists, and used stainless steel from cosmic jetsam to make their shovels, axes, and ploughs.

In March 2007 Popov began writing an interactive Internet blog, his 'live journal', inviting comments from readers on issues of the day. It remains active, and its archive and readers' responses run to thousands of pages.[24] In 2012 Popov published @rbeit: shirokoe polotno, based on this blog, which continues his attacks on the Soviet Union and its vestiges in the post-Soviet present, as well as the corruption of the present. It is structured in two parts: his own musings, or rather those of 'the writer Gdov', then questions on the text as in a school textbook. Part Two consists of readers' responses and questions, and Popov ends the book with a 'thank you' to all his correspondents. The enterprise is indeed new to Russian literature, whereby the writer actively engages in an interaction with his reading public, seeking both approval and consensus.

The forty-four chapters, or scenarios, of Part One all follow the same pattern: the writer Gdov sits down to write a 'broad canvas' of some aspect of Russian life or history, then becomes so 'emotionally agitated' that he is unable to work further. Thus, in Chapter XLI he considers Russia's 'special path', and the author then asks 'Does Russia have a special path?', and if so what is it?[25] To which he receives the following replies: 'Russia's special path lies in its constant search for that special path', 'If Russia has a special path, then any other country also has'.[26] Popov's penultimate question to his audience is 'Do people live correctly?', which elicits the reply 'God, what rubbish!'[27]

It remains to be said that Popov's work may attack and discredit a lost world, and lament the injustices of the new, but it still foregrounds the absurd as the one unchanging aspect of Russian life through the decades and centuries. His work remains quintessentially Russian in its affirmation of the unique place of the writer and the written word, and the conflation of the individual and collective experience as valid autobiography, or what has become known as 'life writing'. In true Gogolian tradition, he lambasts the corrupt and laughs at absurdity, and his work is imbued with a social conscience. Through the power of the word Popov seeks to cauterize the social wounds and address historical injustice.

Popov as a post-Soviet writer is more than a grumpy old man railing against the iniquities of society and life, such as the 'kitsch', 'trash', and '*popsa*' (tri-

---

[24] <http://evgpopov.livejournal.com>.
[25] Evgenii Popov, *@rbeit: shirokoe polotno, Internet-roman* (Moscow: Astrel', 2012), p. 165.
[26] Ibid., p. 548.
[27] *@rbeit*, pp. 181, 562.

vial pop culture) of the modern age; rather, he is very much an angry old man aware that he has little in common with the new Russia. Popov remains a satirical, and often very funny, writer, but in a country, as he says, that is without good-natured, instinctive humour or jokes, 'bez khokhm'. But no matter how bad things are, Popov assures us, two things will always remain in Russia: people will always read books and drink vodka.[28]

Epithets consistently used to characterize the work and personality of Nikolai Gogol' are 'contradictory', 'perplexing', and 'enigmatic'. It is commonly accepted that Gogol''s social criticism is an externalization of his battle with his inner demons, as Richard Peace explains with reference to *Dead Souls*:

It has acute significance for Gogol both as artist and man; for [. . .] he subjectivizes reality, so that in depicting the external world, he is to a large extent describing himself. In this process the device of inversion plays an important role: the neuroses, perversions, anxieties which Gogol feels within himself are projected onto the external world so that they may be purged through mockery. It is as though Gogol is saying: 'it is not I who am odd, it is the world that is odd'. In this way his writing brings personal reassurance. Gogol, critical of himself, appeared to be critical of external reality, and so it came about that his works were interpreted as an indictment of Russian society and its values. Indeed, for Gogol to see the world as odd he needed corroborative evidence of the incompetence, abuses, and injustices of the real world itself.[29]

While there is no evidence of Popov's 'neuroses, perversions, anxieties', he too externalizes his anger and indignation. As Zsuzsanna Kalafatics says, his 'laughter reveals the simulacra of habitual concepts and relationships and exposes the intricate connections between phenomena and things, that is, the absurdity of Soviet life'.[30] The 'absurdity of Soviet life' is now replaced by the grotesqueness of post-Soviet corruption, inequality, and lawlessness, 'the ambivalent Russian ugliness [*bezobrAziia*] (and maybe shapelessness) [*bezObraziia*] that by the beginning of the third millennium had reached cosmic proportions'.[31]

Popov's own experience and thoughts, or those of his ciphers, are paramount: they express the truth of the age, and attack its injustices and absurdity. Modern society has lost its moral foundation, its culture, its ability to laugh out loud. Literature is impotent in that it cannot put right the wrongs of

---

[28] 'Russkaia literatura luchshe, chem seks', p. 136.
[29] Richard Peace, *The Enigma of Gogol: An Examination of the Writings of N. V. Gogol and their Place in the Russian Literary Tradition* (Cambridge, Cambridge University Press, 1981), pp. 293–94.
[30] Zsuzsanna Kalafatics, '"Pushkin i Gogol' — vot istinno dvuglavyi orel": Postmodernistkaia interpretatsiia gogolevskoi traditsii v proze E. Popova', in *Gogol' i 20 vek: materialy mezhdunarodnoi konferentsii, organizovannoi doktorskoi programmoi ELTE 'Russkaia literature i kul'tura mezhdu Vostokom i Zapadom'*, ed. by Zsuzsa Hetényi (Budapest: Dolce Filologia VIII, 2010), pp. 122–31 (p. 125).
[31] 'Gogol': real'nost voobrazheniia', p. 171.

history, but it remains important as the only means of expressing despair and disgust. But literature, the written word, is also important in that it shows very clearly how he, Gdov, Bezobrazov, and others have become marginalized by the new market realities, a denigration clearly seen as a betrayal of fundamentally Russian cultural values. These values remain sacrosanct, because, as he says towards the end of 'Oskal', only the writer retained his humanity during the Soviet period, a humanity that is threatened by the material indulgence of the new Russia but which still (barely) survives.

In his public utterances Popov names Vladimir Voinovich and Vasilii Aksenov as paragons of 'freedom' during the dark days of Soviet repression, but his strongest endorsement is for the role of the literary journal:

> I think that the role of the literary journals has only increased, because for many Russian intellectuals they are the only means of escaping the savagery and forced head-first immersion into this brave new world [. . .]. In this eroded world, where all kinds of *popsa* rule, literary journals are the solid ground that has clear professional and moral outlines.[32]

As culture and the values of humanism associated with it are increasingly threatened and marginalized in the new Russia, Evgenii Popov's highly personalized narrative remains a beacon of cultural authority, a lament for the loss of past certainties, and an uncertain voice in an uncertain present. Like Nikolai Gogol' in the nineteenth century, Popov exposes the 'real' Russia: a country of brutality, indifference, and grotesque absurdity. In Popov's writings and reflections on Russia's 'stunted democracy', it is not difficult to hear an echo of Gogol''s famous metaphor and question from the end of *Dead Souls*:

Не так ли и ты, Русь, что бойкая необгонимая тройка несешься?... Русь, куда же несешься ты? Дай ответ. Не дает ответа.[33]

And are you, Russia, not like the nimble fleet-footed troika that tears forward?... Russia, where are you heading? Give an answer. It does not give an answer.

UNIVERSITY OF BATH DAVID GILLESPIE

[32] 'Literaturnye zhurnaly: chto zavtra?', *Znamia*, 2008, no. 1, 191–205 (Popov's contribution, p. 201).
[33] Nikolai Gogol', *Mertvye dushi*, in N. Gogol', *Povesti. Mertvye dushi* (Moscow, Ast-Olimp, 1996), pp. 529–30.

THESAURUS OF THE UNSPEAKABLE: *THANATOPRAXIS* IN KHARKIV'S TALES OF TRAUMA

> One cannot prove anything. One can only show it. One can only flare up with it. One can only believe it. One can only be forced to believe it.
>
> (Iurii Tsaplin)[1]

One wintry night, walking home from a knight-themed party, three merry young men with swords come across a white statue in a cold dark park. They dare each other to behead it, and after much effort, on the fifth blow, one succeeds. As his drunken friends celebrate the statue's demise, the decapitator suddenly falls to his knees, vomiting violently. The dotingly picturesque description of this abrupt physical reaction, along with its sound effects ('He gagged, then rattled, and snowflakes melted in his hoarse breath'), constitutes the most vivid part of a tiny, 150-word story 'Briug' (1996) by Kharkiv writer Iurii Tsaplin.[2] Its close but decontextualized snapshots of distress, such as snow vanishing in the nausea-infused breath of the statue's executioner, are an example of an intriguing trend in contemporary Ukrainian literature.

This trend, found primarily among the younger generation of writers, consists of detailed but fragmentary references to violence that explicitly lacks any definitive explanation or setting. 'Briug' tells us about the attributes of the asphalt below our perpetrator, for instance, but mentions nothing of the streets surrounding this scene. It also steers clear of omniscient third-person glances at internal monologues. Rather, it works more like a selective and externally narrated cinematic shot. This storytelling technique utilizes a combination of two approaches: a heightened degree of descriptive focus on a microcosmic level, and a general incomprehensibility of narrative on a macrocosmic level. Mingling tormented bodies with chopped texts, this metonymic necrorealism[3] engages with the concepts of suffering and death in concentrated ways that render trauma more approachable: one disembodied dose of horror at a time. This article proposes an analysis of this curious literary technique, which I call *thanatopraxis*, and links it to Ukraine's complicated recent past.

---

[1] Iurii Tsaplin, 'Spirit instead of Human', in *Malen'kii schastlivyi vecher* (Kharkov: Lestvitsa Marii, 1997), pp. 42–51 (p. 46). Unless otherwise noted, all translations from Russian and Ukrainian are mine.

[2] Ibid., pp. 56–57 (p. 57). The curious parallel to Don Giovanni's fate—a man brought down by a statue for his violence—is obscured here by the explicit, real-life details of physical sickness.

[3] Necrorealism was a movement that arose in Leningrad in the early 1980s as a reaction to the ideological aspect of Soviet life. Necrorealists dealt closely with death, its symbols, and its processes. For an in-depth discussion of this phenomenon see Alexei Yurchak, 'Necro-Utopia: The Politics of Indistinction and the Aesthetics of the Non-Soviet', *Current Anthropology*, 49 (2008), 199–224.

'The subconscious of the last Soviet generation preserves the dreams and secrets' of the collapsed country, wrote Mark Lipovetsky, adding that 'on the brink of epochs it produces new hybrid phantoms with particular intensity'.[4] Let us take a look at some of these phantoms, as found in imaginative writing. They come from three short stories, all fragmented, with little apparent plot and startling—or absent—endings. The authors, who were at various stages of adolescence when the Soviet Union collapsed, hail from Kharkiv, a diverse and dynamic borderland city that arguably serves as one of the main cultural hotbeds for Lipovetsky's hybrid phantoms.[5] We have already mentioned Tsaplin, the author of 'Briug'; his 'Spirit instead of Human' (*Dukh vmesto cheloveka*, 1995) is a nameless narrator's rambling account about vile spirits which brutally attack and possess his friend. Andrei Krasniashchikh's 'The Currant Demon' (*Smorodinovyi bes*, 2003) consists of a collection of similarly enigmatic references to a crime that is never fully revealed. All we know is that it involves an alleged slaughter of children. Finally, Oleh Kotsarev's 'The Lybids'ka Depot' (*Depo na Lybids'kii*, 2008) is a tale about a remorseful ghost that haunts a former tram depot, until his chance encounter with one post-Soviet woman changes everything.[6]

In contrast to the trauma-oriented texts of the previous generation of Ukrainian writers—such as Iurii Andrukhovych, Iurii Gudz', Iurii Izdryk, Oksana Zabuzhko—the dizzying dashcam action of the younger writers' narration aims to expose and explore how pain feels, rather than to address or uncover the truth and meaning behind it. These three authors—Tsaplin, Krasniashchikh and Kotsarev—were children when Vasyl Stus, a Ukrainian dissident poet, declared a hunger strike and died in a labour camp for political prisoners in 1985. Their stories do some similar things in two languages, Ukrainian and Russian: they urge the reader to dive into, and perhaps even to own, the symptoms of distress they portray, while problematizing any conclusion one might try to take away. This is a way for the current generation to assert its right of impact (that is, a right to be affected) by the historical ordeal usually claimed by its predecessors.

In another short story by Tsaplin, 'Glue' (*Klei*, 1996), an old grandfather urges his grown-up grandson to put a shattered vase back together. The grand-

---

[4] Mark Lipovetsky, *Paralogii: transformatsii (post)modernistskogo diskursa v russkoi kul'ture 1920–2000-kh godov* (Moscow: Novoe literaturnoe obozrenie, 2008), p. 408.

[5] The literary memory-scape of Kharkiv, historically one of the most literature-infused cities in the nation, is the focus of my doctoral dissertation, 'Where the Currents Meet: Frontiers of Memory in the Post-Soviet Fiction of East Ukraine' (University of Cambridge, expected 2013). For a more detailed discussion of the city, and for further bibliographic references, see Tanya Zaharchenko, 'Polyphonic Dichotomies: Memory and Identity in Today's Ukraine', *Demokratizatsiya: The Journal of Post-Soviet Democratization*, 21 (Spring 2013), 241–69.

[6] Andrei Krasniashchikh (b. 1970); Iurii Tsaplin (b. 1972); Oleh Kotsarev (b. 1981); quoted in my translation from Russian (Krasniashchikh, Tsaplin) and Ukrainian (Kotsarev).

son broke it when he was only two years old, but its pieces have been carefully preserved. 'Do you honestly think I can fix this vase?' asks the young man respectfully after some time. And the elderly man responds crossly: 'Just keep gluing' ('A ty klei. Ty klei').[7] Time has not calmed his frustration about this loss (the toy that hit the vase remains 'idiotic' despite the cushion of years). For retribution or for consolation, the grandfather expects some effort from his grandson to put things right, regardless of whether or not it is a realistic undertaking.

Such expectations are acutely familiar to many representatives of the first post-Soviet generation. To reflect this struggle, until the fallen empire and its post-collapse shrapnel of the 1990s are laid to rest—names verbalized, monuments built, dark spots illuminated, institutions restructured, and fragments of the broken vase finally filed away—writers will continue to serve us up with bizarrely assembled pieces of a shattered whole: *A ty klei. Ty klei*. This article examines the expression that this general framework finds in fiction.

Expressing the Unspeakable

Vitaly Chernetsky describes a novel by Serhii (Serhiy) Zhadan, another Kharkiv-based writer, as 'endowing with a voice a previously unrepresented identity', referring to eastern Ukrainian urban youth.[8] This potent voice could be approached as a combination of many intonations: young, bilingual, thoughtful, searching, and almost always slightly ironic. Despite the natural variations within these intonations, however, they share some main themes. One such theme marries detailed depictions of bodily harm to the general opaqueness of its circumstances, both amplified to the point that helps render horrific events fairly mundane.

This literary device can be termed *thanatopraxis*, from the Greek *thanatos* (death) and *praxis* (practice).[9] It consists of two narrative tactics: zooming in to an exaggerated level of representation of death, and tearing up the storyline to render its circumstances fairly unintelligible. Both of these strategies work to the same effect: they allow the overall gruesome picture to remain beyond any given prosaic screenshot. To use Erich Auerbach's language of 'creating

[7] Tsaplin, 'Klei', in *Malen'kii schastlivyi vecher*, pp. 13–15 (p. 15). In a rare case of grammatical concurrence between English and Russian, *klei* is a noun for glue as well as an imperative form of the corresponding verb.

[8] Vitaly Chernetsky, 'From Anarchy to Connectivity to Cognitive Mapping: Contemporary Ukrainian Writers of the Younger Generation Engage with Globalization', *Canadian–American Slavic Studies*, 44 (2010), 102–17 (p. 111).

[9] In proposing this term I rely on its conveying the apophatic praxis of death in literature, with only distant connections to the similarly named mortuary science and Jacque Derrida's consequent use of *thanatopraxie* to explore what might be referred to, with much simplification, as textual embalming.

a foreground and background', *thanatopraxis* plays in a peculiar way on the dynamic between excessive foreground and recessive background.[10]

This combination of selective auxesis (broadly understood as overstatement) and meiosis (understatement) results in a routinization of horror, an effect achieved by simultaneously emphasizing its bodily mechanics and obscuring its human context. Horror is thus routinized because this approach advances its 'anti-sentimentality', to use James Wood's term.[11] By sabotaging the process of narration a reader would normally rely on to comprehend a story and react to it, *thanatopraxis* renders the horrible processable in pieces.

In his insightful book *How Fiction Works*, Wood notes how 'cinematic' the modern narrative becomes after Flaubert. A section aptly entitled 'The Awful and the Regular' focuses on 'the zoomlike action of the lens, as it gets closer and closer to the corpse'. This zoomlike action in Wood's analysis, interestingly, is fairly non-selective: pointing to an ant that drags 'some sort of bundle' along the upper lip of a dead soldier in Stephen Crane's *The Red Badge of Courage*, Wood plausibly exclaims: 'The protagonist seems to be noticing so much, recording everything! [. . .] Would any of us actually see as much?'[12] As if in response to this observation, the literary *thanatopraxis*—which aims to process rather than to record—opts for a very different kind of zoom technique. Writers drop the bigger picture and the general detail of Wood's examples, and add an unstable dashcam effect to the very selectively focused lens of their prose. If Crane had been practising this technique, we might have learnt much more about that ant's 'bundle' without catching a single glimpse of the corpse, its position, or even its location.

A new kind of literary cinema emerges: mortality is carefully inserted into narratives that combine details of human destruction with a striking lack of clarity and consistency regarding the circumstances of violence portrayed. The underlying assumption is that some phenomena cannot be verbalized or described, but they can be felt and experienced.[13] An example of this idea can be found in Psalm 34, which calls to the believer to 'taste and see that the Lord is good'.[14] Here, two of our five senses are directly engaged in grasping a concept. As a technique, *thanatopraxis* targets senses and rejects explicit elucidations as well:

---

[10] Erich Auerbach, 'Odysseus's Scar', in *Mimesis: The Representation of Reality in Western Literature*, trans. by Willard R. Trask (Princeton: Princeton University Press, 1953; repr. 2003), pp. 3–23 (p. 45).

[11] James Wood, *How Fiction Works* (New York: Picador, 2009), p. 46.

[12] Ibid.

[13] Though linked with Hannah Arendt's understanding of *praxis* as an essential aspect of the active life, *vita activa*, the use of this notion as proposed here is also grounded in its applications in spirituality. In the context of the divine, *praxis* refers to a first-hand encounter with concepts that cannot be comprehended through the mere rationality of the mind.

[14] Psalm 34. 8 <http://www.biblegateway.com/passage/?search=Psalm+34> [accessed 20 December 2012.]

The modern person [...] is not endowed with such fibres of the soul that could receive the electrodes of the literary word about fear—and the physical, the painful, is the only way I can imagine delivering information about the incredible physiological intensity of this feeling.[15]

Invited to immerse ourselves in abounding confusion, we as readers edge closer to the characters: like them, we are left without any answers or some sort of reality control group to measure the storyline against. In essence, we become their witnesses, or even their jury. Unsurprisingly, in these cases the jury often finds itself deadlocked.

Nikolai Gogol', too, offered us a thesaurus of the macabre, while often keeping us in the dark about the larger context and problematizing possible conclusions. His texts, however, are more reminiscent of epic poems. The great knight's entrance in 'A Terrible Vengeance' (*Strashnaia mest'*, 1831), for instance, is hardly short of spectacular: 'What knight of inhuman stature gallops below the mountains, above the lakes, reflected with his gigantic horse in the still waters, his endless shadow flitting terribly over the mountains?'[16] A few decades later, Oleksa Storozhenko, a writer from the town of Poltava, close to Kharkiv, incorporated a similar Gothic motif into 'Devil in Love' (*Zakokhanyi chort*, 1861). Storozhenko's lyrical, singsong prose also builds on otherworldly material, intertwining reality and fantasy and leaning heavily into the folkloric tradition.[17] Both Gogol' and Storozhenko, however, arguably sought to create an image of Ukraine as a poetic place, shrouded in legends and beauty. Post-Soviet thanatopraxic writers have no such goal. Their universe shifts from their predecessors' all-encompassing country to an individual world of total inner turmoil, unchecked against anything external. They become novelists who, in Wood's terms, 'want us to inhabit a character's confusion, but will not "correct" that confusion, refuse to make clear what a state of nonconfusion would look like'.[18]

For example, in Andrei Krasniashchikh's 'The Currant Demon' a group of rather dubious witnesses—in a textbook example of unreliable narrators, to use the term coined by Wayne C. Booth[19]—construct a story of the murder of several children. These witnesses' halting descriptions ('Blood on the floor. Lots of blood. Literally puddles of blood. Blood on the walls, on the fur-

---

[15] Tsaplin, 'Spirit instead of Human', p. 48.

[16] Nikolai Gogol', 'A Terrible Vengeance', in *The Collected Tales of Nikolai Gogol*, trans. by Richard Pevear and Larissa Volokhonsky (New York: Vintage, 1999), pp. 64–105 (p. 94).

[17] For more on this see Svitlana Krys, 'Folklorism in Ukrainian Gotho-Romantic Prose: Oleksa Storozhenko's Tale about Devil in Love (1861)', *Folklorica: Journal of the Slavic and East European Folklore Association*, 16 (2011), 117–38.

[18] Wood, p. 13.

[19] Wayne C. Booth, *The Rhetoric of Fiction* (Chicago: University of Chicago Press, 1961), pp. 158–59.

niture, and a whole sea under the sideboard'[20]) are evocative of the famous horror flashes in Stanley Kubrick's 1980 classic *The Shining*, where a river of blood gushes out of opening elevator doors.[21] But while the evil presence in Kubrick's film acts through a distinct agent, Jack Torrance (though its actual cause or source is concealed), the perpetrators in Krasniashchikh's text stay entirely obscure. Even more importantly, it remains unclear whether any crime has taken place at all. Drawing the violence from his country's past and inserting it into the present, Krasniashchikh and his fellow writers leave it up to erratic narrators and bewildered readers to navigate the details and attempt to construct a bigger picture. Zooming out, indeed, is one thing such authors are not overly concerned with.

This intense focus on details serves to conceal the odd deficiency of agency in these accounts. And agency is, in fact, one of the main themes raised by thanatopraxic texts. The narrative of Krasniashchikh's 'Demon' ends with an unknown speaker (an accomplice?) trying to comfort an unknown offender by outlining a pyramid of responsibility for his alleged malevolent deed. The proposed scheme assigns divine omnipotent forces ('god, for making you this way') to the top gradation of blame, while the anonymous addressee fits cosily on the very bottom.[22] A comparable negotiation of responsibility takes place in 'Spirit instead of Human' by Tsaplin. This short story from his collection of 'Novellas of the Sleeping World' (*Novelly spiashchego mira*) describes the similarly incoherent destruction of a man named Masich by bloodthirsty spirits summoned by a nameless narrator, who appears to be as unreliable as they come. 'I'm not making excuses,' he professes. 'To whom should I justify myself? Do you really think it was easy to give Masich away?'[23] This narrator spends the entire story trying to convince us that he is not liable for what happened to the unfortunate Masich, attributing it instead to higher forces at play. At the end of both stories, the reader is left wondering what the hell (literally) just happened in them. Akin to the black holes of Zhadan's *Voroshylovhrad* (2010), these texts urge us to fill in the unknown in order to make sense of the narrative.[24]

At the start of this article I emphasized the trauma-based aspect of these

[20] Andreï Krasniashchikh, 'The Currant Demon', in *Park Kul'tury i Otdykha* (Kharkov: Tyazh-promavtomatika, 2008), pp. 210–19 (p. 213).

[21] Interestingly, Stephen King's novel does not include this and other famous moments of Kubrick's film. It has been noted that 'most memorable aspects of the film—the ones that have become embedded within popular discourse—are not in the book. It tends to be the brief, wordless shots that resonate most' (Karina Wilson, 'Book vs. Film vs. Mini Series: The Shining', *Litreactor*, 26 June 2012 <http://litreactor.com/columns/the-shining-book-vs-film-vs-mini-series> [accessed 15 May 2013]).

[22] Krasniashchikh, p. 219.

[23] Tsaplin, p. 47.

[24] For a more detailed discussion of deliberate textual voids that lure the reader into co-imagining, see Tanya Zaharchenko, 'While the Ox is Still Alive: Memory and Emptiness in Serhiy

works. It is therefore worth pointing out that the two stories share another important trait: allusions to, and descriptions of, overpowering forms of fear. 'The air smelled of thunder and our fear,' muses the first witness of 'Demon'— 'In turmoil none of us knew what to think. A black, very black sky opened up over our souls.' The protagonist of 'Spirit' echoes: 'Just fear. Total fear. Nothing but fear. [. . .] Fear lasts for ever.'[25] This disorienting dread is not only supernatural; it is also incommunicable. 'You cannot feel this fear, cannot comprehend it, cannot survive it, no matter how much I describe it in an abstract evil voice,' insists Tsaplin's narrator, while some of Krasniashchikh's witnesses spend entire paragraphs on apparent linguistic gibberish.[26] These testimonies to incommunicability set a backdrop for narrating crimes that are incomprehensible as well. Incomprehensible, that is, except through *praxis*. 'One cannot prove anything. One can only show it. One can only flare up with it. One can only believe it. One can only be forced to believe it,' ruminates the narrator of 'Spirit' before offering a haphazard account of another man's—Masich's—violent demise.[27]

These two short stories, 'The Currant Demon' and 'Spirit instead of Human', engage in *thanatopraxis* in so far as their authors attempt to convey death through detailed and often bizarre close-ups, without explanation. While pools of blood fill Krasniaschikh's mystical 'bad apartment', which had brought death to its previous tenants as well, Tsaplin's vicious spirits tear out Masich's intestines, stomach, and kidneys (in that carefully articulated order). And to top off these writers' general focus on the mysteries of human agency, it is not just the parties responsible for these atrocities who remain nameless or missing from the narratives. Where the perpetrators are vague, victims can be indistinct as well. To add to the overall confusion, or perhaps to emphasize it, neither crime leaves a body. The children simply vanish from the evil apartment, and the poor stitched-up Masich continues to wander around as before, albeit now with an evil spirit inside. And then the stories end—without culmination, elucidation, or even conclusion.

This can be perceived as an intriguing inversion of Alexander Etkind's hypothesis of misrecognition, which states that 'Though no single narrative can embrace the Soviet terror, the story of intrafamilial misrecognition can serve as its allegory.'[28] In Etkind's examples, those who are closest to people released from labour camps fail to recognize them on their return. In our

Zhadan's *Voroshylovhrad*', *Canadian Slavonic Papers/Revue canadienne des slavistes*, 55 (2013), 45–70.
  [25] Krasniashchikh, p. 212; Tsaplin, 'Spirit instead of Human', p. 48.
  [26] 'I am exercising in discursive practice, especially tautological writing and psychotic narrative', the author dutifully declares when his turn comes to testify in the story (Krasniashchikh, p. 215).
  [27] Tsaplin, 'Spirit instead of Human', p. 46.
  [28] Alexander Etkind, 'A Parable of Misrecognition: *Anagnorisis* and the Return of the Repressed from the Gulag', *Russian Review*, 68 (2009), 623–40 (p. 640).

examples, it is the rest of the world that overlooks essential transformations within the characters—a demon that enters a father; an evil spirit that now controls Masich—while the narrator alone is not fooled, and is understandably terrified by the reality he is facing. In an example of boundaries often blurred in Kharkiv fiction, the incongruous style of narration of both stories leaves the line between sanity and psychosis rather vague: this recognition-despite-disguise may or may not be evidence of madness. In other words, it may or may not be a sound judgement. But in either case, it feels acutely real to its subject. The isolated, unshared nature of this private knowledge serves an important purpose: it underlines the characters' quintessential solitude.

Both narrators have had a traumatic past prior to this point. Faced with their experiences, and having lived to tell the story, they alone know what happened, and they cannot (or do not want to) formulate it. 'Something has happened, but no one except me had any idea what it was,' whispers Krasniashchikh's child narrator before staying entirely alone (*odin-odineshenek*) under the table in the bad apartment. Meanwhile, the soul of Tsaplin's disturbed storyteller 'shudders in a mute scream' when the possessed Masich smiles at him on a busy street. Oblivious passers-by are deaf to his unvoiced agony. In essence, both stories are about tête-à-tête encounters between speakers and their tortured memories of a nameless personal catastrophe. In other words, these are indeed tales of trauma.

Surviving the Unspeakable

In an analysis of Nadezhda Mandel′shtam's recurring nightmare about seeing her imprisoned husband, Osip, and asking him desperately: 'What is being done to you "there"?', Etkind notes the lack of any appropriate concept that could replace the notion of 'there'. The nightmare could not refer to the Gulag by name, he suggests; instead, an unspecified 'grammatical fiction' was necessary.[29] In Bulat Okudzhava's short story 'Girl of my dreams' (*Devushka moei mechty*, 1985), a mother returns home from labour camp, and her son's need to know the unspeakable keeps him constantly on the brink of asking 'How was it *there*?'[30] In 'Demon', hiding under the table as night approaches, the children worry: 'What was happening *there*, near the sideboard? [...] Are they being tortured or something?' And Tsaplin's narrator warns: 'All that talk about how a human life is worthless is nothing but journalism. It has a worth, it does. *There* they know exactly how much. The spirits know.'[31]

This unarticulated, shapeless *there* (my emphasis) runs through all these

[29] Ibid.
[30] Bulat Okudzhava, 'Devushka moei mechty' <http://royallib.ru/read/okudgava_bulat/devushka_moey_mechti.html> [accessed 24 December 2013].
[31] Tsaplin, 'Spirit instead of Human', p. 46.

accounts like a grey thread, signalling the catastrophe behind them. 'The text of the novel itself—the text of memory—is unable to accommodate the horror of murder,' wrote Lipovetsky of Osip Mandel'shtam's thirty-page novella *The Egyptian Stamp* (*Egipetskaia marka* (1928).[32] This can help explain the torn-up, piecemeal stylistics of both 'Spirit' and 'Demon'.[33]

In his study of *The Egyptian Stamp* Lipovetsky notes that 'its entire stylistics aim to conceal, rather than to reveal, the trauma that generated this text'.[34] He proceeds to suggest that the novella plays out both the demise and the resurrection of this trauma's subject, allowing the Author to survive while his other self, the character Parnok, is swallowed by eternity. Like the stories we have examined so far, *The Egyptian Stamp* assigns a special active role to fear: 'Fear takes me by the hand and leads me.'[35] Akin to the 'intensive processing' of Parnok's death,[36] the *thanatopraxis* of our two writers substantiates the endangerment of the 'I'—the driving force behind a post-catastrophic being. Suffering that encroaches upon the 'I' is recognized and explicitly announced in both stories: 'Each of us thought: what if I am next?' in one and, in the other, 'We would both have been killed'. This angle of personal involvement, of the mere possibility that the 'I' could cease to exist, sheds light on otherwise odd tales: they are not just post-traumatic witness narratives, as we concluded in the preceding section; they are narratives of direct participants in traumatic events. One is told by a possible survivor; another, by a possible perpetrator.

Indeed, the extent of these characters' tormented isolation can be linked to another direct effect of trauma: depersonalization, an anomaly of self-awareness. In Okudzhava's 'Girl' the returned mother is unable to process her son's questions and to respond in the first person: 'Are you hungry?'—'Me?' (*khochesh' est'? — ia?*).[37] Likewise, the protagonist of 'Spirit' is worried that it was not really he who knocked on his doomed friend's door that fateful night, and it was 'I—not I' (*ia — ne ia*) who screamed frenziedly when the spirits attacked them both.[38] Meanwhile, the multiple 'I's of narrators in 'Demon'

---

[32] Lipovetsky, p. 108.

[33] This approach parallels the 'compromise by which the command of reality is carried out piecemeal', which Freud ascribed to post-traumatic melancholia. See Sigmund Freud, 'Mourning and Melancholia', in *The Pelican Freud Library*, trans. by James Strachey, XI (Harmondsworth: Penguin, 1984), pp. 245-68 (p. 253). Etkind points out that such rhetoric also emulates 'the piecemeal logic of torture, which also manipulates parts of the body with the aim of changing the whole of truth, integrity, and history' (Alexander Etkind, *Warped Mourning: Stories of the Undead in the Land of the Unburied* (Stanford: Stanford University Press, 2013), p. 236).

[34] Lipovetsky, p. 80.

[35] Osip Mandel'shtam, *Egipetskaia marka*, in *Sobranie sochinenii*, 4 vols (Moscow: Art-Biznes-Tsentr, 1993), II, 465-95 (p. 494).

[36] Lipovetsky, p. 91.

[37] Okudzhava (as n. 30 above).

[38] Tsaplin, 'Spirit instead of Human', pp. 43, 50.

scatter around until they lose all borders and encompass God himself (*ia — bog; ia vse videl*).[39]

In this struggle of the self—a first-person dilemma, if we build on Bernard Williams's 'one-person conflict'[40]—the 'I' fights a losing battle for intact survival within the text. This is rooted in yet another shared trait of the two stories: both protagonists worry about having done something illicit. When the adults leave for the evening, Krasniashchikh's children hide under a table and try to fetch candy from the other room, which launches their demise: 'We should not have done this!'[41] Tsaplin's nameless hero fancies himself a medium and, together with his doomed friend Masich, deliberately evokes the spirits that proceed to attack them, despite having plainly stated that 'Spirits should not be summoned'.[42] In one way or another, along with issues of agency, remorse and regret enter both narratives. And part of the struggle of the 'I' in these stories is rooted in processing guilt, and in negotiating blame, following an act of rule-breaking that preceded both catastrophes. Bargaining for redemption under the heavy weight of potential responsibility, the 'I' gives ground in its struggle for continued demarcation (wholeness) within the plot, and the readers watch it shatter. Like the mother in Okudzhava's story, these protagonists cannot stop examining: 'Me?'

In fact, Tsaplin's self-professed medium in 'Spirit' explicitly refers to his account as 'Recollections of pain. Of an irreversible impact'.[43] A desperate attempt at inner justification emerges amidst his ramblings, veiled safely in unsystematic references to shamans, scholars, and Jesus. There are situations in which morality must be discarded at once, he insists, or one's life will end. This, he assures us, is not a confession; it is a survival manual. He proceeds to explain that 'merciless' and 'unsentimental' fear destroys individuality—it erodes the 'I' (*strakh razrushaet 'ia'*) that had tried, foolishly, to put morality above survival. A key to the whole story emerges amidst this reasoning: if the mind refuses to carry out its responsibility of preserving the body, 'natural selection' will, unsurprisingly, take that mind away (*otberet razum*). Mental anguish, bordering on mental illness, stands behind the (textual) shattering of the 'I'.

In response to harrowing reality, it appears, texts can react with sickness just as people do. Iurii Gudz', author of *Ne-My* (*Not-Us*, 1998), described his novel as precisely a story of the illness of a literary text (*istoriia khvoroby*

[39] Krasniashchikh, 'The Currant Demon', p. 215.
[40] Bernard Williams, 'Conflicts of Values', in *Moral Luck: Philosophical Papers 1973–1980* (Cambridge: Cambridge University Press, 1981), pp. 71–82 (p. 73). In contrast to Williams's 'one-person conflict', which refers primarily to an internal moral struggle, by a first-person dilemma here I mean an existential one: not what one should do, but whether (and who) the 'I' really is.
[41] Krasniashchikh, p. 211.
[42] Tsaplin, 'Spirit instead of Human', p. 47
[43] Ibid., p. 48.

literaturnoho tekstu) that gobbles up its own author.[44] Mark Andryczyk argues that Gudz' links mind, body, and text to express a 'state of abnormality'.[45] Subsequent generations appear to have inherited this condition as part of their historical lot.

The ambiguous beings whom Tsaplin's survivor has processed and presented to us as uncanny and invincible—as spirits that should never be summoned, but that he proceeds to summon nevertheless—at one point break his and his friend's fingers. 'It works in a horrible way,' he remarks earnestly, 'one can't quite think of anything when your fingers are being broken.'[46] A violent event must have taken place in this person's life, at least in his life as he perceives and articulates it. This catastrophe, whether external or internal, has left him alive but affected by guilt. Struggling with his role in the larger scheme of things, he obsessively offers reasons for how everything worked out, to the point of incoherence. One of the causes of this concealed agony could be survivor's syndrome. 'I am a monster,' he notes matter-of-factly at the start of the story.[47] It was not easy to give up a friend, but one human being must always be surrendered to the spirits once they are summoned.[48] In the character's mind, he made a choice that had to be made. Or so he would fiercely like to believe.

Tsaplin's angst-ridden narrator might find a place near Nadezhda Mandel'shtam and Mykhailo Osadchy, who questioned the reality of loss and of survival long before he did. Osadchy's prison memoir *Cataract* (*Bil'mo*, 1968) uses similar techniques, such as stream of consciousness, to do so. At one point Osadchy describes his imprisoned self as a small, clumsy table, which no one can find a place for.[49] He tackles the reality of being a victim and a survivor. Meanwhile, Krasniachshikh's 'Demon' questions another (highly related) reality—that of perpetration. Osadchy, who hailed from the nearby Sumy oblast', created a surreal atmosphere to convey absurd and awful life events. And Krasniachshikh offers us a set of garbled and often absurd testimonies that are hard to distinguish from a game and (at times) even a farce. 'They're all playing,' confirms the author.[50] He explains that the characters

---

[44] Iurii Gudz', 'Ne-My', *Kur'ier kryvbasu*, 103 (199), 8–54 (p. 23) <http://ygoodz.blogspot.co.uk/2009/08/blog-post_6173.html> [accessed 10 July 2013]. The expression 'istoriia khvoroby' also refers to a patient's medical records.

[45] Mark Andryczyk, *The Intellectual as Hero in 1990s Ukrainian Fiction* (Toronto: University of Toronto Press, 2012), p. 77.

[46] Tsaplin, 'Spirit instead of Human', p. 44.

[47] Ibid., p. 43. Survivor's syndrome, or survivor's guilt, was a recognized diagnosis until 1994. It is now redefined as a significant symptom of post-traumatic stress disorder (PTSD). See American Psychiatric Association, *Diagnostic and Statistical Manual of Mental Disorders DSM-IV*, 4th edn (Washington: American Psychiatric Press, 1994).

[48] Tsaplin, p. 46.

[49] Mykhailo Osadchy, *Bil'mo* (Paris: Smoloskyp, 1971), p. 13.

[50] Andrei Krasniashchikh, interview with the present author, 17 April 2012.

and the readers engage in a mutually 'unattainable task' of penetrating each other's worlds. The former try to (re)enter reality, and the latter seek to recognize everything as a game with no direct links to their life. As a result of this impossible duality, descriptions of a crime scene mingle with shopping lists and haphazard medical arguments against the amputation of one's hoofs.[51]

This can be approached as a kind of *steb*—a type of humour which, in literature, is 'often expressed through reducing the plot to absurdity'.[52] Essentially, it is irony formed during, and informed by, the times of conceptualism. According to sociologist Boris Dubin, *steb* consists of provocatively depreciating certain symbols through their demonstrative use in a parodic context.[53] In the case of 'Demon', this is true not only of, for instance, demonic attributes to be medically amputated, but also of larger concepts, such as testimony (garbled), witness (unreliable), truth (questionable). Referring to *steb* discourse, Alexei Yurchak contends that its instances 'refused every possible binary distinction, always balancing in multiple zones in-between'.[54] As observed above, one of the distinctions that get blurred in the process is the line between seriousness and play, allowing the 'in-between' condition to penetrate and inform contemplations of victimhood and perpetration in fiction. And this draws fiction into reality—for, as we know, the boundary between victim and perpetrator was particularly faint under the Soviet regime.[55]

Thus, the historical conditions that give rise to *thanatopraxis* form a grey area that both thrives on and suffers from ambiguity, and is evocative of Giorgio Agamben's 'zone of indistinction'.[56] Like Osadchy's remembered self, who is neither a free individual nor a clumsy table, or Mikhail Lermontov's demon, who belongs to neither heaven nor hell and is neither darkness nor light, stories such as 'The Currant Demon' and 'Spirit instead of Human' are informed by paradoxes that help bring imaginative writing ever so close to the intricate nature of reality itself.[57]

---

[51] Here one might enjoy discreet parallels with Mikhail Bulgakov's *The Master and Margarita*.

[52] Antonina Plat, 'Iumor, ironiia, steb — chto eto takoe?' <http://zhurnal.lib.ru/p/plat_a_n/humour.shtml> [accessed 20 December 2012]

[53] Boris Dubin, 'Kruzhkovyi steb i massovye kommunikatsii: k sotsiologii kul'turnogo perekhoda', in *Slovo — pis'mo — literatura: ocherki po sotsiologii sovremennoi kul'tury* (Moscow: NLO, 2001), 163–74.

[54] Alexei Yurchak, *Everything Was Forever, Until It Was No More: The Last Soviet Generation* (Princeton: Princeton University Press, 2006), p. 252.

[55] For instance, it has been argued that Soviet labour camps were unlike the Nazi ones in that 'some of the perpetrators ended up in the gulag just a few months or years later than their victims' (Etkind, *Warped Mourning*, p. 86).

[56] 'Testimony [about the camps] [. . .] takes place where the silent and the speaking, the inhuman and the human enter in a zone of indistinction in which it is impossible to establish the position of the subject' (Giorgio Agamben, *Remnants of Auschwitz: The Witness and the Archive*, trans. by Daniel Heller-Roazen (New York: Zone Books, 1999), p. 120.

[57] Mikhail Lermontov wrote in 'The Demon': 'to ne byl angel-nebozhitel' [. . .] to ne byl ada dukh uzhasnyi [. . .] ni den', ni noch', — ni mrak, ni svet!' ('Twas not an angel that redeems,

Traversing the Unspeakable

As a perpetrator, Tsaplin's narrator—like Lermontov's demon—is also a sufferer. This fusion was of interest to the preceding generation of Ukrainian writers as well. In Iurii Izdryk's novel *Votstsek* (1997), for instance, the title character suffers from a mental condition that causes him to lock his family in a basement in order to protect them from the world. After the police free them, he is locked up in a mental institution, where he struggles desperately with names and faces that continue to haunt him.[58]

This elusiveness of the perpetrator–sufferer frontier is also evident in a short story by Kharkiv writer Oleh Kotsarev entitled 'The Lybids′ka Depot' (*Depo na Lybids′kii*). Of the three main texts analysed in the present article, this one is the least fragmented. Its plot follows an old tram depot through a turbulent 'epoch of changes'.[59] As the Soviet Union collapses, the depot is privatized (which happened on a mass scale during those years[60]) and turned into a supermarket. But during this reconstruction one of the new co-owners is found murdered on site, in a makeshift grave of concrete. No proper investigation ensues, and the perpetrators are never identified.

The disturbed remains of the murdered co-owner, Vyshnevets′kyi, give rise to a ghost that begins to haunt the premises. He is particularly fond of breaking and shattering doors, even during the supermarket's busiest shopping hours. But he also seems drawn to remaining bits and pieces of the old tram depot: preserved spots of old paint, for instance. The narrator suggests that Vyshnevets′kyi, who worked in the depot's management before the 'epoch of changes' arrived, is tortured by 'the sin of privatization': 'How else can one explain the ghost's unexpected nostalgia for the times of the tram?'[61] Guilt-ridden for his role in the depot's illicit dismantling, its former manager, now a desolate ghost, boards a translucent otherworldly tram once a month and dashes around the streets where the rails used to be, yelling and causing quite a few scares.

Intriguing parallels with Gogol′'s Akakii Akakievich emerge from this

[. . .] 'Twas not a fiend from Hell below, [. . .] Not day, not night, not dark, not bright': trans. by Archibald Cary Coolidge in 'The Demon', *Slavonic Review*, 4 (1925), 278–307 (p. 288)). Lermontov's demon not only belongs somewhere between heaven and hell, but also is both guilty and pitiable: the reader is supposed to feel his longing, pain, and loneliness. And speaking of agency gradations, none of it is his choice—arguably, it is the fault of the one who made both him and Tamara.

[58] Iurii Izdryk, *Votstsek* (Ivano-Frankivs′k: Lileia-NV, 1997).

[59] Oleh Kotsarev, 'Depo na Lybids′kii', in *Neimovirna istoriia pravlinnia Khlorofituma Pershoho* (Kyiv: Smoloskyp, 2009), pp. 48–55 (p. 48).

[60] For a study of 'economic shock' following the collapse of the USSR, and of the human toll of mass privatization, see David Stuckler, Lawrence King, and Martin McKee, 'Mass Privatisation and the Post-Communist Mortality Crisis: A Cross-National Analysis', *Lancet*, 373.9661 (2009), 399–407.

[61] Kotsarev, p. 51.

darkly comic description. Like the manager Vyshnevets'kyi, the clerk Akakii Akakievich haunts the living and hungers for revenge in the celebrated story 'The Overcoat' (1842). But our manager cannot obtain his revenge because the weight of guilt is also on his shoulders, contaminating the purity of the post-mortem fury depicted in 'The Overcoat'. After all, he played a role in his own demise when he engaged in financial manipulations. Here 'A Terrible Vengeance' surfaces once more: sometimes, as the cruellest punishment, one is deprived of the possibility of avenging oneself. Helpless and cursed, the great corpse in 'Vengeance' grows larger underground from gnawing his own bones in agony. And Vyshnevets'kyi descends into his own underworld, in the form of the defunct tram system he keeps retracing.

But one evening, a down-to-earth woman named Lina sees Vyshnevets'kyi hovering miserably in mid-air in the supermarket. Intent on buying cigarettes, and busy contemplating whether or not to purchase a snack as well, she is quite annoyed with the apparition. With a curse she shoves the pensive phantom out of the way. This physical contact, a worldly acknowledgement of his existence, suddenly unbolts the gateway that the door-breaking ghost himself never managed to open: it reverses the passage of time and launches the locale's temporal transformation into its memory of itself. The supermarket vanishes, and Lina finds herself surrounded by old trams. Roaming around to find an exit, she gets pulled into one of them and ends up riding around the city with Vyshnevets'kyi all night. In the morning, upon getting home, she gives birth to a sparrow. These ethereal rides become a regular occurrence for the rest of her life, and her birds all settle on the roof of the former depot. The story ends with the narrator informing the reader of this fact.

Vyshnevets'kyi was both the perpetrator of a crime (large-scale financial fraud) and the victim of one (murder), fitting right in with the reality-questioning worlds of Tsaplin's and Krasniashchikh's narratives. He is both immaterial and tangible, both dead and able to give rise to life (no matter how tiny). Trapped between two epochs of the same locale, he represents the notion of a phantom of locality, not just of person: the spectre of the depot, where Lina finds herself after cursing and shoving the forlorn ghost, is a site of memory of years long gone.[62] It is also a site of criminal activity, in at least two instances: illegitimate privatization of state property, common in the 1990s, and the subsequent disposal of Vyshnevets'kyi's body. Ruled by the aftershock of these transformations and traumas, the shifting eras even cut off Lina's mobile signal—notifications of missed calls arrive only when she gets home. The sparrow is born shortly afterwards.

According to *The Continuum Encyclopedia of Animal Symbolism in Art,*

---

[62] 'Site of memory' is a term coined by Pierre Nora. See his *Realms of Memory: Rethinking the French Past*, trans. by Arthur Goldhammer (New York: Columbia University Press, 1996).

the sparrow is a symbol of 'divine awareness of even the lowliest creatures'.[63] And when portrayed exiting a cage, it serves as 'a symbol of the human soul escaping the material plane and ascending to heaven'. The painless emergence of a sparrow from a woman's body, then, illustrates deliverance, release, which leads to the appeasement of a regretful and unavenged ghost.[64] Importantly, Vyshnevets'kyi finally looks content and 'dreamy' on that shared tram ride. One wonders whether Lina became pregnant through the ear, and whether it was the telling of his story that released the ghost from his turmoil.

Vyshnevets'kyi's travelling back in time on his unearthly tram—or, rather, his merging time, past and present, during his wild rides, with their agonized recitals of remembered passages from books he had never read—failed to console him. But when he takes Lina along, both are hooked. In addition to his recitals, the intrinsic nature of memory is represented powerfully by the phantom tram's travelling only through those streets that had once contained its rails. This evokes the connections the tram system used to enable, destroyed with the coming of the new epoch. Haunted by such recollections, and haunting the place of their convergence, Vyshnevets'kyi finds some comfort in the company of a listener. The life-affirming allegory of birth introduces a future into his past–present entrapment.

But why on earth does the practical-minded Lina, a woman capable of cursing and shoving a floating spectre because it got in her way, continue to seek him out 'like a lunatic'? Her own creator calls her a former 'woman-tractor'—though this description applies to Lina's 'metaphysical power' back in the 1980s and 1990s, and not now.[65] Now, once again repeats Kotsarev, 'the times have changed'. So the author makes sure to refer, albeit fleetingly, to this character's past in the previous century, as well as to some drastic changes she underwent after it ended. An inhabitant of a new epoch with lifelong links to the old one, Lina is in need of healing, too. Like us, she is a direct (and troubled) witness to 'the brink of epochs' Lipovetsky mused about.

This brings us back full circle to the subject of trauma. In literature, the cultural meaning of death and resurrection of the main hero has been linked to a wish to resurrect time, to start a new 'normal' cycle of history in the light of the existing painful one.[66] But how does one interpret the sizeable place given by contemporary Kharkiv writers to insanity, or at least to the possibility of insanity? That the plot might be the result of confusion or madness is signalled

[63] See Hope B. Werness, *The Continuum Encyclopedia of Animal Symbolism in Art* (New York: Continuum, 2003), s.v. 'Sparrow', p. 384 (in reference to Matthew 10. 28–30).

[64] A dove leaving a human body would have holier associations; but a dove would also suggest death, the loss of the soul. In contrast, the sparrow is a down-to-earth, everyday little bird, and its emergence does not seem like death. It is more of an *otdushina*: a release and a relief. I am grateful to Sibelan Forrester for these contemplations.

[65] Kotsarev, p. 53.

[66] e.g. Lipovetsky, p. 322.

in 'Depot' with linguistic pointers such as a 'mad tram' (*shalenyi tramvai*) or 'like a lunatic' (*mov lunatyk*). This is illuminated, too, by the account of a tram-related psychosis in another of Kotsarev's short stories, 'A Tram Incident' (*Tramvainyi intsydent*, 2006). Michael Wood's concept of drunk reality described by a sober observer could be an apt one in this context.[67] We can understand an intoxicated person's take on the world swaying around him, but how do we process a world that sways despite an observer's sobriety—a world that is just not okay? 'Ghosts, vampires, werewolves, and other beasts help authors and readers discuss history that is not comprehensible by other means. Such was the Soviet period,' suggests Etkind.[68]

In addition to the Soviet legacy, however, writers who deal with the turmoil of the 1990s face the challenges of describing a very different epoch. On top of the previous era's control from above, which in a post-traumatic sense has not yet been fully worked through, they must also process the post-Soviet general indifference. American poet Stephen Dunn (b. 1939) lamented a similar state of affairs in his poem 'Because We Are Not Taken Seriously' (1981):

> Some night I wish they'd knock,
> on my door, the government men,
> looking for the poem of simple truths
> recited and whispered among the people.[69]

Dunn's lyrical hero dreams of being a poet whose 'loneliness, finally, is relevant', and places the ghosts of Mandel'shtam and Lorca on his shoulder. Stripped of the value of the forbidden, indifference shakes one of the main pillars that supported literature on terror: the weight of the writer's voice. Contemporary authors in Ukraine must work without this dark but powerful resource. Without it, 'ghosts, vampires, werewolves' still emerge, because the catastrophe must still be processed. But they traverse pieces of torn text and broken narratives that reflect the chaos of the 1990s.

Andryczyk highlights the 'numerous examples of the prevalence of the sick intellectual protagonist in the prose of the Eighties Writers'. This is an 'invariant' of their texts, he maintains, attributing it to 'the general state of disorientation and chaos that engulfed Ukraine together with euphoria' when the Soviet Union collapsed.[70] The protagonists we are seeing in the country's newest fiction, however, are anything but intellectuals. Their creators, too, have largely lost the status of cultural hero in post-Soviet society—a role that was still accessible to their predecessors. And while the previous generation of writers tended to include psychiatric hospitals in the narratives of their

---

[67] Michael Wood, 'In Reality', *Janus Head*, 5.2 (special issue on Magical Realism) (Fall 2002), 9–14.
[68] Etkind, 'Stories', p. 657.
[69] Stephen Dunn, *New and Selected Poems: 1974–1994* (New York: Norton, 1994), p. 112.
[70] Andryczyk, p. 81.

'sick intellectual protagonist', the younger authors appear to have dropped this medical verdict. In a way, it was too explanatory for them. Their suffering characters are a part of our drunk reality instead.

The landscape of fiction changes: terror and oppression, which the older writers struggled to make sense of, allowed for a relative continuity of anguish, which could find its way into texts that attempted to address it. There was a source, the state, which consistently bred the pain that fuelled the writing. Post-Soviet indifference and emptiness are a different kind of foe: like Vyshnevets'kyi, they float dejectedly in mid-air and break things in helpless fury as people shove them out of the way in search of cigarettes and snacks.

Hence, today's younger writers have layers of trauma to address: like a palimpsest, or like a burial ground with several strata of bones, where each tier needs a different kind of understanding. As a result, they do not shy away from death in the slightest, but its reasons and perpetrators are no longer the main focus. These authors are more interested in how things feel, how things impress themselves upon a human being—thus, *thanatopraxis*. As the post-Soviet generation attempts to make sense of its heritage—to embrace the reverberations and repercussions of the mangled vase they are presented with—eras shift, and texts fall apart.

Writing about the Unspeakable

'Poetry will remain irreplaceable for us as long as there are no other means of communicating the incommunicable,' writes Tsaplin in 'A Small Joyful Evening' (1995).[71] In this context, prose plays a similar role. 'I think one must write in a complicated and slightly incomprehensible way,' he explains. 'This is required by the subject of writing. [. . .] If you want to write simply, you want to lie.'[72] The argument, Tsaplin proceeds to clarify, is not that complex writing reflects the actual substance of things, but that it captures their essence. *Thanatopraxis*, the literary tactic of extreme close-ups on death amidst a frayed narrative, is part of this effort to capture the essence of what is otherwise indescribable. If this practice is to be honest—if one does not 'want to lie'—then the text must reflect the actual incongruity of experience.

In 'The Reading' (*Chtenie*, 1995) Tsaplin offers another argument for the disconnectedness of contemporary prose. He readily admits that the hectic nature of modern life does not allow for the 'honest' reading of complex texts that he himself has called for. So he proposes a method of 'new reading' that consists of irregular, 'unsystematic' explorations of several random pages at a time. Because this technique presumes using a text in ways unplanned by its

[71] Tsaplin, 'Malen'kii schastlivyi vecher', in *Malen'kii schastlivyi vecher*, pp. 5–10 (p. 10).
[72] Tsaplin, 'O pisanii i postizhenii', ibid., pp. 26–27 (p. 26).

author, concludes Tsaplin, there is only one solution: to start writing in ways that presuppose 'new reading' in the first place. That is, in self-sufficient fragments. The narrator of 'Reading' maintains: 'If the socio-historical conditions force us to read in a new way, then we must write books that can and should be read that way.'[73] Whether this method is really 'new' might be the subject of some debate (think, for instance, of the Oulipo, or of works by Milorad Pavić[74]), but what is clear is that some contemporary Ukrainian writers do follow this advice.

In his preface to Kotsarev's collection of short stories, Sashko Ushkalov, another young writer from Kharkiv, observes that Kotsarev's texts often end unexpectedly, as if they have no end at all.[75] Likewise, 'Briug', mentioned at the start of this article, ends with one of the drunken gentlemen contemplatively attempting to roll the statue's head while his friend vomits nearby. It concludes with the satisfyingly laconic 'the head rolled poorly' (*golova katalas' plokho*). Fragmentation of texts, indeed, includes not only abrupt endings and disconnectedness within longer narratives, but incongruous short stories as well—not unlike works by the well-known Russian absurdist Daniil Kharms. In 2007 an eloquent reviewer mused:

[. . .] fiction is more than just a device for transmitting information or learning about reality or dissecting problems. Fiction is about simultaneously outing and satisfying our innate desire for narrative. Kharms, admittedly, does more of the former than the latter.[76]

So do our writers. Pieces consisting of a few brief paragraphs without an immediately apparent or an entirely coherent plot—an abridged type of *zarisovki*—are, for instance, Kotsarev's *Podorozh*, *Zhinka z shampurom*, *Nema*, *Zaduma*, *Tumbochka i zyma*; Tsaplin's *Briug*, *Veselaia truba*, *Detskaia noch'*; and, though longer, arguably Krasniashchikh's *Teogonivo* (dedicated to 'early Tsaplin') or *Illiuzion*.

In his piece on Kharms, George Saunders highlights 'a fresh respect for, and (importantly) suspicion of, storytelling itself', which results from our reading of such texts. We are reminded that a narrative is but 'a trick a writer does with language'. But while Kharms's brilliant creations may have resulted primarily from his innate intolerance for artifice, as Saunders argues, the writers covered

[73] Tsaplin, 'Chtenie', ibid., pp. 35–38 (p. 38).
[74] Oulipo ('Ouvroir de littérature potentielle'), founded in 1960, was a group of writers and mathematicians who experimented with unusual writing techniques. Italo Calvino's *If on a Winter's Night a Traveller* (1979) is one captivating example. Serbian author Milorad Pavić (1929–2009) is known for novels written in unconventional formats, such as a dictionary (*Dictionary of the Khazars*, 1984) or Tarot cards (*Last Love in Constantinople*, 1994). They can be read effectively from any point.
[75] Sashko Ushkalov, 'Made in Kotsarev', in Kotsarev, *Neimovirna istoriia*, pp. 5–9 (p. 8).
[76] George Saunders, 'Soviet Deadpan', in *The New York Times*, 9 December 2007 <http://www.nytimes.com/2007/12/09/books/review/Saunders-t.html> [accessed 1 July 2013].

in the present article are arguably tearing up and zooming in on their texts in an effort to convey the conglomeration of layers of incomprehensibility and responsibility they face as post-Soviet authors. By creating their swaying worlds around sober observers (us), they are keeping us aware that all of it is still there to be calmed, excavated, and addressed. Violence enters the present in exactly the way it feels: convoluted, perplexing, and immediate.[77] People whose lifetime is heavily punctuated by history end up punctuating their stories in fierce, unexpected, yet captivating ways.

Conclusion

The three short stories discussed in this article are reflections of their writers' intensive and creative processing of topics similar to those that affected the grandfather in Tsaplin's 'Glue': loss and reckoning with loss. All three authors get particularly involved with the overlapping frontier between victims and perpetrators. The last speaker of 'The Currant Demon' implores: 'You know, pal, don't tell anyone about this. You've told me, and that's enough. I myself sometimes think that we're the ones who killed them.'[78] This vagueness of perpetration might be one reason why both Tsaplin's and Krasniashchikh's prose includes a story in which the main characters either watch their own funeral or interact with their own grave.[79] Another reason, of course, could be the need for burial before one can move on. Kotsarev does not produce a similar cemetery setting, but he does come up with a story in which the narrator gets trapped in a train sent to haunt him, and eventually escapes from it in a way that strongly resembles a death experience. In the end, he sits by a peaceful heavenly river and watches his feet turn golden in the water.[80]

Lidiia Ginzburg wrote that events occurring within one's consciousness can reach a level that renders empirical experience useless.[81] Indeed, these intense inner processes can obscure (or enhance) reality itself. In 'The Dreamer', for instance, Tsaplin contemplates a person who walks down a familiar street: 'He walked here last time and dreamt of something distinctly, with details—and

---

[77] Sibelan Forrester has pointed out yet another possible layer of complexity for this generation: 'A particular kind of discomfort: maybe it's not my fault that these people weren't buried properly, but they're wandering and haunting as ghosts. Does my fear of them and desire to escape them put me on the same side as those who repressed them?' (email to the author, 22 March 2013, following presentation of an earlier draft of this article at a conference at the University of Pennsylvania on the same day).

[78] Krasniashchikh, p. 219

[79] Krasniashchikh, 'Karusel'', in *Park Kul'tury i Otdykha*, pp. 29–36; Tsaplin, 'Mertvye i zhivye', in *Malen'kii schastlivyi vecher*, pp. 16–17 (p. 16).

[80] Kotsarev, 'Zminy u rozkladi', in *Neimovirna istoriia*, pp. 145–57.

[81] Lidiia Ginzburg, *Zapisnye knizhki. Vospominaniia. Esse* (St Petersburg: Iskusstvo-SPB, 2002), p. 71.

now he remembers it, and is uncertain: it's imagined, but it also existed.'[82] The line between reality and fiction, between one's external and internal worlds, grows ever so vague. All kinds of spectres from the past start crossing it unhindered, because there is no actual border between the past and the present in reality—and 'even less so in the realm of magic'.[83]

This article has argued that the practice of *thanatopraxis*, or selective zooming in on death, is one of the tactics writers have utilized to approach these post-Soviet phantoms. A fusion of deconstruction and naturalism renders apparitions of death more accessible. These apparitions cannot be conveyed merely 'with an abstract evil voice', as the anguished survivor of 'Spirit' lamented. But, as Psalm 34 suggests, they can be tasted and thus glimpsed, albeit inwardly. *Thanatopraxis* is one way to achieve this effect in literature. Traversing the post-catastrophic grey area of overlapping frontiers and thriving in a 'zone of indistinction', it utilizes a new variety of 'piecemeal rhetoric'[84] to offer a type of 'new reading' that fits and illuminates the haunted historical period it represents.

UNIVERSITY OF CAMBRIDGE   TANYA ZAHARCHENKO

[82] Tsaplin, 'Mechtatel'', in *Malen'kii schastlivyi vecher*, pp. 39–40 (p. 40).
[83] Alexander Etkind, 'Stories of the Undead in the Land of the Unburied: Magical Historicism in Contemporary Russian Fiction', *Slavic Review*, 68 (2009), 631–58 (p. 635).
[84] Freud, 'Mourning and Melancholia'.

REVIEWS

The Metamorphoses of Fat: A History of Obesity. By Georges Vigarello. Trans. by C. Jon Delogu. New York: Columbia University Press. 2013. xiii+261 pp. £20.50. ISBN 978-0-231-15976-0.

Every now and then a work comes along which at once compellingly establishes a developing field as worthy of academic interest and yet pushes its parameters beyond that which has come before. Georges Vigarello's *The Metamorphoses of Fat* is such a work, expertly rendering the history of the overweight body at once compelling and ground-breaking. Most importantly, Vigarello takes traditional methodologies focusing upon medical understandings and artfully weaves them into the social context in which they were formed: from medieval French courts to the publishing houses of the Revolution, and to the total cross-media domination of today's world.

Vigarello traces the evolution of the larger body from big to fat and from fat to outcast. In the medieval period bigness was not necessarily negative, large size being allied with strength and power. The criticisms that did come from some clerics and doctors focused on the sin of gluttony. The concept of 'fat' still did not really exist, with big people being written about only when they had reached the extremities of size. In the fifteenth century this all changed. In the setting of the court, where refinement became the order of the day, self-control was praised, as largeness became associated with the lower classes. Still, however, the interest was in morality rather than aesthetics: fat people might be flawed, but they were not necessarily ugly. During the Renaissance this shifted again—rather than moral sins the larger person became associated with ideas of slowness and heaviness. As fat became seen as more of a danger to health, doctors' attention was drawn to the variety of ways in which it could be treated, exploring in particular new kinds of diet and restraining clothing. By the eighteenth century this slowness had become linked to a lack of efficiency, and many Revolutionary prints used the image of the bourgeois getting fat and doing nothing while the poor starved. At the same time, the Enlightenment gaze created the first attempts to measure bodily size, with a particular interest in the circumference. As individualization rose, fatness became part of an individual's identity, something to be discerned and assessed. By the nineteenth century, gender distinctions in size really come into force; women's fatness had always been less permitted, but by the modern era this had turned into continual pressure to be thin, while large size could still indicate social gravity for some men. For the first time, progress in the understanding of combustion revolutionized awareness of the importance of food intake and diet, and led to widespread categorization of size, whereby height was cross-referenced with weight. With the decline of the corset and the rise of the flapper figure, the lanky silhouette of today and the pressure to be thin without the assistance of restraining clothes were born. Fatness has become an economic issue, increasingly associated with poverty and discussed in terms of cost to the state. Experiences of being fat have shifted from indulgence to physical suffering, and to today's martyr figure, at war with a body that has become part of their identity.

This work represents all that is best in new histories of the body. Moving away from simple medical conceptions, it shows how attitudes towards and experiences of the body are embedded in complex social, cultural, and economic dynamics. Held back at times by minor flaws in what is overall an excellent translation, this is nevertheless an exciting addition to the field.

UNIVERSITY OF SHEFFIELD   ANNA JENKIN

Medicine and Narration in the Eighteenth Century. Ed. by SOPHIE VASSET. (SVEC, 2013:04) Oxford: Voltaire Foundation. 2013. viii+260 pp. £60. ISBN 978-0-7294-1065-6.

This is a very strong collection of essays from expert contributors based on a conference at the Maison Française in Oxford, 2008. Sophie Vasset has done a good job in ensuring that these pieces interact with each other and, although they consciously offer no overarching 'metanarrative' of narrative, they are keenly aware of the historical and literary complexities in such work, and make a rich contribution to the study of both European literature and medicine in the period.

The volume is divided into four parts. In the first, Alexandre Wenger's essay on Diderot's deployment of medical case histories in *La Religieuse* is a direct example of how medicine provides materials for the novel. Sophie Vasset's examination of the controversies and pamphlet wars consequent on John Ranby's *Narrative of the Last Illness of the Earl of Orford* (1745) reveals the literary nature of medical narratives, and the way in which prose style and command of narrative was a requirement for medical authority and respectability.

Shifting focus in the second section to epistolarity, so central to this age of the literary letter and diagnosis by post, Philip Rieder's essay on physician Louis Odier's correspondence makes the important point that case studies stressed the individual and subjective nature of disease, rather than a Foucaultian clinical gaze, and that novel-reading affected the way medics expressed themselves in their own medical prose. David Shuttleton takes the opportunity to highlight the importance of the Cheyne–Richardson correspondence on the wider literary and medical culture of the period as well as for the writing of Richardson himself, where valetudinarianism 'was an essential part of Richardson's established literary persona as a man of feeling' (p. 80). Dealing more squarely with the novel, in their essay Hélène Dachez and Sophie Vasset focus on the social construction of Clementina's disease in the 'polyphonic narration' (p. 83) of Richardson's *Sir Charles Grandison*.

In the third part, 'Illness as Narrative', Rudy Le Menthéour argues that Rousseau's self-narration of his melancholy and vapours was an attempt to control his public image. Catriona Seth demonstrates how the conflicts around smallpox inoculation cut across medical and literary texts, and how literary texts might be useful to medical writers, a theme picked up constantly across this book. Gavin Budge, in

'Smollett and the Novel of Irritability', mines a very interesting theme: the distinction between irritability and sensibility, which are terms very closely linked in both medical and literary writing. Budge argues for Smollett as a novelist of irritability, but tends to give examples of irritability that are from later in the period than Smollett, and which fit much better with the Brunonian medicine of the Romantic period proper. This essay helpfully paves the way for further research in this complex and important area.

The fourth section of the volume, 'Medical Strategies and Narrative Devices', begins with Sylvie Kleiman-Lafon showing that Bernard Mandeville's *Treatise of the Hypochondriack and Hysterick Diseases* is both a literary and a medical work, and that it effects a cure, of a talking sort, through its very form. The crucial role of medical material in both political and novelistic writing, as manifested in the spectacular figure of the oculist in German culture, is amply proven in Helge Jordheim's essay. Hugues Marchal's analysis of 'poetic and medical codes in Jean-François Sacombe's obstetric epic, *La Luciniade*' (p. 211) emphasizes the increasingly important role of science to the epic genre.

This excellent collection is an essential part of the growing and crucial body of scholarship that has been demonstrating the dynamic interaction between literature and medicine in the period, linked as the two discourses are by the common mode of narrative.

NORTHUMBRIA UNIVERSITY   CLARK LAWLOR

Formative Fictions: Nationalism, Cosmopolitanism, and the Bildungsroman. By TOBIAS BOES. Ithaca, NY: Cornell University Press. 2012. xii+202 pp. $65 (pbk $21). ISBN 978-0-8014-5177-5 (pbk 978-0-8014-7803-1).

Tobias Boes calls his book 'a cosmopolitan interpretation of the German *Bildungsroman*' (p. 2). His theory is that the genre is best understood as an effect of historicist-informed nationalism, but that this is always complicated by local elements resistant to incorporation into 'the normative regime of the nation-state' (p. 3). This is why the novels referred to as *Bildungsromane* are shaped by teleological expectations but routinely disappoint them. Boes points out the significant gap where the story of an individual and the 'emplotments' employed by nations fail to come together in a vision for collective identity. Furthermore, there are transnational forms of historical emplotment that will not conform to national forms, and these not only complicate the Idealism-influenced anticipation of closure that has misled criticism, but also produce the possibility of comparing and contrasting the particular vicissitudes of German identity with those arising in analogous literature from other national cultures. One other important modification made by Boes to the received wisdom about the genre is that, rather than seeing *Bildung* as normative, it is seen as a performative notion, reacting to consciousness of (different kinds of) historical, as well as personal, changes.

One of the original features of this argument is that it promotes Karl Morgenstern from the status of a footnote in the history of the *Bildungsroman* (as the person who coined the term without fully comprehending what he had done) to the source of several of the structuring ideas of the revision offered here: the implied (but missing) link between individual and national identity, and the performative (that is to say educational) role of the novels in regard to the reader. This developed use of Morgenstern is a good example of how Boes unites history and theory: we learn much more about the empirical circumstances of Morgenstern's intervention than we think we want to know, but this careful contextualization then generates the theoretical framework for the whole study.

The other, more important, original feature here is how that framework allows Boes to situate his contribution between the two houses of *Bildungsroman* criticism between which there is usually only sporadic dialogue, namely the one that operates entirely within German literature and the Goethean paradigm, and the other that takes the term very broadly as one of the leading 'natural' genres of world literature.

Boes gives a splendid close reading and intellectual-historical contextualization of *Wilhelm Meisters Lehrjahre*. The elaborately artificial ending of Goethe's novel is much illuminated by the idea of historicist-national thinking tempered by cosmopolitanism. The following three comparative essays are on Karl Immermann's *Die Epigonen* with Stendhal's *Le Rouge et le Noir*, Gustav Freytag's *Soll und Haben* with George Eliot's *Daniel Deronda*, and Alfred Döblin's *Berlin Alexanderplatz* with James Joyce's *Portrait of the Artist as a Young Man*. They fulfil the comparatist promise of the study by patiently drawing out the parallels between the ways in which respective and differing failures to find national form for the formation of the individual generate the 'cosmopolitan remainders' that permit comparison between novels all stamped with the difference of their own cultures.

A couple of minor complaints: it would have been worth mentioning that it is not at all clear that Döblin wanted the subtitle of his novel to be as it is, especially since Boes places some importance upon the appearance of the word 'Geschichte' in it (p. 128 onwards). More pedantically, the production company of *Berlin: Die Sinfonie der Grosstadt* was not Ufa, but Fox-Europa-Produktion (p. 129).

A slightly more major criticism is that the final chapter, on Thomas Mann's *Doktor Faustus*, becomes too complicated in its attempt to see in Mann's portentous allegory a continuation and conclusion of the argument. It is a risky undertaking to try to integrate Mann's own labyrinthine and self-conscious pathos about the fate of Germany with a reasoned analysis of the relation between historicism and allegory. Yet this overcomplication is certainly not representative of the intellectual style of the rest of the study. On the contrary, Boes handles many and difficult relevant bodies of thought, both historical and theoretical (Franco Moretti and Friedrich Meinecke, for instance), with exemplary clarity, writing in fluent and precise academic prose free of unnecessary jargon. What is more, he situates his work as a whole lucidly and creatively between the disciplines of German Studies and comparative literature, thereby enriching both of them and striking a blow for the ability of literary study to refresh itself at a time when the humanities are in sore need of the kind of inventiveness and confidence in them that Boes displays.

JESUS COLLEGE, CAMBRIDGE   MICHAEL MINDEN

International Bohemia: Scenes of Nineteenth-Century Life. By DANIEL COTTOM. Philadelphia: University of Pennsylvania Press. 2013. 354 pp. $59.95. ISBN 978-0-8122-4488-5.

Few nineteenth-century cultural types can have been so widely praised and reviled, or so multiply and conflictingly defined, as the bohemian. Daniel Cottom's ambitious book does not claim to give an exhaustive account of the life of this figure; as its subtitle suggests, it focuses instead on particular places, moments, and texts, each at once representative and unique, in which the term took on particular importance. Yet the effect obtained by this approach is impressively cornucopian, taking in works by major and forgotten authors from France, Britain, Germany, Italy, and the United States. In seven satisfyingly varied chapters, Cottom explores the rich cultural nexus of bohemianism, 'a form of cultural protest' with textual and real-life manifestations (p. 83). The book balances and interweaves anecdotal accounts of life in the bohemian milieux of nineteenth-century Paris and New York with detailed literary readings of writing by Henri Murger, George Eliot, Bram Stoker, Walt Whitman, Arthur Conan Doyle, and a host of others. Cottom's wide-ranging approach does full justice to the multiplicity of the bohemian stereotype, its centrality (both as fetish and bogey-man) to the nineteenth-century imagination, and its evolution across the century.

Cottom's obvious attraction to bohemian figures does nevertheless produce a somewhat idiosyncratic image of some of the works he considers. Thematic books are not to be reproached for focusing on their theme, of course, but Cottom's argument reveals a curious tendency to suggest that the very *absence* of any reference to bohemianism in a work is somehow compelling evidence of its relevance to that work. Thus we read, for instance, that 'the success with which [Whitman] internalized bohemianism may be measured by the fact that nineteenth-century reviewers of his publications did not think to mention it', and that 'Whitman's craft in writing and repeatedly revising his poems throughout his life makes the word *bohemian* stand out by its very absence in his corpus' (p. 152). Now seeing the world thus, through bohemian-tinted spectacles, can yield fascinating results: Dracula-as-bohemian is an intriguing idea, to be sure, and the interpretation of *Dracula* presented here is persuasive and exciting. But the results can also be rather odd—as is the case with Cottom's reading of George Eliot's *The Mill on the Floss*, which not only posits Maggie Tulliver as a sort of *grisette manquée*, but even reprimands Eliot for her 'heartbeaking' failure to make her heroine a true bohemian who follows her passions to their logical conclusion (p. 67). 'Why couldn't she have written *The Mill on the Floss* so that it was something more like, for instance, Christine Reid's *A Daughter of Bohemia* (1874)?', asks Cottom (p. 67). Why indeed? And what about that *Anna Karenina*, while we're at it? What a downer! Why couldn't Tolstoy have made it more like *Desperate Housewives*? One hardly needs to be a Leavisite to understand that moral conflict was at the heart of Eliot's work; as far as she was concerned, the jury was still out as to whether learning to love oneself really was the greatest love of all, or whether in fact we might have a duty to others as well. Yet Maggie's terrible ethical choice is reduced by Cottom to mere conformism.

The 'pro-hemian' *parti pris* at work in Cottom's dismissive reading of Eliot matters because it is arguably symptomatic of a broader sentimentalism in the book, which at times reads as much like a vindication of those plucky bohemians as a study of a cultural and historical trope. Still, even that reading has the very real merit of being original and provocative, and many of Cottom's most unexpected textual references are grounded in scrupulous, perceptive tropological work. The book is moreover written with pace, brio, and energy, in an accessible, demotic style. The importance of its topic and the breadth of its ambition make it a worthwhile read for nineteenth-centurists and general readers alike.

KING'S COLLEGE LONDON   ANDREW J. COUNTER

The Decadent Republic of Letters: Taste, Politics, and Cosmopolitan Community from Baudelaire to Beardsley. By MATTHEW POTOLSKY. Philadelphia: University of Pennsylvania Press. 2012. viii+232 pp. $59.95; £39. ISBN 978-0-8122-4449-6.

Two aspects of Baudelaire's aesthetic underpin Matthew Potolsky's argument for a revisionist reading of Decadent community: his encounter with the works of Poe and his list of titles of potential articles for *Le Hibou philosophe* (*The Philosopher Owl*), a projected journal from 1852 that never came to fruition. Baudelaire's reading, translation, and critical discussion of Poe is emblematic of a transnational reception and circulation of texts within a community of like-minded readers and writers, similarly evident in the cross-pollination between Gautier, Swinburne, Pater, Huysmans, and Wilde, not to mention all the other writers beyond the Anglo-French fields. Potolsky's book adapts its title from one of Baudelaire's proposed pieces for *Le Hibou philosophe*, 'La République des lettres'; another title, 'Les Ouvriers de la dernière heure', is used for the Introduction, which argues that Decadence should be seen not in terms of a retreat into apolitical individualism but as an active counterculture *avant la lettre*, a loosely affiliated community brought together by alienation from contemporary society and a hankering for an earlier form of republican civic humanism. Using Ferdinand Tönnies's distinction between *Gemeinschaft* (community) and *Gesellschaft* (society), Potolsky presents Decadence as a communal stance towards culture which is based on a family resemblance rather than a single doctrine, characterized by shared taste and exchange (borrowing, judgement, and production). Schiller's observation that taste is political provides an illuminating context for this debate: Potolsky shows how the writers associated with Decadence manifest the whole spectrum of political views, from reactionary to anarchist with all points in between, frequently changing within an individual's career (as in the case of Baudelaire), or even at the same time. If there is a common enemy, it is perhaps the twin pillars of liberalism and nationalism; here Potolsky argues that the libertine tradition is relevant as an aesthetic-political approach to freedom and an alternative to nineteenth-century bourgeois modernity. The predominant view of Decadence that comes out of the book is a correction not simply of Nordau's view of degeneration, but also of Bourget's view of atomization on both political and stylistic levels. Most importantly, it shows how the trope of considering Huysmans's character Des Esseintes in *A rebours* as the epitome of Decadence results in a misleading conception of the term as being synonymous solely with rejection, isolation, passivity, and a turning towards the past.

The Introduction is followed by five discrete chapters that explore different aspects of Potolsky's view of Decadence as a cosmopolitan community. Chapter 1 describes how Baudelaire never loses his interest in community, even as he becomes more conservative after the failure of the Second Republic: ironically, he becomes a critic of what might be perceived as the decadent 'zoocracy' of the Second Empire, which shows how fluid the term can become. His belief in the importance of an aesthetic elite for the public good—a form of shared enlightened artistic despotism, perhaps—reveals the paradoxical nature of this Decadent republicanism, with alienated outsiders forced to find a community, not least because of the economic consequences of the decline in patronage. Potolsky ends this chapter with an interesting discussion of Alfred de Vigny's little-known 1832 novel *Stello*, which proclaims the idea that the republic of letters is the only one whose citizens are truly free. The second chapter focuses on the politics of appreciation, examining the tributes to Baudelaire in Gautier's preface to the posthumous 1868 edition of *Les Fleurs du mal* and Swinburne's elegy 'Ave atque vale' from the same year. Potolsky argues that both Gautier and Swinburne view Baudelaire's Decadence as a source of political revival, proposing an emerging alternative polity to the contemporary hegemony, based on the aesthetic politics of internal exile. Chapter 3 explores the notion of Decadent canonization, outlining how Decadence challenges the national canon(s) through alternative corpora of texts; the examples here are taken from Pater's *The Renaissance* and Huysmans's *A rebours*, both of which contain extensive cataloguing of familiar and obscure sources. In the case of *The Picture of Dorian Gray*, reading the 'Yellow Book' (*A rebours*) initiates Dorian into the Decadent community in the same way that reading Petronius and Baudelaire *inter alios* initiates Des Esseintes himself; Potolsky also shows how Michael Field's *Sight and Song* similarly encapsulates an alternative canon of literature and ekphrases of Renaissance paintings. The fourth chapter looks at the tension between Decadent pedagogy and public education, challenging Fichte's analogy between school and nation in its delineation of an alternative 'aesthetic-didactic nexus', illustrated here by several examples of the Pygmalion story (including Sacher-Masoch's *Venus in Furs*, Rachilde's *Monsieur Vénus*, and Vernon Lee's *Miss Brown*). Chapter 5 casts a synoptic eye over some versions of Decadent community, locating them in a theoretical framework informed by Jean-Luc Nancy's notion of 'literary communism' and Michael Warner's work on 'counterpublics'; yet even this draws on new examples to illustrate its thesis, discussing two unfinished works: Pater's *Gaston Latour* and Beardsley's *The Story of Venus and Tannhäuser*. The book ends with a refreshing postscript, a close reading of Mallarmé's memorial sonnet 'Hommage'/'Le Tombeau de Charles Baudelaire' that interprets 'pubis' not as a sexual reference but as an allusion to the Latin word *pubes*, referring to the adult male population. For Potolsky, Mallarmé recuperates Baudelaire as a public figure representing his community, symbolized by the street light depicted in the poem; similarly, Baudelaire emerges from Potolsky's own book as a more complex figure, both modern and anti-modern, Decadent and anti-decadent.

The Decadent Republic of Letters is a rewarding and stimulating study of the nineteenth-century literary field that wears its impressive erudition with a pleasurable lightness. My one reservation concerns the opening claims that Decadence was a movement with a manifesto (p. 3) or 'produced a remarkable number of collective manifestos' (p. 6): the evidence for this seems to rest principally on Luca Somigli's work on manifesto-writing, but considering Anatole Baju's editorial 'A nos lecteurs!' in the first issue of *Le Décadent* (April 1886) as a manifesto is a contentious point, and the same objection can be raised against similar claims for 'textes manifestaires' by Gautier, Bourget, and others. In fact the lack of a manifesto would actually support Potolsky's overriding argument that Decadence is an amorphous stance that continues to permeate our culture today (did the hippies or the punks need manifestos?), and this minor caveat does not detract from the overall quality of the work, which demonstrates how Potolsky has successfully written himself into the Decadent community.

UNIVERSITY OF LEEDS   RICHARD HIBBITT

Modernism and the Orient. Ed. by ZHAOMING QIAN. New Orleans: University of New Orleans Press. 2013. 294 pp. $24.95. ISBN 978-1-60801-074-5.

In recent studies of modernism there has been an increasing emphasis on its global context, marked by multilingualism, cultural transfer, and creative adaptation. This collection of twelve essays, based on the third International Conference on Modernism and the Orient which took place in Hangzhou, China, in 2010, contributes precisely to this burgeoning field of study. The term 'modernism' is used to indicate a time-span from the late nineteenth to the second half of the twentieth century in predominantly Anglo-American and Irish contexts, Marcel Proust being the only exception. Half of the essays focus on 'high' Modernist writers such as Ezra Pound, T. S. Eliot, Virginia Woolf, James Joyce, W. B. Yeats, Robert Frost, Marianne Moore, and Proust. The others cover two 'proto-modernists', Oscar Wilde and Emily Dickinson, and three 'post-war modernists', Louis Zukofsky, Harry Guest, and Lee Harwood. The 'Orient' in this book refers to Japan and especially China. One of the contentious points that Zhaoming Qian hopes to demonstrate is that 'Of the Orient, the Far East proved more productive than the Near East as a source of literary models for twentieth-century Western writers' (p. xiv). The volume revisits a group of works by modernist writers that manifest their individual as well as collective fascination for, or in Qian's words 'instinctive affinity' (p. xvi) with, Far Eastern art, literature, and thought.

Most of the essays are well documented. In some cases the documentary discovery itself is highly original. Ronald Bush's essay on Pound and the figure of Buddhist bodhisattva centres on his close examination of the poet's unpublished manuscripts or avant-texts of *Pisan Cantos* in Italian and English. Qian's essay on the late Moore and Taoism is based on the newly discovered recording of Moore's 1957 lecture 'Tedium and Integrity', which, as Qian insists, 'provides essential clues about the development of Moore's late modernist poetic' (p. 214) manifest in *O to Be a Dragon* (1959) and *Tell Me, Tell Me* (1966). Christine Froula takes surprisingly varied approaches to 'Proust's China'. She astutely explores the historical details in and behind one of the most celebrated paintings in Proust's *A la recherche du temps perdu*, Vermeer's *View of Delft*, highlighting various fascinating Sino-Dutch connections in Vermeer's time. Many of the findings seem to anticipate Proust's characters' remarks on Chinese objects centuries later. This is further supported by details of Proust's close contact with Jean-Louis Vaudoyer (who reviewed the Vermeer exhibition) and by the genesis of the passage on Bergotte's death. The overall argument revolves around modernists' '"new" historic sense of our time' (p. xv) (Ezra Pound) as well as André Benhaïm's claim about Proust's intention to '"disorient" radicalized ideas of France, Frenchness, and the nation' in the context of 'a new century of nationalist violence and ethnic persecution' (quoted by Froula, p. 75). This article is certainly one of the most extensive exegeses of what is often seen as an intriguing connection between Bergotte's artistic regret and his final revealing observation of an essential detail in Vermeer's painting, 'the tiny section of yellow wall', which is compared to 'a precious Chinese work of art' (p. 81).

There are some fine examples of comparative study. Zhang Longxi's essay on Wilde and Zhuangzi's Taoist philosophy, Qiping Yin's examination of Frost's poetic imagery in Taoist perspective, and Ira Nadel's study of Joyce and Chinese writing are refreshing rereadings of canonical texts. Their approaches move smoothly from the traditional notion of 'influence' to what one might call 'confluence' studies, as their analytical foci gradually shift from empirical textual evidence to aesthetic and poetic cross-fertilization. On the other hand, some scholars may find Fen Gao's reading of Woolf's notion of truth in the light of Chinese poetics slightly forced and schematic, precisely because her approach completely breaks away from influence studies and cross-culturally compares two 'similar' concepts, which may appear historically and epistemologically difficult to justify in Woolf's case.

Because of the relatively unfamiliar Far Eastern angle, a good amount of 'new' material is almost guaranteed even for specialists in modernism. Scholars and students working in comparative literature are likely to benefit most from this book. However, it makes little effort to problematize traditional concepts of modernism as an elitist, anti-Romantic/Victorian, and male-dominated artistic and literary movement. How important is this Far Eastern Orientalism to the overall Modernist movement and how could this 'new' perspective challenge any of our received understandings of modernism? These questions could have been taken further. On a minor note, the English translations of *Ru Shi* and *Chu Shi* should be matched in reverse order on page xix—a tiny error, but one that could be misleading for those unfamiliar with Chinese terminology.

UNIVERSITY OF EDINBURGH   SHUANGYI LI

Literature and Psychoanalysis. By JEREMY TAMBLING. Manchester: Manchester University Press. 2012. vi+169 pp. £60 (pbk £12.99). ISBN 978-0-7190-8673-1 (pbk 978-0-7190-8674-8).

At the beginning of this book, Jeremy Tambling explains why he is interested in studying the key texts of three major psychoanalysts—Sigmund Freud, Melanie Klein, and Jacques Lacan—and applying their findings to the study of literature. Those authors 'have decentred "man" from being the centre of his own world' (p. 6): they have shown 'the ego that it is not master in its own house but must content itself with scanty information of what is going on unconsciously in its mind' (p. 5). What Freud says about literature, then, enables 'some exciting ways of considering it' (p. 6): literature's essence might eventually be 'that it has no essence. Its precise words turn out to be not quite what is meant to be said, because language condenses and displaces' (p. 13). Psychoanalysis has also circulated a large number of concepts and expressions that literary scholars cannot ignore: Oedipus complex, Freudian slips, *déjà vu*, death drive, superego, the uncanny, and so on. Finally, no approach to theory can 'fail to engage with Freud's legacy, and his legacy as, substantially, that theory's diversity' (p. 6). The first two chapters of the book—devoted to Freud's decentring work and to analyses of literary texts in the light of Freud's discoveries—have an introductory approach and target interested but not highly knowledgeable readers. Subsequent chapters are more testing and challenge competent readers, sometimes with rather cryptic references. Complex texts by Freud, Klein, and Lacan, and by authors as different as Wilfred Bion, Jacques Derrida, W. R. D. Fairbairn, Julia Kristeva, and D. W. Winnicott, are used to discuss what memory and guilt may mean in Freud, the significance of the mother in literature and psychoanalysis, the mechanisms of introjection and projection in the development of the infant as described by Klein, and the roles that alienation, the Imaginary, the Symbolic, and the Real play in Lacan's thought.

Tambling claims the right to be selective in his choice of topics, and the texts written by the authors he studies are so many and dense that few would argue with him. The criteria that drive his selection, however, are rather vague. He is interested in what is relevant for literature—but what is not? He repeatedly stresses his personal fascination with 'that sense of repressed meanings being always a potential in the text', with the liberation entailed in 'statements that mean the opposite of what they say' (p. 13) and in the assumptions that 'truth' cannot be 'single, unitary' (p. 23), that 'we cannot ask "what did Beckett really mean by Godot?" in

Waiting for Godot' (p. 97); but these statements may also be problematic. On the one hand, if we need psychoanalysis to achieve that fascination and to experience that liberation, why is this so? Isn't the authority that one relies on connected to the scientific component of Freud's work, to his and his colleagues' pursuit of some truth, or at least to the understanding of some ambiguity, in the care of their patients? On the other hand, the claim (in the blurb on the back cover) that 'all those who have wondered what Freud really said [. . .] will want to read this book' might be accidental, or ironic, but Tambling seems to partially contradict himself a few times. Focusing, for example, on the *Studies in Hysteria* (1895) and on related studies published by Freud ten years later—and neglecting 'The Aetiology of Hysteria' (1896) and its implications—looks like an overly neat way to reach the single 'truth' that Freud 'was gendering hysteria as female' (pp. 2, 58). Freud discussed only women patients in the *Studies*, but he very interestingly referred to men in 'The Aetiology' (pp. 207-08 of the *Standard Edition* used in this study).

This said, Tambling's book is thought-provoking, especially when it deals with writing as madness in Chapter 8. It elicits a good number of possible interpretations from the literary texts it quotes, such as Wordsworth's *The Prelude; or, Growth of a Poet's Mind* in Chapter 5. The discussion of Lacan's ideas, in Chapter 6, is one of the clearest one can read. The bibliography is wide-ranging, from Jacopone da Todi to Rossellini, and the connections highlighted between distant texts are extremely interesting. Some remarks on how to translate Freud's German into English are also very useful.

University of Exeter   Luciano Parisi

In Dark Again in Wonder: The Poetry of René Char and George Oppen. By Robert Baker. Notre Dame: University of Notre Dame Press. 2012. xiv+238 pp. $36; £24. ISBN 978-0-268-02229-7.

At the beginning of what he describes as his book's very long conclusion, Robert Baker asserts that Char and Oppen 'are poets as concerned with the question of freedom as with the question of the whole in which they find themselves' (p. 121). Much of the rest of the book attests to the fact that this claim is at once very likely true and at the same time peculiarly difficult to explain by way of detailed specificity. Given that it is a basic intention of *In Dark Again in Wonder* to establish common grounds between two poets who do not ostensibly share any—'Char's work [. . .] represents many of the things Oppen most distrusted in poetry' (p. 10)—Baker's arguments and observations incline consistently and necessarily towards abstraction. Trying to uncover deep connections between such disparate poets means that found affiliations are at once remote and profound. Indeed, the subtitle of the long conclusion, 'Revisions of Axial Age Metaphysics in the Age of Modernity', gives the reader an idea of just how far Baker must look to find shared concerns. The decision to make a case for comparison based on such elemental relations is purposive (and not by any means a fault). It seems to me that the critical inclination to aggrandize rather than discriminate constitutes Baker's basic critical ethos, one exemplified by an effort to see similarities despite obvious differences, and shared associations despite certain peculiarities. The basic term of relation, as the book's title suggests, is 'wonder', a quasi-religious and somewhat variously construed manifestation of poetical and philosophical belief. In one typical passage, for example, he writes: 'If one could, as I've said, characterize this way of seeing as Heideggerian or Marcelian, one could also characterize it as Emersonian, Whitmanian, Stevensian. Our lives take place within this ultimately unfathomable whole, appalling and benevolent at once, perpetually erosive and perpetually disclosive at once' (p. 100).

Among the book's signature conceptual and argumentative strategies is the suspension of considerations of aesthetic difference, analysing instead poems and/or sequences according to a logic of accumulative paraphrase in which several conversant but perhaps not exactly parallel readings of this or that important impulse in Char's or Oppen's work are enumerated before quoting a few lines of poetry, as in: 'Time is a source of the layering of depths and horizons, of the slopes between the given and the invisible, the immediate and the not yet. "Lend to the bud, in leaving it the future, all the brightness of the deep flower", Char writes in "Companions in the Garden"' (p. 19). What is curious about this approach is that frequently the poetry quoted by way of example serves to clarify Baker's commentary, rather than vice versa, so that the verses under inspection become evidentiary clarifications of the analyses which precede them. At one point Baker claims somewhat enigmatically that '[a]ll that we engage in thought exceeds all that we think'; he then immediately quotes from Oppen without much further comment or ado:

> Clarity
> In the sense of *transparence*,
> I don't mean that much can be explained.
>
> Clarity in the sense of silence.
>
> (p. 93)

The final chapter—to this reader's mind the most important and useful—suspends its focus on the individual titular poets for long periods, opting instead for impressive and wide-ranging accounts of Romantic and existential philosophical and religious thought, exploring ideas that not only inform the poetries written by Char and Oppen, but the work of numerous other 'philosophical' poets influenced by 'the long modern conflict between an historicist sociology and a romantic existentialism' (p. 6). In sum, Baker has written a comprehensive study of how modernist European and American poetry continues to internalize philosophical oppositions by looking beyond the discrete outputs of the two poets it names in its title. In this sense, it will be of equal interest to anyone concerned with Char's œuvre, Oppen's work, or with the intellectual history of Western religion, philosophy, and art in the twentieth century.

Universität Bayreuth   Michael Kindellan

Conversing Identities: Encounters between British, Irish and Greek Poetry, 1922-1952. By KONSTANTINA GEORGANTA. Amsterdam and New York: Rodopi. 2012. x+224 pp. $65. ISBN 978-90-420-3563-8.

Conversing Identities 'presents a panorama' of the British-Irish and Greek cultures 'brought in dialogue through travel, immigration and translation set against the insularity imposed by war and the hegemony of the national centre', claims the cover of this book. Konstantina Georganta delivers: her book offers a very readable analysis of the poetic and broader literary intersections between British, Irish, and Greek poetry during three crucial decades of the twentieth century (1922-52). These decades coincide with turbulent times in Greece (the Smyrna Disaster in the aftermath of the First World War, rising European Fascism and the inter-war Greek dictatorship of Metaxas, the Nazi/German Occupation of the Second World War, and the destructive Civil War). These events are reflected in Georganta's careful contextualizations of her topics and subjects. Greece is certainly at the forefront, both geographically (extending beyond the country's current national borders) and symbolically (encompassing ancient through modern language and culture, with a solid presence of Homer). Much of Georganta's book is further devoted to the insights that British and Irish poets have shared *about* Greece, that is, to these travellers' receptions (plural, indeed) of modern Greece and of Hellenism at large.

Georganta's original dissertation topic has, in the pages of this book, matured into a discerning reflection on modernism, aesthetics, literature, and art across European borders. Her book is particularly strong in its discussions of the Greek poets Palamas, Cavafy, and Seferis, but the reader will learn a tremendous amount also about the less-known Demetrios Capetanakis, who made the journey to the British metropolis (based on the author's meticulous archival research). British and Irish poetry is tellingly represented by T. S. Eliot, John Lehmann, Louis MacNeice, William Plomer, and W. B. Yeats. W. H. Auden, Elytis, Nikos Engonopoulos, E. M. Forster, Joyce, Kostas Karyotakis, and a few French poets receive brief but necessary attention. Georganta has admirably kept the focus on the essence of literary modernism, and eloquently attests to its potential to establish 'mobility across frontiers' (pp. 4, 11, 31). Prominent and productive also are her guiding themes of memory, tradition, cultural ruins, symbolic transfers, the search for identity and authenticity, and geographical and psychological displacement (the unreal city, the homeland utopia, city and hinterland, diverse diaspora). Palpable, too, is the impact of modernist building construction and infrastructural design as well as of new technologies such as radio broadcasts, with the classicist, translator, and traveller Louis MacNeice among its pioneers and masters. Despite his xenophobia and imperial anxieties, Mr. Eugenides, Eliot's displaced hero of *The Waste Land*, becomes symbolic of the cross-cultural encounters and of the fraught historical times. William Plomer's writings capture a journey of the early 1930s, on the escape from what he himself called 'insular complacency' (p. 55), whereas John Lehmann 'attempted to construct a return to the bones of the Mediterranean to heal a sense of homelessness' (p. 149).

The crisp analysis of Georganta's book shows solid theoretical awareness but is not dictated by theory. The seven chapters are rounded off by an Introduction, Conclusion, extensive bibliography, and handy index. The author's writing style remains lucid throughout and the copious notes provide apt clarifications and further references. The quality of the book's illustrations, however, leaves a lot to be desired. I recommend that Rodopi redo the illustrations if the book were to be published online in the near future.

UNIVERSITY OF FLORIDA   GONDA VAN STEEN

A Critical Edition of the Complete Poems of Henry Howard, Earl of Surrey. Ed. by WILLIAM MCGAW. Foreword by WILLIAM A. SESSIONS. Lewiston, NY: Mellen. 2012. xcix+536 pp. £114.95. ISBN 0-7734-2917-4.

At the beginning of his Foreword, the eminent Surrey scholar William A. Sessions exclaims, '[a]t last an edition of the poems of the Earl of Surrey that is intellectually comprehensive and textually accurate—and completely accessible to all readers of this great innovator of poetry in English' (p. i), and as the reader winds his or her way through this mighty tome it becomes increasingly difficult to resist this conclusion. William McGaw has performed an invaluable service to sixteenth-century scholarship in completing this ambitious project. He himself acknowledges in his prefatory discussion that this *Critical Edition* has had a long and eventful gestation period: its origins look back to academic conversations of 1979. In 1993 the unfinished typescript became 'seemingly irrevocably locked in an outdated Apple Macintosh' and was not fully retrieved until 2004 (p. v). After this eleven-year hiatus, the project was resumed and saw the light of day in 2012. With this publication, McGaw establishes a corpus of Surrey's work which extends to fifty-nine poems: forty-four songs and sonnets; eleven biblical paraphrases with two prologues; and two books of the *Aeneid*.

If, in the sixteenth-century accounts of the earl, it is often difficult in the praise devoted to him to distinguish between his lofty achievements as a poet and his equally dazzling profile at the court of Henry VIII, in the intervening centuries he has all too frequently slipped from critical and reader attention. Thus, scholars and students alike have found themselves relying on ageing editions and anthologies to gain access to this major Tudor poet while, in the twentieth century, his contemporary Thomas Wyatt enjoyed renewed interest from editors and critics alike—often in the guise of a precursor to Donne.

Carefully researched and fluently introduced, McGaw's edition finally unveils for modern scrutiny the breadth of Surrey's poetic achievements, taking into account his roles in transforming the Petrarchan sonnet into English, his creative skills in the forging of English blank verse, and his significant investments in the English elegiac tradition: 'Whatever its origins, Surrey's blank verse was a striking but, more importantly, astute innovation. Lack of rhyme allowed Surrey not only the prosodic but also the grammatical freedom to follow Virgil's thought patterns and imitate his verse paragraphs [in his translations of the *Aeneid*]' (p. xxxi). Initial discussions focus upon Surrey's biography, poetic diction, and chosen poetic modes: 'Not only is Surrey not an archaist but also he is, surprisingly for his age, mostly non-proverbial in his thought [compared with Wyatt]' (p. xxvi). Subsequently, however, more thorny and, ultimately perhaps, more revelatory discussions examine the difficulties surrounding questions of textual dating, methods of composition, and textual transmission: 'the chronological order of Surrey's poems is problematic and [. . .] no manuscript or publication authority [exists] for placing Surrey's collected poems in any particular order' (p. lxxxii).

One of the other major contributions of this edition is its attention to the intertextual nature of Surrey's poetic undertakings, and McGaw offers sustained and valuable treatment of his French but, most particularly, Italian poetic influences in his commentaries in the latter half of the collection. In terms of the presentation of the poetic texts themselves, this reader initially looked for a tripartite division to the page which might have included the lively material from the endnotes, instead of a bipartite structure where the eye was left to ponder the text and its variants. However, on reflection, this format perhaps allows the contours and diversity of Surrey's poetic output to be rendered more evident as the shorter lyrics are swiftly placed in conversation with the biblical paraphrases and translations. McGaw rightly draws attention throughout this volume to the achievements of Tottel's *Songes and Sonettes* and *Certain Bokes of Vergiles 'Aenaeis' Turned into English Metere by the Right Honorable Lorde, Henry Earle of Surrey* (both 1557) during the reign of Mary I and to those of more modern editions, such as Emry Jones's *Surrey: Poems* (Oxford: Clarendon Press, 1964) in disseminating Surrey's poetry to a wider audience. Indeed, rather unexpectedly, McGaw follows Jones's lead in his own Introduction in concluding that 'in all his work [Surrey's] inclination was to adapt material rather than be original [. . .]. As a courtly maker, Surrey was by definition a derivative poet' (p. lii).

The Introduction in its present form is substantial, extending to just short of a hundred pages. Nonetheless, this reader would have liked a little more sustained attention devoted to the problematizing of such questions of 'originality' (see above) in early Tudor culture, to the artistic environment of courtly 'makers' during the reign of Henry VIII, and indeed to Surrey's textual negotiations with his British (*as well as* his continental and antique) predecessors: McGaw raises some lively questions of the influence of Chaucer's *Troilus and Criseyde*, for example, on Surrey's erotic writing, and, indeed, Skelton's interest in the elegiac mode might also have offered greater pause for consideration in this context. Nonetheless, the valuable achievement of this critical edition is never in question. It showcases Surrey's work in a manner hitherto unknown and will clearly become a mainstay of Surrey scholarship for the future.

BANGOR UNIVERSITY ANDREW HISCOCK

Edmund Spenser: A Life. By ANDREW HADFIELD. Oxford: Oxford University Press. 2012. xxi+624 pp. £25. ISBN 978-0-19-959102-2.

A thorough, up-to-date biography of Edmund Spenser, considered by his contemporaries as the greatest English poet of the late sixteenth century, is long overdue. Apart from Willy Maley's skeletal *A Spenser Chronology* (London: Macmillan, 1994), there has been no Life since A. C. Judson's volume for the Variorum Edition of Spenser's *Works* in 1945 (*The Life of Edmund Spenser* (Baltimore: Johns Hopkins University Press, 1945). Innumerable new details relevant to the life have since emerged, and there have been fundamental shifts in perspective, particularly on Spenser's career as a colonial settler and official in Elizabethan Ireland. Andrew Hadfield and Oxford University Press are thus to be applauded for undertaking a substantial new biography. Hadfield's breadth of reading and his coverage of relevant details are impressive. He has not only traversed the vast forests of Spenserian scholarship and criticism, both recent and historical (approximately half the volume consists of footnotes and bibliography), but also, most valuably, explored the byways of sixteenth-century intellectual, political, economic, and religious networks, in London, Cambridge, and Ireland, which may have influenced Spenser or with which he may have engaged. For Hadfield, 'writing a biography is as much about establishing the contexts [. . .] as it is about startling archival discoveries' (p. 10). By piecing together a jigsaw of clues and allusions, he sheds new light on crucial aspects of Spenser's life: family connections in Northamptonshire; the network of sponsors and companions that conditioned his schooling and university education; and the official services and advantageous land deals that established his family among the other pioneering gentlemen settlers in Munster. The contexts Hadfield elaborates are indeed highly suggestive, although, in the absence of many 'startling archival discoveries', key aspects of Spenser's life (his family origins, his ambitions, the circumstances of his death) remain tantalizingly elusive.

If the bare archival witnesses of Spenser's life—financial records, official correspondence, and dates and details of publications and printers—yield sparse clues, the writings of Spenser himself, and of others close to him, particularly the published letters of Gabriel Harvey, offer more promising material. Hadfield is fully alive to the complex problem of Spenser's self-representation—he quotes Richard McCabe's description of Spenser's works as 'self referential but seldom autobiographical'—and mainly handles the poetry with tact (McCabe, 'Edmund Spenser', in *The Cambridge Companion to English Poets*, ed. by Claude Rawson (Cambridge: Cambridge University Press, 2011), pp. 53–71 (p. 53); cited in Hadfield, p. 401). There are, nevertheless, some surprising readings. The shepherd's slaughter of the wolf in sheep's clothing in the September eclogue of *The Shepheardes Calender* ('[He] let out the sheepes bloud at his throte') is interpreted as showing that 'even wolves are part sheep' (pp. 116–18). Hadfield's argument is that Spenser sympathized with the ideas of the Family of Love, a shadowy group tolerant of Roman Catholicism, and that the fable criticizes Bishop Young (the shepherd) for undiscerning persecution of the Familists. Hadfield contends that Spenser was throughout his life more sympathetic to Catholicism than has been recognized and that in, for instance, the Blatant Beast episode in Book VI of *The Faerie Queene*, 'pre-Reformation religion is the locus of stability, security and culture' (p. 225).

For a book that will undoubtedly become the authoritative biography of Spenser, there are a shocking number of irritating minor errors and typos. Two sonnets 'in alexandrines' (p. 92), which Hadfield thinks may be experiments, turn out, when quoted (complete with typo), to be, after the first two lines, in old-fashioned Poulter's Measure; and a letter, illustrated in facsimile, is twice described as being from O'Neill and dated 31 August 1580, when the facsimile clearly displays a different letter dated 29 August (pp. 158–59). Sentences are sometimes difficult to navigate (two examples on page 270), a large percentage of quotations contain typos, and even Spenser's name gets misspelt. Such carelessness disappointingly mars what is otherwise a thoroughly valuable book.

UNIVERSITY OF READING   ELIZABETH HEALE

Drama and the Transfer of Power in Renaissance England. By MARTIN WIGGINS. Oxford: Oxford University Press. 2012. xii+151 pp. £62. ISBN 978-0-19-965059-0.

Contemporary politics were one of the taboo subjects for professional dramatists in the early modern period in England. A casual satiric reference to James I's Scottish knights had the authors of *Eastward Hoe* in prison with their noses and ears in danger. Editions of Shakespeare's *Richard II* published in the lifetime of Elizabeth had to appear with the abdication scene omitted. Even though the events in question happened two hundred years before, the very fact that a monarch was represented publicly abdicating his throne was too touchy a subject for the paranoid queen. But what if it was the state itself that sought to make theatrical capital out of topical events? Martin Wiggins, in this intriguing and learned study, argues that at key moments of the transfer of power in England, drama was one of the instruments of government propaganda.

Wiggins, no doubt drawing on his research for *British Drama 1533–1642: A Catalogue* (the first three volumes of which have appeared; Oxford: Oxford University Press, 2011–13), picks out five specific dates for illustrating his thesis. In 1535, when Henry VIII was enforcing the Act of Supremacy, a pageant staged as part of the city's Midsummer Watch in an episode drawn from the Book of Revelation showed 'a group of clerics being beheaded' with 'the character doing the cutting [. . .] a representation of King Henry himself' (p. 7). At the Christmas season of 1558–59, in the immediate wake of Queen Elizabeth's accession, a masque was performed, according to one contemporary observer, with 'crows in the habits of Cardinals, [. . .] asses habited as Bishops, and [. . .] wolves representing Abbots' (p. 23). The strong anti-Papist message was appropriate as the new queen returned the realm to Protestantism after the reign of her Catholic sister Mary, though Wiggins interestingly shows that this sort of fervently Protestant, anti-authoritarian drama was soon to be reined in by Elizabeth. A number of instances are given of the 'performances' that smoothed the accession of James I in 1603: a sycophantic invitation to him to hunt on his progress down from Scotland, and a court masque by Queen Anne with recycled clothes from the wardrobe of the dead Elizabeth. The elaborate and expensive pageants planned for the new King Charles I's formal entry into the City of London in 1625 were finally cancelled after a year's preparation, in part, Wiggins argues, because the King did not feel the need for such validation: 'he simply was the rightful King of England, despite all controversy' (p. 92). The year 1642 is a different case. No pageants signalled the shift of power from King to Parliament; on the contrary, Parliament put an end to any potentially politically significant shows by shutting down the theatres, though for contingent rather than absolutely ideological reasons, as Wiggins shows.

The difficulty with this investigation, as Wiggins admits, is that there are virtually no texts extant. The 'drama' that did (or did not) accompany the transfer of power in each case has to be reconstructed from accounts of costumes used, knowledge of generic practice for court masques, city pageants, and ceremonies, and from the gossipy and often scandalized reports of ambassadors to foreign states. Bricks have to be made with the wispiest pieces of straw, or sometimes no straw at all. Speculation as to whether the invitation to James to hunt 'at the northern edge of Sherwood Forest' would have involved references to Robin Hood produces what Wiggins accepts is a 'rickety tower of hypothesis' (pp. 47–48). Much of the book is arcane literary detective work but no less fascinating for that, extending our sense of what constituted drama in Renaissance England, and how it could be used to massage public opinion as power shifted from one regime to another.

TRINITY COLLEGE DUBLIN   NICHOLAS GRENE

Swift and Science: The Satire, Politics, and Theology of Natural Knowledge, 1690–1730. By GREGORY LYNALL. Basingstoke: Palgrave Macmillan. 2012. xi+209 pp. £50. ISBN 978–0–230–34364–1.

What is Swift's relationship to Enlightenment? If we consider that question from the perspective of his attitude to science, it would seem that he was its implacable foe. Swift is usually regarded as hostile to scientific and technological progress. When he has the King of Brobdingnag give the following opinion, Swift might appear to envisage a role for science in agricultural improvement: 'whoever could make two Ears of Corn, or two Blades of Grass to grow upon a spot of Ground where only one grew before; would deserve better of Mankind, and do more essential Service to his Country, than the whole Race of Politicians put together' (*Gulliver's Travels*, Book II, Chapter 7, repr. in *The Essential Writings of Jonathan Swift*, ed. by Claude Rawson and Ian Higgins (New York: Norton, 2010), pp. 311–502 (p. 399)). In context, though, the King has just refused to learn the secret of gunpowder, a malevolent invention of diabolical science; and in the Lord Munodi Swift creates a character who has entirely traditional methods of rendering nature fruitful, as if the cornfields might double their yield through some means that was itself 'natural'.

Gregory Lynall's knowledgeable and nuanced book presents a different view of Swift's attitude to science. His conception of that relationship is fully alive to the distinctive and disconcerting aspect of early eighteenth-century satiric practice: that those who wrote satire were not necessarily inveterate enemies of their targets. Those who think, for example, that John Gay wrote *The Beggar's Opera* (1728) because he despised Italian opera are very wide of the mark. Characteristic of the satire sometimes termed 'Scriblerian' is its way of utilizing the creative energy of those writers and literary forms that it simultaneously affects to excoriate. So it is, Lynall argues throughout this book, with Swift's attitude towards science.

Lynall has two related conceptions of Swift's scientific satire that render it less unenlightened and marooned by history than it may seem: he sees it as opportunistic, and he sees it as particular. Taken together, these vantage-points imply that Swiftian satire does not always result from a deep and utopian analysis of how the way things are falls short of the way things could be. Sometimes it results from a desire to ridicule particular individuals and particular literary or philosophical works: it takes opportunities, settles scores, alleviates spleen; 'animosities for and between individuals and institutions over single matters could boil over to encompass all affairs' (p. 9). Lynall's main achievement in this book, therefore, is to put into circulation new contenders for the particular objects of Swift's satire in the *Tale*, the *Battel*, *Gulliver's Travels*, and the poem 'Directions for a Birth-day Song'.

Lynall makes a strong case for the argument that a principal target of the *Meditation upon a Broom-Stick*, and even of the *Tale*, is Robert Boyle's so-called 'meletetics', his *Occasional Reflections upon Several Subjects*—even if it is difficult to see why this relatively harmless work should have been so firmly in Swift's sights (pp. 19–20). Through close reading of the Spider and Bee episode in the *Battel*, Lynall argues that Swift is in dialogue with Thomas Burnet's *Sacred Theory of the Earth* (1698) and with John Keill's *Examination* of Burnet's book (1698). Elsewhere, Isaac Newton is placed firmly back on the agenda as a target for Swift's anti-mathematical animus in Book III of *Gulliver's Travels*. The context for this is convincingly Irish: as Master of the Mint, Newton had been responsible for an assay of Wood's coins that showed them to be of proper weight. Swift ridiculed Newton's naivety, in the *Drapier's Letters*, for imagining that the sample sent by Wood was in any way typical of the coinage as a whole. Unworldliness on this scale is what makes Newton into a Laputan. Lynall's least convincing chapter is his final one on Swift's 1729 poem 'Directions for a Birth-day Song'. Here, two brief passages that refer to Queen Caroline's interest in metaphysical speculation and to Dr Samuel Clarke, who was known to have tutored her in such esoteric matters, provide Lynall with a somewhat slender hook upon which to hang the heavy coat of an examination of early-century materialism, deism, and Socinianism.

Even if this final chapter reads like the work of an editor who does not know when to end his gloss, Lynall is usually aware of the allegorizing and reductivist dangers that inhere in the kinds of source-hunting upon which he has embarked. He senses the tension between arguing that Swift is a complex satirist and identifying the specific individuals and their works that lie behind passages such as

Section ix of the *Tale*. He pilots us through this Scylla and Charybdis successfully for most of this engaging and absorbing book.

UNIVERSITY OF NOTTINGHAM   BREAN S. HAMMOND

Early Modern Poetics in Melville and Poe: Memory, Melancholy and the Emblematic Tradition. By WILLIAM F. ENGEL. Farnham: Ashgate. 2012. ii+191 pp. £62.66. ISBN 978-1-4094-358-6.

William Engel explores the conjoined topics of memory, death, and literary form, especially chiasmus, in this and earlier works to expose the interplay between reader response to form and theme in the light of the varied codes and images descended through the English literary traditions of the Renaissance and the seventeenth and early eighteenth centuries. Engel establishes through copious illustrations the power of chiasmus in binding together and providing shape to two works in particular—Melville's 'The Encantadas' and Poe's 'The Raven'—but his avowed aim is not only to assess structure but also to examine the broader function of establishing dynamic memory images which involve allegory, pagan gods, and architecture to express the authors' sense of enclosure and loss. In 'The Encantadas', Engel finds the matched sides of the equally split ten chapters to reflect on each other, beginning and ending with the idea of death and the potter's field. Between those bookends he finds balancing elements of the physical world leading to metaphysics in the early chapters mirrored in the later ones by the turn to mundane social realities discovered through the histories of human residents of the islands. In so doing, Engel establishes his basis for textual echoes and thematic reduplications which he unravels in convincing complexity, exploring not only images and literary devices, but also sound echoes and interlingual puns.

Often enough, when Engel seems to be getting furthest from rational relationships, the introduction of a historical source provides impressive underpinnings for his thematic insights, providing the reader with intriguing challenges. In 'The Raven', Engel's search generalizes as well into the deciphering of Poe's playfully coded messages and his transference of echoes not only within the structure of the poem but also leading outward to other sources, including various French references refracted by Poe's theories of hidden structure and the deciphering of lost meaning. Architecture and the architectural provide 'The Raven' with a form that contains the memory of pain and loss, presided over by the bust of Pallas over the chamber door. Numerology helps unlock its consistency and chiastic progression. In each of these cases, Engel teases out the intended elaborations of the emotions of mortality in interesting ways that give the works greater power than their already formidable reputations suggest, and which bring Engel himself to a rhetorical climax in the expiration and inspiration of breath as the ultimate bodily expression. In his own words, chiasmus provides 'a reshaping of the order of thought that takes form finally as an allegory at odds with its own mechanisms of generating meaning' which exhausts the forms which Poe and Melville have employed (p. 159). Scholarly readers should find the intricacy of Engel's arguments engaging and thought-provoking, and, one would hope, the source of a broader appreciation of both of these powerful works as representative of the canons from which they come.

UNIVERSITY OF NEW HAVEN   DAVID E. E. SLOANE

Modernizing George Eliot: The Writer as Artist, Intellectual, Proto-Modernist, Cultural Critic. By K. M. NEWTON. London: Bloomsbury. 2011. viii+230 pp. £55. ISBN 978-1-84966-494-3.

The essays in this volume, which in part bring together in revised configuration K. M. Newton's thinking on George Eliot over some years, are loosely grouped into three sections around the areas announced in the book's title: the author's intellectual, aesthetic, and cultural concerns. The 'modernizing' aspect of the first section, on George Eliot's intellectual achievements, is its endeavour to reorient contemporary views of George Eliot towards appreciation of her as an original, rather than derivative, thinker who made a significant contribution to developments in nineteenth-century European thought. Successive chapters deal with Eliot's critical appropriation of Darwinian, Byronic, and Kantian world-views, and her rigorous testing—especially in her early fiction (*The Mill on the Floss*, *Felix Holt*) and poetry ('The Spanish Gypsy')—of the implications, possibilities, and limitations of these thought-systems in a secular world of lost absolutes. Natural selection, Romantic individualism, and rationalist morality are presented not so much as antagonists to George Eliot's preoccupation with transcendence or sublimation of animal egotism through socially habituated consciousness, but as the intellectual medium within which her distinctive philosophy takes shape.

The central and most consistently convincing portion of the book turns to the (albeit more familiar) issue of George Eliot's anticipation of modernist formal practices, particularly in *Middlemarch* and *Daniel Deronda*. The starting-point for this study is the famous pier-glass metaphor from *Middlemarch*—long a favourite with deconstructionist critics: the phenomenon by which multitudinous and arbitrary scratches on a mirror's surface appear to be concentrically arranged around any lighted candle which happens to be held against it is explicitly offered by the narrator as a quasi-scientific analogy for the delusions of egoism and the necessary subjectivity of reality construction (George Eliot, *Middlemarch*, ed. by David Carroll (Oxford: Oxford University Press), p. 261 (Chapter 27)). The essential relativism of *Middlemarch*, as figured also in the dominant web imagery, heralds, argues Newton, the perspectivism of later modernist fiction. More, one defining hallmark of the 'classic realist text' (p. 6), the omniscient narrator, is also subject to the novel's dialogic vision—self-consciously offered as one interpreting, and sometimes deliberately alienating, voice among many others. George Eliot's mature realist fiction combines the further modernist traits of dialectical allusiveness in respect of past literatures and reliance on myth. *Daniel Deronda* is a precursor of Joycean narrative: firstly, in synthesizing and revising aspects of novelistic predecessors—specifically, the romance elements of Scott's historical fiction, of Austen's marriage plots, and of Dickens's social criticism; secondly, via its story of Deronda's discovery of Judaic origins, in harnessing to realist prose the resonance and power of ancient mythology. The proto-modernist formal experimentation of the larger novels is showcased in miniature in *Silas Marner*. The novella draws ironically on fairy tale and myth, it is argued, in order to demonstrate the distance of the latter's simple moral order from the aggressively individualist and mercantile ethic of a post-industrial world, thus critiquing the very Victorian values which the work is often seen to recommend.

The third and most ambitious section of the book seeks to defend and rescue George Eliot's late works—*Daniel Deronda* and *The Impressions of Theophrastus*—from their reductive caricaturing as (respectively) proto-Zionist and racist texts by postcolonialist readings of the last decade or so. Against the either/or logic of political critics, Newton sets the both/and habits of George Eliot's thinking, which signal a break with Enlightenment rationalism equivalent to that of Derrida in the twentieth century. The ethical and cultural tests of George Eliot's late work are prototypical examples of 'undecidability' in the Derridean sense of a decision having to be taken without guarantee that it is the right one (pp. 163–64, citing 'Hospitality, Justice and Responsibility: A Dialogue with Jacques Derrida', in *Questioning Ethics: Contemporary Debates in Philosophy*, ed. by Richard Kearney and Mark Dooley (London: Routledge, 1999), pp. 66–68). It is unclear how this deep-seated cultural relativism accords with the affirmation of belief systems which Newton scrupulously acknowledges to be present in George Eliot's work, from *The Mill on the Floss* to *Daniel Deronda*. How far George Eliot's brand of relativism is fundamentally akin to postmodern scepticism, and how far it is the particular product of a more immediately post-religious world, is one question cumulatively begged by this body of work. It is also striking that this revisiting of former work often does not incorporate more recent insights in the field. (A chapter on George Eliot's relation to Darwin and evolutionary thought without apparent awareness of the seminal work of Gillian Beer and Sally Shuttleworth is distinctly odd.) But this volume's key and welcome accomplishment is to reverse the terms of much critical thinking in relation to George Eliot over the last thirty years. The author emerges not as the outmodedly conservative and conventional writer of twentieth-century critical construction, but as an intellectual and literary mammoth of proportions incommensurate with the narrow dogmatism of ideological critiques.

University of Liverpool   Josie Billington

A Historical Guide to Henry James. Ed. by John Carlos Rowe and Eric Haralson. (Historical Guides to American Authors) New York: Oxford University Press. 2012. vi+271 pp. ISBN 978-0-19-512134-6.

Oxford University Press's Historical Guides to American Authors professes to be 'an interdisciplinary, historically sensitive series that combines close attention to the United States' most widely read and studied authors with a strong sense of time, place, and history'. Designed for students (and teachers) of American literature, each volume in the series is comprised of 'historical essays written on subjects of contemporary social, political, and cultural relevance'. Though unacknowledged as such, one of its defining features, then, is an attempt to marry the potentially competing demands of 'historical' criticism and contemporary 'relevance'. John Carlos Rowe and Eric Haralson's *Historical Guide to Henry James* adheres closely to this broad critical and pedagogical framework, which has the added benefit of distinguishing it from other recent companion-style collections on James. After an editorial Introduction and a 'capsule biography', the volume contains five core essays by established James scholars under the section-heading 'Henry James in his Time', each of which explores and summarizes a different historical field of recent criticism: gender studies focusing on the 'New Woman'; media studies and new technology; race and empire; sexuality and queer theory; and James's position within (post)modernity. The volume is completed by an Illustrated Chronology of James's life—again emphasizing broader historical contexts—and a Bibliographical Essay, providing an overview of James's reception from contemporary responses to the modern 'James industry'.

The methodological orientation of the volume is at its most effective when the historical contexts of James's writing are established as important sources of his continuing (or increasing) relevance to today's readers, and somewhat less convincing when the differences between late nineteenth- and early twenty-first-century cultural contexts are elided. A good example of the former is Stuart Culver's essay, 'Objects and Images: Henry James and the New Media', which makes the interesting observation that James's lifetime spanned two 'technological environments' for 'producing and circulating images and information' (p. 94): the mid-nineteenth-century innovations of telegraphy, photography, and steam-powered transportation and the 'more instantaneous' technologies of the early twentieth century, including automobiles, typewriters, and motion pictures. Some of these technologies played a significant role in the development of James's fiction and literary style, and he maintained a critical engagement with new technology throughout his life; to realize this places the contemporary reader on a historical continuum with James's experience of modernity. Similarly, Sara Blair's essay, 'Henry James, Race, and Empire', situates James's early travel writing and the 'international theme' of much of his fiction within the context of late nineteenth-century American nationalism, imperial aspiration, and constructions of racial identity, while Haralson's 'Henry James and Changing Ideas of Sexuality' usefully reminds students that James's career coincided historically with the 'ascendancy of sexual discourse itself'—an 'epistemic shift in Western societies' familiar to readers of Foucault (pp. 170–71). The issue of sexuality notoriously raises the spectre of historical anachronism, but Haralson and other contributors succeed in balancing the interpretative claims of gay and queer studies with the historical conditions of James's writing. The use of the term 'New Woman' in Martha Banta's discussion of James's relationship to the political history of female emancipation seems less historically precise and potentially a source of confusion: in most recent criticism the New Woman is a specific cultural phenomenon of the *fin de siècle*, whereas here it ranges in application from the 1840s through to the First World War. Finally, a rather incongruous feature of this volume is its lack of stylistic consistency in terms of notation and referencing: whereas one of the essays is extended by almost ten pages of discursive endnotes followed by a five-page bibliography, others contain either no bibliography or no notes at all. One might have expected a book in a series of this kind to follow established presentational guidelines, as indeed its list of contents follows a set format.

UNIVERSITY OF LEEDS   RICHARD SALMON

Wyndham Lewis and the Cultures of Modernity. Ed. by ANDRZEJ GĄSIOREK, ALICE REEVE-TUCKER, and NATHAN WADELL. Farnham: Ashgate. 2011. xiii+265 pp. £55. ISBN 978-1-4094-0054-7.

Revaluation of Wyndham Lewis has expanded more or less steadily ever since his centenary in the early 1980s, and Victor Barac suggests in this volume that his work 'continues to attract more attention and respect from a widening public' in the twenty-first century (p. 200). 'Attention' and 'respect', though, have not always been easily or persuasively combined, where Lewis is concerned, and *Wyndham Lewis and the Cultures of Modernity* continues to practise some of the elisions often employed in earlier phases of his revaluation, particularly where his disreputable 1930s politics are concerned. A few of the twelve essays in this anthology consider Lewis's anti-Semitism, but only one—and then only for part of its length—looks closely at his 1930s Hitlerism. Lewis, true enough, was not altogether uncomplicatedly a Fascist in the 1930s, but nor were his earlier views altogether uncomplicated by Fascism. Several essays could usefully have explored further this aspect of his thinking, in relation to his outlook on modernity and his cultural criticism in general.

Patchy in its coverage, as well as in the quality of some of its essays, *Wyndham Lewis and the Cultures of Modernity* sometimes shows too clearly its origins as conference proceedings. Yet its overall aims are in other ways a sensible corrective to earlier strategies in Lewis's revaluation—ones often inclined to claim too much for him on the grounds only of his work as a creative writer or artist. As this volume's Introduction insists, Lewis needs also to be read for his critical output: in terms of his 'location within the larger constellations of early twentieth-century cultural debates', and in his role as 'a philosopher-critic who produced distinctive appraisals of modernity' (p. 5). Looking back at one of several huge cultural critiques he produced in the 1920s, *Time and Western Man* (1927), Lewis himself remarked, early in the 1950s, that 'in that bleak fortress there is still much loot' (*Rude Assignment* (London: Hutchinson, 1950), p. 194). Sixty years later, *Wyndham Lewis and the Cultures of Modernity* demonstrates at several points how much 'loot' still remains, and what critical purchase it offers on modernism, modernity, and early twentieth-century culture generally. This demonstration is developed effectively in several essays distinguished by detailed knowledge of the 'constellations'—of individuals as well as ideas—in which Lewis worked in the years before the Great War, and in the decade that followed it. In an essay on 'Wyndham Lewis, Charlie Chaplin and Cinema', Scott W. Klein portrays Lewis not only as an aloof 'philosopher-critic', but also minutely subject to pressures, emotional and intellectual, from his artistic environment and from complicated personal relationships. Dominika Buchowska shows in similar detail the substantial differences, even hostilities, prevailing among the artists whom Lewis tried to corral together as Vorticists in the pre-war years. Jodie Greenwood examines equally closely contemporary responses to Lewis's Vorticist journal, *Blast*, along with the responses *Blast* itself made to contemporary idioms of advertising and typography.

Similarly close attention to events responsible for Lewis's outlook, and to the forms his responses took, figures in Paul Edwards's 'Wyndham Lewis and the Uses of Shellshock: Meat and Postmodernism'. Edwards traces through *The Childermass* (1928), and much of Lewis's later writing, attempts 'to accommodate somehow a trauma that was for him unassimilable', and to deal with the Great War 'as a historical event and as a cultural and political after-effect in the 1920s' (pp. 227, 230). Lewis was one of fairly few modernist writers in English to experience the Great War directly, as a combatant. It left him convinced that the placid culture of the pre-1914 years had been no more than, in his words, 'the stunt of an illusionist' (p. 224). The uses Lewis made of this radical conclusion—its critical implications for modernism; its sense of established culture as veil, deception, or illusion—are well worth recovering or revaluing. At its best, *Wyndham Lewis and the Cultures of Modernity* offers some productive ways of doing so.

UNIVERSITY OF EDINBURGH   RANDALL STEVENSON

No Accident, Comrade: Chance and Design in Cold War American Narratives. By STEVEN BELLETTO. Oxford: Oxford University Press. 2012. viii+206 pp. £40. ISBN 978-0-19-982688-9.

Cold War studies show no sign of abating, and Steven Belletto opens his examination of Cold War narratives with a clear and valuable insight: that Western polemics against Communism often exploited the notion of chance, which was excluded from the strict official line of Marxism. He introduces his subject through the mysterious figure of Jerzy Kosinski, a Pole who came to the USA on forged documents and who then made a career for himself as a novelist. Kosinski developed a close friendship with the biologist Jacques Monod, whose study *Chance and Necessity: An Essay on the Natural Philosophy of Modern Biology* (trans. from the French edn (1970) by Austryn Wainhouse (New York: Knopf, 1971)) was subsequently woven into Kosinski's fiction. Belletto's stated purpose here is to move beyond containment as a model for Cold War narratives, and he has useful insights to offer on non-fictional works such as Daniel Bell's *The End of Ideology* (Harvard: Harvard University Press, 1962), which argued—spuriously—that the West had somehow moved beyond ideology to embrace individualistic chance.

As soon as Belletto moves on to the fiction of the period, however, problems begin to arise with his rather schematic opposition between Marxist determinacy and Western unpredictability. As he himself admits, Flannery O'Connor's fiction has a vested interest in Catholicism which stands behind her treatment of accidents. Also, William Burroughs demonstrates a lifelong ambivalence towards the official conspiratorial narratives he repeatedly evokes only to ridicule. One of the attractions of paranoid narratives is that they offer so many interconnections, a point which critics such as Peter Knight have explored to good effect (see, for example, *Conspiracy Culture: From Kennedy to the X Files* (London: Routledge, 2000)). Belletto rehearses relatively familiar arguments on Pynchon's first novel *V.* (1963), which counterpoints its action between the paranoid Stencil, who sees plots everywhere, and the slapstick Benny Profane, who stumbles from one scrape to another. The very term 'plot' implies either conspiracy or the principle of rational connectedness underlying a narrative, and Pynchon, along with many of his contemporaries, catches the reader in the awkward double bind of seeking connections which we are also encouraged to ridicule. When Belletto turns to Nabokov, yet another variable emerges—the effect of chance in self-conscious fiction. Cold War homophobia becomes the interesting local focus of a discussion of *Pale Fire* (1962), which nicely brings out unexpected dimensions of that novel's many references to secrets.

One of the most useful and effective aspects of *No Accident, Comrade* is that it suggests connections within quite a disparate body of fiction. Thus, an account of the textual intricacies of *Pale Fire* segues into an examination of chance in African American fiction. As Belletto rightly argues, the narrator in the Brotherhood sections of Ralph Ellison's *Invisible Man* (1952) develops a suspicion of Marxism because it seems to deny his own agency. At the same time, however, it could be argued that Ellison is describing a growing suspicion of *all* cultural narratives, even liberationist ones, precisely because they position the individual within sequences not of his own making. Two other areas of this fiction are discussed by Belletto—nuclear accident and the applications of game theory, both famously connected in *Dr. Strangelove* (1964). A work such as Eugene Burdick and Harvey Wheeler's *Fail-Safe* (1962) introduces contingency when a tiny component malfunctions within a defence computer. A parable-like warning is thus given about an exaggerated faith in military technology, just as satirical applications of game theory highlight the appalling risks involved in gambling with millions of lives. Much of Belletto's study sets Marxist determinacy against a Western insistence on contingency, but many novels of nuclear war (such as Mordecai Roshwald's *Level 7* (1959)) describe a kind of mirror logic where the defence establishments, and therefore ways of thinking, of East and West have bizarrely come to resemble each other. One of the main points of *No Accident, Comrade* is to alert us to the general, complex importance of chance, and, for all its limitations, this is what it does. Belletto has opened up an approach which can be profitably applied to fiction dealing explicitly with the Cold War and also to neglected classics such as Luke Rhinehart's *The Dice Man* (1971).

UNIVERSITY OF LIVERPOOL   DAVID SEED

Aggressive Fictions: Reading the Contemporary American Novel. By KATHRYN HUME. Ithaca, NY: Cornell University Press. 2012. xiii+200 pp. ISBN 978-0-8014-5001-3.

According to Kathryn Hume, the defining feature of much contemporary American fiction is an unmitigated hostility towards its audience. Writers routinely inflict on their readers the 'mental equivalent of pissing on your shoes [while] holding a knife to your throat' (p. ix). The impressive breadth of *Aggressive Fictions* suggests that Hume has repeatedly subjected herself to this type of literary assault. Her study explores the dynamics involved in this cycle of abuse and seeks to pin down five types of 'aggression' within the House of Contemporary Fiction. Firstly, Hume detects spleen in *narrative speed*. Recent novels exhibit an 'excessive rapidity' in their blurry deluge of characters, events, and details (p. 14). Secondly, she bemoans the preoccupation of contemporary novelists with *complaint*. While readers may sympathize with the subject of suffering and oppression, they are likely to be alienated by a voice which is 'high-pitched, whiny and even hysterical' (p. 41). 'Complaint fiction' is divided into writing that indulges in 'self-centred complaint' about, for example, sexual abuse and 'political diatribes' which harangue readers for their complicity in patriarchal oppression, capitalist excess, white racial hegemony, animal cruelty, and environmental devastation (p. 51). Thirdly and fourthly, aggressive fictions carpet-bomb the reader with visceral imagery that is *grotesque* and *violent* (pp. 77–114, 115–40). Finally, the frantic fracturing of 'reality' and 'identity' in this sadistic œuvre *destabilizes ontological certainties* and plunges the reader into a philosophical tailspin (pp. 141–43).

Hume concedes that aggressive fictions 'do not form a tidy subgenre', and yet her definition of the key term is so expansive that it threatens to become a supragenre (p. 171). 'Aggression' is used in this study as a blanket term to be thrown over almost any novel that includes acts of violence or explicitly political commentary, that upsets a reader's values, that is formally challenging and experimental, or that requires more than a minimal level of interpretative effort. Defined in this way, 'aggressive fiction' is perhaps less convincing as a label for recent prose than as the raison d'être for the American novel itself. The alternative to aggressive fiction is somewhat tentatively traced. Fictions would apparently qualify as 'unaggressive' when they allow the reader to 'enjoy the success and happiness of sympathetic characters', with 'the traditional happy ending in which lovers marry and family members or friends are reunited'. 'Unless they are dismissive Marxists or feminists', Hume argues, 'most readers enjoy the ending of Jane Austen's *Pride and Prejudice*' (p. 3). Such comments appear to be targeted at a very specific audience. *Aggressive Fictions* is littered with pronouns which some readers may find collusive if not coercive. The 'you', 'we', and 'one' Hume has in mind are 'ordinary readers' who are 'middle class' and belong to the 'mainstream' (p. 13 and passim). Evidence to support the claim that members of this group are uniformly 'outrag[ed] and repell[ed]' by aggressive fictions is patchy (p. 8): in place of detailed ethnographic research Hume relies on occasional anecdotes concerning responses to specific novels by her students and friends. There may be others who unashamedly enjoy aggressive fictions, but they will tend to belong to a specific 'ethnic, racial, gender-oriented, political, or religious group' (p. 8). One such coterie would appear to be literary critics and theorists. Aside from an exhaustive survey of theories of the grotesque, *Aggressive Fictions* largely fails to engage either with critical theory or any scholarship on contemporary American fiction (while claiming to have identified 'an aspect of recent fiction that criticism has ignored' (p. 164)). Hume seems to want to position herself as an amateur arbitrator who can bridge the gap between experimental writers and a mass audience. While some of her readings are unapologetically and perhaps polemically aggressive towards aggressive fictions, there are points at which Hume appears to gesture towards an apology for the genre. The concluding chapter, for instance, foregrounds the possibility that a bruising submission to aggressive fictions can be emotionally, intellectually, politically, and even spiritually invigorating. Whether the gentle reader will be persuaded to swap a Jane Austen wedding for the company of a knife-wielding textual ruffian who urinates on her footwear remains to be seen.

LOUGHBOROUGH UNIVERSITY   BRIAN JARVIS

The Fabliaux: A New Verse Translation. Trans. by NATHANIEL DUBIN. Intro. by R. HOWARD BLOCH. New York: Liveright. 2013. xxxiv+1027 pp. £19.99. ISBN 978-0-87140-357-5.

In the course of a conversation in *Le Pescheor de Pont-sur-Seine* concerning the importance of sexual relations within marriage the husband says to his wife, who has stated that she loves him because of his love and the clothes and food he provides for her: 'I frequently make a great effort for you. | No wife will ever love her husband | because of any garment | as much as for doing what I am telling you about' ('Je m'en esfors por toi sovent. | Ja fame por nul garniment | n'amera si bien son mari | com por fere ce que je di', ll. 47–50, my translation). These lines are rendered by Nathaniel Dubin as: 'I push myself to do my stuff | for your sake. Clothes are not enough | to keep a wife's love; satisfaction | depends much more on fucking action.' Clearly those who seek a crib or a faithful line-by-line translation of the original text will be disappointed by what Dubin has done. But he offers a great deal more than simply transposing Old French words into English, as his translations are literary creations in their own right. He retains all the various semantic elements of the original text, recasts or reinterprets key aspects of his material, and remains faithful to its rhythms and rhymes. Essential, of course, when translating comic texts such as these, is to maintain humour through witty and unusual rhymes. In *Le Fevre de Creeil* ('The Blacksmith of Creil') the blacksmith's servant is well endowed: 'About his balls I'll not keep mum [rhymes with 'become'], | hanging between his arse and pizzle | like mallets sculptured with a chisel, | befitting such a master tool. | Ready for action, as a rule, | on the qui vive his member stood, | its head uncovered, with its hood | thrown back, like monks who harvest pears! | (these words are true, your author swears!), | red as an onion grown in Spain, | its one eye open wide to drain | off a great quantity of juice, | and you could toss inside and lose | a fava bean from Lombardy | and still not stop its flow of pee' (ll. 24–38). Of the eight rhymes here not one is based on the rhyming words in the text. Nothing is omitted: 'as a rule' is poetic licence for 'toz jors', 'your author swears' is a filler, and 'Spain' replaces the French commune of 'Corbueil' (Corbeil).

Dubin sustains his high-quality translations through sixty-nine fabliaux (over 16,000 lines of text). Importantly, his versions are clearly anchored in a thorough knowledge of the nuances of the original language. They are based on his own new editions of the texts, for which he has used the diplomatic editions and critical texts in the *Nouveau recueil complet des fabliaux* (*NRCF*), ed. by Willem Noomen and Nico van den Boogaard, 10 vols (Assen: Van Gorcum, 1983–98). Such a large corpus of fabliaux within one volume constitutes a valuable resource for scholars (but cross-references to the volumes of the *NRCF* would have been welcome). Dubin is to be congratulated on satisfying the needs of scholars and the general reader. He informs us that he has translated twice as many fabliaux as are found in this volume, and it is to be hoped that these will soon be made available to us.

UNIVERSITY OF LIVERPOOL   GLYN S. BURGESS

1511–2011, Philippe de Commynes: droit, écriture. Deux piliers de la souveraineté. Ed. by JOËL BLANCHARD. (Cahiers d'Humanisme et Renaissance, 100) Geneva: Droz. 2012. x+377 pp. SwF 43. ISBN 978-2-600-01543-1.

In 2011 several events took place to commemorate the life and work of Philippe de Commynes, who died in 1511. This volume is a collection of essays presented at one such event: a conference in Orléans on the interpretation and perception of Commynes's *Mémoires*. These famous writings deal with the reign of Louis XI, king of France, and the wars which he waged against the Burgundian dukes and Italian lords in the second half of the fifteenth century. As a Flemish nobleman and councillor of Louis XI, Commynes was well placed to comment on these events, and used them to moralize about the time in which he lived, and the ethics of politics. Commynes is therefore often called the French Machiavelli, although several authors in this book rightly argue for abandoning this sobriquet. Commynes is more a representative of medieval thinking than the Italian writer. He is an advocate of political dialogue, and argues that negotiation should be at the core of politics. Commynes's writings are less based on theory than Machiavelli's, because the events which the royal councillor witnessed gave him enough empirical data to prove his arguments. The *Mémoires* therefore read as a kind of journal, full of lively details about late medieval politics, and make Commynes worthy of commemoration.

This collection of essays does not add many new details about the *Mémoires* or about their author. Its editor, Joël Blanchard, has already published several excellent books on Commynes and his work (including a complete new edition of the *Mémoires* and the *Lettres* of the Flemish nobleman). It does, however, contain good case studies, which deal with many aspects of the texts and life of Commynes. The subtitle is a little misleading, for the discussion is not limited to juridical matters and issues about the writing of the *Mémoires*. Neither is the concept of sovereignty central to most essays; the Introduction does not explain why this word figures in the subtitle, nor does it give a satisfactory definition of *souveraineté*. The topics considered are more diverse, including: Commynes's views on the Spanish and the English (Stéphane Péquignot, Jean-Philippe Genet, Gilles Lecuppre); the use of poison as murder weapon (Franck Collard); the perception of Commynes in England (Michael Jones) and in the nineteenth century (Catherine Emerson). The essays of Jan Dumolyn and Marc Boone on Commynes's Flemish background are also of interest, as they outline that the genre of the *Mémoires* and the discourse used in them in many respects reflect literary and ideological practices in his homeland. Christoph Mauntel and Klaus Oschema point to an often ignored aspect of Commynes's work, namely the use of emotions in his discourse. Remarkably, the *mémorialiste* often cited emotions as a cause of some events, such as the defeat of Charles the Bold on the battlefield of Nancy in 1477. Commynes suggests that Charles's outburst of anger and his often irrational behaviour meant that the mighty duke could not be seen as a lawful lord. Therefore the *Mémoires* legitimize the victory of his sworn enemy, the French king, who is depicted as a fair monarch.

The moral lesson which Commynes learns from the events which he witnessed is that law, justice, and rationality should be at the basis of any rule. Consequently, war is legitimate if it is waged against 'bad lords' and tyrants (as Jean-Louis Fournel shows). These assumptions put Commynes's *Mémoires* at the crossroads of the Middle Ages and more modern times, and show that *droit* is at the centre of his work and, but not exclusively, of this volume.

UNIVERSITY OF LEUVEN JELLE HAEMERS

Fiction and the Frontiers of Knowledge in Europe, 1500–1800. Ed. by RICHARD SCHOLAR and ALEXIS TADIÉ. Farnham: Ashgate. 2010. xi+172 pp. £55. ISBN 978-1-4094-0865-9.

The nebulous interface between fiction and early modern philosophy, science, medicine, or law will never look quite the same after this collection of erudite essays, so lyrically presented by Richard Scholar and Alexis Tadié. Isabelle Pantin reveals how the physician Fracastoro lacked medical proofs or philosophical explanation for the origins of syphilis, and so preferred to speculate through the liberating medium of poetry. The resultant poetic space bridges the gap between myth and reality, creating a vast medical/poetic interface useful for medics and syphilis sufferers alike. Any reader who may heretofore have neglected *if*-clauses need look no further than Wes Williams's web of hypotheses linking Ronsard, Montaigne, Corneille, and Pascal. Potential past worlds are evoked through fictional hypothesis, hovering low over the Cleopatra's nose school of history as Williams's nuanced reading unveils subtle reflections on contemporary French civil war. While ultimately recognizing mankind's own limitations, Williams masterfully combines close linguistic analysis with subtle criticism of literature, philosophical thought, politics, self-exploration, and early modern historicity. In another rich trajectory, Isabelle Moreau probes philosophical, scientific, and fictional models from Descartes and Gassendi to Bernier, through exploration of the epistemological and moral dimensions encompassed within the term *fiction*. She traces legal and theatrical fiction and perceived planetary movements, and ultimately examines the collision of truth, reality, and rules, against hypotheses, constructs, and falsehoods. The various uses made of fiction, including scientific theory, legal fiction, and political theory, in Hobbes's system of philosophy are analysed by Luc Foisneau, who argues that Hobbes's 'system' is a descriptive rather than a performative term, where fiction functions in order to bring a scientific paradigm shift into clearer focus, namely the move away from the Aristotelian theory of sensation and towards a new all-encompassing scientific exemplar. Robert Mankin also explores the displacement of Aristotle by European modernity, through dexterous examination of the self-fashioned personal versus philosophical identity for both Locke and Hume. In a highly original reading of the *Lettre sur les aveugles*, Kate Tunstall subtly argues that Diderot's treatment of Molyneux's Problem, or the role of judgement in sense perception, has routinely been misunderstood precisely because of artificial disciplinary frontiers erected between philosophy and literature. She hints that Réaumur's refusal to admit Diderot to witness his eye operation is the fictional springboard or construct necessary to facilitate the subsequent methodical reasoning and hypothesis so richly elaborated within the *Lettre*. Moreover, she admits that when compared with the cruel butchery of a contemporary eye operation, Diderot's philosophizing on blindness was clearly more humane and enlightened. Anne Simonin investigates the post-Revolutionary Terror, and posits its foundations in a legal fiction wherein truth and falsehoods are inextricably intertwined, with judicial interpretations perilously accepted as reality, and during which rulers acted 'as if' France were in a state of siege with previous laws suspended, thus potentially proffering treacherous repercussions for modern-day French law. These essays, replete with fiction and hypothesis, are inspirational in their execution and breadth, and will be enjoyed by anyone engaged in early modern fiction and thought.

UCD DUBLIN   SÍOFRA PIERSE

Les Costeaux; ou, Les Marquis frians. By JEAN DONNEAU DE VISÉ. Ed. by PETER WILLIAM SHOEMAKER. (MHRA Critical Texts, 31) London: MHRA. 2013. viii+82 pp. £9.99. ISBN 978-1-907322-33-4.

Published anonymously, this short play was attributed in the eighteenth century to Deschamps de Villiers, although Peter William Shoemaker has enough faith in Chappuzeau's seventeenth-century attribution to Donneau de Visé, which he backs up in his Introduction to this edition with both textual and circumstantial evidence, to include it on the title-page. The title requires some explanation, and Shoemaker duly provides it: the word designates individuals who had the reputation of having such refined taste that they would drink wine from grapes grown on only a small number of vineyard slopes (*coteaux*); however, these people were not just wine snobs, they were food snobs too, and, although wine is discussed, it is this latter aspect which is more important here. The plot of the play is no more than a pretext to bring together three such characters—with the addition of a *raisonneur* figure to highlight the ridiculousness of their views—and to allow them to talk while waiting for a meal that never materializes. The comedy of manners is intensified by the fact that these three are not just self-styled gourmets, but are also parasites who turn up at meal times at the houses with the best food in order to avoid eating at their own expense. The play is droll enough, and interesting for the way that it homes in on this particular fashion, but it is also very short; one cannot help feeling that the author could have made the conversation that is its principal raison d'être last rather longer. Shoemaker includes as an appendix three other texts that talk about food fads similar to those mentioned in the play: Boileau's third *Satire*, the portrait of Cliton from *Les Caractères*, and two letters by Saint-Évremond. As well as providing interesting notes on the text, he also situates it well in its historical context: a time when there was a huge vogue for cookery manuals, when the values of local and seasonal food were being promoted, when the provenance of products was seen as being enormously important, and when the old heavy cooking was being rejected in favour of a more delicate style in which spices did not mask the true flavour of the ingredients, which were instead allowed to speak for themselves. Plus ça change...

SWANSEA UNIVERSITY   DEREK CONNON

Dissonance in the Republic of Letters: The Querelle des Gluckistes et des Piccinnistes. By MARK DARLOW. London: Legenda. 2013. x+229 pp. £45. ISBN 978-1-907975-54-7.

As Mark Darlow points out, the Querelle des Gluckistes et des Piccinnistes was simply the last in a series of literary quarrels during the eighteenth century in France, the most famous of which were the Querelle des Anciens et des Modernes and the Querelle des Bouffons. There are similarities between it and the other quarrels of the century, not least because the Querelle des Bouffons also concerns opera, but Darlow argues persuasively that this later quarrel, although less studied, has special features which make it worthy of our attention. Marie-Antoinette's support of Gluck, for instance, was one, but not the only, aspect of the dispute which gave it a political significance that was not confined to the court.

In chapters entitled 'Opera Reform on the Eve of Gluck's Arrival', 'From *Iphigénie en Aulide* to *Orphée*', 'Simplicity without Primitivism', 'Talking about Opera', and 'Resolution?', Darlow, after starting with the background to the quarrel, charts a chronological course through his subject, but in many respects it is the various aspects of the affair and the issues raised by it that he homes in on en route that constitute the more important part of the study. For instance, it prolongs discussions that had also contributed to the Guerre des Bouffons about the suitability (or not) of the French language for musical setting; it raises questions about how literary quarrels conform to codes of etiquette and politeness; there are issues surrounding the extent to which contributors depicted themselves as individuals or members of a group, and were prepared to take responsibility for their views or preferred the cloak of anonymity; and questions arise about the extent to which Gluck and Piccinni were symbols of wider issues rather than the true subjects of the discussion. And, of course, such disputes on the subject of music not only extended theories of music, they also developed the way that writers wrote about it. Yet, if one striking feature of Darlow's study is how little of it is actually about music itself, in the sense of its style and techniques, this is an accurate reflection of the way that the writers who are his main subject approached the topic themselves, for, in general, they were writers and not musicians, and so lacked the technical expertise to engage in an entirely musical discussion. Darlow quotes generously from a wide selection of the many texts that contributed to the quarrel, from the writings of well-known authors to anonymous pamphlets. His profound and thoughtful study should be of interest not only to music specialists, but to anyone with an interest in eighteenth-century aesthetics and ideas.

SWANSEA UNIVERSITY   DEREK CONNON

The Sentimental Theater of the French Revolution. By CECILIA FEILLA. Farnham: Ashgate. 2013. xv+258 pp. £55. ISBN 978-1-4094-1163-5.

In this highly detailed work, the lens of sentimentality is very effectively used to analyse the theatre, dramas, and broader culture of the French Revolution. Pointing out that the most performed plays of the decade were not political or patriotic tragedies, but rather sentimental dramas and comedies, Cecilia Feilla asserts that 'Revolutionary theater was remarkably and undeniably sentimental' (p. 4). However, the sentimentality of the Revolutionary stage is not restricted to questions of genre or content, but rather encompasses the period's attitude towards the role and duty of theatre. It was believed that it was the emotional connection between play and audience that would lead to a new, 'improved' society, as the 'theater was capable of acting upon the audience, and through the tears shed, through the movements of the heart and soul, could produce the ideal and virtuous community represented on stage' (p. 62). Thus, the attraction of tragedies such as Voltaire's *Brutus* (1730) was not simply its potentially political subject matter, but its 'moral and emotional effect on the audience [. . .] its ability to foster sympathy' (p. 185).

A selection of the decade's most popular plays, such as Beaumarchais's *L'Autre Tartuffe; ou, La Mère coupable* (1792) and Chénier's *Fénelon; ou, Les Religieuses de Cambrai* (1793), are analysed in their Revolutionary context, demonstrating how, despite seeming to have little in common, they are united in their emotional impact on the audience. In aiming to elicit sympathy from spectators, they—and sentimental theatre in general—'created the possibility for a truly united social body where, in reality, such unity did not exist' (p. 63). Greater attention is given to Voltaire's *Brutus* (1730), Collot d'Herbois's *La Famille patriote* (1790), and François de Neufchâteau's *Paméla; ou, La Vertu récompensée* (1793), whose performance led to the arrest of both its author and the actors of the Théâtre de la Nation in September 1793. This focus on the sentimental in relation to key Revolutionary plays offers an intriguing perspective on how these compositions were viewed and understood by audiences, but also provides valuable insights into such questions as the role and importance of virtue, vows, and national festivals. In particular, Jacobin politics and the execution of Louis XVI are addressed in some detail, ensuring that sentimentality's impact on Revolutionary events is analysed in full.

Yet while such case studies are used to great effect to illustrate Feilla's argument, her examination of Revolutionary theatre is not restricted to individual plays, but extends to the considerable impact of sentimentality and the Revolution on acting and performance. A variety of sentimental tableaux—in art, literature, and the theatre—are also carefully analysed to show how their emotional connection with spectators 'provided a means and model for political participation, and a codification of politics in affective terms' (p. 90). Consequently, as Feilla convincingly argues, sentimentality is not separate from politics, but 'was the very cloth from which Revolutionary theater, and Revolutionary culture more generally, was cut' (p. 10). This is a highly informative work that places Revolutionary theatre at the centre of political and cultural developments. While it will be of value to anyone with an interest in the plays under discussion, it should be especially compelling to those working in the area of eighteenth-century theatre, culture, and politics.

UNIVERSITY OF EXETER   CATRIN FRANCIS

The French Idea of History: Joseph de Maistre and his Heirs, 1794–1854. By CAROLINA ARMENTEROS. Ithaca, NY: Cornell University Press. 2011. xiv+362 pp. $59.95. ISBN 978-0-8014-4943-7.

Joseph de Maistre has long been studied not in his own right, or in his historical context, but rather at a series of removes, through the medium of the partial and sometimes even caricatural accounts of his thought produced by his various admirers and detractors: Comte, Baudelaire, and Barbey d'Aurevilly in the nineteenth century, Caillois, Cioran, and Isaiah Berlin in the twentieth, to cite only a few prominent examples. None of these versions of Maistre quite managed to do justice to the Savoyard counter-Revolutionary polemicist, theosophist, and political theorist. Owen Bradley came much closer to conveying a sense of Maistre's achievement in his *A Modern Maistre* (Lincoln: University of Nebraska Press, 1999). However, it is Richard Lebrun who has done the most in recent times to give Maistre his voice back in the anglophone world, latterly with the able support of Carolina Armenteros. This book represents the fullest articulation of her own distinctive position, following on from her recent spate of excellent articles.

Armenteros's Maistre is unlike any hitherto described by either anglophone or francophone scholarship. Many received opinions are either cast into doubt or overturned, for the most part very convincingly. Armenteros pulls off this trick by distinguishing between Maistre the polemicist and Maistre the theorist: it is the polemicist, with his lucid prose, paradoxes, and provocations, who has tended to live on in the literary historical imagination, even as the theorist has tended to be forgotten. Maistre the polemicist appeared simply to repudiate the Enlightenment and the Revolution it had spawned; Maistre the theorist engaged with his foes on their own ground, using their own weapons. It is not always clear to what extent Maistre was in control of this process of engagement, as Armenteros herself points out: 'before dying, Maistre, horrified, understood that the Revolution had pervaded everything, that it had slipped even into the finest cracks of his own philosophy' (p. 30). Nevertheless, Armenteros's Maistre, born out of dialogue with Rousseau, emerges as a much more nuanced and controlled thinker than has hitherto been allowed. Maistre's innatism and the value he places on intuition are balanced, in Armenteros's reappraisal, by his hitherto unsuspected empiricism and love of reason; his authoritarian politics are shown to flow out of a concern for freedom; his emphasis on unitary sovereignty is shown to lead him towards a pluralist Europeanism. More generally, Armenteros's stress on Maistre's historicism allows her to produce the most convincing and coherent account yet of Maistre's undeniable influence on French historiography of the nineteenth century, whether of the right or the left. One of Armenteros's many achievements is to pull apart and make sense of Maistre's reputation as a reactionary champion of throne and altar paradoxically championed by a French left seemingly in thrall to authority—an *idée reçue* articulated, with what may appear an ironic lack of irony, by Flaubert: 'je viens d'avaler *tout* l'odieux Joseph de Maistre. Nous a-t-on assez scié le dos avec ce monsieur-là! Et les Socialistes modernes qui l'ont exalté! à commencer par les Saint-Simoniens pour en finir par A. Comte. La France est ivre d'autorité, quoi qu'on dise' (*Correspondance*, ed. by Jean Bruneau and Yvan Leclerc, 5 vols (Paris: Gallimard, 1973–2007), IV: *Janvier 1869–décembre 1875* (1998), p. 642). In the process, she demonstrates how Maistre, not himself a historian, came to shape the French idea of history in the first half of the nineteenth century. Anyone interested in studying Maistre on his own terms should start with this excellent, lucid, erudite, and highly original book, but also bear in mind that the Maistre it reveals would probably have proved unrecognizable to most of his contemporaries.

ORIEL and UNIVERSITY COLLEGES, OXFORD   FRANCESCO MANZINI

Mapping Memory in Nineteenth-Century French Literature and Culture. Ed. by Susan Harrow and Andrew Watts. Amsterdam: Rodopi. 2012. 328 pp. €66. ISBN 978-90-420-3458-7.

In introducing this varied and illuminating volume, which emerges from the 2008 conference of the Society of Dix-Neuviémistes, Susan Harrow and Andrew Watts note both the importance of memory studies on recent critical and historiographical work, and the limited impact they appear to have had on nineteenth-century French studies. The volume sets out to redress this lacuna by exploring in seventeen essays 'the ways in which memory informs individual consciousness and inflects collective experience' (p. 20). The latter part of this double approach is clearly influenced by Pierre Nora's work on *lieux de mémoire*, and sure enough, Nora's imaginative understanding of the various cultural objects and practices around which collective memory might coalesce is shared by many of the contributors here. Indeed, the word 'culture' in the title of this volume is perhaps more than usually operative, and the choice of primary phenomena by the various authors says much about the present shape of nineteenth-century French studies. Where once a volume on memory in this period might have been expected to offer a number of contributions on Romanticism, for instance, *Mapping Memory* makes only passing references to Chateaubriand and Lamartine, while Nerval, astonishingly, figures not at all. The study of Romanticism is currently at a low ebb, of course, but the same can hardly be said of Baudelaire, one of the century's most influential artists on the theme of memory—yet one who, again, receives no substantive attention here (though he is mentioned in the late Ben Fisher's study of Catulle Mendès's anthological work). While these absences do feel, at least a little, like omissions, the volume testifies conversely to the breadth of research interests in the discipline and to the innovative approach to defining textual and cultural objects of study adopted by scholars working on nineteenth-century topics. Colette Wilson's investigation of the (non-)commemoration of the Paris Commune in Parisian street nomenclature, Elizabeth Emery's account of an attempt in 1898 to revive the medieval *fête des fous*, Luc Nemeth's elucidation of popular involvement in the Dreyfus Affair, and Rémi Dalisson's study of the evolution of national festivals across the century are but the most striking examples of the general attention paid here to phenomena located outside standard literary, and indeed textual, canons. Other chapters on life writing (Brian Martin on soldiers' memoirs; Lucy Garnier and Cécile Meynard on Stendhal's journals), criticism (Tim Farrant on nineteenth-century responses to Rabelais), and visual art (Melanie Vandenbrouck-Przybylski on watercolours commemorating the Iron Gates expedition) also serve to broaden the admirable disciplinary reach of the volume.

Still, nostalgic souls will find plenty of more squarely literary studies here as well, those *grands absents* notwithstanding: no fewer than three chapters on Flaubert (Richard Saint-Gelais on *Madame Bovary*; Mary Orr on *La Légende de saint Julien l'hospitalier*; and Carmen Mayer-Robin on *La Tentation de saint Antoine*), and individual contributions on Balzac's *Le Lys dans la vallée* (Owen Heathcote), Zola's

La Faute de l'abbé Mouret (Émilie Piton-Foucault), Barbey d'Aurevilly's *Un prêtre marié* (Francesco Manzini), and the *Album zutique* (Denis Saint-Amand). Many of these studies place their key texts into theoretical and intertextual relations with the nineteenth century's own vital practices of retrospection; Orr, for instance, places *Saint Julien* in subversive dialogue with the spirit of official nineteenth-century historiography (as embodied in Michelet), while Manzini finds in *Un prêtre marié* echoes of the synthesis of history and theodicy to be found in Joseph de Maistre's writings on the Revolution. In combination, these approaches offer an intellectually satisfying exploration of an important topic, and a precious snapshot of the state of nineteenth-century French studies: inventive, interdisciplinary, and perhaps a tiny bit forgetful.

KING'S COLLEGE LONDON   ANDREW J. COUNTER

Text, Image, and the Problem with Perfection in Nineteenth-Century France: Utopia and its Afterlives. By DANIEL SIPE. Farnham: Ashgate. 2013. ix+218 pp. £55. ISBN 978-1-4094-4776-4.

This book explores how the utopian imagination comes increasingly to reflect on its own limits and contradictions in a body of texts and images selected from the Romantic period to the *fin de siècle*. It locates this self-problematizing characteristic squarely within the development of utopian cultural production itself in this period, rather than necessarily in those dystopian conceptions which succeed it in the subsequent century. For Daniel Sipe, the metaphysical ideal to which the image of the perfect society was tied in the Classical period has, in post-Revolutionary France, come to be displaced by what he calls its 'afterlife': a quality at times self-critical and conflicting, and born of a disquieting new sensibility towards the centrality of individual pleasure, madness, and desire in nineteenth-century French visions of utopia.

An early chapter surveys François-René de Chateaubriand's *Atala* and discusses the socially oriented function of the poet as set forth by Victor Hugo in his 'Fonction du poète'. A particular focus here is the foregrounding of the wayward passions of characters such as Chactas and Atala in *Atala*; these are read as undermining critically the restraints implied by Chateaubriand's vision of social harmony, thereby implicitly signalling that the utopia may fail to redirect or sublimate fully the energies and passions of those who participate in it. One of the most innovative parts of the book is its critique of Étienne Cabet's *Voyage en Icarie*, which overturns a certain view of that utopia as a rationalist monolith from which antagonism and passions are absent. An extended discussion of Cabet's text presents the case for a more historicized, and literary, understanding of the work, centring on plot, characterization, and intrigue; Sipe argues convincingly that the economy of pleasure which ostensibly governs the lives of the citizens of Icaria is itself undercut by the citizens' own private desires and transgressions.

A more pictorial focus is adopted in later chapters on Grandville and Gustave Courbet. The discussion of Grandville and Taxile Delord's parodic *Un autre monde* contemplates, among other things, their undermining of nineteenth-century taxonomies, and their accompanying pursuit of images of alterity through the ludic visual reassembling of elements of the known world. Meanwhile, the section on Courbet shows how that artist's experiments in self-portraiture were intended to mark out a model of creative work that was neither typically bourgeois nor bohemian. In the context of some of Courbet's most famous self-portraits, Sipe goes on to consider the symbolic function of artistic madness in figuring an image of alterity. *The Origin of the World*, for its part, is presented ambitiously as 'a perversion of the utopian space of social interaction' (p. 164).

The study's underlying concern with desire, violence, and the rise of mechanistic conceptions of social interaction culminates persuasively in a final chapter concerned with the figure of the female automaton in narratives by Charles Barbara and Villiers de l'Isle-Adam. This final chapter completes the book's narrative of a shift within the utopian imagination from an ethical ideal of happiness to a more dubious concern with the optimal management of libidinal exchange, from social vision to a technocratic regime of fetishized objects and unconscious drives. Conversant with the work of Fredric Jameson, Louis Marin, and Lyman Tower Sargent, this story of a rising self-critical anxiety and unease is a compelling one, which makes an original and highly important contribution to the study of utopian thought in modern French culture.

University of Glasgow   Greg Kerr

Simone de Beauvoir and the Politics of Ambiguity. By Sonia Kruks. Oxford: Oxford University Press. 2012. xiv+203 pp. £18.99. ISBN 978-0-19-538143-6.

In her Introduction Sonia Kruks defines her multiple audiences: Beauvoir scholars, scholars in political philosophy and theory, as well as social critics and political activists. Coming from a feminist and literary angle to Beauvoir's work, I have certainly found this book enlightening.

Kruks writes for an English-speaking readership without presuming any prior knowledge, and her exposition of Beauvoir's political ideas is a model of clarity, the only criticism I have being errors in the quotations in French. Her thesis is compelling and the message from Beauvoir her text expounds is strangely comforting. Throughout her life and writings—not just her political essays—Beauvoir insisted on the ambiguity set at the heart of human existence, which stems from the fact that we are both body and consciousness. The corollary to this ambiguity is the unavoidable risk of failure inherent in any human action, even political judgement. I personally have found this acknowledgement liberating and encouraging.

Kruks's book is made up of five fairly discrete chapters (three of which have already been partially published), a bibliography, and an index. In her first chapter, 'Humanism after Posthumanism', Kruks argues that a consequence of Beauvoir's concept of embodied subjectivity is that she advocated an 'ambiguous humanism— that is [. . .] a humanism that is aware of its own limitations and necessary failures'

(p. 22). In 'Theorizing Oppression' Kruks explores the mechanisms of oppression, and shows that Beauvoir offers other sources beyond her use of Hegel's master–slave dialectics to help us think about oppression. Drawing on three works by Beauvoir— *The Second Sex* (trans. by Constance Borde and Sheila Malovany-Chevalier (New York: Knopf, 2010)), *America Day by Day* (trans. by Carol Cosman, foreword by Douglas Brinkley (Berkeley: University of California Press, 2000)), and *The Coming of Age* (trans. by Patrick O'Brian (New York: Putnam, 1972))—Kruks is able to categorize three means by which oppression is perpetuated: asymmetrical recognition for women, indifference to blacks, and aversion from the old. Chapter 3, 'Confronting Privilege', takes Beauvoir as an example of how to deal with privileges. Rather than trying to shed one's privileges, as progressives may unsuccessfully attempt to do, why not redeploy these privileges to help the oppressed, as Beauvoir did, using her high profile to further the cause of, for example, women and the FLN in Algeria? In 'Dilemmas of Political Judgement' Kruks contrasts Beauvoir's nuanced view on how we form a political decision with rationalist models, and compares it with Hannah Arendt's thinking on the question. Again, it is Beauvoir's conception of human beings as embodied, situated existences that drives her to envisage all the other factors, besides reason, that come to bear on how we arrive at a political judgement. Kruks shows the complexities of the process through a study of *The Mandarins* (translated by Leonard M. Friedman (London: Fontana, 1972)), and the character of Henri Perron in particular. Finally, Kruks envisages 'The Question of Revenge' in 'An Eye for an Eye' (in *Simone de Beauvoir: Philosophical Writings*, ed. by Margaret A. Simons, trans. by Kristina Arp (Urbana: University of Illinois Press, 2004) pp. 245–60), written in 1946 in the wake of Robert Brasillach's trial and death sentence for his collaborationist, anti-Semitic activities. It is noteworthy that Kruks questions Beauvoir's decision not to sign the petition drawn up by French intellectuals to try and save his life, given the fact that Beauvoir held the view that revenge serves no useful purpose and is bound to fail. To finish, Kruks supposes that Beauvoir's reaction to the truth and reconciliation commissions would have been positive, in spite of their shortcomings in fulfilling people's desire for revenge.

Thus presented, Beauvoir's politics of ambiguity offers a humane middle way between the extremes of liberal rationalism and poststructuralism. This monograph should secure Kruks's place next to Michèle Le Dœuff and Toril Moi, who battle convincingly to show Beauvoir's continuing relevance to contemporary thinking.

SWANSEA UNIVERSITY   CATHERINE RODGERS

Black and Blue: The Bruising Passion of 'Camera Lucida', 'La Jetée', 'Sans soleil', and 'Hiroshima mon amour'. By CAROL MAVOR. Durham. NC: Duke University Press. 2012. xvi+193 pp. £16.99. ISBN 978-0-8223-5271-6.

Black and Blue is a beautifully produced book. The inside covers are reproductions of the cyanotype *Papaver* by Anna Atkins, an X-ray-like representation in light blue of a slightly bruised, faded poppy, followed by a totally black page (recto and verso).

Then a photograph of a woman blissfully asleep. The same sequence is repeated at the end of the book in reverse except that there is now also a photograph of the same woman, awakened, smiling, looking knowingly at us. Besides being one of the characters in the short film *La Jetée* by Chris Marker (Argos Films, 1962), could she be an image of the reader? Carol Mavor's book certainly has the potential to wake us up, open us to new levels of meaning and appreciation, not only of the four works she studies, but of a wealth of other artists she mentions. It is interspersed with black-and-white photographs, and following the text are eighteen full-page colour plates. Seven black pages, containing only the titles of the Introduction, the four chapters and the two author's notes, punctuate the text, recalling the black pages of the cover, the black leader of Marker's film *Sans soleil* (Argos Films, 1982), and the black of the book's title.

While *Black and Blue* is certainly a scholarly study of four French post-war political works, all 'guilty of *beauty*' (p. 12), it is much more than that. It is also a consideration of the symbolic value of the colours black and blue and a reflection on anamnesis. It is both a public and a very private book, in which the author expresses her own blue and black feelings: her mother's Alzheimer's disease, her discovery as a child of racial prejudices, as a teenager of the bombing of Hiroshima. Sadness envelops her text, which is marked by the 'hurt of war, love, of time like a bruise' (p. 15). Her beautiful, poetic style, shot through by pithy statements, makes reading her text a sensuous experience, shot through at times by pain.

Her own reflection is mainly informed by Proust's *A la Recherche du temps perdu* (4 vols, Paris: Bibliothèque de la Pléiade, 1987–89) and Barthes. The punctum for her of Barthes's analysis of photography in *La Chambre claire: note sur la photographie* (Paris: Gallimard: 1980), translated as *Camera Lucida*, is his use of 'ô négresse nourricière' (p. 74) to qualify the 'Aunty' in James Van der Zee's portrait of a black family, struggling as she does with Barthes's potential racism. Her perspective on *La Jetée* is that it is a 'fairy tale for adults' (p. 54), a political, post-apocalyptic 'dystopia, with the hope of utopia' (p. 60), a remake of *Vertigo* (dir. by Alfred Hitchcock, Universal Pictures, 1958), a rewriting of Lewis Carroll's stories of Alice, and 'Marker's desire to escape the hands of time' (p. 75). The black leader of *Sans soleil* is what engages her the most in this 'epistolary film' (p. 95), since with it Marker approaches the Kernel of the film, to use Nicholas Abraham's terminology: the happiness that the three Icelandic children fail ultimately to represent. It is this same Kernel she is looking for in *Hiroshima mon amour* (dir. by Alain Resnais, Argos Films, 1959) and finds in the marble which rolls into the black cellar where the young French woman is kept prisoner and which stands for life and memory.

Just as one cannot reduce a photograph or a poem to its intellectual content, I cannot do adequate justice to Mavor's synaesthetic work and can only encourage you to experience it for yourself.

SWANSEA UNIVERSITY   CATHERINE RODGERS

A History of German: What the Past Reveals about Today's Language. By JOSEPH SALMONS. Oxford: Oxford University Press. 2012. xv+396 pp. £70 (pbk £19.99). ISBN 978-0-19-969793-9 (pbk 978-0-19-969794-6).

In his Introduction the author comments on the number of books available on the history of German and outlines the significant differences between these and his own work. However, he overlooks one vital point, viz. that this is now the only available book on the subject in English. The excellent works by R. E. Keller (*The German Language* (London: Faber, 1978)) and C. J. Wells (*German: A Linguistic History to 1945* (Oxford: Clarendon Press, 1987)) were allowed to go out of print several years ago—and as they appeared decades ago, they are no longer up to date with the immense amount of research on the subject which has appeared since. The present work, by one of the most eminent contemporary scholars in the field, thus fills a gap which has been keenly felt for some time by those teaching university courses on this topic.

However, the topic is potentially huge, and there is room for many different approaches. This becomes obvious when one compares the present work with Peter von Polenz's compendious *Deutsche Sprachgeschichte vom Spätmittelalter bis zum Gegenwart* (Berlin: de Gruyter, 1991-99), which in three volumes of over 1600 pages deals only with the period from the late Middle Ages. He also deals almost exclusively with the development of the language in a social and political context, with very little detail on the diachrony of linguistic structures. Salmons's focus, on the other hand, is not dissimilar to Keller's, in that his primary interest is in the history of linguistic forms, although external factors are by no means ignored, especially in the later periods, and he also follows more traditional practice in taking the story back to the origins of German in Indo-European. In essence, his primary aim is the one given in the subtitle: to show students whose first language is not German how looking at the history of the language can reveal much about those features of the language which seem most characteristic (or even odd).

The book had its origin in material prepared for university courses, and the author's enthusiasm for the subject, his estimable command of current research, and his desire to communicate it to students are evident throughout. It is to be hoped that the companion website (<http://www.historyofgerman.net/index.html>), which contains a large set of exercises for students, will continue to be updated with new references. A consequence of this is that the book at times gives the appearance of a set of topics to be dealt with in a course rather than a narrative history for the independent reader. Some topics, such as complementizer agreement (pp. 321-22), seem to have been included more for their theoretical interest than because of their significance in the history of the German language. And, despite the assertion to the contrary on the flyleaf, enagaging seriously with much of the material in the book will require a quite sophisticated background in general or historical linguistics.

The presentation of individual topics is generally excellent, and the author's insistence (p. 354) that any theory or proposed analysis should be supported by complete and accurate data must be warmly welcomed. This can be illustrated by the account of the controversy regarding the use of main-clause word order after *weil*, which, as Salmons shows (pp. 322–24), is an instance of the 'recency' illusion, a feature which has been thought new over the last few decades but which has actually been present as a variant for a considerable time. Almost every topic covered involves serious discussion of opposing views, as with the vexed issue of the origin of the dental preterite (pp. 78–79). Although clearly an introductory textbook cannot deal in detail with the complex phonological issues which seem to vitiate both major explanations, the reader who wishes to pursue the matter further is provided with references to the most recent definitive work on the subject.

The general presentation of the book is good, with copious helpful illustrations, tables, and maps, and there are relatively few misprints in the actual text (some are already listed on the website). However, a number of errors of detail have slipped in which would need to be corrected in subsequent editions. For instance, the preterite of Gothic *hlaupan* (p. 76) would presumably have been *haihlaup* (although the form is not attested in the extant texts); the lateral *l* is not generally vocalized in Alemannic dialects (p. 126); *Name* is not a weak noun in modern German (pp. 153 and 299); the case forms of the numeral *zwei* are used in all genders, not just the neuter (p. 155); many Low German dialects (especially North Saxon) do exhibit apocope (p. 244)—and map 14 referred to on page 244 does not illustrate the extent of apocope; *geist* and *wald* never had neuter gender (p. 245); *sehen* never had the participle form *gesagen—gisewan* is attested with grammatical change in OHG, although this form is infrequent.

The provision of separate indexes for languages, authors, and topics is very much to be welcomed, but here, too, there are occasional slips, with nothing on 'clitic' to be found on page 67 or on Goethe on page 330. The bibliography is comprehensive and immensely useful, taking up over twenty-five pages, but the entries fail to adhere to any recognized bibliographical convention consistently, with much variation in the use of capitals in titles. It is to be hoped that such breakdowns in the copy-editing process can shortly be eliminated in a subsequent edition; this book has been a desideratum for too long.

UNIVERSITY OF MANCHESTER   MARTIN DURRELL

Innovative Schriftlichkeit in digitalen Texten: Syntaktische Variation und stilistische Differenzierung in Chat und Forum. By GEORG ALBERT. (Diskursmuster— Discourse Patterns, 3) Berlin: Akademie Verlag. 2013. 208 pp. €79.80. ISBN 978-3-05-006273-0.

Language use in the new media in German as a field of research has been growing for over a decade, often focusing on the perceived 'conceptual orality' of communication in the new media, alongside its 'medial literacy'; that is to say, it is often regarded as speech written down. In this monograph, Georg Albert makes a novel contribution to this field, taking issue with the conceptual orality approach and shedding light on the nature of linguistic innovation as found in everyday communication in the new media. He focuses on innovative uses of the German modal verbs (including the peripheral *brauchen*) and is thus in a position to offer novel findings on the changes which these verbs are currently undergoing and to illustrate how the level and nature of these innovative changes vary in different online media.

Albert argues persuasively against the traditional view of computer-mediated communication as conceptually oral (p. 60). Some of his views may not meet with universal agreement; see, for instance, his rejection of the classification of emoticons as markers of emotionality and informality (p. 63), or his criticism of the view that the graphic rendering of non-verbal information is 'compensation' for the absence of this type of information from prototypical writing, which he counters by positing that chat participants wishing to compensate for this lack could simply have telephoned one another instead (p. 65). Nonetheless, his critical discussion of the semiotics of digital media (Chapter 3) is vital reading for all who are interested in the nature of online language use.

The corpus of data, which is analysed both quantitatively and qualitatively, comprises two sources: *c.* 2 million words of text from chat protocols and over 366,000 words of text from the forums of an elite dating website. The data were extracted by means of a concordancing program and then manually coded. Throughout the monograph, comparisons are drawn between the chat and forum data. The language used in the latter source is strongly norm-conformant (and, therefore, not necessarily typical of language use in forums). Although Albert does note the norm-consciousness of the users of the elite dating forums (pp. 153–55), the possible atypicality of the forum data may have skewed the chat vs. forum comparisons. A desideratum for future research is therefore the study of other, less 'highbrow' forum data, which might show language use in chats and forums to be less divergent than this investigation suggests.

Albert emphasizes the importance of taking into account the language users and their interests, as well as the inventory of graphic means and stylistically different variant constructions available. It is demonstrated that linguistic 'innovation' need not refer only to a completely new construction, but rather to a new use of a particular construction, and that something that is innovative to one language user will not necessarily be so to another language user. Albert's chat data show more innovation than his strongly norm-conformant forum data. For instance, 71% of the *brauchen* tokens in the chat data involve an infinitive without *zu* (i.e. following prototypical modal verb use), while a similar proportion of *brauchen* tokens in the forum data involve an infinitive preceded by *zu* (i.e. the norm-conformant non-modal structure) (p. 113). Furthermore, the norm-divergent use of a modal verb with no infinitive (as opposed to norm-conformant use without an infinitive) is much more frequent in the chat data than in the forum data (p. 121).

Albert's findings, based on the careful and detailed analysis of two different types of everyday online language use, offer valuable insights into the developments affecting the German modal verbs, into the nature of communication in online situations, and into the nature of innovation in language. As such, this book is of relevance to scholars with an interest in syntax, sociolinguistics, pragmatics, as well as in the use of German in everyday situations.

UNIVERSITY OF NOTTINGHAM   ALAN K. SCOTT

Schreiben und Streichen: Zu einem Moment produktiver Negativität. Ed. by LUCAS MARCO GISI, HUBERT THÜRING, and IRMGARD M. WIRTZ. (Beide Seiten: Autoren und Wissenschaftler im Gespräch, 2) Göttingen: Wallstein. 2011. 360 pp. €24.90. ISBN 978-3-8353-0850-3.

How and why do writers sometimes delete part of what they have written, and what can the relation between writing and deleting reveal about these writers' texts? These are just two of the questions explored in this generally engaging volume which illustrates amply, and sometimes beautifully, that deletions can be far more exciting than the bone-dry stuff of philology they are often made out to be. The volume is refreshing also in the approach it takes to 'texts': most contributors, many of whom are involved in producing historical-critical editions, view the literary text as a dynamic process, moving the focus away from the end product, the default object of literary interpretation. Some contributors even argue that what we come to call 'literature' is fundamentally predicated on deletions, invoking Jean Bellin-Noël's punning term *litté-rature* to suggest that literature begins with *rature*, deletion—literature as 'delete-rature', a view which some may find frivolous. At any rate, the genuine merit of this volume is its proposition that writers' deletions constitute a sort of 'documentary materiality' (p. 23), and that deletions, far from effacing or cancelling what has been written by hand, typed, or printed, leave ample material traces which are significant in and of themselves as well as in relation to the altered or new stage of the text. In other words, deletions can be understood as a cultural practice that is dialectically bound up with writing, a truly 'productive negativity', as the book's subtitle has it.

The volume comprises fifteen academic essays, arranged chronologically by subject, and is augmented by three concluding statements from contemporary Swiss writers. Most of the essays focus on a single author, a specific text, or specific contexts of production and publication, as is the case with the pieces on Droste-Hülshoff, Raabe, Robert Walser, Friedrich Glauser, and Erica Pedretti (who also contributes a short statement). These essays do a good job of illustrating specific issues. For this reviewer, the better contributions are those that contextualize a writer's individual practice of deletions, as Claas Morgenroth does in his piece on Heine's *Lutezia*, which argues that the deletions and substitutions Heine carried out as a result of intervention by the censors must be understood as active reflections of political events surrounding the text and as attempts to sharpen and refine genuinely political writing. Other essays opt for poetics and aesthetics as their context. Marcel Lepper and Felix Christen each read Hölderlin's idiosyncratic practice of deleting words in terms of a poetics of paradox, a material version of Romantic irony that destabilizes language and representation. Other practices of deletion keep the emerging or resulting text and its interpretation radically open-ended, as Thomas Richter shows in his account of the genesis of Rilke's *Aufzeichnungen des Malte Laurids Brigge*, while Alexander Honold reads Musil's *Mann ohne Eigenschaften* and the author's anticipatory 'Nachlass zu Lebzeiten' as enacting the fundamental paradox between writing and its denial.

Other essays are concerned with several authors. Hubert Thüring explores a range of media, theories, and tropes of negativity around writing and deleting, and illustrates these beautifully with a passage from Kafka's first notebook and from Nietzsche, showing how deletions both disrupt and enable the production of the text, and come to function as an exploration of what escapes the subject's rational control or indeed the writing subject itself. Sandro Zanetti's essay likewise uses a broader range of examples to show the ways in which deletions can be understood as an achronological unfolding of modernist poetics, including Beckett's redaction of published texts for their stage production, Kafka's use of deletion in order to decontextualize what was written, Celan's deletions that carry over hidden poetological meanings, and Arno Schmidt's unwieldy typescript novel *Zettels Traum*, which exploits typos to make literary and historical allusions. Ulrich Weber's excellent piece on Friedrich Dürrenmatt begins where Zanetti leaves off: Weber reveals the extent of revision and intervention in the late Swiss writer's final writings, which are generally regarded as an example of impromptu, improvisational postmodernism; for Weber, Dürrenmatt's deletions are a deliberate tactic which calls into question authorial control and textual representation, and consequently he punningly calls them 'Streiche' (pranks). The volume largely eschews any attempt to provide a typology or taxonomy of 'Streichungen' in modern German-language writing, thus demonstrating, for this reviewer, the rich potential of what Uwe Wirth calls a 'materialbezogene *Philologie des Konkreten*' (p. 45)—so long as it pertains to individual writers and their contexts. As well as challenging the often tacit assumption or philological ideal of the finished text, the essays largely avoid the opposite danger of fetishizing the deletion itself. In fact, they frequently point to, and skilfully explore, what Lepper calls the indeterminacy of the poetic process (p. 92). This is probably where deletions, paradoxically, make their lasting presence felt.

GOLDSMITHS, UNIVERSITY OF LONDON   ANDREAS KRAMER

Heights of Reflection: Mountains in the German Imagination from the Middle Ages to the Twenty-First Century. Ed. by SEAN IRETON and CAROLINE SCHAUMANN. (Studies in German Literature, Linguistics, and Culture) Rochester, NY: Camden House. 2012. ix+395 pp. £55. ISBN 978-1-57113-502-5.

'Great things are done when men and mountains meet', mused William Blake (*Gnomic Verses*, 1). When those men are Germans, it is almost inevitably a poem, novel, painting, musical composition, or film that results. The present volume traces in a series of essays the 'conceptions and representations of mountains in the German-speaking intellectual tradition over the course of approximately one thousand years' (p. 17).

In their introduction the editors briefly define 'the meaning of mountains' from the basic geological and topographical facts to their symbolic value in various religious traditions. Dan Hooley's 'Prelude' provides a fascinating survey of the mystery of climbing in antiquity from Euripides to Seneca, culminating in Petrarch's renowned ascent of Mt Ventoux. Albrecht Claasen follows with a knowledgeable overview of medieval German poets, who, while not blind to mountains as physical barriers, in general display no 'specific interest in mountains per se' (p. 50).

The 'paradigm shift' (p. 57), according to Caroline Schaumann's careful analysis, appears in Albrecht von Haller's idealizing poem 'Die Alpen' (1732). Anthony Ozturk's necessarily sketchy account traces 'the Alpine sublime' in German, French, and English art and literature from Thomas Burnet and Edmund Burke to John Ruskin, with glances along the way at such figures as Wordsworth and C. D. Friedrich. Sean Franzel considers texts by Schiller, Fichte, and Goethe in which 'the sublime operates as a narrative motor that propels observations of self and others forward' (p. 108) before turning to Hegel as representative of premodern writers who regard mountains simply as boring.

Six essays then treat specific texts. Heather I. Sullivan's 'ecocritical' reading of the three mountain scenes in *Faust* shows that Goethe shifts the perspective from the sublime to the material realm and the actual difficulties of mountain ascents, including climatic conditions. Peter Arnds applies the terminology of Heidegger, Foucault, Nietzsche, and Freud to Tieck's *Der Runenberg* to reveal theoretical aspects of that novella. Sean Ireton's wholly original view of *Nachsommer* shows that Stifter's *Bildungsroman* is at the same time a 'Bergroman' in which the hero's mountain experiences constitute an essential aspect of his spiritual education. Johannes Türk looks at the familiar association of 'elevation and insight' in Thomas Mann's *Zauberberg* as a specific 'regional epistemology' (p. 248) that exposes insights into human physiology offered by the various stages of acclimatization in the atmosphere of Davos. Scott Denham establishes parallels between Hans Castorp's experience on his 'magic mountain' and the Alpine experiences of figures in W. G. Sebald's fiction: notably Dr Henry Selwyn in *Die Ausgewanderten*, who regards as the high point of his life his months of climbing in the Bernese Oberland. Olaf Berwald considers the extreme mountaineering in Christoph Ransmayr's lyrical novel *Der fliegende Berg* as an allegory for 'the risks of vertiginous reading' (p. 334).

Another trio of essays turns from European mountains to various peaks elsewhere in the world: the 'discourse of tropicalization' (p. 146) that characterizes Georg Forster's reports of the mountains in Tahiti (Sabine Wilke); nineteenth-century depictions of Kilimanjaro in the context of the 'mountains of the moon' (Christof Hamann); and the mythicizing adaptations in modern film and fiction of Alexander von Humboldt's failed attempt to scale Chimborazo in the Andes (Oliver Lubrich).

In an insightful analysis of Richard Strauss's *Alpensinfonie* Peter Höyng shows how that tone poem, tracing the tragic life of the Swiss artist Karl Stauffer, presents mountains as 'a metaphor for the ultimate Other, opposing [. . .] the evils of a decadent modernity' (p. 237). Three essays then look at the treatment of mountains in film: as places of redemption in Arnold Fanck's popular 'Bergfilme' of the 1920s (Wilfried Wilms); the quasi-religious significance of Himalayan Nanga Parbat, the 'mountain of destiny' (p. 285) that captured the German consciousness of the 1930s (Harold Höbusch); and the 'cognitive mapping' and 'proprioceptive spatial orientation' (p. 304) underlying Werner Herzog's mountaineering films (Roger Cook).

The nineteen essays, almost uniformly well informed and mostly written in a refreshingly jargon-free prose, offer stimulating introductions to certain aspects of mountains in the German imagination but, inevitably, do not constitute a complete account. Where, for instance, is Schiller's *Der Spaziergang* or the entire genre of German elegies with their customary mountain locus (Theodore Ziolkowski, *The Classical German Elegy, 1795–1950* (Princeton: Princeton University Press, 1980), pp. 27–54), or Hermann Broch's 'Bergroman' (mentioned but not discussed)? As one might expect from a self-confessed 'devoted and close-knit group of climbing partners' (p. ix), their essays focus exclusively on the heights: on mountains as sublime. But missing are the equally important depths of the mountain: its mines and caverns as images of the soul (Theodore Ziolkowski, *German Romanticism and its Institutions* (Princeton: Princeton University Press, 1990), pp. 18–63). Many German writers, from Novalis to Dürrenmatt and Grass, were more familiar with the interiors of mountains than with their peaks. In sum, while the volume brilliantly displays Marjorie Hope Nicolson's 'mountain glory', it lacks a good dose of the corresponding 'mountain gloom'.

PRINCETON UNIVERSITY   THEODORE ZIOLKOWSKI

Literarische Entdeckungsreisen: Vorfahren — Nachfahrten — Revisionen. Ed. by HANSJÖRG BAY and WOLFGANG STRUCK. Cologne: Böhlau. 2012. 376 pp. €49.90. ISBN 978-3-412-20764-9.

In a partially contrapuntal move, the age of the globalization and the Internet, of increased global interaction and mobility, has sparked new fascination with the physical exploration of the world during Europe's colonial expansion at a time when the white patches on Europe's geographical and mental maps were shrinking, making the discovery of the unknown—such as the mysterious sources of the Nile and remote polar regions—increasingly difficult in both logistical and epistemological terms. As the editors of the volume in hand note, German literature since the 1980s has seen a wave of literary engagement with the adventure and myth of these colonial journeys of discovery, starting with significant postmodern novels, such as Christoph Ransmayr's *Die Schrecken des Eises und der Finsternis* (1984) and Sten Nadolny's *Die Entdeckung der Langsamkeit* (1983), through a range of novels revisiting the exploration of Africa and the Pacific, to recent best-sellers, such as Ilija Trojanow's *Der Weltensammler* (2006) about Richard Burton and Daniel Kehlmann's *Die Vermessung der Welt* (2005) about Alexander von Humboldt. Inspired by postcolonial studies and new interest in cultural history, including shifting notions of space, scholarship has now followed suit.

Following in the footsteps of the volume *Ins Fremde schreiben: Gegenwartsliteratur auf den Spuren historischer und fantastischer Entdeckungsreisen*, ed. by Christof Hamann and Alexander Honold (Göttingen: Wallstein, 2009), and involving some of the same contributors, *Literarische Entdeckungsreisen* draws on semiotics and poststructuralism for its conceptual framework, as well as on the methodology of researching 'colonialism as culture', a highly productive field of interdisciplinary research in the German humanities since the later 1990s (see e.g. *Kolonialismus als Kultur: Literatur, Medien, Wissenschaft in der deutschen Gründerzeit des Fremden*, ed. by Alexander Honold and Oliver Simons (Tübingen: Francke, 2002)). The volume, which is based on a conference in Erfurt and Gotha in autumn 2009, is clearly not aiming to give a *comprehensive* account of the fascination in contemporary German literature and film with exploration, discovery, and liminal experience more generally; and the final section on literary representations of travel to Italy and the global South is particularly selective. Instead, the twenty chapters by established and younger researchers from Germany, the USA, Canada, and Cameroon focus on the epistemology of colonial exploration and the political and aesthetical challenges of its narrative representation: while the explorers of the eighteenth to early twentieth centuries were themselves compelled to follow in the footsteps of those before them, depending on preconceived knowledge and ideas that made the craved discovery of the genuinely unknown beyond the ultimate frontier thoroughly elusive, literary engagement with their adventures, accounts, and aspirations today is by definition a retracing and rereading of stories, myths, and phantasms from the European archive, giving these texts a 'meta-textual' (p. 11) dimension even where they do not subscribe to an explicitly metafictional aesthetic. At the same time, the editors point out from a postcolonial perspective that such literary rereading of European cultural history, and the renewed fascination with crossing ultimate frontiers, necessarily runs the danger of perpetuating and restaging colonial fantasies and 'imperial violence' (p. 10). One of the guiding questions therefore is to what extent contemporary literature and film have moved on from colonial narratives.

The editors' brief preface and their sketchy outline of some of the tropes of narratives of exploration are followed by a first section devoted to polar expeditions around 1900 and their cultural representation. These are seen by Wolfgang Struck and Bettine Menke as particularly poignant examples of the established discursive universe of colonial exploration and its cultural construction, which affected historical adventure as much as its meta-discursive literary 'rereading' today. Philipp Felsch explores the imaginative power of nineteenth-century cartography with regard to the North Pole, while Sabine Frost traces some of the same patterns in a postmodern travesty of science fiction (Ransmayr's *Der fliegende Berg*, 2006).

The second set of essays is devoted to contemporary literary engagement with the exploration of Africa, a prominent theme of the past fifteen years. Considering novels such as Trojanow's *Der Weltensammler* and Thomas Stangl's *Der einzige Ort* (2004), Hansjörg Bay explores the politics of postcolonial and postmodern aesthetics, asking to what extent such advanced narratives are still complicit in perpetuating elements of colonial discourse despite promoting critiques of colonial thought and language. Going back in time, Christof Hamann reconstructs the history of rereading that links Raabe's *Stopfkuchen* (1890) back to François Le Vaillant's South African travel account (1790) and its influential retelling by Joachim Heinrich Campe (1792)—a line continued, as Axel Dunker shows, in Hamann's own novel *Usambara* (2007). John K. Noyes argues convincingly that Urs Widmer's seminal *Im Kongo* (1996) exposes 'the historical and geographical foundations [...] of the colonial view of the world' and the constructedness of European subjectivity (p. 175), while David Simo discusses an African response to European discourses about Africa, Yambo Ouloguem's novel *Le Devoir de violence* (1968), seen as a break with the first generation of postcolonial literature.

The third section looks more generally at some of the tropes and counter-discourses involved in German representations of the tropics, in particular with regard to South America. Examples include Robert Müller's *Tropen* (1915; Dietmar Schmidt), Alfred Döblin's *Amazonas* trilogy (Pierre Kodjio Nenguié), the myth of El Dorado and Werner Herzog's film *Aguirre oder der Zorn Gottes* (1972; Sabine Wilke), and Brazilian film-maker Nelson Pereira dos Santos's *Como era gostoso o meu francês* (Jörg Dünne). John Zilcosky draws on Freud and psychoanalysis to read colonial cross-cultural encounters against the grain, highlighting the uncanny experience of how close to the European self the supposedly alien others often turned out to be.

The last section concerns travel to Italy and the Pacific, including August von Goethe's engagement with his father's famous Italian travels (Rupert Gaderer), the thoroughly imperialist wave of forgotten German educational novels about China, written around 1900 in the context of the Boxer uprising (Yixu Lü), the prominent European discourse about Tahiti, right through to Felicitas Hoppe's *Pigafetta* (1999; Ortrud Gutjahr), Alex Capus's literary rereading of Stevenson's *Treasure Island* (Sabine Zubarik), and, returning to Ransmayr, the question of an ethics of travel writing, seen as a mode of European self-reflection (Volker Mergenthaler).

The volume offers significant findings on the grammar of narratives of exploration, both during the colonial period and today, along with some perceptive and thoughtful textual and intertextual analysis. More research could have been invested into the historicity of such narratives and the reasons behind the recent upsurge in literary interest in the theme.

University of Nottingham   Dirk Göttsche

Popular Revenants: The German Gothic and its International Reception 1800–2000.
Ed. by ANDREW CUSACK and BARRY MURNANE. (Studies in German Literature, Linguistics and Culture) Rochester, NY: Camden House. 2012. vii+
309 pp. £55. ISBN 978-1-57113-519-3.

Derrida's conflation of intertextuality with spectrality means that this book could be about anything. There is an inevitability about the arrival of the clever-absurd claim 'all stories are [. . .] ghost stories' on page 255 (admittedly quoted from elsewhere, but with acquiescence, if not approval). On the other hand, the ghost of Derrida prevents the book from being Dryasdust empirical literary history. The editors and contributors walk a tightrope between establishing exactly what 'Gothic' means in the discipline of German Studies, and the German component in the genre of the Gothic, for which it was always an advantage if the tale concerned was either actually, or at least claimed to be, translated from the German. Both aspects are then placed in the reception context announced by the subtitle.

The editors provide an introductory essay each, Andrew Cusack articulating the challenge lucidly, and Barry Murnane taking on the task of defining the issue from the German Studies angle. Here the focus becomes a little blurred. After an excellent contextualization of the popular discourse in Germany at the end of the eighteenth century and a thought-provoking account of the nineteenth-century afterlife in German letters of Gothic elements, the narrative becomes rather random in its references to, for instance, Kafka and *Metropolis* (while it is left to Andrew Webber many pages later to remind the reader of the *obviously* Gothic elements in Lang's film). Perhaps Murnane has taken on too much for such a short space: but can one really claim that Heiner Müller was 'Germany's most internationally prominent dramatist of the twentieth century' (p. 33)? Perhaps Brecht wasn't Gothic enough for this take on German literary history.

Thereafter one has twelve essays (most of them 'evolved' from a 2009 symposium in Dublin) treating the elusive topic in a great variety of ways. Jürgen Barkhoff and Silke Arnold de Simine's contributions are (very good) translations (we are not told by whom) of illuminating examples of intellectual history (on the contemporary anthropological context of *Der Geisterseher*, and the differing literary and political horizons of expectation revealed through scrutiny of the English translations of Benedikte Naubert's novels, respectively). Victor Sage's contribution is a fascinating piece of literary history on the genealogy of the 'fantastic' traced through the relation between Sir Walter Scott and E. T. A. Hoffmann. Cusack offers a case study—that of J. C. Mangan's association with the influential *Dublin University Magazine*—of the real role the Gothic played in 'cultural transfer' from the German source to an entirely distinct political and religious environment, with its own discursive logics. With Mario Grizelj (who is careful to use the word 'grisly' in his second paragraph) a more technical perspective reveals changes in the implied mediality of different kinds of hermeneutic fright in texts by Joseph Alois Gleich, Hoffmann, and Edgar Allan Poe. If 'mediality' betrays the familiar Derridean erosion of sense, the claim that 'life in modernity is structured like a gothic novel'

(p. 128) promises to further subvert the possibility of sensible judgement, but in fact comes in a very interesting essay, by Jörg Kreinbrock, on the Gothic implications of idealist thought made flesh in Heinrich Heine's treatment of German philosophy. Monika Schmitz-Evans turns the topic towards the Romantic relationship between text and music by reporting on Robert Schumann's Jean Paul-influenced early novel fragment *Selene*. Kreinbrock and Schmitz-Evans, in their different ways, evoke the function of ghost stories as expressions of historical perplexity about how to talk about anything non-empirical—surely the core issue of the whole book. Webber's close reading of Hoffmann and Weimar film meets the challenge of linking the Gothic sensibility of literature with the intrinsic uncanniness of the film medium brilliantly. It is not completely clear what Peter Arnds wants us to think about the mass of material he clusters around the Pied Piper of Hamelin story. His piece seems to be as much about the inner Dionysian structure of National Socialist psychology (a little too glibly, perhaps) as it is about Wilhelm Raabe's Novelle *Die Hämelschen Kinder*. Here, and in Catherine Smale's original and perceptive essay on the haunting from the past in the post-Wall German present in texts by Irina Liebmann and Christa Wolf, the topic's potential for excessive elasticity is possibly manifest. Two other essays, however, define their subjects very crisply in relation to the Gothic: Matthias Bickenbach examines talk *about* ghosts in Fontane, something which indisputably existed in reality, even if ghosts themselves do not ('Innstetten' has two 'n's in its first syllable, by the way), and Murnane illuminates the connection between cultural geography, serious modernism, and the popular Gothic in an excellent essay on Gustav Meyrink's *Der Golem* and other texts in their relation to Prague.

Although always threatening to disseminate itself into thin air, this volume provides concrete evidence of Slavoj Žižek's claim, in Paul A. Taylor's words (*Žižek and the Media* (Cambridge: Polity, 2010), p. 59), that 'a full understanding of what it is to experience reality as a human being requires acknowledgment that the spectral has a very real effect'.

JESUS COLLEGE, CAMBRIDGE   MICHAEL MINDEN

Poetischer Fetischismus: Der Kult der Dinge im 19. Jahrhundert. By DOERTE BI-
    SCHOFF. Munich: Fink. 2013. 486 pp. €59. ISBN 978-3-7705-5042-5.

The concept of the fetish is understood in this study in three interrelated ways: in an anthropological sense as an inanimate object to which magical powers are attributed; in a Marxist sense as a commodity invested with value beyond its actual practical value (*Warenwert* vs. *Gebrauchswert*); and in a Freudian sense as a part, attribute, or representation of a person that is desired or admired in that person's (or any potential sexual partner's) stead (see page 447). The common denominator of the three aspects is that the fetish serves as a substitute for something that is absent—and presumably more genuine, whole, or meaningful than the surrogate. All three of these uses offer productive perspectives from which to unravel the nineteenth century's intellectual signatures and psycho(patho)logical make-up in that the deconstruction of fetishism in literature reveals how the respective texts show up and play out the themes, concerns, and phobias of a fissured, unruly, and, in its modernizing dynamics, incomprehensible age.

Several discursive fields where these uncertainties are played out come into view: the construction of alterity (attributed to alleged colonial fetish worshippers), the exculpation of complicity in the excesses of economic objectification by projecting responsibility upon others (for example, Jews as alleged agents of a capitalist commodification of interpersonal relationships), and the disintegration of gender demarcations and sexual configurations manifest in fetishist eroticism. The material in which motifs and symbolism related to the complex of fetishism feature is varied and sometimes surprising. Among others, the following texts are discussed: Goethe's *Faust II* (with special emphasis on the Helena theme); Hauff's *Kaltes Herz* and Chamisso's *Schlemihl*; Hoffmann's *Fräulein von Scuderi* and Arnim's *Melück*; Vischer's *Auch Einer*; Stifter's *Nachsommer*, 'Kalkstein', *Abdias*, and 'Die Streichmacher'; Grillparzer's *Jüdin von Toledo* and *Armer Spielmann*; the three tales 'Regina', 'Don Carrea', and 'Berlocken' from Keller's collection *Das Sinngedicht*; Oskar Panizza's *Der Corsetten-Fritz*; and Sacher-Masoch's *Venus im Pelz*. Several of these texts participate in discourses that only later became condensed into systematic theories, but all, in Bischoff's reading, defy representation and signification in any conventional sense.

This study is not for the faint-hearted or theoretically uninitiated. It demands of its readers an acceptance that every (textual) phenomenon implies its own negation, that every agent is, at the same time, a recipient, that every act of (imaginary) commodification contains the potential to salvage some (aesthetic) autonomy through performative acts, that signification is never unambiguous or finite. It also demands of its readers a trust in the validity of analytical categories involving processes such as 'stillstellen', 'unterlaufen', 'aushebeln', 'verschieben', 'engführen', or 'aufs Spiel setzen'—to name but a few of the terms that occur on almost every page. The reader must not, however, expect any concrete indicator as to how exactly the fetish complex relates to historical reality—over and above, that is, serving as a diagnostic tool for the 'Verdinglichung des Menschen im Zeitalter von Warenökonomie und beginnender Massenproduktion' (p. 325). What the study attempts to achieve is probably most succinctly expressed in the blurb on the back cover that culminates in the following claim: 'Die poetische Produktivität, die sich mit dem Kult der Dinge verknüpft, liegt, wie gezeigt, darin, dass Konstruktionen von Eigenem und Fremdem, korrekter und korrupter Objektbeziehung, wahrem Ding und Warending, als solche inszeniert werden und so Performativität und Materialität kultureller Symbolisierung lesbar werden.' What the study does not reveal, however, is *how* the texts become readable: as parable, allegory, intervention, reflection, engagement, emplotment—or perhaps as something else?

NATIONAL UNIVERSITY OF IRELAND MAYNOOTH   FLORIAN KROBB

Bridal-Quest Epics in Medieval Germany: A Revisionary Approach. By SARAH BOWDEN. (MHRA: Texts and Dissertations, 85/Institute of Germanic and Romance Studies (University of London) Bithell Series of Dissertations, 40) London: MHRA and the Institute of Germanic and Romance Studies (University of London). 2012. viii+184 pp. £9.99. ISBN 978-1-907322-46-4 (pbk 978-1-907322-96-9).

The opening sentence of this monograph sets out its objective with admirable clarity: 'The aim of this study is to do away with, once and for all, the genre labels of *Spielmannsepik* and *Brautwerbungsepik*, which have been regularly applied since the late nineteenth century'—with the phrase 'once and for all' encapsulating the thoroughness, ambition, and rigour the author brings to the undertaking.

The two problematic genre labels are associated with a set of rather disparate texts which have been grouped together on the grounds of supposedly subcourtly, popular style and the recurrent motif of overseas travel to win a bride (or to reclaim a stolen bride). There has been long-standing dissatisfaction with these genre labels, particularly with *Spielmannsepik*, and it has become conventional to deploy them with scare quotes or preface them with 'so-called'). Nonetheless, as Sarah Bowden demonstrates in the introductory chapter, critics have been reluctant entirely to jettison the view that the texts are linked to each other through recourse to common narrative schemata and should therefore be read primarily against each other. Bowden argues that the presence of a motif (such as that of a bridal quest or of travel to/around the Orient) in a text is not sufficient to constitute evidence of a narrative schema, let alone of a genre with 'ideal criteria [. . .] against which every text containing the motif is to be judged' (p. 25). In the subsequent four chapters she therefore goes on to provide individual readings of four texts (*König Rother*, *Salman und Morolf*, the *Münchener Oswald*, and *Grauer Rock*) which direct the reader 'away from the hitherto dominating context of Spielmannsepik or Brautwerbungsepik' (p. 25).

Each of these chapters constitutes an innovative and compelling engagement with the text in question. The analysis of *Salman und Morolf* is particularly enjoyable. This text—which tells the story of how Morolf twice recaptures the unfaithful wife of his brother Salman (Solomon) and eventually solves the problem by killing her—has traditionally been treated as an 'inverse' bridal-quest epic which derives its meaning from the way in which it distorts the conventions of the presumed genre. However, Bowden argues that for this view to be valid, 'there must be a genre and a norm to comply with in the first place', and concludes that 'if the bridal-quest motif is simply a story-motif that can be used flexibly and in a variety of contexts, then *Salman und Morolf* cannot upturn conventions, because there are none to be upturned' (p. 94). Instead, she offers a reading that foregrounds the significance of corporeality as an element of personal and social identity, and the construction of desire as a motivating force, both within the narrative and on the level of the reading experience.

Bowden's style is clear, lively, and elegant. As well as making a definitive statement on the question of the genre of these texts, this book also offers insightful interpretations that are likely to make the texts in question more accessible and appealing to students.

ORIEL COLLEGE, OXFORD   ANNETTE VOLFING

'The Chronicle of Prussia' by Nicolaus von Jeroschin: A History of the Teutonic Knights in Prussia, 1190–1331. Trans. by MARY FISCHER. (Crusade Texts in Translation, 20) Farnham: Ashgate. 2010. xi+306 pp. £60. ISBN 978-0-7546-5309-7.

About the life of Nicolaus von Jeroschin we know little—but we can be confident that his literary activity took place in the first half of the fourteenth century; that he was, by his own account, a chaplain in the Teutonic Order; and that he was the author of two known works in German. One, a life of St Adalbert, has survived in a single fragment, but Jeroschin also wrote a history of the Order from 1190 to 1331 which has been transmitted in several manuscripts. Mary Fischer presents an English translation of the latter in her book, which can be seen against the background of at least two areas of interest in recent research: chronicle studies and the literature of the Teutonic Order. The *Encyclopedia of the Medieval Chronicle*, ed. by Graeme Dunphy (Leiden: Brill, 2010), is now a major point of reference on the former, and Fischer herself has made a number of contributions in English to the latter field, which has tended to be dominated by work in German, such as Gisela Vollmann-Profe, *Krieg im Visier* (Tübingen: Niemeyer, 2007).

There is much of interest in Jeroschin's chronicle, from an account of the Order's founding (pp. 29–35), through the establishment of its first base on the Vistula (pp. 62–63), to the relocation of its headquarters from Venice to Marienburg (pp. 254–55). This narrative, in which campaigns against the pagan Prussians and Lithuanians occupy centre stage, is interspersed with passages on Christian warfare (e.g. pp. 51–62), events in the wider world (e.g. pp. 181–83), and details such as the appearance of two giant fish in Prussian rivers in 1331 (pp. 294–95). The translation, which renders the rhyming couplets of the original in English prose, generally reads well, although some of the longer paragraphs might have been broken up (or at least an indication given of how the divisions relate to those in the edition and ultimately the manuscripts). Fischer draws attention to the fact that 'some repetition which is dictated by line length and the rhyme scheme has been omitted [. . .] for the sake of clarity' (p. 17), but this does not always account for what is arguably a wider tendency to pare down the phrasing of the original. It might be felt that something is lost of Jeroschin's style without a significant increase in clarity when, to give two examples, the goodwill of past popes is said to have made the Order 'illustrious' (p. 35) rather than 'irlûchtit und irhabin' ('resplendent and respected', perhaps; l. 900), or the German adverbial 'in vlêndir vlîe' ('imploringly'; l. 23308) is omitted from the injunction that the lay brothers 'should pray' (p. 255) to Mary during the difficult year of 1309.

The translation is accompanied by an Introduction, bibliography, and index. It is particularly helpful that a commentary is also provided in notes that can easily be consulted at the foot of the page, rather than being printed in a separate section as is often the case in translations of this kind. The notes for the most part elucidate historical details and identify parallel passages in the Bible, and will be a real help in making the text accessible to a wide audience. In this respect, it is perhaps a pity that the book does not provide further background information, particularly in the Introduction, for non-specialist readers. No reference is made, for example, to online material such as the relevant entry in the *Handschriftencensus* project (www.handschriftencensus.de/werke/487), a standard point of reference on the manuscript transmission of works in German, which includes a link to a colour reproduction of the earliest manuscript of the chronicle. Likewise, Ernst Strehlke's 1861 edition of the German text has been digitized (e.g. <www.books.google.de/books?id=YX8OAAAAYAAJ>), and allows readers to gain a first-hand impression of the original behind the translation. The transmission of Jeroschin's work and the salient features of his compositional technique are both mentioned in the Introduction, but these freely available resources enable readers to go beyond what is said there even if they do not have access to an academic library in the first instance. Similarly, the Latin chronicle by Peter von Dusberg that provided Jeroschin with his main source is discussed, but readers who plan to look more closely at the relationship between them should be aware that a new edition of it is now available (*Piotr z Dusburga: 'Kronika Ziemi Pruskiej'*, ed. by Jarosław Wenta and Sławomir Wyszomirski (Wodzisław Śląski: Księgarnia Średniowieczna, 2007)).

From the perspective of literary studies, more might also have been done to introduce an English-speaking readership to the work that has been done in German on the literature of the Teutonic Order, or to consider how the chronicle is constructed as a literary text rather than being 'just' a historical source. When Jeroschin begins with a prayer to the Holy Trinity, for instance, the notes make no mention of the tradition behind this device, of which the prologue to Wolfram von Eschenbach's *Willehalm* is perhaps the most famous example in medieval German literature. The treatment of Jeroschin's rhetorical colour in individual passages as described above might thus be seen as a counterpart to the perspective on the text adopted in the accompanying material.

Translation strategies, though, are a subjective matter; and even if their relevance, like that of the text, to wider themes such as the relationship between history and literature could have been explored more extensively, the book ultimately deserves to be judged on its own terms. It sets out to approach Jeroschin's chronicle primarily in terms of its historical interest, which it conveys very well indeed, as well as giving tantalizing hints of its literary significance.

UNIVERSITY OF OXFORD   ALASTAIR MATTHEWS

Handbuch kultureller Zentren der Frühen Neuzeit: Städte und Residenzen im alten deutschen Sprachraum. Ed. by WOLFGANG ADAM and SIEGRID WESTPHAL. 3 vols. Berlin: de Gruyter. 2012. 2348 pp. €458. ISBN 978-3-11-020703-3.

Critics of the Holy Roman Empire have often lamented its lack of a single capital, but it is precisely the rich legacy of its polycentric character, comprised as it was of over three hundred princely courts, seventy ecclesiastical territories, and more than fifty imperial cities with their often distinctive political, economic, social, and cultural features, that shaped the regional and municipal diversity and heterogeneity still visible in Germany today. In contrast to other countries where a relatively narrow group of people directs the affairs of an entire nation, the multiplicity of administrative, economic, and cultural centres in the empire provided an opportunity for a much wider range of people to make their mark—it was, as Leibniz observed in 1679, 'ein herrliches Mittel dadurch sich soviel Leute hervor thun können, so sonst im Staube liegen müsten' (p. xxxiv). This excellent book, or rather, this monumental work—a product of the interdisciplinary Institut für Kulturgeschichte der Frühen Neuzeit (IKFN) at the University of Osnabrück—aims to serve as a guide to the characteristic features of a selection of towns, showing in particular how they each developed between 1500 and 1800 but with a particular focus on the seventeenth century. As such it will be an essential aid to anyone studying cultural aspects of the early modern period, valuably complementing such works as Werner Paravicini's four-volume *Höfe und Residenzen im spätmittelalterlichen Reich* (Ostfildern: Thorbecke, 2003–12). The coverage is not comprehensive—only fifty-one towns are dealt with. These are: Augsburg, Bamberg, Basel, Berlin and Potsdam, Breslau, Coburg, Danzig, Darmstadt, Dillingen, Dresden, Elbing, Emden, Frankfurt am Main, Görlitz, Gotha, Gottorf, Halberstadt, Halle, Hamburg, Heidelberg, Helmstedt, Ingolstadt, Jena, Kassel, Cologne, Königsberg, Köthen, Leipzig, Lübeck, Magdeburg, Mainz, Marburg, Munich, Münster, Nuremberg, Osnabrück, Prague, Regensburg, Rudolstadt, Speyer, Strasbourg, Stuttgart, Trier with Koblenz, Tübingen, Ulm, Weimar, Weißenfels, Vienna, Wittenberg, Wolfenbüttel and Braunschweig, and Würzburg. The editors themselves regret the omission of Erfurt, Frankfurt an der Oder, Herborn, and Salzburg, and one could certainly add Innsbruck to this list (though to some extent this particular deficiency can be remedied by reference to the extensive coverage of the political, ecclesiastical, and cultural history of that town in *Tyrolis Latina: Geschichte der lateinischen Literatur in Tirol*, ed. by Martin Korenjak and others (Vienna: Böhlau, 2012)). What a small selection of towns this is becomes evident, the editors themselves note, when one recalls that the topographical index to Georg Christoph Hamberger and Johann Georg Meusel's *Das gelehrte Teutschland oder Lexikon der jetzt lebenden teutschen Schriftsteller*, 5th edn, 23 vols (Lemgo, 1796–1834; repr. Munich: Saur, 1979) lists some 2,300 localities, of which at least a hundred could be regarded as culturally important inasmuch as they had a significant number of writers associated with them. The fifty-one towns covered do, however, represent a wide range of municipalities: some predominantly Catholic (e.g. Cologne and Regensburg), some Protestant

(Frankfurt, Nuremberg); university towns (Helmstedt, Ingolstadt, Jena, Tübingen, Wittenberg); Hanseatic towns (Elbing, Hamburg, Lübeck); towns ruled by an ecclesiastical dignitary (Bamberg, Mainz, Trier, Würzburg); others with secular rulers (e.g. Dresden, Weimar, Wolfenbüttel).

Each entry consists of eleven standardized sections: 'Geographische Situierung', 'Historischer Kontext', 'Politik, Gesellschaft, Konfession', 'Wirtschaft', 'Orte kulturellen Austauschs', 'Personen', 'Gruppen', 'Kulturproduktion', 'Medien der Kommunikation', 'Memorialkultur und Rezeption', and 'Wissensspeicher', followed by a bibliography tailored to the town in question. Each entry runs to about forty to fifty pages, though inevitably some will be rather shorter than others (notably Emden, Gotha, Helmstedt, Marburg, Rudolstadt, and—surprisingly—Vienna). Each article is written by one or more specialists, sixty-two in all, among them such authorities as Kaspar von Greyerz on Basel, Helen Watanabe-O'Kelly on Dresden, Wilhelm Kühlmann on Heidelberg, Jens Bruning on Helmstedt, Klaus Conermann on Köthen, Detlef Döring on Leipzig, Karl Vocelka on Vienna, and Jill Bepler on Wolfenbüttel and Braunschweig. The section headings listed above indicate the scope of each entry. Most of these headings are self-explanatory, but a few require elucidation. Thus 'Orte kulturellen Austauschs' covers such institutions as the Frankfurt fair and the city's libraries, coffee-houses, and theatres (pp. 553–59); the university, Thomasschule, and Nikolaischule, the libraries and the Deutsche Gesellschaft at Leipzig (pp. 1263–70); the monasteries and schools of Regensburg (pp. 1709–15); and the Hohe Carlsschule, attended by Schiller, at Stuttgart (p. 1899). 'Personen' of course covers notable individuals in all walks of life, from potentates and patricians to writers and scholars in various disciplines, while 'Gruppen' refers to such diverse entities as the literary salon known as the 'Kreis der Empfindsamen' in Darmstadt, whose members enthused over Sterne, Richardson, and Ossian (p. 351), the chapter of Cologne Cathedral comprising eight prelates and sixteen noblemen (p. 1112), and the Freemasons in Vienna with their lodges 'Zur gekrönten Hoffnung' and 'Zur wahren Eintracht', to which Haydn and Mozart belonged (p. 2184). Under 'Kulturproduktion' we find discussion of court festivals, ballet, musical activities, and the theatre, for example at Königsberg, where from 1605 the 'Englische Komödianten' and other itinerant actors performed (p. 1190). 'Medien der Kommunikation' surveys printing, publishing, and bookselling in each town (though in rather less detail than in such works as Christoph Reske's *Die Buchdrucker des 16. und 17. Jahrhunderts im deutschen Sprachgebiet* (Wiesbaden: Harrassowitz, 2007) and David Paisey's *Deutsche Buchdrucker, Buchhändler und Verleger 1701–1750* (Wiesbaden: Harrassowitz, 1988), neither of which is included in the general bibliography). Particularly useful, though, is information about newspapers and journals published in each town, for example the Strasbourg *Relation aller Fürnemmen und gedenckwürdigen Historien* of 1605 (p. 1867) and the Wolfenbüttel *Aviso, Relation oder Zeitung* of 1609 (p. 2282), Germany's two oldest newspapers, or the *Casselsche Zuschauer*, modelled on *The Spectator* (p. 1079). Under 'Memorialkultur' is included information about such topics as the celebrations in 1617 marking the centenary of the Reformation or the lamentations over the death of King Gustavus Adolphus in battle in 1632 (for instance, at Strasbourg, p. 1869). The opaque term 'Wissensspeicher' refers to repositories of information about the individual towns: archives, libraries, and museums. Each entry includes a small number of illustrations showing old maps, townscapes, or significant buildings, which certainly adds to the interest of the book.

Although the standardized headings within the articles to some extent facilitate the task of making comparisons between different towns—should one wish to know, for instance, how the 1617 and 1717 anniversaries of the Reformation were marked in different towns—the lack of a fully comprehensive index of names and concepts must be regarded as a serious inconvenience and deficiency in a work of over 2,300 pages.

LONDON, INSTITUTE OF MODERN LANGUAGES RESEARCH   JOHN L. FLOOD

Language and Enlightenment: The Berlin Debates of the Eighteenth Century. By AVI LIFSCHITZ. (Oxford Historical Monographs) Oxford: Oxford University Press. 2012. xii+231 pp. £60. ISBN 978-0-19-966166-4.

It has long been customary, in discussing theories of the origin of language in eighteenth-century Germany, to locate the decisive breakthrough in Herder's prize-winning essay of 1771 on that subject. But while he rejected both the Christian theory of divine instruction and the naturalistic theory that language gradually developed out of emotive cries and onomatopoeic sounds, Herder in fact avoided the question. Instead of explaining the origin of language as a temporal transition from a pre-linguistic state, he simply declared that language is an integral part of human nature and has existed as long as human beings themselves.

What this book shows is that the above issues, and other related ones, had already been debated at length in connection with the topic set by the Berlin Academy in 1759 on the reciprocal influence of language and the opinions of those who use it. Among the intractable problems discussed were that of the relationship between the 'natural' and 'artificial' (or conventional) aspects of language, and how human beings could have agreed to use language without language being already in existence.

Two figures stand out in the ensuing discussions, namely the Göttingen theologian and orientalist Johann David Michaelis and the French philosopher André Pierre Le Guay de Prémontval, a member of the Berlin Academy and friend of Lessing.

The competition of 1759 was won by Michaelis, and an extended edition of his essay was published in French translation in 1762 and in English in 1769. His conclusion that language and opinion interact and evolve over time is already close to Herder's thinking, as is his contention that language is essentially democratic, since it is shaped by the entire community—and not just the educated classes—of those who use it. It is none the worse for that, he believes, and so-called 'primitive' languages are generally more 'natural' and poetic than their more sophisticated successors (Michaelis had attended Robert Lowth's lectures in Oxford on the poetic richness of the Hebrew Scriptures).

Prémontval, who had himself suggested the topic of the 1759 competition, reinforced Michaelis's conclusions by arguing that the use of the vernacular is always preferable to that of dead or non-native languages. He affords the ironic spectacle, in that age of Gallomania in continental Europe, of a French philosopher opposing the widespread use of French in Germany (as in the Berlin Academy) and urging wider use of the more authentic vernacular. All these developments reinforced the emergent conviction in Germany, more fully explored in recent times by Reinhart Koselleck and others, that language and thought are perspectival in character, reflecting the historical and geographical circumstances of the societies from which they emanate.

As Avi Lifschitz convincingly argues, the Berlin debates on language are also part of a much wider debate on human origins in the European Enlightenment; and they are not, as maintained in Isaiah Berlin's once influential studies of Hamann and Herder, the product of a 'Counter-Enlightenment' which led directly to nineteenth-century Romanticism. This illuminating monograph is a welcome addition to our knowledge of the middle years of the German Enlightenment. Though on occasion digressive, as on the early history of the Berlin Academy (pp. 65–69) and on Michaelis's role in planning the ill-fated expedition of 1761–67 to Arabia (pp. 104–09), it retains the reader's interest throughout. The author's use of unpublished material—especially relating to the important but neglected figure of Michaelis—is a further commendable feature.

SIDNEY SUSSEX COLLEGE, CAMBRIDGE   H. B. NISBET

Briefwechsel und Gespräche. By GOTTLIEB WILHELM RABENER. Ed. by E. THEODOR Voss, with the assistance of JAN MÜLLER. 2 vols. Göttingen: Wallstein. 2012. 579 pp. (vol. I); 352 pp. (vol. II); 74 ill. €69. ISBN 978-3-8353-0991-3.

Anyone who thinks that editorial philology is a dry and dusty affair will do well to spend some time with E. Theodor Voss's new edition of Gottlieb Wilhelm Rabener's correspondence. A labour of love, twenty years and more in the planning, its ambition is to gather not only all of Rabener's surviving letters and all the letters he received, but also all the references to him in the correspondence of his contemporaries, as well as other documentary traces both during and after his lifetime, excluding only (a few exceptions aside) the memoranda he wrote in his professional capacity as tax inspector and civil servant in the service of the Saxon state.

Rabener (1714–1771) was a significant figure in what one might call the Gellert generation in German literature, who began publishing in the 1740s, midway between Gottsched and Lessing. He was chiefly associated with the group of the 'Bremer Beiträger' and was the acknowledged satirist in that circle. His *Sammlung satirischer Schriften*, collected in four volumes (1751–55), made him famous in his own lifetime, if not much beyond it. The last complete edition of his works appeared in 1839.

To anyone wondering whether this minor man of letters deserves the royal treatment he receives here—the equivalent, only scaled down in bulk, of Goethe's complete correspondence, the several *Begegnungen und Gespräche* recorded by his contemporaries, and collections such as Bode's *Goethe in vertraulichen Briefen seiner Zeitgenossen*—Voss has an eloquent answer: 'Die Wiedergewinnung unseres Autors stand [. . .] im Zeichen der ihm in seiner Zeit und uns in unserer Zeit zugemuteten Zerstörungen und Verluste und galt zugleich der ihm und seiner Zeit eigenen Besonderheit geistesheller Präsenz und entsprechender Diktion, deren spürbares Stillerwerden im Geräusch unserer Zeit Impulse des Rettens auslöst, wie Lessing sie kannte bei der "Rettung" verkannter oder vergessener Autoren, die heute wie ehedem auf die Mittel einer immerfort notwendig bleibenden Philologie angewiesen sind' (I, 57). Beyond this impulse of preservation and rescue, Voss's sympathy for his author is palpable and infectious. And the letters do not disappoint. The spirit and wit of the satirist carries over into them—but also the gentleness and patience that seem, paradoxically, to have been among the personal qualities that endeared him to his friends.

The edition prepared by Voss (and his helpers: see II, 24–27) is more than the sum of its parts. As he points out in his Introduction, the documentary value of each letter often only becomes clear when it is seen in sequence and compared with other sources. Voss's commentary in the second volume expertly helps the reader make the connections, explaining the context for each letter, filling in biographical and historical details, and putting the relevant cross-references in place. Rabener was well connected in the literary world of his time, but was also close to important figures at court in a time of crisis for Saxony. Thus both the literary and the political historian of the period will find much that is of interest here. A detailed index provides a useful tool for research.

Voss has considerably augmented the previously known documentary sources. In the correspondence alone, he has unearthed thirty-two previously unpublished letters, out of a total of 186. It is a melancholy thought that this itself represents only a fraction of the number Rabener is known to have written and received. The destruction of his papers began in his own lifetime, during the bombardment of Dresden by the Prussians in 1760, described in an impressive letter by Rabener of 12 August of that year, here (in one of the edition's major new finds) reproduced in its original form for the first time. The second, and more thorough, destruction of Dresden in February 1945, together with similar losses across Germany, has resulted in further depredations. Yet Voss's diligent research shows how much can still be retrieved. He found relevant documents in Dresden itself, but others as far afield as Tartu (Dorpat) and Stanford University. This ought to give hope and encouragement to other scholars who, like him, suspect 'daß weite Bereiche des vermeintlich "hinreichend" erforschten deutschen 18. Jahrhunderts erst noch zu entdecken sind' (II, 16). Voss's Introduction to the edition gives the reader a powerful sense of the excitement generated by piecing together the clues that made informed archival searching possible, and of the feeling of triumph when the trails led him to new discoveries. This is a winning plea in favour of positivist philology, seen not as a form of mere necessary drudgery, but as a pursuit engaging the whole person in the quest. One comes away resolved to devote a new energy to the 'Reanimation stummgewordener Hinweise in Referenzwerken wie Goedeke' (II, 13).

Voss believes that one major result of his labours will be an 'anders zu lesender Rabener' (I, 48): 'Dem Konzept der [. . .] auf Neugewinn unbekannter und auf Wiederaneignung vergessener Texte eingerichteten vorliegenden Edition lag von vornherein der Gedanke zugrunde, daß mit einer Öffnung und Erweiterung des Rabnerischen Text-Ensembles auch unbeirrbar quellenfern und geschichtsfern behauptete Festschreibungen unseres Autors in Bewegung geraten müßten' (I, 50). He wants to challenge the critical consensus that for all its elegance and wit, Rabener's satire was rather tame, by comparison with the ancients or Swift, or even his own slightly older German contemporary, Christian Ludwig Liscow. He is no doubt right that the professions of goodwill towards religion and crowned heads in the preface to the first part of the *Satirische Schriften* should not automatically be taken at face value; and he is able to point to contrary, half-concealed political points in both the letters and the satires. Whether this will be quite enough to overturn Rabener's reputation for mildness is another question. In his letter to Bodmer of 28 April 1752 (I, 177–79), Rabener defends his preface and the immunity it grants against satirical attack both to religion and to individuals (as opposed to types). In that same year, he announced to Friedrich von Hagedorn that he would publish only one last volume of the *Satirische Schriften* in his lifetime, among other things because he feared the effects on his character of a darkening of his mood: 'Ich kann es nicht leiden, wenn ein Satiriker zu mürrisch, zu böse, und zu traurig ernsthaft wird' (22 May 1752; I, 184). Voss points out that he continued writing satires even after this volume appeared in 1755, with the intention that they would appear in a posthumous edition. Voss suspects that they would have revealed a blacker, angrier Rabener, and that he was merely exercising political prudence while he was still alive and employed as a civil servant. We will never know: the intended *Nachlaß* fell victim to the Prussian cannons in 1760. But even if we accepted Voss's conjecture, the need for political discretion would itself confirm the claim, made towards the end of the century by Friedrich Maximilian Klinger, that legal and cultural conditions in Germany were not favourable to anything like the cutting energy of Swiftian satire (Klinger, *Betrachtungen und Gedanken* (Berlin: Verlag der Nation, 1958), pp. 469 and 483). And when we reflect that Dean Swift evidently found no conflict between holding ecclesiastical office and wielding the satirist's pen, whereas Rabener notes as a matter of course that his fellow 'Bremer Beiträger' Johann Andreas Cramer and Johann Adolf Schlegel had to cease writing 'scherzhaft[e] Verse' and 'munter[e] Satiren' once they were ordained (to Friedrich von Hagedorn, 22 May 1752; I, 185), we are again reminded of the inhibitions and prohibitions that curtailed the satirical impulse in eighteenth-century Germany.

This brief discussion shows that the editor is right to hope that these volumes will prompt the reader's 'eigene Suchbewegung' (I, 78). Different questions will lead down different paths through the documents. There are more riches to be found here than can be exhausted at a single sitting. With this meticulous, exemplary collection Voss has done eighteenth-century German literary scholarship a major service.

St Peter's College, Oxford   K. F. Hilliard

Schriften des Herzens: Briefkultur des 18. Jahrhunderts im Briefwechsel zwischen Anna Louisa Karsch und Johann Wilhelm Ludwig Gleim. By Jon Helgason. Trans. from the Swedish by Jana Mohnike. Göttingen: Wallstein. 2012. 325 pp. €29.20. ISBN 978-3-8353-1020-9.

Jon Helgason's monograph joins a number of scholarly studies of the epistolary genre in the eighteenth century, many, like this one, showing a particular interest in questions of gender (e.g. Becker-Cantarino, Nikisch, Nörtemann, Vellusig); and it further builds on work done in the last twenty-five years on Gleim and Karsch (e.g. Pott, Nörtemann, Schaffers). His particular focus is on the letters the two poets exchanged in the first three years of their acquaintance. He draws on the edition of the correspondence by Ute Pott and Regina Nörtemann (*'Mein Bruder in Apoll': Briefwechsel zwischen Anna Louisa Karsch und Johann Wilhelm Ludwig Gleim* (Göttingen: Wallstein, 1996)), which contains approximately a third of the entire corpus; he does not refer to any unpublished letters. The textual basis of his study is thus rather narrower than it might seem from the title.

Helgason chooses not to follow the correspondence as it unfolded. He rarely discusses an individual letter as a whole; nor does he engage in much sustained close reading. Rather, he selects individual passages to illustrate points he has already formulated discursively. Though the effect can often be telling, the perhaps unintended consequence is to make the letters seem secondary to the larger case he is arguing. This impression is augmented by the frequent recourse he has to themes from literary history, gender studies, and discourse analysis to guide his remarks.

These themes are brought to bear on a larger question that is Helgason's primary interest: the 'Bedeutung des Briefgenres für den Modernisierungsprozess und besonders für das, was man als moderne Individualisierung bezeichnet' (p. 19). He believes that just as the whole of the eighteenth century was labouring to give birth to the 'modern individual' (p. 37), eighteenth-century literature (at least in its 'bürgerlich' manifestations) was trying to resolve 'das Problem des persönlichen individuellen Ausdrucks' (p. 163)—the problem, that is, of 'authenticity', of the correspondence of inner thought and feeling with public expression. His thesis is that while Gleim tried and failed to resolve this problem, his correspondent Karsch used the materials he provided to make the breakthrough to a 'bürgerlich gefärbte Ausdrucksästhetik' (p. 92), one which anticipated the 'Literaturauffassung der Romantik' (p. 164).

This is an all too familiar narrative, in which a totalizing reading of eighteenth-century literature forces every genre, every work, every author into a single development towards an elusive ideal. Once upon a time it was thought that the development towards authentic individuality culminated in the *Sturm und Drang* Goethe, in opposition to the artificial rococo culture of his youth. There is a certain pleasing novelty in the way Helgason now makes that same culture the incubator of pre-Romanticism. But in truth this only shows how arbitrary the whole narrative is.

Much that Helgason has to say about Gleim's literary politics or about role-play in his correspondences is valuable and interesting. But the framework for the discussion is fatally flawed. Confidence in his real knowledge of the period is not increased by his apparent belief that Daphnis is the name of a shepherdess (p. 111) and that eighteenth-century Ansbach was part of Bavaria (p. 126), or by such claims as 'Im 17. Jahrhundert schrieb man Liebesmanuale, während der Roman im 18. Jahrhundert eine entsprechende Funktion erhält' (p. 236). The style—whether of the original or of the translation—is frequently odd. The profit the reader will gain from Helgason's study is not in proportion to the labour that evidently went into it.

ST PETER'S COLLEGE, OXFORD   K. F. HILLIARD

Der andere Goethe: Die literarischen Fragmente im Kontext des Gesamtwerks. By KARINA BECKER. Frankfurt a.M.: Peter Lang. 2012. 460 pp. €69.90. ISBN 978-3-631-63178-2 (ebk 978-3-653-01743-4).

In his *Aesthetics* of 1750, Alexander Gottlieb Baumgarten equates beauty with completeness, while the near-contemporary Johann Joachim Winckelmann describes the Apollo Belvedere as the most perfect of all sculptures, enabling Karina Becker to position Goethe at the intersection of contradictory perspectives. By way of introduction, a bewildering array of different types of fragment must first be revisited: these range from short notes and sketches to larger works produced with the intention of mimicking the dilapidated relics of antiquity. Becker investigates each type (*étude*, 'Torso', 'verhüllter Torso', *croquis*, and others) with the aid of handsome reproductions of Cézanne's paintings and sketches.

It is a curious fact that scholarship has taken a more positive view of Schiller's fragments than of Goethe's, and while few would now agree with the assessment of these as 'Tiefstand von Goethes dichterischem Schaffen' (thus Lieselotte Blumenthal in *Weimarer Beiträge*, 7 (1961), 1), our knowledge of texts such as *Das Mädchen von Oberkirch* and *Breme von Bremenfeld* will remain severely limited while these are excluded from most standard editions.

Becker begins with the Promethean types of the *Sturm und Drang* phase. 'Große Kerle' give way to 'göttliche Widersacher' (Ahasver, Faust), and these are replaced by lampoons and political satire. The fragmentary quality of all drama is nowhere more clearly evident than in the *Faust-Dichtungen* that kept the poet busy for much of his life. Each successive version, each scene, and each speech can be presented as a fragment designed to conceal more than it reveals. And while Becker sees this not only as appropriate but also as inevitable, hers is a socio-political reading that is often specific and controversial: the Meerkats in the Witch's Kitchen are Christian rulers who wantonly ignore their God-given mission (p. 94); Gretchen readily succumbs to Faust because her brother has been conscripted into the army and is therefore not available to provide necessary moral guidance (p. 125).

Unfinished texts possess an insidious lure, as early Kafka exegetes were quick to appreciate. Becker cannot avoid straying onto unsafe ground by speculating about how a fragment would have continued. According to her, the closing words of the *Faust*-Fragment should read 'Warum hast du mich verlassen?' (p. 103). The problem becomes ever more evident as we approach the French Revolution, a frustrating subject for a poet who abhorred the lower orders ('Pöbel') while being unable to support the corrupt aristocracy of the *ancien régime*. It may be for this reason that Goethe's many attempts to grapple with the political realities of the day remain incomplete and relatively unknown: *Die Reise der Söhne Megaprazons*, *Die ungleichen Hausgenossen*, *Die Mystificirten*, *Der Zauberflöte zweyter Theil*, *Der Groß-Cophta*, as well as the Grecian tragedies *Nausikaa*, *Iphigenie von Delphi*, and *Ulysses auf Phäa* all date from this period. Here Becker reaches remarkable insights, with Achilles featuring as the democrat ('Citoyen' is the preferred label), and Odysseus and Alcinous as 'failed citoyens'—the former too deceitful, the latter too illiberal. Given Goethe's displeasure at even relatively mild revolutionary activity, such as the overthrow of King Charles X of France, it is challenging to read his middle-period fragments as advocating social change (p. 224).

The otherness of Becker's Goethe lies in areas which are still under-investigated: his determination to resist Prussia's encroachment on Saxony, his efforts to prevent the forced recruitment of young men into the army, and his frequent but usually futile attempts to curb Jupiter's (Carl August's) profligate spending. *Iphigenie auf Tauris* may anticipate a harmonious *Fürstenbund*, and yet remain a fragment: 'Weil [. . .] von Gerechtigkeit und Gleichheit kaum etwas zu spüren ist, bleibt der letzte Vers unvollständig' (p. 146).

Overall, this is a well-conceived study that manages to illuminate key themes of little-known works and almost succeeds in persuading us that the 'other' Goethe is more deserving of attention than the one we already know. It might have been even more convincing had the author been able to resist the temptation to speculate, over-confidently in places, on how the fragmentary works were to have continued.

UNIVERSITY OF KENT   OSMAN DURRANI

Who Is This Schiller Now? Essays on his Reception and Significance. Ed. by JEFFREY L. HIGH, NICHOLAS MARTIN, and NORBERT OELLERS. (Studies in German Literature, Linguistics, and Culture) Rochester, NY: Camden House. 2011. xviii+494 pp. £60. ISBN 978-1-57113-488-2.

There can be no doubting Schiller's topicality. His plays *Die Räuber*, *Wallenstein*, *Maria Stuart*, and *Die Jungfrau von Orleans* raise the issues of terrorism, whistleblowing, incarceration of political opponents, and armed struggle on behalf of ethnic groups. This substantial volume, which derives its title from a question posed by Samuel Taylor Coleridge in 1794, recognizes a need for new descriptors of both man and dramatist. The time has come to put aside the familiar exampaper questions and, taking our cue from Coleridge, ask what 'this Convulser of the Heart' can offer the present world with its present dilemmas. Answers are duly supplied in twenty-seven essays, in English and German. These are thematically grouped into five sections on drama and poetry, aesthetics and philosophy, history and politics, reception, and, finally, 'Schiller Now'.

Co-editor Jeffrey L. High sets the scene in an Introduction that locates the poet/dramatist within contexts that range from the Declaration of Independence to George Lucas's *Star Wars*. The central section on aesthetics may occasionally stray from the overall objectives of the volume; here, successive papers draw attention to the origins of and influences on Schiller's thought, to Baumgarten, Meier, and Kant, where one might have expected more in the way of parallels with today's aesthetics. David Pugh's reference to the much-quoted line 'Der Mensch ist nur da ganz Mensch, wo er spielt' cries out for linkage to current definitions of 'ludic man'.

Yet it is also in the dramas that opportunities are missed. Norbert Oellers provides an interesting reading of Wallenstein's downfall, which he attributes to vacillation between Max's exuberant idealism and Buttler's hard-nosed realism within the general's evidently split mentality; yet there is no reference to modern research into Wallenstein's motivation nor does the author refer to the medical phenomenon of bipolarism, which is obliquely postulated in this essay. The sensitively argued piece by Ritchie Robertson places *Maria Stuart* within a wide context of literary responses to the Scottish Queen, but takes the story no further than Swinburne's tragedy of 1881. Modern historians operating in the wake of Antonia Fraser are ignored, as is Ulrich Heising's ground-breaking production (Düsseldorf, 1980), which compellingly sketched out a context of contemporary issues, principally feminism. Papers by T. J. Reed and John A. McCarthy rightly seek to rehabilitate aspects of Schiller's work as a historian and as a scientist.

In line with the editors' central concern, repeated attempts are made to look at recent productions and draw parallels with present-day icons. Jeffrey L. Sammons brings us into the modern world by recalling Schiller's place in Bruno Francke's twenty-volume edition of *German Classics* for the US market, whose launch unfortunately coincided with the sinking of the liner *Lusitania*, whereupon *sauerkraut* became 'freedom cabbage', Schiller Park (in Columbus, Ohio) became Washington Park, and the project's editor resigned his Harvard professorship. Sammons comments drily, 'it would not be accurate to regard his resignation as entirely voluntary' (p. 342), a reminder that in the twentieth century, culture and politics will emerge as close bedfellows. Jörg Robert's piece on Max Kommerell's *Der Dicher als Führer in der deutschen Klassik* (1932) reveals more about Kommerell than Schiller; here the young poet's adulation of Goethe allegedly replicates the young academic's adulation of Stefan George. Henrik Sponsel puts in a robust if predictable defence of Schiller against those who condemn him, and with him much of the German Enlightenment, for facilitating latter-day Fascism.

The editors' brief is fully observed when Dennis Mahoney picks up Robertson's narrative about *Maria Stuart*, albeit a good deal further down the line, by taking a close look at the Broadway staging of 2009 and at scenes parodied by Goetz, Brecht, and Hildesheimer. This is one of a few pieces that firmly locate Schiller in the post-9/11 world of fanaticism and the 'enhanced interrogation' (p. 414) of suspected enemies of the state. A different but no less relevant note is struck by Gail K. Hart's analysis of modern strategies designed to open up new perspectives on the poet's 'wound', to which some traditionalists have responded with horror. But, Hart argues, if chemists can teach the Periodic Table through the medium of rap, why should we not search for common ground between Schiller and our pupils (p. 431)? Paul Kerry reflects on Schiller's thoughts on freedom, identity, and republicanism within an increasingly transnational Europe, something that was initially suggested by F. J. Lamport in 'Schiller and the "European Community"' (*MLR*, 93 (1998), 428–40). Finally, it is left to Walter Hinderer to establish a connection with the book's cover by revealing comically gruesome details of the ultimately futile quest for the deceased poet's skull. This essay was evidently translated from a German original; surely the phrase '12 May 1945, three days after Schiller's 140th Birthday' (p. 453) must result from confusion of *Todestag* and *Geburtstag*?

Although it does not quite live up to the promise of its title, this collection of conference papers demands attention not least for the great variety of approaches chosen by its well-qualified contributors, all of whom share the common aim of liberating Schiller from his traditional role as the junior member of the Weimar partnership. While some of its chapters could sit comfortably under the heading 'Who was this Schiller then?', the bulk of the constituent material gives us a Schiller still vibrantly alive—now, and in the foreseeable future.

UNIVERSITY OF KENT　　　　　　　　　　　　　　　　　　　　　OSMAN DURRANI

German Women's Writing of the Eighteenth and Nineteenth Centuries: Future Directions in Feminist Criticism. Ed. by HELEN FRONIUS and ANNA RICHARDS. London: Legenda. xii+192 pp. £45. ISBN 978-1-906540-86-9.

The front matter of this handsome book gives a good impression of the problems it faces and discusses. The cover features two women, inhibited by clothing, nature, and each other, looking in opposite directions. Page v introduces the gatekeepers of publication: fourteen out of the nineteen members of the Legenda editorial board, including the chairman, are men. Conversely, the 'Notes on the Contributors' (pp. x–xii) detail twelve women and one (co-authoring) man. The 'Contents' (pp. vii–viii) then show that the book is divided almost exactly between theory and practice (in that order).

Thus, of the diverse scholars who originally gathered in Oxford in 2008 to discuss the future of 'their' discipline, Anne Fleig, Anke Gilleir, Helen Fronius, Hilary Brown, and Susanne Kinnebrock with Timon B. Schaffer suggest 'New Approaches'; while Charlotte Woodford, Linda Kraus Worley, Jennifer Askey, Stephanie Hilger,

Annette Bühler-Dietrich, and Katharina von Hammerstein offer 'Case Studies'. In her Introduction Anna Richards lays the groundwork, detailing the possible threats to traditional feminist literary criticism from theory, pluralism, and deconstructive gender studies, and arguing that, while German Studies have been less affected by these developments than other disciplines, that field too has evolved along broadly similar lines in the same period. And in reviewing the contents of the book, she is quite specific about where the future of feminist criticism lies: in a non-essentialist return to the author and the text; in continued archaeology and historical contextualization; in a comparative approach; and in a broadening of the field to include not only 'proto-feminist' texts, but also apparently 'conservative' ones. The concern, she says, 'is to bring to light neglected women's writing, offer a nuanced, sensitive understanding of its particular characteristics, and broaden our historical understanding of women's experience' (p. 11).

To an extent, the case studies fulfil these objectives. But so did Gisela Brinker-Gabler in 1978 (*Deutschsprachige Dichterinnen vom 16. Jahrhundert bis zur Gegenwart* (Frankfurt a.M.: Fischer)) and indeed Heinrich Gross in 1882 (*Deutschlands Dichterinen und Schriftstellerinen*, 2nd edn (Vienna: Gerold)). And although statistics quoted refer to thousands of unknown women authors, almost all those presented here have been researched elsewhere. Ebner-Eschenbach and Gabriele Reuter are famous, Marlitt and Frieda von Bülow well known. The sentimental novel and 'Mädchenliteratur' are familiar genres. Laura Marholm and Rosa Mayreder are the subjects of relatively recent biographies. And amazingly, Henriette Frölich's *Virginia* was republished in East Germany in 1963. Moreover, in this book comparison is actually rare, and the category 'conservative' is seldom questioned. Myths scotched in one essay resurface in another. And the readings are not always sophisticated in literary terms.

Thus the book's structure, like its title, ultimately collapses: the future has not yet happened. Yet it is glimpsed here—and it will indeed necessarily entail killing off and reviving the female author and the female reader, undoing and redoing gender, sexuality, and herstory, embracing pluralism and firing the canon. And it will only have been achieved once the gatekeepers become contributors and all critics—including men—are doing feminist criticism.

QUEEN MARY UNIVERSITY OF LONDON   ROBERT GILLETT

Metamimesis: Imitation in Goethe's 'Wilhelm Meisters Lehrjahre' and Early German Romanticism. By MATTIAS PIRHOLT. (Studies in German Literature, Linguistics, and Culture) Rochester, NY: Camden House. 2012. 220 pp. £55. ISBN-13: 978-1-57113-534-6.

There is much to admire in Mattias Pirholt's study. It is tenaciously argued, well documented, and he is thoroughly conversant with much of the High Theoretical exegesis of Romanticism in general and of the Romantic novel in particular that has been in evidence over the past three decades. As a literary genre the novel had, in the eighteenth century, a somewhat uphill struggle to gain respectability. It was regarded as disreputably episodic, untidy, all plot and no purpose. Yet—and this emerges very clearly from Pirholt's study—by the early nineteenth century it had acquired enormous sophistication, not just in terms of theme (the complexity of individual selfhood) but also mode (a thoroughgoing ability to reflect on its own performance as imitation of human experience).

Pirholt begins with *Wilhelm Meisters Lehrjahre*, and then goes on to consider *Lucinde*, *Heinrich von Ofterdingen*, and *Godwi*. For him, the Romantic novel is supremely the kind of narrative whose energy is to be found less in its referentiality than in its high self-consciousness. At one point he writes: '[T]he romantic work reproduces mimesis metapoetically as a representation of representation. It reflects the representational conditions of the work itself, rendering it what I would like to call a *metamimetic* space' (p. 4). He is splendidly acute in tracing the ramifications of this process through the Romantic novels at the centre of his enquiry. And on occasion he brings us close to the feel of a particular novel—as when he comments on the interplay of remembering and forgetting, of 'repetition and remembrance' (p. 132) in Novalis. But I could not help wondering if the level of abstraction at which he argues does not produce a certain sameness. Take the following remark (on *Lucinde*): 'the novel mimetically represents the difference of mimetic representation as well as the act of transgressing this differentiating void, an act that the difference enables' (p. 81). Or again, on *Heinrich von Ofterdingen*: 'Fiction as the production of truth through appearance constitutes a mimetic formation that is a self-contained simulation of life and at the same time a representation of reality' (p. 141). For him *Godwi* is a novel that embodies an acute awareness of sociocultural change—indeed it goes so far as to formulate a 'fundamental negation of the ideological premises of romanticism' (p. 157). Pirholt's study is a demanding one, and he brings us close to some important instances of the novel form as a largely discursive, essayistic, philosophical enterprise.

At one point he writes: 'Novalis is able to produce what Goethe failed to do in *Wilhelm Meisters Lehrjahre*: the complete synthetic sign or a self-contained simulation of life, which, through the infinite process of mimetic repetition, is capable of annihilating difference' (p. 142). To which some readers (myself included) might respond with pleasure at Goethe's failure. Not least because, in the midst of Pirholt's sternly metamimetic enquiry, it is a great relief to encounter some common-or-garden mimesis. By this I mean some recognizable characters—particularly a protagonist who both learns and forgets, who advances and backslides—a recognizable society, with certain institutions (particularly the theatre), and a narrative that sometimes attends to practicalities (the charm and limitation of a puppet theatre, the sheer effort of putting on a play, the links between art and its artefacts and commodification). Goethe's novel, like its Romantic followers is, of course, profoundly self-aware; but perhaps it has the signal virtue of establishing the mimetic contract first before the meta-meta-energies are unleashed.

More often than not all novels need to touch base with their substantial (rather than glitteringly discursive) condition—although even that substantial condition is, of course, an experiment, a conjecture, a fiction. We cannot prove Emma Bovary's existence; all we can do is read the novel in which she figures. But once we do read and enter into the mimetic contract, what was mere assumption and conjecture, an 'as if', becomes utterly absorbing and truthful. Of course the meta-awareness is still there; we know that we are making believe, that we are colluding in a fiction. But we do so in the name of the truthfulness that literature has to offer: not Revealed Truth, not empirically provable Truth, but a truthfulness in respect of our actual or imagined experience. It is a response which we need now more than ever as we find ourselves surrounded by all kinds of fundamentalisms (religious, scientific, secular).

UNIVERSITY COLLEGE LONDON   MARTIN SWALES

'Im Freien?' Kleist-Versuche. By ROLAND REUSS. Frankfurt a.M. and Basel: Stroemfeld. 2010. 400 pp. €48. ISBN 978-3-86600-072-8.

The volume collects eighteen essays written over a period of twenty-five years and originally published in the *Kleist-Blätter*, the companion series to the critical edition of Kleist's works by Reuß, Peter Staengle, and Ingeborg Harms. Some of them take decisions made in that edition as their starting-point, but none of them is narrowly conceived as a contribution to editorial scholarship only. They constitute, rather, a bold and significant contribution to Kleist studies in the broadest sense of the word. The advantages Reuß brings to this undertaking are an intimate knowledge of the works, acute intellectual sophistication, and a clear and bold set of interpretative principles.

These principles have been characterized as deconstructive (by Manfred Koch in a review for the *Neue Zürcher Zeitung*); and indeed Reuß makes occasional use of Lacan and Derrida. But it would be misleading to leave it at that. Reuß's Introduction pokes fun at the 'Verlockungen der jeweils durchs Dorf gejagten Alphadiskurse' of 'theory' (in the emphatic sense of the word), and recommends, as an 'ideales Korrektiv', a 'Sich-Einlassen auch auf die kleinsten scheinbaren Nebensächlichkeiten', of the kind an editor has to deal with, as a guide to the 'Eigensinn' of the works (p. 8).

What Reuß recommends, he practises. No variant spelling, no punctuation mark is too small to escape his notice, and often it is these features that stand at the centre of his interpretations. He has no interest in integrative, structural accounts of the works (e.g. Aristotelian readings of the plays); his method does not place us in the middle distance, as it were, where we might be able to take in the action and the characters at a glance, but right up close to the fine grain of the text. Since Reuß believes that Kleist's works are deliberately composed of fragments (for him, they are all 'broken jugs'), and that they function, in the first instance, by destroying synthesizing narratives and structures of meaning, he is not troubled by the consequences of his method; indeed he would no doubt argue that it is the ideal correlative of Kleist's own idiosyncratic creativity.

Since the readings Reuß produces are so dependent on his method, and since he practises that method so consistently, it is worth spelling out some of its features. In general, one can say that he adopts a principle of maximal (multiple and best) meaning in textual details against the background of scepticism about the normalizing tendency of discursive language, plot, and character psychology (all of which characteristically fail in Kleist's work, as Reuß repeatedly notes). 'Intentione recta gebraucht, ist [Rede] nicht geeignet, etwas zu offenbaren, was nicht schon zuvor bekannt gewesen wäre' (p. 150). Since Kleist does want to reveal something, his words must therefore be read obliquely. A number of hermeneutic principles come into play to make this possible. One is a variant of the old editorial principle of the *lectio difficilior*, here understood as the reading that adds maximal information to the text, as opposed to banal explanations (e.g. of a particular spelling as a typesetting error) which subtract from it. Another is keeping open indefinitely all meanings of a word or utterance; undecidability, the suspension of meaning between two or more possibilities, creates meaning beyond the limits of binary logic. Etymological, rare, or even punning meanings of words are often more valuable than the overt and obvious ones. (An example: 'Kleists Texte legen es nahe, mit dem Wort 'Platz' immer auch die Gedanken des "Auseinander-" und des "Aufplatzens in Stücke" zu verbinden' (p. 55, n. 4).) Bold interpretation is generally to be encouraged; a number of times a kind of self-exhorting meta-commentary urges the interpreter not to be deterred by timid common-sense objections, but to go on the attack (see e.g. pp. 83–84). In that spirit, allegoresis is given free rein, as for instance when the scene in 'Das Erdbeben in Chili' in which the collapsing walls of the prison temporarily prop each other up and allow Jeronimo to escape is read as an image ('Bild') of the liberty briefly afforded to the subject by the destruction of conventional structures of meaning—the *locus classicus* for the catastrophe that has to precede any attempted jailbreak from the prison-house of language (p. 150).

Perhaps the boldest of Reuß's hermeneutic suggestions is that lines of verse should systematically be read as semantic (not merely rhythmical) units in their own right, independently of the sentences of which they form a part. The passage where he most clearly articulates this principle deserves extensive quotation: 'Die Versgrenze ist *an sich* überhaupt kein rhythmisches Phänomen, sondern der Ort, wo Rede in Nichtrede und diese zurück in Rede übergeht: Anzeige eines Innehaltens oder Unterbrochenwerdens meinender Rede. Durch den entstehenden Rückstau *innerhalb* des Verses bildet sie, gerade dort, wo sie in Konflikt zu den "normalen" syntaktischen Einschnitten steht, syntaktisch-semantische Einheiten *sui generis*, die *auch* für sich gelesen und interpretiert werden müssen' (p. 384, n. 38). The application of this principle can be studied in Reuß's discussion of *Amphitryon* (pp. 61–65) or in the closing essay on Goethe's 'Ein gleiches' (pp. 384–96).

One might imagine that a microscopic focus could only produce microscopic results. This would be a mistake. The point of Reuß's interpretative method is to see *multum in parvo*. There is a palpable longing in his essays for Kleist's work not to mean this or that thing only, but to yield some piercing insight into the largest truths. The fragmentation of ordinary meaning in Kleist's texts creates absences and gaps in which epiphanic revelations can briefly appear. 'Intentione recta gebraucht, ist [Rede] nicht geeignet, etwas zu *offenbaren*' (my emphasis): and 'Offenbarung' is what Reuß is after. The exegetical origin of some of Reuß's hermeneutic methods is matched by his quasi-theological desire for plenitude of meaning. Punctuation marks are graphic stigmata (pp. 84 and 150), the imprint of a higher order of meaning on the body of the text. Kleist's texts are a membrane ('Diaphragma' (p. 153)) through which we can sense the pulsing of his very being, a linguistic penumbra around the apophatic site of 'unverzerrte Kommunikation' from an uncorrupted source (p. 78). Something transcending the fallen world of instrumental reason and regimented language and thought can thus show through the lines of the texts. For Reuß, Kleist's work is evidence of 'das Wissen, daß über die Bedeutung der Texte etwas entscheidet, was zwar mit diskreten Buchstaben, Semantik, den Ordnungen der Syntax und des Diskurses etwas zu tun hat, von diesen Systemen letztlich aber auch völlig unabhängig ist' (p. 52). Reading for that 'etwas' is an act of faith (p. 79), undertaken in the 'Hoffnung einer Begegnung' for which criticism can only prepare the way: 'Ob und wie [die Hoffnung] eingelöst werden kann, ist nicht mehr Thema der Literaturwissenschaft oder der Ästhetik' (p. 154).

Reuß's book rests on considerable learning, but it is itself not an ordinary piece of scholarship. It is an exhilarating but also a troubling work. Reuß has only contempt for the methods of conventional criticism and the readings they generate. Common sense and the practices of conventional literary interpretation will always have a hard time against interpretative licence and the multiplication of hermeneutic methods, especially when the former is so ingeniously exploited and the latter is so intelligently applied as they are here. For boldness is always more attractive than caution, and pluralism more appealing than consensus. But perhaps the test should be a pragmatic one. Here the advantage of plurality may lie on the other side. For one merit of more conventional readings is that at least the works are able to say different things; whereas in the end, for all the inventive variety of ways in which they go about it, Kleist's texts, as Reuß sees them, all spell out the same things: the inadequacy of language and communication, the impossibility of self-possessing subjectivity, the failure of instrumental thinking, and the (generally frustrated) desire to throw off the normalizing constraints of language and culture and escape 'ins Freie'.

Nevertheless, literary criticism would be much poorer without the kind of radical challenge that Reuß's essays present. Kleist's provocative originality has never been in doubt, but it shines forth with renewed brilliance from this remarkable volume.

St Peter's College, Oxford   K. F. Hilliard

Johann Peter Hebel und die Moderne. Ed. by Achim Aurnhammer and Hanna Klessinger. Freiburg i.Br.: Rombach. 2011. 233 pp. €42. ISBN 978-3-7930-9672-6.

The title puts the cart before the horse. The personnel consists of the usual suspects Kafka and Canetti, Bloch and Benjamin, Sebald and Stadler. Less familiar figures such as Klaus Nonnenmann get disproportionately short shrift. The absence of Heidegger appears accidental but feels programmatic; the presence of Brecht seems deliberate but looks gratuitous. The themes are familiar: calendar, history, theology, Judaism, Enlightenment. The range of Hebel texts discussed is reprehensibly narrow and the concentration on 'Unverhofftes Wiedersehen' seems both excessive and unjustified. For whole stretches, Hebel disappears completely. And the authors have learnt from him neither stylistic elegance nor the art of the ending. Yet this volume of proceedings from a conference marking Johann Peter Hebel's 250th birthday is a genuinely important and exciting contribution to scholarship. Why?

The book is thorough and conscientious. After Günter Saße's article on 'Der konservierte Bergmann' and Fabian Lampart's on Franz Fühmann's *Im Berg* we need never again send Hebel down the mines. In his article on 'Canetti, Kafka und Klaus Nonnenmann' Wilhelm Kühlmann not only analyses, but reproduces Kafka's famous dedication to Ludwig Hardt. And with its generous footnotes, Monika Schmitz-Emans's article on 'Zeitmodelle' just about exhausts W. G. Sebald's Hebel essay. The book is methodologically careful. Writing on 'Kunert, Strauß und Theobaldy', Thorsten Fitzon adumbrates a threefold model for the reception of 'Kalendergeschichten'. Co-editor Achim Aurnhammer subjects Heimito von Doderer's *Sieben Variationen über ein Thema von Johann Peter Hebel* to productively minute, though not always unexceptionable, analysis. And Günter Oesterle, in contrasting 'Benjamins und Blochs Deutung des Erzählers Hebel', impressively exemplifies the dialectic of modernity on which the whole volume turns. Not least in Alexander Honold's article on Alexander Kluge's *Chronik der Gefühle*, Hansgeorg Schmidt-Bergmann's on Arnold Stadler, and Kathrin Klohs's on 'Zeitgenössische Kalendergeschichten im Dialog mit Hebel', the book repeatedly offers overwhelming glimpses into what Hebel is actually up to and why that still matters. And we are also made aware—nowhere more obviously than in co-editor Hanna Klessinger's account of Botho Strauß's *Unerwartete Rückkehr*—of the sins Hebel does not commit as a writer. Moreover, the book frankly lays bare its own contradictions, notably in the context of a round-table discussion between the two editors, Ulrike Draesner, Andreas Maier, and Karl-Heinz Ott. When Ott comments 'man kann ihn auch nicht wirklich mit Stadler [oder] Bichsel in Verbindung bringen' (p. 215), he both negates Schmidt-Bergmann's position and questions Schmitz-Emans's attempts to include Bichsel in her 'Zeitmodelle'.

Ott's remark 'im Grunde ist er der Nicht-Moderne' (p. 219) also sheds new light on the 'und' of the book's title. In this view, it is not so much what links Hebel and modernity that matters as what sets him apart from the other authors discussed. When it comes to brevity, wisdom, limpidity, and complexity, only Kafka and Benjamin are in the same league. In his generic range, Hebel outdoes even them. In that sense, Hebel really does come first. And the title is not the wrong way round after all.

QUEEN MARY UNIVERSITY OF LONDONROBERT GILLETT

Literatur im Jahrhundert des Auges: Realismus und Fotografie im bürgerlichen Zeitalter. By SABINE BECKER. Munich: edition text+kritik. 2010. 388 pp. €39. ISBN 978-3-86916-049-8.

Sabine Becker's richly rewarding and engaging study *Literatur im Jahrhundert des Auges* is an attempt to rewrite the history of German bourgeois Realism. Taking polite issue with two classic studies of literature and photography by Gerhard Plumpe (*Der tote Blick: Der Diskurs der Photogaphie in der Zeit des Realismus* (Munich: Fink, 1991)) and Erwin Koppen (*Literatur und Photogaphie: Über Geschichte und Thematik einer Medienentdeckung* (Stuttgart: Metzler, 1987)), Becker argues that the invention and rapid dissemination of photography as a technology of representation were central to and to a large extent constitutive of nineteenth-century German Realism. While this point has been made with respect to, for example, French and British Realism, the relationship between photography and Realism in Germany has remained relatively underexplored. Becker not only makes good this lack, but develops a series of powerful literary-historical theses about the genesis and particularity of German Realism.

Becker starts by questioning the view that German Realists fundamentally rejected photography. The corpus of Realist texts, she argues, seldom thematizes photography, and this goes hand in hand with a denigration of the new medium in aesthetic debates about Realism. Structured around the binaries of man/machine, soul/apparatus, interiority/exteriority, and, ultimately, life/death, such debates pitted the mechanical reproduction of material reality via an optical and chemical process against the artistic transfiguration of experience through subjective creativity. And yet Realist authors were far more accepting of the medium in their private lives, writing about photography in letters and, in some cases, becoming competent amateur practitioners themselves. This apparent paradox leads Becker to rethink the history of bourgeois Realism from the point of view of media history.

Realist literature, Becker argues, developed in competition with but also in parallel to photography. While it sought to distance itself from photography in order to assert the capacity of literature to address those aspects of subjective experience that fell outside the domain of the photographic, it evinces specific structural similarities with photography which attest to the common anthropological and ideological underpinnings of Realist literature and photography. Both were a product of profound changes in human perception, and in particular in the culture of seeing, that emerged around 1800, and they were intimately related to a desire for precise registration of external reality that Becker sees as characteristic of bourgeois positivism. And despite the differences conditioned by their specific modes of production and consumption, both were ultimately cultural responses to the same set of social concerns: the bourgeois need for self-representation and self-assertion; the need to negotiate an identity position poised between the collective and the individual; the need to address both everyday external reality and subjective interiority; and the desire to preserve the past. Photography and literary Realism also, as Becker shows, share certain formal similarities, such as a concentration on the detail and the moment, the tendency to arrest time, and the valorization of the individual perspective. Becker is careful to note the limitations of the analogy, to make space for the specificity of photography and literature, while also highlighting that the influence of the former on the latter goes much further than had hitherto been realized in the German context.

Literatur im Jahrhundert des Auges is lucidly written, learned, and consistently interesting (even if it does become occasionally repetitive over the course of its 387 pages). If there is an omission here, it is that Becker sidelines the repressive functions of nineteenth-century photography: its involvement in institutions of surveillance and ideologies of otherness. Nancy Armstrong's *Fiction in the Age of Photography: The Legacy of British Realism* (Cambridge, MA: Harvard University Press, 1999) offers a sophisticated account of this other aspect of photography's influence on fiction, in the light of which Becker's book seems more optimistic than might have been expected. While some of the bolder historical claims with which she concludes might invite revision, though, this is a valuable addition to the growing scholarship on literature and the visual media. It does not revolutionize our understanding of photography or German Realism, but it does allow us to understand how profound the interference was between the two systems of representation. More importantly, it allows us to see this interference as part of far-reaching social changes that arose from the specific condition of the nineteenth-century German bourgeoisie. This is a significant achievement.

DURHAM UNIVERSITY   J. J. LONG

The German Bestseller in the Late Nineteenth Century. Ed. by CHARLOTTE WOODFORD and BENEDICT SCHOFIELD. Rochester, NY: Camden House. 2012. 286 pp. £55. ISBN 978–1–57113–487–5.

In a cultural-studies perspective, literary history cannot be confined to those authors and works which the older German tradition of criticism and scholarship based on late eighteenth- and nineteenth-century aesthetics singles out as belonging to 'Höhenkammliteratur' (the prominent literary canon), as opposed to a so-called 'Trivialliteratur' (trivial literature) that caters for the uneducated mass reader. In reality literary production has always been a complex multidimensional space that undercuts such dichotomous blending of cultural reach and aesthetic merit. Since the socio-historical and feminist reappraisal of popular writing in the 1970s, literary research has provided ample evidence of the problematic politics of canonization, of the need to consider non-canonical works when exploring cultural history, and the abundance of significant German nineteenth-century literature that straddles the perceived boundary between the popular and the ambitious. The edited volume in hand, which is based on a conference at the University of Cambridge in 2009, takes a fresh and highly productive look at German best-selling novels and novellas written between the 1840s and the early 1900s. It combines socio-historical enquiry into the history of literary writing, publishing, and reading with a particular focus on 'the fertile crossover between so-called high literature and works written for the mass market' (p. 2). The case studies include the obvious suspects—such as Gustav Freytag's *Soll und Haben* (1855), Felix Dahn's *Ein Kampf um Rom* (1876), and the woman writer E. Marlitt—along with authors who are less prominent today but well worth reconsideration, such as Berthold Auerbach, Wilhelm Jensen, Clara Viebig, or Bertha von Suttner. They also offer a very instructive rereading of canonical works from the perspective of their (not always instant) popular success, such as Stifter's and Storm's novellas or Thomas Mann's *Buddenbrooks* (1901). In other cases, such as the travel writer Balduin Möllhausen, Gabriele Reuter, or Margarete Böhme, the conditions of their popular success were too historically specific to survive the period.

The twelve chapters in this book, written by established Germanists as well as younger researchers, are well researched and thoughtful almost throughout. Many are highly successful in combining socio-historical enquiry with in-depth literary analysis. Charlotte Woodford's Introduction and Katrin Kohl's case study of Marlitt provide background information on the development of book production, the literary market, and reading skills, as well as on the emergence of lending libraries, popular journals (in which novels and novellas were serialized), and mass production in the nineteenth century. Most case studies use biographical and paratextual information to assess the authors' responses to the 'modern' literary market and the challenges of professional authorship. All chapters mark the intersections between the underlying history of literary poetics (from Romanticism and *Vormärz* through Realism to Naturalism, *Heimatkunst*, and Modernism), particular narrative genres (such as romance, melodrama, the family novel and the social novel), the shifting broader socio-political context, and period-specific themes and public concerns that the best-sellers were seen to address. The mid and late nineteenth century's fascination with 'realism' and 'authenticity' itself points to cultural resonance as a condition of literary success across a diverse readership. The volume also includes examples from the literary canon (such as Stifter, Raabe, Thomas Mann) whose enduring significance is based on a dual strategy of working with popular formats while also addressing a more demanding audience. Several case studies include comparison with English-language literature in order to discuss similarities and differences in the history of best-sellers in the two languages.

UNIVERSITY OF NOTTINGHAM   DIRK GÖTTSCHE

Private Lives and Collective Destinies: Class, Nation and the Folk in the Works of Gustav Freytag. By BENEDICT SCHOFIELD. (MHRA Texts and Dissertations, 81/Bithell Series of Dissertations, 37) London: MHRA. 2012. 219 pp. £19.99. ISBN 978-1-907322-22-8.

While Gustav Freytag's centrality to our understanding of German literature, culture, and mentality during the second half of the nineteenth century, and specifically of the literary movement of *Bürgerlicher Realismus*, has long been recognized, engagement with the author's work has largely concentrated on his *Grenzboten* programmatics, his best-seller *Soll und Haben*, and, to a much lesser extent, on the two late works *Bilder aus der deutschen Vergangenheit* and *Die Ahnen*. Benedict Schofield's study redresses this imbalance by including the author's entire output in his investigation of Freytag's literary campaign to forge a German national identity, namely, in addition to the aforementioned works, the early volume of poetry *In Breslau* (1845), the four dramas of the 1840s, the *Nachmärz* plays *Die Journalisten* (1852) and *Die Fabier* (1859), his biography of the politician Karl Mathy (1869), his *Technik des Dramas* (1862), the novel *Die verlorene Handschrift* (1864), and his work for the journal *Im neuen Reich* (after 1871). The result of the analysis is a surprising consistency of preoccupation throughout his career and a remarkable concentration on a handful of motifs (above all, marriage across class divisions). While the concrete function of the works might have changed between the three historical eras (*Vormärz*: aspirational; *Nachmärz*: programmatic; post-unification: consolidatory and affirmative), Freytag's general aim remained the same from the 1840s to the 1880s: to propagate a German national identity by demonstrating that allegedly eternal characteristics of the German *Volk* are consolidated in contemporary middle-class virtues and orientations so as to form the nation. The aristocracy becomes redundant if it fails to submerge itself into the bourgeoisie; the working class hardly ever comes into view at all.

A strength of the study is its clarity and thematic focus. Occasionally, though, this is achieved to the detriment of some nuance and differentiation: a word on the relationship between *Bildung* and *Besitz* as the central planks of bourgeois self-understanding, a distinction between ruling petty princes, landed gentry, and titular or service nobility in the discussion of interclass marriage (here, all three are subsumed under the label 'aristocracy'), and some recognition of the specifics of the nineteenth century's historical imagination might have helped to identify certain complexities in Freytag's arguments and their position in wider discourses. To illustrate the last point: it must be doubtful whether Freytag's depiction of the marriage of Marie of Burgundy to Maximilian of Habsburg in his early play *Die Brautfahrt; oder, Kunz von der Rosen* (1841) really contributed to the creation of 'a myth about the birth of the German nation' (p. 49), given that the historical incident exemplifies dynastic rather than national politics and an expansion beyond the geographical and cultural borders of the nation as envisioned by proponents of both a *großdeutsches* and a *kleindeutsches* settlement, and given the prevalent view that the Habsburg inheritance of the Low Countries triggered centuries of strife and bloodshed (the Thirty Years War being, among so many other things, a conflict about the status of the Netherlands) in which the middle-class progressive German sympathies, as shaped by Schiller's historiographies, firmly lay on the side of the Anti-Habsburgs. Also, rather too many typing errors remain, some of them significant (for example, when 'ausrotten' becomes 'retten' and Ludolf Wienbarg becomes 'Weinbarg'; both p. 71). Nonetheless, the book represents a valuable contribution to the field and enhances our understanding of Freytag's strategy and agenda in no small measure.

NATIONAL UNIVERSITY OF IRELAND MAYNOOTH   FLORIAN KROBB

Vienna is Different: Jewish Writers in Austria from the 'fin de siècle' to the Present. By HILLARY HOPE HERZOG. Oxford and New York: Berghahn. 2011. 289 pp. £22; $95. ISBN 978-0-85745-18.

Nexus: Essays in Jewish Studies, vol. 1. Ed. by WILLIAM COLLINS DONAHUE and MARTHA B. HELFER. Rochester, NY: Camden House. 2011. 246 pp. £50. ISBN 978-1-57113-501-8.

As different as these two volumes are at first sight, they demonstrate the continued fascination of American academics with Jewish literature and culture in the German-speaking world. Thanks mainly to the doyen of German-Jewish studies in the United States, Sander L Gilman, this interest is not confined to the historical era but extends to the most recent times, albeit with a greater emphasis on Jewish writers in Germany than on those in Austria. Hillary Hope Herzog's book sets out to close this gap: it not only demonstrates the continuity of Jewish literature since the late nineteenth century across the historical fissures of the twentieth century into the second millennium, it also focuses on Austria.

Herzog's presentation of the power of tradition in Austrian Jewish literature is reminiscent of what Claudio Magris, whom she does not mention, achieved in the 1960s for Austrian literature more generally. Indeed, among the writers featuring in her corpus are some of the most prominent representatives of what Magris had identified as the 'Habsburg myth' (Claudio Magris, *Der habsburgische Mythos in der österreichischen Literatur* (Salzburg: Müller, 1966)). While myth does play a role in *Vienna is Different*, it is more the myth of the place—as the quotation in Herzog's title suggests—than the conservative idyll that Magris had posited as the common denominator of Austrian literature from the age of Joseph II to the early twentieth century. Like Magris, Herzog identifies loss of the empire as the principal creator of the myth. This loss, which arguably had an even greater impact on Austrian Jews than on the rest of the population, was exacerbated by the Holocaust.

The strength of *Vienna is Different* lies in its combination of historical contextualization with individual case studies. In the earlier periods these include, alongside the obvious names, less-known authors such as Adolf Dessauer, whose novel *Großstadtjuden* (1910) advocates mixed marriage between Jews and non-Jews as a solution to the *Judenfrage*; and Felix Salten, whose 1909 collection of feuilletons *Das österreichische Antlitz* (Berlin: Fischer) shows the author of *Bambi* as a *flâneur* roaming the city of Vienna. It is curious, though, that some important names are missing in Herzog's coverage of the most recent period. Although she writes about Elfriede Jelinek, who does not herself stress the Jewishness of her father, Anna Mitgutsch, who identifies herself as a Jew and has produced some very interesting novels on Jewish themes, does not feature. Herzog confines herself to those writers who are now most readily associated with contemporary 'Jewish' Vienna: Robert Schindel, the Menasses, Doron Rabinovici, and Ruth Beckermann. Excluded are such exciting and increasingly recognized authors as the Russian Jewish immigrants Vladimir Vertlib and Julya Rabinowich, and the essayist Hazel Rosenstrauch. André Heller is referred to only as the editor of Theodor Herzl's feuilletons but not as the author of *Schlamassel* (1993), a series of Viennese vignettes which would have supported Herzog's thesis of the continued importance of Vienna in the work of Jewish writers in contemporary Austria.

The nature of the second volume under review here exempts it from issues of coverage. *Nexus* is a new biennial publication that is designed as the interface of the study of German and Jewish culture. As such it promises to offer a range of articles whose focus is on theoretical, literary, and literary-historical studies, or on more general cultural issues. Essays in this first volume engage with topics ranging from the impact of the Digital Humanities on German-Jewish studies and the proposal to conceptualize the relationship between Jews and non-Jews in terms of Jewish difference instead of anti-Semitism, to the re-examination of George Mosse's well-known thesis of the centrality of *Bildung* in the process of Jewish emancipation, and the reshaping of Holocaust symbols in the art displayed in Jewish Museums. The volume also includes new approaches to well-known Jewish writers such as Kafka, and a discussion on how a lesser writer by the name of Clementine Krämer subverted *Heimatliteratur*, a genre not commonly associated with Jews. It is clear that this review cannot do justice to the depth of the topics treated in *Nexus* 1, although each would deserve closer attention. What is most impressive about a number of these essays is that the argument their authors develop with reference to specific texts could be appropriated for other texts offering similarly new insights. A particularly striking example of this, it seems to me, is Nicola Behrmann's comparative assessment of Hugo Ball's and Walter Benjamin's ideas about language. The author outlines how similar experiences of personal loss lead these writers to develop similar doubts about the representability of experience through language and to 'focus on the magical potential of language' (p. 163). It could be pointed out that, with reference to the rupture caused by the Holocaust, the magical potential of language as a response to catastrophe has gained in significance. Indeed, one of the striking features of most recent Austrian Jewish literature is the deployment of the magical. In Doron Rabinovici's story 'Papirnik' (1994) as well as in his novel *Suche nach M.* (1997) the magical is proposed as the language in which the children of survivors engage with their parents' traumatic experience. More explicitly still, Julya Rabinowich's mythical figure of the Spaltkopf in her eponymous debut novel from 2008 not only appears—especially in the author's drawings—as an uncanny reincarnation of Benjamin's *Angel of History*, but the magical also frequently interrupts and comments on this modern *Bildungsroman*. Rabinowich, who was uprooted as a child from her native St Petersburg and grew up in Vienna, is dealing in this autobiographically inflected novel not only with her personal trauma but also with that of her maternal grandmother's suppressed Jewishness.

Herzog's *Vienna is Different* constitutes an informative guide to the continuities in Austrian Jewish literature during the long twentieth century and will be an excellent handbook for students in the field. The biennial journal *Nexus*, on the other hand, promises to contribute new and exciting perspectives to our understanding of German-Jewish philosophy, literature, and culture.

UNIVERSITY OF SOUTHAMPTON   ANDREA REITER

A Poet's Reich: Politics and Culture in the George Circle. Ed. by MELISSA S. LANE and MARTIN A. RUEHL. Rochester, NY: Camden House. 2011. 349 pp. £50. ISBN 978-1-57113-462-2.

Writing about Stefan George's politics is a difficult task: his poetry 'does not make political statements', as Raymond C. Ockenden comments (p. 111). Early in his life, George vowed to stay away from politics, yet he also challenged the barriers between ethics and aesthetics: his work changed the way his friends lived their lives. Eventually, representatives of almost every political persuasion laid claim to George.

Several chapters in the present volume—which goes back to a conference held in Cambridge in 2002—explore this interplay between poetry, critical practice, community, and reception. Ockenden, in what must be the best chapter-length overview of George's works, analyses both their criticism of modernity and the alternatives they propose: George believed in friendship as a practice in which 'excessive rationalization' is overcome (p. 101), even as he began to lose faith in its power to change society. Rüdiger Görner, in his insightful chapter on Friedrich Gundolf's Rilke essay, calls for an aesthetic theory that explores 'what it means to adhere to the circle principle, both as a pattern of composition and structure of reception' (p. 81). One of the circle's myths was 'Maximin', the poetic account of a divine appearance seen by George in Maximilian Kronberger, a poet who died at the age of sixteen. Ute Oelmann carefully states that while 'Maximin' was 'the product of George's creative ingenuity, it was sustained by the alliance of love and friendship that was his Circle' (p. 30). In marked contrast, Adam Bisno claims with stale psychoanalytical arguments that George, by 'stressing the pedagogical function of love between men and boys, legitimized his desire' (p. 46); Bisno thus dismisses George's love, pedagogy, and poetry as a façade for his 'corporeal attraction' to men. Robert E. Lerner's lucid analysis of Gertrud Kantorowicz's attitude towards women, Jews, and Germans (which Lerner surprisingly identifies as the central concerns of *Der Stern des Bundes*, p. 58) sheds light on the only woman to publish in *Blätter für die Kunst*. Richard Faber compellingly shows how conceptions of Europe by mid-century politicians and intellectuals from Adenauer to Ziegler resonate with George's world-view. These chapters are fascinating; it is a shame that what could have been another excellent chapter—Bertram Schefold's piece about the economists around George—was 'partially rewritten by the editors' (p. 194), as its first footnote indicates. Schefold, one of the leading George scholars, has published his authorized version elsewhere ('Politische Ökonomie als "Geistes-wissenschaft"', in *Studien zur Entwicklung der ökonomischen Theorie*, ed. by Harald Hagemann (Berlin: Duncker & Humblot, 2011), pp. 149–210).

In his highly informative overview of 'public perceptions of George's poetry in the Weimar period', David Midgley points out what is so unusual about the relationship between George and politics, citing Herbert Marcuse: '[George's] Reich kam nie — weil er im Grunde nie eins wollte' (p. 118). George's apolitical stance notwithstanding, his volume *Das neue Reich* does exist, and it *is* George's Reich. The present volume could have made an important contribution to George studies by illuminating this tension, by interrogating the terms 'Reich', 'politics', and 'culture', and by more fully acknowledging existing publications on George's social and political vision. For example, Ulrich Raulff establishes in *Kreis ohne Meister* (Munich: Beck, 2009) that George's friends exerted considerable political and cultural influence until at least 1968, yet the Introduction claims that 'the curious interplay between politics and culture in the George Circle' came to an end either with Hitler's rise to power or with the Stauffenberg brothers' failed conspiracy in 1944 (p. 11). The editors are puzzled by the ambiguities (pp. 8, 150, 228) of George's politics, arguably because his poetry is missing from their view. Melissa S. Lane's chapter deals with the way in which George's friends used their interpretations of Plato—the 'founder-legislator-leader-master-poet-lover-educator' (p. 134)—to support 'a politics of education, legislation, love, self-cultivation, and self-abnegation before a leader' (p. 150). Her chapter is riddled with factual inaccuracies which are each quite minor but distort the picture as a whole. Martin A. Ruehl's innovative reappraisal of Ernst Kantorowicz's nationalism is, unfortunately, marred by several conflations of writings and their reception.

Three chapters present starkly diverging assessments of George's influence on National Socialism. Robert E. Norton reiterates his view that George laid 'the intellectual groundwork' for Hitler by 'merging the aesthetic with the political' (p. 284), citing as evidence Hitler's love of 'theater and opera, film [and] literature', which, however, rank among the things that George enjoyed least. Peter Hoffmann states that Hitler's adversaries Claus and Berthold von Stauffenberg 'never abandoned their loyalty' to George while at the same time asserting that '[a]scribing Stauffenberg's deed to George's teaching and influence [. . .] is mere speculation' (p. 304). Thomas Karlauf points out that it makes no sense to see Hitler's actions as the 'implementation' of George's ideas and still characterize the resistance leaders as George's loyal followers (p. 317); he has 'little doubt' that their deed was informed by 'the values of the George Circle' and, in turn, George's poetry (p. 321).

This volume tackles important questions but it remains a patchy affair; it often contents itself with ambiguity, and tends as a whole to rely on the immediate appeal of its core terms. By not translating the complex term *Reich*, it seems to suggest that George's 'Reich' is the Third Reich (no one would speak of the Holy Roman 'Reich'). Some of its chapters leave too many open questions; other analyses, however, provide incisive contributions to English-language research on George and the relationship between poetry, ethics, and politics.

UNIVERSITY OF BRISTOL   CHRISTOPHE FRICKER

German Expressionism and the Messianism of a Generation. By LISA MARIE ANDERSON. (Internationale Forschungen zur Allgemeinen und Vergleichenden Literaturwissenschaft, 150) Amsterdam and New York: Rodopi. 2011. 210 pp. €42. ISBN 978-90-420-3352-8.

Lisa Marie Anderson offers an informative account of the place of Messianism within German Expressionism, and discusses the controversies that have attended the Expressionist phenomenon both in the decade of its greatest prominence and in attempts by critics and historians ever since to come to grips with it. The book shows how Expressionism has been variously characterized as attitude, sensibility, or style; as world-view and ethos; as an aesthetic movement, a form of secularized religiosity, a confused mix of revolutionary sentiment decoupled from political efficacy. Remaining open to all of these possibilities, Anderson reads Expressionism, in particular Expressionist drama, as an instantiation of the Messianic, best understood through its relation to the longer traditions of Messianism—Jewish, Christian, revolutionary—on which it feeds. The book traces key Messianic figures of rupture, apocalypse, revelation, and redemption from biblical and other sources, and finds them reworked and resignified by the Expressionist generation.

The central chapters contain detailed readings of plays by Ernst Barlach, Georg Kaiser, Ernst Toller, and Franz Werfel; in fact, the discrepancy in the title as given on the cover (*German Expressionism and the Messianism of a Generation*) and as the header of each left-hand page (*German Expressionist Drama and the Messianism of a Generation*) suggests that the book was originally conceived as a study of these dramatists, with the focus later being broadened to encompass reflections on Expressionist Messianism more generally. Anderson is generous in her provision of plot summaries and close readings; readers familiar with key texts of the Expressionist decade revisit them afresh, from Kaiser's *Von morgens bis mitternachts* (1912) through Werfel's *Mittagsgöttin* (1919) to Toller's *Hinkemann* (1923). The less widely known plays of the older Barlach, better known as a sculptor than as a dramatist, are represented here by *Der arme Vetter* (1918), *Der Findling* (1922), and *Die Sündflut* (1924). The decision to structure the discussion thematically, instead of chronologically or by author, makes for a strongly comparative study, with the texts being read against each other rather than in isolation or as part of an œuvre.

The firm anchoring in textual evidence makes it surprising that the book does not engage in a more sustained way with questions of stylistic exhaustion, derivativeness, or parody. What is most striking about much of the material considered here is its rhetorical excess. While the focus on motif and theme reveals continuities and differences across the playwrights' treatment of various topoi (Eden and Babylon, eucharist and resurrection), this approach tends to marginalize stylistic questions.

Barlach's monologues are accused (twice) of turgidity, but otherwise there is a tendency to quote without critical gloss on the often remarkable—in places remarkably derivative—linguistic gestures of Expressionism. Where the author offers her own translations, these, while largely accurate, risk stylistic flattening: a passage from Georg Kaiser's 1919 essay 'Mythos', for instance ('Buntem Paradiesbaum pflückt kecke Menschenhand Frucht aus — und sausender Engel verweist mit donnerndem Schwert in ewige Zerrüttung', p. 56), is translated into a normalized prose which restores the missing articles. The book's conclusion—that the Expressionists for the most part failed to transcend the false radicalism of their own proselytizing mode (p. 181, a view developed from the line of critique inaugurated by Lukács)—is arrived at thematically and conceptually, rather than via the stylistic symptoms displayed by the material under discussion.

The study is most persuasive where it focuses on Nietzsche's centrality in shaping the attitudes and rhetoric of the Expressionists. Nietzscheanisms of various hues are read as distinctive brands of Messianism, often in a syncretist blend with Jewish and/or Christian elements; the tension between desacralizing and resacralizing impulses is carefully teased out; and due attention is paid to the problematic political trajectories of Nietzsche reception in this period. The discussions of Nietzsche (as forerunner) and Ernst Bloch (as Expressionist Messianist) complement the dutiful references to the by now familiar Benjaminian landmarks—weak Messianism, homogeneous empty time, angel of history, now-time shot through with splinters of the Messianic, strait gate through which the Messiah may at any moment enter. The book sets out the key ingredients of modernist Messianism in its Expressionist inflection. Readers less inclined to take Messianism at its word may wonder at the questions Anderson poses in her concluding chapter (how does the past shape the Messianic future? can we force the end? what agency do humans have with respect to the fulfilment of the Messianic promise? who or what can save us?), but they will certainly gain valuable insights into the stylistic inflation and conceptual exhaustion of Expressionism's 'poetics of hysteria' (Richard Murphy, 'The Poetics of Hysteria: Expressionist Drama and the Melodramatic Imagination', *Germanisch-Romanische Monatsschrift*, 40 (1990), 156–70), which—despite the *Erneuerungspathos* it repeatedly invokes—attests most of all, perhaps, to the disorientation of the war generation.

DURHAM UNIVERSITY   CAITRÍONA NÍ DHÚILL

Thomas Mann in English: A Study in Literary Translation By DAVID HORTON. (New Directions in German Studies, 8) London: Bloomsbury. 2013. 248 pp. £60. ISBN 978-1-4411-6798-9.

Discussing English translations of Thomas Mann in recent years, David Luke, Timothy Buck, and others have focused on the work of his authorized translator, Helen Lowe-Porter, and have found it frequently inaccurate and generally unsatisfactory. While such studies have scored some good points, they have, as David

Horton contends, been based on the unexamined assumption that the translator ought to produce an exact equivalent to the original text. This seemingly commonsense assumption fails to consider that the original text is polyvalent and unstable; that the meaning which the translator seeks to transfer is not simply given, but results from innumerable acts of interpretation; and that the translator, by definition, inhabits a different cultural milieu from that in which the source text was composed. Instead of aiming at an impossible equivalence, the translator should try to produce a distinct text that offers a similar array of indeterminacies to that of the original.

Horton bases his analysis on a thorough knowledge of recent translation theory. Since his book reflects the development of translation studies from an impressionistic and judgemental exercise to a technical and descriptive discipline, it is not always easy reading, and one encounters such sesquipedalian monsters as 'operationability' (p. 15) and 'explicitation' (p. 17). There are, however, few terms that will be unfamiliar to educated readers (I confess that I had to look up 'anastrophe' and 'cataphoric' in dictionaries). It is a relief to find that Horton is sceptical about the possibility of any universal scheme for describing translations. He suggests that translations cannot be described solely by linguistic means. Translation studies must depend in some measure on the aesthetic intuitions of the literary critic.

Since his approach is descriptive, Horton first reconstructs Lowe-Porter's implicit assumptions about translation. Like Constance Garnett and many other contemporaries, she assumed that a translation should read as smoothly as though it were an original English text. Some of her recent critics assume unthinkingly that a translation should foreignize the original, forgetting that the result is not necessarily felicitous. Horton himself does not always abstain from judgement: he explicitly prefers John Woods's more modern version of *The Magic Mountain* to Lowe-Porter's, which reminds him of Galsworthy.

Horton then addresses a series of issues in translation. He applies a sophisticated linguistic and statistical apparatus to compare the two translations of *Der Zauberberg*, both in detail and with reference to the 'macrostylistic' level—i.e. how far the two translators have consistently rendered Mann's leitmotifs. He next deals with the specific problem of translating titles. Here we learn that Mann suggested giving *Der Erwählte* the English title *Gregory, Son of Sin* (why does this seem so hilarious?) and that his American publisher vetoed the English title *Lotte in Weimar* on the grounds that customers would not be able to pronounce it when asking for it in a bookshop. We then have considerations of the presentation of speech and thought in *Buddenbrooks*, where versions of *erlebte Rede* and the novel's range of dialects pose various problems; John Woods has been blamed for making Permaneder speak 'Mississippian' (p. 161), but what better solution is there? Modes of address ('Du/Sie') constitute a further range of problems, especially in *Der Zauberberg*, and though it is not Horton's business to propose solutions, practising translators should find this discussion particularly useful. Finally, the often unexpected effects of syntax are considered with reference to *Der Tod in Venedig*. Horton shows in a detailed comparison of the versions of its opening paragraph by Lowe-Porter and the late David Luke that the latter, one of her severest critics, seriously underestimated the difficulty of achieving equivalence between original and translation.

Based on thorough expertise and on a comprehensive command of the surprisingly extensive secondary literature on translating Mann, Horton has made a major contribution to the field. Henceforth anyone who wants to comment on translations of Mann must first read and digest this book. While it has something to offer all readers of Mann, its precise linguistic analyses and its sensitivity to literary effects may be especially timely for critics venturing into the new field of cognitive literary studies (illustrated e.g. by Emily Troscianko, 'The Cognitive Realism of Memory in Flaubert's *Madame Bovary*', MLR, 107 (2012), 772–95) and applying the insights of academic psychology to literary texts.

The Queen's College, Oxford \hfill Ritchie Robertson

Spaces for Happiness in the Twentieth-Century German Novel: Mann, Kafka, Hesse, Jünger. By Alan Corkhill. (German Life and Civilization, 57) Oxford: Peter Lang. 2012. viii+203 pp. £32. ISBN 978-3-0343-0797-0 (ebk 978-3-0353-0225-7).

Happiness, as Alan Corkhill points out in the follow-up to his study *Glückskonzeptionen im deutschen Roman von Wielands 'Agathon' bis Goethes 'Wahlverwandtschaften'*, Saarbrücker Beiträge zur Literaturwissenschaft, 78 (St Ingbert: Röhrig Universitätsverlag, 2003), has always proven 'tantalisingly elusive' (p. 1), and book-length studies on the subject are indeed few and far between. And yet, exploring the complex ways in which people experience and express happiness is a central function of literature, arguably as important as the current fascination with trauma, violence, and war. While happiness discourses range from the philosophical via the pedagogical, psychological, and spiritual to the socio-political, they always reflect the *Zeitgeist* and are rooted in intellectual traditions. Corkhill argues that writers act as therapists to their own protagonists and, by proxy, to their readers. He sets out to test the validity of his thesis by analysing seven canonical German texts: Thomas Mann's *Der Zauberberg*, Franz Kafka's *Der Prozess* and *Das Schloss*, Hermann Hesse's *Siddhartha*, *Der Steppenwolf*, and *Das Glasperlenspiel* as well as, interestingly, Ernst Jünger's *Heliopolis*.

In addition to literary analysis, Corkhill employs four interrelated theoretical frameworks: Eastern happiness philosophies which teach self-mastery and spiritual enlightenment, the psychologization of happiness according to Sigmund Freud and C. G. Jung, the application of Flow theory as propounded by Mihaly Csikzentmihalyi, and the identification and appraisal of 'spaces of happiness' based on Gaston Bachelard's 'topoanalysis' and Michel Foucault's 'heterotopoanalysis'. There is also a subtle philological approach at work, which, though not systematically, explores the semantic uncertainty of expressions describing a happy disposition—bliss, serenity, cheerfulness, contentment, joy, gladness, pleasure, etc.

Der Zauberberg is shown to demonstrate that the modern human condition entails snatching and even immortalizing brief moments of happiness, reflecting the tension between the 'Errichtung des allgemeinen Glücks' (Settembrini) and the experience of a happiness resulting from the stimulation of desire (Madame Chauchat), while Kafka's protagonists suffer from guiltless guilt and anxiety which not only inhibit happiness temporarily but produce conditions which lead to permanent unhappiness. For Hesse, the acquisition of individual happiness is not a quick fix but a long struggle towards self-knowledge and serenity. Whether 'Sinnen- und Liebesglück' or more cerebral states of happiness, Hesse's goal is the 'Bereicherung unserer Glücksmöglichkeiten' without denying their elusiveness. In a lucid exploration of Hesse's meditative essay *Glück* (1949), Corkhill focuses on fleeting 'moments' of happiness in childhood memories, though the discussion would have benefited greatly from Flavia Arzeni's excellent study *An Education in Happiness: The Lessons of Hesse and Tagore*, trans. by Howard Curtis (London: Pushkin Press, 2009). Ernst Jünger's depiction of the inhumanity of regimented happiness (recently revisited by Juli Zeh in her *Corpus Delicti*) foresees the end of social utopias, though it is unclear whether individuals can do without a Faustian 'Augenblick des Glücks'.

The study has no happy ending: 'the novels do not offer clear-cut resolutions to fundamental ontological, epistemological and existential conundrums concerning the nature, quality and meaning of happiness' (p. 148). That is not to say that the effort was in vain—far from it. Great literature, as Corkhill persuasively demonstrates, challenges uncritical appropriations of happiness as a lifestyle or commodity, negotiates the vast spaces colonized by subjective feelings of happiness, and shapes the very ideas that allow us to generate them in the first place.

I have two slight reservations. 'Glück', according to Herbert Marcuse in his *Versuch über die Befreiung* (Frankfurt a.M.: Suhrkamp, 1969), is an objective condition that requires more than subjective feelings: our (material) happiness is directly linked to suffering elsewhere. While Corkhill acknowledges the political dimension of happiness, this discussion remains largely confined to 'the great happiness dialogue' in *Heliopolis*, and focused more on technocratic solutions than their consequences for the population. The other problem concerns the focus on 'felicitous spaces' necessitated by the author's decision to read the texts in the light of 'topoanalysis' and 'heterotopoanalysis', a strategy that seems somewhat laboured in comparison with the very convincing discussion of happiness as a timeless experience in *Der Zauberberg*.

This should not detract from what has been achieved here: an impressive exploration of fictionalized constructs of happiness, new readings of familiar texts with interesting juxtapositions, and a sustained argument for the re-evaluation of the happiness phenomenon.

UNIVERSITY OF LEEDS INGO CORNILS

Franz Kafkas Handschrift zum 'Schloss'. By MATTHIAS SCHUSTER. Heidelberg: Winter. 2012. 552 pp. €74. ISBN 978-3-8253-6071-9.

Only a few years ago, the critical edition of Kafka's works edited by Malcolm Pasley and others (*Kritische Ausgabe der Werke von Franz Kafka* (Frankfurt a.M.: Fischer, 1982–)) seemed the last word in the accurate reproduction of Kafka's manuscripts. After extensive criticism by Hartmut Binder and others, and especially after this ferocious broadside by Matthias Schuster, it looks decidedly battered. The apparatus is indeed inconvenient to use, as Schuster complains (p. 46); the division into 'Tagebücher' and 'Nachgelassene Schriften' is artificial; the introduction of Eszett, which Kafka did not use in his manuscripts, is pointless, and doubly so since the recent spelling reform. All this qualifies, but surely does not much diminish, our gratitude for texts which are a clear advance on those provided by Max Brod.

Schuster maintains, however, that the Kritische Kafka-Ausgabe is not such an advance on Brod after all. It shares Brod's purpose of providing a handy reading edition. It imputes to Kafka the intention of ultimately producing a final text, and therefore banishes to the textual apparatus all the alterations and revisions that show how Kafka thought about his text as he produced it. By tidying up Kafka's text, it creates a misleading impression of coherence and homogeneity, and makes us forget that the three novels are really texts in flux. It even follows Brod's practice of intervening in Kafka's text, as when, in the heading of a section of *Der Process*, the name 'Beck' is changed to 'Block', the name borne by Huld's client in the body of the text. (See *Der Proceß*, ed. by Malcolm Pasley (Frankfurt a.M.: Fischer, 1990), Apparatband, p. 147.)

The only reputable method of reproducing manuscripts not prepared for publication by the author, in Schuster's view, is that adopted by Roland Reuß and Peter Staengle in their Historisch-Kritische Ausgabe, namely facsimile reproduction accompanied by a diplomatic transcription. Granted, this needs to be done anyway, so that posterity will know what the manuscripts looked like after, despite expert conservation, they have crumbled away. But it does not help towards providing a reading edition for non-scholarly readers. Without the prospect of producing a paperback edition for the mass market, Fischer would hardly have financed the costly Kritische Kafka-Ausgabe. Schuster's concession—'Unbestritten besitzen leicht zu rezipierende Leseausgaben ihre Berechtigung, vor allem für nichtwissenschaftliche Rezipienten' (p. 63)—implies that if such 'Rezipienten' ('Leser' are apparently extinct) are not obliged to struggle with a facsimile, they are being shamefully mollycoddled.

Nevertheless, Schuster has a strong case. It would be valuable to have a reading edition which acknowledged that the text of *Das Schloss* is much less tidy than it seems. Schuster shows that the so-called 'Fürstenzimmer-Fragment', beginning 'Der Wirt begrüsste den Gast' (*Das Schloß*, ed. by Malcolm Pasley (Frankfurt a.M.: Fischer, 1982), Apparatband, p. 115), along with other cancelled passages whose relation to the main text Pasley did not perceive, cannot be sharply severed from the main text. We need especially what Schuster calls an alternative ending, in which a villager reports K.'s account of his meeting with Bürgel (see *Das Schloß*, Apparatband, pp. 420–24) and adds malicious and disparaging comments.

The bulk of Schuster's book consists of close readings of Kafka's manuscript text, bringing out especially the complex narrative perspective, which is far less focused on K. than has hitherto been recognized. Friedrich Beissner's argument for narrative 'Einsinnigkeit', now generally dismissed, could never have withstood a careful reading of *Das Schloss*. Schuster further brings out the problems of perception (as in the unintelligible description of the Castle), the characters' tendency to idealize the bureaucrats which the narrative repeatedly undercuts, the frequency of insincerity and play-acting, the constant efforts by K. and the villagers to manipulate one another, and the way in which the villagers internalize and reproduce the system of domination under which they live. While inevitably these readings cover much familiar ground, they are astute enough to provide many new and refreshing insights, even when they are not based on what we can no longer call textual variants. This is in short an important book which must be taken into account by any future academic study of *Das Schloss*.

THE QUEEN'S COLLEGE, OXFORD   RITCHIE ROBERTSON

Kafka for the Twenty-First Century. Ed. by STANLEY CORNGOLD and RUTH V. GROSS. Rochester, NY: Camden House. 2011. 286 pp. £40; $75. ISBN 978-1-57113-482-0.

The essays in this volume are all worth reading; they are also well written and cogently argued because they have been expertly edited. Often they are provocative, sometimes opening up new avenues into parts of Kafka's œuvre (the coverage is not intended to be comprehensive), sometimes, just as productively, re-exploring old ones. I found Ritchie Robertson's 'Kafka, Goffman, and the Total Institution', which is about power, and John Zilcosky's '"Samsa war Reisender": Trains, Trauma, and the Unreadable', which analyses the hero of *Die Verwandlung* as if he were the traumatized survivor of a train crash, the most innovative. Other readers may particularly appreciate Walter Sokel's contribution on Kafka as an avid reader of Nietzsche; he works from the texts rather than biographical evidence, which does not exist in this case. Roland Reuß, in contrast, contributes his usual harangue, which becomes increasingly obscure, on the need to take into account the way Kafka wrote in his notebooks, since he was sometimes wont to incorporate line and page breaks as calligraphic marks that contribute to the meaning. At the end, Reuß is defending Brod against the assembled experts who made the Fischer Edition, which seems bizarre if he is interested in philological accuracy. It is perhaps curious, though given the accumulation of scholarly material and the complexity of the subject-matter entirely understandable, that the younger scholars are less original. The essays by Uta Degner ('What Kafka Learned from Flaubert'), Katja Garloff ('Kafka's Racial Melancholy', a reading of 'Ein Bericht für eine Akademie'), and especially Jacob Burnett ('Strange Loops and the Absent Center in *The Castle*) are erudite and elegantly formulated but they are essentially restatements of known positions.

As Ruth V. Gross explains in her Preface, the point of origin for the book was a 'Kafka at 125' conference which took place in North Carolina in 2009 (which was in fact 126 years after his birth). *Kafka for the Twenty-First Century* is the result, so she explains, of genuine discursive collaboration, with papers other than those by the four keynotes (Reuß, Robertson, Sokel, and Zilcosky) being circulated in advance and discussed in the round. The essays apparently represent only around half of the conference contributions, and the two editors make a good stab at arguing that they fit together in a way that is as good as if they had been commissioned at the outset. While the volume essentially offers a snapshot of current American interests, taken together the essays do in fact set out a fairly coherent agenda for Kafka Studies over the coming years and even decades. As this is the editors' declared intention, I will try in what follows to tease out some of the critical and ideological implications of that agenda.

With all due respect to Gross, the agenda has a distinctly Corngoldian inflection. Thus Doreen Densky ('Proxies in Kafka: *Koncipist* FK and *Prokurist* Josef K') takes the *Amtliche Schriften* as an integral part of the œuvre. Gross and Corngold explain (and quite rightly) in their excellent Introduction why we should all do so, though in this volume it does come at the expense of Kafka's at least equally brilliant letters. The accent elsewhere is on metaphor (Mark Harman, 'Torturing the Gordian Knot') and perspective (Peter Beicken, 'Kafka's Visual Method')—i.e. on form. Content, for example in the shape of Elizabeth Boa's three-pronged study *Kafka: Gender, Class, and Race in the Letters and Fictions* (Oxford: Clarendon Press, 1996), is sidelined, and significantly Boa gets just one mention in the index. This is a shame: if the editors and contributors disagree with her approach, this merits debate. Kafka can still be approached through culture, but not through politics or feminism, queer studies or psychoanalysis, which all appear to have had their day. He is no longer radical in any identifiable way, as he was at various points over the previous century in all of those domains. If the demography of the volume is anything to go by, Kafka is the preserve of academically established and consequently ageing males (all four keynotes are men whose combined age must approach 300) and youthful females (the five women contributors must have less professional experience between them than Corngold's stated forty plus years at Princeton). Yes, Kafka Studies is still dynamic, and—more to the point—Kafka's writings are as central to understanding modernity as they ever were. This is an argument the editors make especially forcefully, but inevitably and thankfully there is much more to Kafka and to the study of his work than is represented here.

SWANSEA UNIVERSITY   JULIAN PREECE

Schriftsteller und Widerstand: Facetten und Probleme der inneren Emigration. Ed. by Frank-Lothar Kroll and Rüdiger von Voss. Göttingen: Wallstein. 2012. 424 pp. €34.90. ISBN 978-3-8353-1042-1.

This volume presents revised versions of papers given at a conference at the Technical University, Chemnitz, in July 2009 to mark the seventy-fifth anniversary of the attempted assassination of Hitler by officers of the Wehrmacht, and it is not without significance that the conference took place under the auspices of, inter alia, the Stiftung 20. Juli 1944. The editors' Introduction states that the remit of the conference was to reassess the position of oppositional forms of cultural expression ('kulturelle Resistenz') and intellectual resistance against Nazism, with particular reference to literature and journalism (p. 9). The volume broadly succeeds in this aim.

The quality of the papers is high, as one would expect from the experts in their fields assembled here, and while to some extent the contributions inevitably go over ground covered previously, the volume as a whole is a valuable contribution to the ongoing debate about the range, forms, contexts, and significance of modes and practices of dissent within the cultural landscape of the Third Reich. There are signs in some of the contributions of a willingness to broach new ways of looking at the often stylized relationship between 'inner' and territorial exile, and in others of a reassessment of the terminological and conceptual difficulties of the key terms 'inner emigration', 'opposition', and 'resistance'. In this last case, the example of the Stauffenberg group stands as a reminder of the need to find a language which differentiates the varieties of intellectual nonconformism and gainsaying from acts of active resistance.

The sixteen contributions are grouped into five sections, focusing on: (1) general and theoretical issues ('Grundfragen'), (2) historical and political perspectives, (3) questions of media and genre ('Vermittlungsformen'), (4) surveys of groups of authors ('Gruppenbilder'), and (5) individual case studies. Specifically, the essays deal with: (1) the 'possibilities and limits' of intellectual resistance (Frank-Lothar Kroll), the problematic history of the concept 'inner emigration' (Hans Dieter Zimmermann), the politics of literature and authors critical of the regime (Jan-Peter Barbian); (2) historical fiction (Günter Scholdt), the concept of Europe among oppositional groups in inner and territorial exile (Boris Schilmar), utopias as an oppositional construct (Georg Guntermann); (3) literary and cultural journals as sites of opposition (Maria Theodora von dem Bottlenberg-Landsberg), travel literature (Gunther Nickel), melancholy in lyric poetry (Erwin Rotermund); (4) the Stefan George circle (Wolfgang Graf Witzthum), Christian confessional poetry (Gerhard Ringshausen), Austrian authors (Herwig Gottwald); (5) Werner Bergengruen (Katja Bergmann), Reinhold Schneider (Hans Dieter Zimmermann), the 'Third Reich' and postmodernity (Hans Dieter Schäfer), the intellectual legitimation and political significance of 'inner emigration' (Rüdiger von Voss).

The discussion of the 'Grundfragen', especially in the first section, is extremely useful. Kroll's introductory essay, for example, stresses that 'inner emigration' authors were often tolerated by the regime because they could provide an 'alibi' for the regime's credibility abroad and, more importantly, a controllable safety valve for feelings of discontent in the Reich (p. 20). Zimmermann's essay is a critical review of the history and reception of the term 'inner emigration', a term which, despite its dubious origins and problematic career since 1945, he reluctantly accepts as serviceable. Barbian's essay is a keen-sighted review of the legalistic, and arbitrary, workings of the culture chambers, and of the spectrum of authors, from those on the 'awkward' political right (such as Wiechert and Pechel) to the 'silent dissidence' of Loerke and Haecker, to the 'active resistance' of figures such as Bonhoeffer and Haushofer. Barbian specifically excludes authors such as Thiess, examples of 'bürgerlich accommodation', from the category of 'inner emigrants'. Scholdt concludes his essay on the oppositional uses of historical tropes with a timely reassessment of consolation and hope as important functions of this coded literature (pp. 122–23). While these must appear somewhat peripheral when compared with heroic acts of resistance and sacrifice, they were nevertheless worth more than the low regard in which many Germanists hold them today.

The volume will be of particular interest to scholars of Bergengruen, who features prominently in the contributions by Kroll, Scholdt, Guntermann, Schilmar, and Bergmann. A real strength of this collection, however, is the wide scope of the papers, touching on neglected as well as familiar figures. It is regrettable, therefore, that no index is provided. This reservation apart, the volume is to be welcomed as marking an important stage in the evolving debate surrounding the phenomena of 'inner emigration' in the Nazi period. By focusing on the complex and often ambiguous nature of individual works and individual authors at given moments, it demonstrates that simple categorizations are inadequate.

UNIVERSITY OF BIRMINGHAM   WILLIAM J. DODD

Brecht and the GDR: Politics, Culture, Posterity. Ed. by LAURA BRADLEY and KAREN LEEDER. (Edinburgh German Yearbook, 6) Rochester, NY: Camden House. 2011. 241 pp. £50. ISBN 978-1-57113-492-9.

A valuable addition to an excellent series, this volume focuses on Brecht's relationship with the GDR: his life and work there from May 1949 when he moved to East Berlin, the GDR's controversial management of his legacy after his death in 1956, and the creative responses to his work before and after the demise of the country. Through careful structuring and judicious cross-referencing, the volume's eleven essays achieve a degree of coherence not always found in similar collaborative enterprises.

In the first of the volume's three parts, David Barnett uses Brecht's own productions of *Puntila und sein Knecht Matti* (1949) and Johannes R. Becher's *Winterschlacht* (1955) to challenge attempts both to depoliticize him by alleging his overriding interest in a timeless human condition and also to deny the importance of his theories to his actual practice in the theatre. Noting 'the bewilderment' (p. 47) of critics in the face of the very diverse modes of poetry Brecht wrote in his final years, Karen Leeder finds in theories of lateness, old-age literature, and late style (notably in Edward Said's work) the unifying principle underpinning the 'late' poetry Brecht wrote in the GDR. Presenting hitherto inadequately considered evidence of the rapid physical deterioration which plagued Brecht's final years, Stephen Parker argues that the public attacks and obvious surveillance to which he was subjected by the SED accelerated the ageing process and brought even closer the early death which was in any case inevitable. In arguing that Brecht's reaction to 17 June was far less sympathetic to the SED's spin on events than critics have often supposed, Patrick Harker sees the well-known entry in his journal on 20 August 1953 ('der 17 juni hat die ganze existenz verfremdet') not as a confession of disillusionment and alienation but as 'undoubtedly Brecht's most optimistic and positive interpretation of 17 June' (p. 94) because it suggests the detachment required to understand the uprising and thereby promote Socialist progress.

Brecht's legacy became the focus of a struggle between the GDR state and the Brecht family, as Erdmut Wizisla shows while cautiously suggesting that, compared with state control, the controversial 'Privatarchiv der Erben' established by Helene Weigel 'may well have been the more democratic principle' (p. 114). In her discussion of the way in which the 70th, 75th, and 80th anniversaries of Brecht's birth were commemorated, Laura Bradley highlights another significant area in which the same protagonists fought for ownership of Brecht's legacy—a legacy to which, as Paula Hanssen argues, the contribution of Elisabeth Hauptmann as Brecht's co-author and editor (to say nothing of the inspiration she offered the Berliner Ensemble) has still not been sufficiently appreciated.

In the concluding section Joy Calico considers the literary and musical responses to Brecht's work of Hanns Eisler and Paul Dessau, seeing in the latter's *In memoriam* a non-hagiographic elegy which reflects the complex relationship between the two men, while David Robb focuses on the creative use made by Wolf Biermann and the group Karls Enkel of the grotesque aspects in Brecht's early work. In the two essays which round off the volume, Moray McGowan focuses on the *Fatzer* fragment, notably its importance for Heiner Müller, and on the remarkable degree of attention it has received since the demise of the GDR, while Loren Kruger considers the numerous productions of *Die heilige Johanna der Schlachthöfe* in recent years, analysing in particular detail those at the Berliner Ensemble in 2003 and in Konstanz in 2010. What both essays assert is the unmistakable relevance of Brecht's work to a critical understanding of the destructive impact of neo-liberalism and globalization on present-day realities.

UNIVERSITY OF BATH   IAN WALLACE

Complicity, Censorship and Criticism: Negotiating Space in the GDR Literary Sphere. By SARA JONES. Berlin and New York: de Gruyter. 2011. 226 pp. €89.95. ISBN 978-3-11-023795-5.

Access to the archives of the SED and Ministerium für Staatssicherheit (MfS or Stasi) has allowed fundamental rethinking of the relationship between *Geist* and

Macht in the GDR. This volume brings together archival research with literary analysis and clear-sighted exposition of political structures to offer an innovative and multi-layered approach to that relationship. Unlike those analyses that see the GDR as a totalitarian *Unrechtsstaat*, and the lines of political and moral allegiance as clear-cut, this subtle and clearly presented volume insists that 'complexity, differentiation, ambiguity and ambivalence' (p. 6) and 'fluid boundaries between opposition and conformity' (p. 21) are the governing tropes of GDR society.

Sara Jones presents three illuminating case studies that reveal contrasting but complementary varieties of self-legitimation, behaviour, and habitus: Hermann Kant (President of the Writers' Union and *Inoffizieller Mitarbeiter* (IM)); Stefan Heym (self-styled 'perpetual dissident', enjoying international prestige and never a Party member); and Elfriede Brüning (conformist writer of middle-brow literature, little known beyond the GDR). In each case she presents archive material (including Stasi files and unpublished correspondence), pre-1989 literary texts, and detailed readings of post-*Wende* autobiographies.

Jones is well aware of the problems of reading these very different kinds of document alongside one another, but uses them scrupulously: allowing the contradictions to speak largely for themselves, patiently teasing out the ambiguities, and always aware of the problems of factual reliability. None of the writers comes out of it terribly well. All are revealed to be busy retouching the relationship between memory and expediency: from Kant's denial that he worked for the Stasi, Heym's self-stylization as intellectually superior while also tacking and manœuvring like everyone else, and Brüning's catalogue of complaints to those in power that dissidents were getting all the glory (and financial incentives) and that her achievements were being sidelined. Fascinating, nevertheless, is the picture that emerges of the power that writers could wield at the right moment if they dared. But more important, perhaps, is the sense that the fault-lines in the GDR went through all walks of life. The tug of war between impulses towards liberalization or conformity, humanity or cowardice clearly go through publishers, journals, reviewers, and functionaries too, presenting a nuanced, sometimes chaotic and very human picture.

Cumulatively these case studies form part of a larger argument on three levels. Firstly, Jones insists on literature's role as part of the 'official discourse' of the GDR, opening it to very successful discourse analysis in line with David Bathrick's work. She also chips away at the notion of anti-Fascism as a meta-ideology that served to ensure loyalty to the state among the older generations in the GDR (though it would have been interesting, of course, to challenge both of these notions by taking as one of her models a much younger writer who had little or no official status in the GDR and saw their own work as a counter-discourse). Finally, in a very suggestive part of her Conclusion, she offers the Church as another model 'space' that might benefit from a similar analysis. Many there, too, were drawn into straddling the divide between power and people in ways not previously understood. Her overall argument, in line with Martin Sabrow, is that such spaces (literature, Church, etc.) serve to reveal the extent to which fraying and disintegration of previously clear-cut values and understandings finally left the GDR 'hollowed-out' in 1989 when pressure was brought to bear on them. This feeds into the broader understanding of the GDR as a 'participatory dictatorship' (Mary Fulbrook, *The People's State: East German Society from Hitler to Honecker* (New Haven and London: Yale University Press, 2005), p. 12) in very useful ways and insists eloquently on the importance of combining political analysis, cultural history, literature, and the place of the individual in all future work. This brisk, confident, and eminently readable volume is a model of how it can be done.

NEW COLLEGE, OXFORD   KAREN LEEDER

'Schreiben mit gespaltener Feder': Peter Rühmkorfs ästhetisch-politisches Doppelengagement. By VERENA PAUL. (Saarbrücker Beiträge zur Literaturwissenschaft, 88) St Ingbert: Röhrig Universitätsverlag. 2012. 593 pp. €54. ISBN 978-3-86110-518-3.

The poet and activist Peter Rühmkorf (1929–2008) is characterized by two photographs that introduce Volumes II and III of his *Collected Works*. One shows him behind microphones in a marketplace somewhere in West Germany during a reading or political campaign; the other depicts him on a balcony meditating over a cat. Alongside Hans Magnus Enzensberger, Martin Walser, and Günter Grass, Rühmkorf was a legend as a poetic activist in his inevitable trench coat with his dark, broad-rimmed hat and often equally broad yet wry or melancholic smile, complemented by a pair of spectacles whose size seems to ensure clarity of vision. Together with the poet Robert Gernhardt, Rühmkorf reinvented a Heine-like sound in German poetry, which distinguished itself by an appealing performative quality coupled with rhythmic structures akin to jazz.

In 1967, on the verge of the student revolts, Rühmkorf identified a special quality that marks out genuine poems, suggesting that they are lie detectors designed to uncover the truth about society and the individual. At the same time Rühmkorf re-established the fairy tale as a form of imaginary discourse (which began in 1980 with *Auf Wiedersehen in Kenilworth*). His diaries and memoirs, all published during his lifetime, complemented one of the richest lyrical œuvres in post-war Germany.

While there are not many critical studies on Rühmkorf, there were a number of significant contributions in the 1980s, starting with Herbert Uerlings (*Die Gedichte Peter Rühmkorfs* (Bonn: Bouvier, 1984)), and more recently Frédérique Colombat-Didier's *La Situation poétique de Peter Rühmkorf* (Bern: Peter Lang, 2000). Verena Paul's erudite investigation of this poet's 'double commitment' in poetry and politics is a welcome addition. Her study is informed by an appreciation of the intrinsic complexity of political 'engagement' through poetic reflexivity. Aptly, she begins her exploration of the 'Doppelengagement' with extensive references to Heine and the challenge his commitment poses for later poets, and goes on to offer a balanced assessment of Rühmkorf's main literary genres. Somewhat surprisingly, she does not begin with his poetry and poetics but puts the essay and fairy tale first—the discursive and the imaginary—followed by his interest in biography, his radio plays, and his failed attempts to enact political commitment on stage. Paul thereby presents us with a comprehensive overview of Rühmkorf's concerns as reflected in the various aspects of his œuvre. To a lesser extent she focuses on themes or motifs and therefore cannot but underrate the overlaps and synergies in Rühmkorf's writings. Moreover, Paul appears to underestimate the sheer delight a virtuoso poet such as Rühmkorf takes in savouring the rich possibilities language can offer.

Paul's study demands much of the reader in terms of length, but it reads well. Mostly she succeeds in engaging the reader's attention in her exploration of the significance of Rühmkorf's 'double engagement'. Occasionally, though, she seems to hide her own stance behind the view of others. This becomes particularly evident when she comes close to discussing the eminently relevant question whether 'Doppelengagement' in Rühmkorf's sense could lead to what Gottfried Benn termed 'Doppelleben'. Moreover, this voluminous monograph suffers from a major deficiency: Paul fails to come up with a satisfactory definition of what 'engagement' means in Rühmkorf's case. This may be a consequence of the fact that she posits an integral 'ambivalence' (p. 147) in Rühmkorf's interest in creating a purely aesthetic (and quasi-magic) engagement through his allegorical fairy tales, and his ambition to 'enlighten' his readership politically. If poetic 'engagement' entailed the pursuit of an ideological agenda (Rühmkorf was never really in danger of that!), he would inevitably betray his allegiance to the 'beauty' of language. But if he only favoured the latter, he risked becoming irrelevant in social and political terms. This is a risk that poets such as Rühmkorf, Grass, and Enzensberger have always been concerned about, while others have primarily aimed to advance poetry 'merely' aesthetically.

A structural point is worthy of mention: Paul's 'summaries' at the end of each chapter initially seem a trifle pedantic, but in most cases they introduce a new aspect or fresh material that would have deserved a somewhat more 'engaging' title. Ironically, a summary is lacking at the end of the monograph, when the reader would expect the various strands to be drawn together in a compelling discursive finale. Instead the study breaks off somewhat randomly with a poem in which Rühmkorf criticizes postmodernism. Nevertheless, Paul's significant contribution persuasively makes the case for re-engaging with scholarship on Rühmkorf, and establishes how contemporary German-language poetry should, or could, learn from the dazzling example of this great bard.

QUEEN MARY, UNIVERSITY OF LONDON   RÜDIGER GÖRNER

Writing and Muslim Identity: Representations of Islam in German and English Transcultural Literature, 1990–2006. By FRAUKE MATTHES. London: Institute of Germanic & Romance Studies. 2011. 266 pp. £25. ISBN 978-0-85457-231-1.

Frauke Matthes explores representations of Islam in terms of transculturation, travel, language, and gender in German-language works by Emine Sevgi Özdamar

(*Das Leben ist eine Karawanserei*, in Chapter 1; *MutterZunge*, in Chapter 4), Ilija Trojanow (*Zu den Heiligen Quellen des Islam*, in Chapter 2), and Feridun Zaimoğlu (*Kanak Sprak*, in Chapter 3; *Koppstoff*, in Chapter 4). These texts are compared with works by Monica Ali (*Brick Lane*, in Chapter 1), V. S. Naipaul (*Among the Believers* and *Beyond Belief*, in Chapter 2), Hanif Kureishi (*The Black Album*, in Chapter 3), and Leila Aboulela (*The Translator* and *Minaret*, in Chapter 4). Most of Matthes's writers are, in her terms, (culturally) 'Muslim'; only Aboulela is an 'Islamic' writer: her personal faith is essential to her literary project (this may also be said of Trojanow, in respect of his Hajj narrative). All German quotations are translated, mostly very well.

Islam belongs to Europe; writers can help explain what this means. Matthes explores the associated complex and delicate questions with erudition. The main focus is on the explication of the German texts, the English serving as contrasting foils. In the international book market, Matthes suggests, readers and critics judge the still emergent German 'transcultural' literature against anglophone norms. She questions this but allows it to structure her study.

There must be tension in such a study between a literary-critical and a social-political agenda. The former is privileged. Matthes's criticism draws on wide secondary and theoretical reading, but the rationale for selecting texts is not clear and the comparisons shed little light on each other. In Chapter 1, the pre-migration first instalment of Özdamar's autofiction sequence is not an obvious comparator with *Brick Lane* for a discussion of concepts of migration, travel, and home in Muslim diaspora settings. Ali's narrative of community (un)settlement in London can be contrasted in too many ways with Özdamar's theatrical individualism set in Turkey. Likewise in Chapter 2, the unabashedly Eurocentric Naipaul's question— why is there an Islamic revival in non-Arab Muslim societies?—is not addressed by Trojanow's bland apologia for the Hajj (his Richard Burton novel might have served better). Chapter 3 tackles depictions of diasporic radical Islamists. *The Black Album* would compare better with some of Zaimoğlu's stories in *Zwölf Gramm Glück*, or the docu-drama *Schwarze Jungfrauen*, than with *Kanak Sprak*, where even what Matthes vaguely calls 'folk Islam' (p. 164) is little in evidence. On the incipiently jihadist rant attributed to 'Yücel, Islamist', which closes *Kanak Sprak*, Matthes only speculates that Zaimoğlu (in 1995) placed Yücel last 'as a herald for the fundamentalist attacks of the 2000s' and that Yücel's proclaimed 'surrender' to God must make him a 'failure' in the view of 'other *Kanaken*' (pp. 164–65). Zaimoğlu is not a seer and his text supplies no responses to Yücel's views; and here 'ergeben' is a translation of 'Islam'.

The Egypt-born, Sudan-educated, Scotland-based novelist Leila Aboulela writes committed Islamic feminist fictions, engaging both Muslim and non-Muslim audiences. Kenan Çayir's *Islamic Literature in Contemporary Turkey: From Epic to Novel* (New York: Palgrave Macmillan, 2007) would have helped to locate Aboulela's work. He analyses a rich body of fiction which propagates and interrogates changing understandings of Islam: much popular fiction ('salvation novels' published on a huge scale since the 1980s) but also challenging literary works. The Islamic novel is now emerging in Western European languages too. It will make a rewarding topic for comparative (also cross-faith) study: narratives of faith tested, lost, redefined, and renewed, and of the competing claims of individual belief, community authority, and secular norms. It is hard to see the point of comparing the devout Aboulela with Özdamar (a socialist with little time for religion, except as a cultural factor) or Zaimoğlu (who defends private, idiosyncratic religiosity against ideologies, and publicly identifies as a Muslim in the face of rampant Islamophobia). The chapter is highly disjointed. A concluding chapter belatedly presents snapshots of Navid Kermani and Zafer Şenocak, German writers who are steeped in Islamic literary and intellectual traditions, and on the British side, Suhayl Saadi (*Psychoraag*) and Gautam Malkani (*Londonstani*), who are not.

Often arguing against undifferentiated understandings of Islam, Matthes nevertheless only differentiates 'Muslim identity' in non-Muslim or universalist terms: in textual performances of gender, sexuality, or linguistic disruption. Divisions between Sunni and Shi'a, Alevis or Sufis, ethnic and political transnational identifications go unmentioned; so does the 'European Islam' proposed by scholars such as Tariq Ramadan and Bassam Tibi. We gain limited insight into general questions of Muslim identity in non-Muslim societies. Both Aboulela (p. 182) and Trojanow (p. 120) note with regret the greater freedom to practise Islam outside Islamic countries: there is no cross-reference or discussion. Even granted that this is a study in literature rather than religion and politics, there are worrying errors. When Naipaul's visit to the Ahmadis in Lahore in *Among the Believers* is cited, Matthes quotes his phrase 'the purest of Muslims' with no further comment about the Ahmadis, or apparent purpose (p. 97). Naipaul wrote (with suave irony): 'The Ahmadis considered themselves the purest of Muslims.' We do not learn from Matthes that the sect follows a nineteenth-century Messiah and is vigorously persecuted in Pakistan and other Muslim countries, or that Naipaul provocatively made it an emblem of missionary Islam. Research into 'Muslim turns' needs firmer grounding in Muslim realities. Nevertheless, Matthes has done future scholars in this area a service by exploring how diverse, shifting Muslim identities are represented by writers both inside and outside the communities of faith and ethnicity

SWANSEA UNIVERSITY TOM CHEESMAN

The Concise CineGraph: Encyclopaedia of German Cinema. Ed. By HANS-MICHAEL BOCK and TIM BERGFELDER. (Film Europa: German Cinema in an International Context) New York and Oxford: Berghahn. 2009. xi+574 pp. £100. ISBN 978-1-57181-655-9.

In 1981 the German imprint Fischer released the first paperback edition of the avant-garde director Hans Richter's 1929 film manifesto, *Filmgegner von heute — Filmfreunde von morgen* (Frankfurt a.M.: Fischer, 1981). An Introduction by the historian and future director of Frankfurt's German Film Museum, Walter Schobert, gives early insight into the revisionist historical impulse that would later fuel the collection reviewed here. Commenting on Richter's enthusiasm for the film medium's visual poetry, Schobert notes, 'Richter's conception [of film art] is [...] more capacious than he himself suggests. Did not the truly great directors of supposedly trivial films show the same mastery in their employment of techniques that Richter [...] propagates as the specific features of the artistic film?' (pp. v–vi).

Schobert's comments highlight the longevity of what is often misleadingly dubbed the 'new' history of German cinema—a history now amplified by Bock and Bergfelder's biographical encyclopedia, a digest for anglophone readers of the Hamburg film research institute CineGraph's comprehensive *Lexikon zum deutschsprachigen Film*, ed. by Hans-Michael Bock and others (Munich: text+kritik, 1984). As this volume shows, Schobert's efforts to extend the reach of German cinema history beyond the art film canon were mirrored from the early 1980s among a new generation of historians who worked with or within an expanding archive sector, within an emerging historical film festival circuit, in university departments and research institutes, to explore a national cinema heritage whose riches extended well beyond Weimar's author-film classics, or the Nazi propaganda and New German cinema canon. Further invigorated by the easy availability of video, or later DVD, editions of restored or rediscovered titles, as well as by more recent online resources including the invaluable <www.filmportal.de>, revisionist film scholarship has spent three decades exploring forgotten or neglected film-historical fields: the cinema of Weimar émigrés, and of exile practitioners after 1933; the German-language popular cinema of genres and stars which, contrary to entrenched myths of Hollywood dominance, has regularly secured the lion's share of the German-language audience; or the co-productions, the migrant and re-migrant waves, the cross-border traffic in personnel, film sounds, and images that demand an extension of 'German' cinema history into the transnational territory of world film.

This volume shows how far German-language film history has travelled since Schobert penned his Richter Introduction in 1981. The editors Hans-Michael Bock, Director of the CineGraph film research institute, and Tim Bergfelder, Professor and Head of Film Studies at Southampton University, have a distinguished joint track record, including their work as co-editors with Sabine Hake of the Berghahn Film Europa series. CineGraph's loose-leaf *Lexikon*, from which the book derives, has become a model for later digital versions of work-in-progress film encyclopedias, most centrally the German film portal, a collaborative venture between CineGraph, the Deutsches Filminstitut, and other partners. What distinguishes the *Concise CineGraph* (and makes it a worthwhile £100 library investment, even in today's cash-strapped times) is the careful targeting of its entries towards anglophone readers. The original German entries were substantially revised for this volume, and it includes an excellent Appendix detailing German film's 'historical and thematic contexts'. The volume also enacts the turn to cultural diversity and transnationalism to which many contemporary film histories merely pay lip service. Individuals are selected, therefore, not solely on the basis of national origins, but by virtue of their significance for German-language film. Hence the inclusion of stars such as the Danish Asta Nielsen, the Polish Pola Negri, the Russian Olga Tschechowa, or such multiply displaced émigrés as Hedy Lamarr or Franziska Gaál. Similarly welcome is the book's inclusion of practitioners across the creative and industrial spectrum, including set designers, producers, composers, and practitioners in influential sister arts, such as theatre, advertising, literary fiction, and fine art.

The Concise CineGraph also suggests a final conclusion on future directions for German-language film history. The volume joins a plethora of period and national cinema overviews targeted over the past decade at students, teachers, and researchers into German-language film. Both for pedagogic reasons and—more centrally perhaps—for heuristic purposes pertinent to future research, the time may be ripe for more focused studies that draw on resources including *CineGraph* not just to identify gaps in the historiography, but to explore in concentrated detail the trickier issues of critical method that are thrown up by a history that centres attention on such figures as the scriptwriter, actor, and director Henrik Galeen (aka Heinrich Weissenberg, aka Heinrich/Henryk Galeen). Growing up in a Central European city—Lviv/Lwów/Lemberg, which has, geopolitically speaking, itself 'migrated' since the early twentieth century between Poland, the Austrian Empire, the Soviet Union, and Ukraine—Galeen shuttled between Vienna, Berlin, Bern, and St. Gallen, worked as scriptwriter on early film classics including *The Student of Prague* (1913), travelled to Britain in 1931 to work among other projects on early sound shorts, then 'turned up in the United States in 1940, where he lived as a recluse in New York and Vermont for the rest of his life' (p. 146). Quite which segment of German-language film history provides a home for Galeen is an issue that is not easily answered: German national cinema? Austrian? British? Ukrainian? Exile, transnational, cosmopolitan film? Precisely for that reason the question is energizing, and it suggests that we may have more work to do before we exhaust the rich seam of historical enquiry that is German-language film.

KING'S COLLEGE LONDON   ERICA CARTER

The Many Faces of Weimar Cinema: Rediscovering Germany's Filmic Legacy. Ed. by CHRISTIAN ROGOWSKI. (Screen Cultures: German Film and the Visual) Rochester, NY: Camden House. 2010. xiii+354 pp. £50. ISBN 978-1-57113-429-5.

Christian Rogowski's Weimar film anthology joins the expanding list of English-language overviews that now sustain German film studies as an established subdiscipline. Published in Johannes von Moltke and Gerd Gemünden's excellent Camden House Screen Cultures series, the volume presents case studies from a Weimar cinema understood as 'predominantly' a cinema of genres and stars (p. 3). Drawing on research by both emerging and established film scholars, the collection develops five key postulates borrowed from the larger contemporary historiography of Weimar film. The first involves a redefinition of the object of study, 'Weimar film' itself. As Rogowski's Introduction indicates (p. 5), a vastly expanded historical corpus is generated by recent shifts from the tired narrative of an author-centred cinema moving in linear fashion from Expressionism to *Neue Sachlichkeit*, to a multilayered history of overlapping genre cycles, heterogeneous audiences, international market and art movements, or cross-media relations between film and the legitimate arts. Hence, for instance, this volume's rich array of genre studies: Jill Suzanne Smith, Barbara Hales, and Christian Rogowski on sex-educational melodramas including social hygiene film (*Aufklärungsfilm*); Philipp Stiasny on the post-First World War anti-Bolshevist genre wave; Richard McCormick on Jewish comedy; Mihaela Petrescu on late Weimar romantic comedies; or Theodore F. Rippey on the *Kulturfilm*, a form of semi-staged documentary that was among the period's most distinctive contributions to international film art. Hence too Valerie Weinstein's engaging star study of Brigitte Helm as the quintessential Weimar vamp, a figure who '[preyed] on ideas of racial pollution' (p. 198) to feed popular fears of gender disorder and sexual decay. Moreover, Weinstein's reading of Helm as a prism reflecting and refracting Weimar social fantasies of 'race' and gender exemplifies the conjunctural approach proposed by Joseph Garncarz in his characteristically astute discussion of Weimar stars. Taking issue with star studies that ignore the cultural specificity of national star systems, Garncarz cites among the specific features of the Weimar system the retention by star actors of control over their public image; the relative secrecy surrounding the private lives of stars; the significance of the legitimate theatre as the culturally dominant medium; and the special importance of stars in an industry that for many years lacked major studios, remaining therefore, Garncarz argues, especially wedded to star promotion as a strategy in the struggle for market share.

A second historiographical premiss shaping this volume is evident in the prominence here of Ernst Lubitsch. Lubitsch makes his mischievous presence felt in McCormick's discussion of his 1920 Oriental fantasy *Sumurun*; his name also surfaces in Cynthia Walk's nuanced discussion of Jewish assimilation films, and in Rogowski's Introduction, where Lubitsch's early comedies and historical epics are identified as path-breaking for the later development of German-language genre film. But Lubitsch is also emblematic of a historiography that locates German-speaking Jews at the forefront of Weimar film history, foregrounding contributions by such further prominent Jewish practitioners as E. A. Dupont, Hans Richter, Robert Siodmak, Rosa Valetti, or Kurt Gerron. This question of social identity in its relation to cinema—evident more recently in Weimar film historiography's (long overdue) concern with Jewish ethnicity—was posed first in the 1970s by a spate of class-based histories of Weimar film, and somewhat later by feminist accounts that explored the intersection of class with sexual and gender identities. In *Many Faces*, the imprint of this third—feminist—historiographical reorientation is visible in Elizabeth Otto's fine-grained analysis of Conrad Veidt's 'masculine masquerades', as well as Petrescu's convincing discussion of romantic comedies that parodically 'rewrite the genre of melodrama in the context of shifting gender relations' (p. 300). Similarly compelling are accounts by Veronika Fuechtner and Nancy Nenno that highlight a fourth shift in historical emphasis towards transnational collaborations and culturally hybrid forms. Nenno's plea for a restoration to canonical status of Viktor Trivas's pacifist *Niemandsland* (*War is Hell*, 1931) thus rests on a moving reading of the film's polyglot African soldier, Joe Smile (Louis Douglas), whom Nenno presents as an emblem of the film's cosmopolitan 'supra-national ideal' (p. 291). Fuechtner, meanwhile, uses a study of collaborations between the early *Heimatfilm* director-turned-Bombay-expatriate Franz Osten, and the producer–actor couple Himansu Rai and Devika Rani, to quash the myth of an early German cinema amenable to containment within national bounds.

Not least in the light of Germany's long and troubled history of state regulation, ownership, and ideological control, the convention was for many years to divide the national film narrative into political epochs from the *Kaiserreich* through the Weimar Republic to Nazism, the Cold War, unification, and beyond. Rogowski's collection shares with other recent histories, by contrast, a periodization deriving as much from cinematic developments as from political cycles or ideological shifts. The result is a welcome attention to the coming of sound as a historical caesura of sufficient significance to warrant four pieces in total: Chris Wahl's informative account of the multi-language versions (MLVs) that were the major studios' initial response to sound film; Ofer Ashkenazi's absorbing analysis of early sound films, including Robert Siodmak's *Abschied* (*Farewell*, 1930) and *Voruntersuchung* (*Inquest*, 1931), whose experimental and cosmopolitan audio-visual aesthetic is read, in contrast to the MLVs' primarily commercial solution, as a 'progressive-liberal' response to the sound film challenge. Equally engaging is Joel Westerdale's account of silent cinema's swansong: experimental films by Walter Ruttmann, Hans Richter, Viking Eggeling—directors who glimpsed in silent film a visual music whose aesthetic potential many viewed as crushed by the advent of sound.

Jaimey Fisher completes the sound film picture with a dense, though ultimately convincing, piece on G. W. Pabst's sonic manipulation of offscreen space in *Westfront 1918*. His article is one of a number in *Many Faces* that help reshape the German cinema canon around titles critically reappraised in the wake of recent DVD release. But this recanonization of film as digital object raises an issue to which Rogowski's collection does not always sufficiently attend. Readers (myself included) may share the enthusiasm of some contributors for 'beautifully restored' prints (Rogowski, p. 212) reissued on DVD. But what borders occasionally on a fetishization of the beautiful DVD also promotes a connoisseurship that misrecognizes aesthetic appreciation as historical analysis. The weakest pieces in this book thus offer thin, largely text-based accounts consisting, in the worst cases, of pedestrian plot retelling, with derivative summaries of existing secondary sources and voluntaristic linkages to contemporary historico-political events.

A stronger editorial hand in these few cases might have helped fully to realize the book's otherwise well-executed project of presenting Weimar cinema in all its 'exciting richness and variety' (p. xii). A possible source of *Many Faces*' occasionally laissez-faire editorial style can, however, be glimpsed in the Introduction. Rogowski is one of numerous contributors who acknowledge their debt to the founding texts of Weimar cinema studies, Siegfried Kracauer's *From Caligari to Hitler* (1947) and Lotte Eisner's *The Haunted Screen* (*L'Écran démoniaque*, 1952). Those works are criticized, however, for their rooting in 'a monolithic notion of national or cultural identity' (p. 2). The argument is of course well founded; but as Rogowski himself makes clear, it is also well-trodden territory: to take only the most recent examples, Thomas Elsaesser's magisterial volume on Weimar cinema's 'historical imaginary', Anton Kaes and Philipp Stiasny's different but related readings of Weimar film as a response to the Great War, or the wealth of feminist accounts of a gendered spectatorship that fractures the homogeneous national consciousness of earlier accounts.

What unites this new historical corpus, despite its critique of earlier Weimar histories, is a commitment to the same practice of social-theoretical speculation that grounded Kracauer's writings in Marxist phenomenology, or Eisner's in an art-historical understanding of Romanticism's legacy in early film. That theoretical commitment is less apparent in *Many Faces*. While many writers (Garncarz, Otto, Westerdale, Rippey, Nenno, Fisher, Petrescu) do develop explanatory frameworks for a simultaneously social-historical and aesthetic understanding of Weimar film, others gesture only obliquely towards critical methodologies. The pot-shots taken by some contributors at Kracauer and Eisner might usefully have been replaced by harder thinking about the problems of evacuating the space of social theory, especially when what supplants it is a celebration of popular cinema's market-induced diversity that is surely every bit as ideologically flawed as were the early theorists' accounts of national mentalities. There are also inevitable absences: there is little here, for instance, on audience; on Austrian film; on theory and criticism; or on the film producers, set designers, scriptwriters, cinematographers, distributors, or exhibitors who shaped modes of production and reception, as well as the textual aesthetics of Weimar film.

These criticisms notwithstanding, *Many Faces* will be recognized as an important book, especially by teachers and researchers for whom the volume's comprehensive bibliographies and filmography, the latter with detailed listings of DVD, video, and archive sources, will be an added bonus alongside the contributors' more discursive historical accounts.

KING'S COLLEGE LONDON ERICA CARTER

From the Womb to the Body Politic: Raising the Nation in Enlightenment Russia. By ANNA KUXHAUSEN. Madison: University of Wisconsin Press. 2013. 242 pp. $29.95. ISBN 978-0-299-28994-2.

Anna Kuxhausen's book on concepts of *vospitanie* offers intriguing new insights into the cultural history of eighteenth-century Russia. She argues that views on pregnancy, midwifery, infant care, and education changed radically during that time. Inspired by Enlightenment ideals, reformers wanted to take action in these matters so that infant mortality would be reduced and young people would grow up to be healthy, virtuous citizens of the Russian state.

The book is divided into six chapters. Chapter 1 discusses the meanings of *vospitanie*, which involved the physical as well as the moral and intellectual aspects of upbringing, as expressed in the writings of various intellectuals. Chapter 2 is dedicated to reforms in midwifery. In particular, it looks at a programme for the education and licensing of midwives proposed by Pavel Zakharovich Kondoidi, which failed because of its top-down approach. Also, Kondoidi struggled to find physicians who could have given classes in Russian and he overestimated the midwives' willingness to carry out his directives. Chapter 3 investigates discussions on the importance of mother's milk. As in many European countries, intellectuals in Russia advocated that mothers should breastfeed their children instead of hiring wet-nurses. Motherhood was not a private matter any more, but had political implications, as nursing mothers were understood to contribute to Russia's prosperity by raising robust children. Chapter 4 looks at recommendations on the care of a child's body. These discussions included ideas about a child's ideal nourishment, such as a frugal diet, the practice of swaddling, or views on the question whether a cold regime was conducive to a child's health. Chapter 5 is concerned with moral instruction for the Empire's youth as it manifested itself in school textbooks, and which combined Enlightenment values with Orthodox teachings. Also, a new ideal of masculinity emerged, which was meant to represent an original Russian national character that predominant French tastes had allegedly rendered effeminate. Chapter 6 explores new notions of girlhood. Kuxhausen convincingly argues that educational institutions for girls (Smolny being the most prominent among them) created a space that allowed young women to prolong their girlhood for a few years before they would enter into marriage and motherhood. This prolonged girlhood offered them opportunities to educate themselves, create networks, and participate in social events.

Kuxhausen carefully points out the gendered nature of the discourses on these topics. New scientific knowledge, which was accessible mainly to men, was regarded as superior to the traditions of child-rearing women had practised in the past. Sometimes the reader might wonder what the reality of childbirth, nursing, upbringing, and education looked like at that time, and to what extent it contrasted with the reforms intellectuals stipulated, yet it is not the goal of Kuxhausen's study to provide answers to these questions.

It is interesting to observe how the notion of virtue played an important part in the suggested reforms, as Kuxhausen repeatedly points out. Kondoidi, for instance, stipulated that midwives should be young, virtuous, and content with a minimal financial compensation for their work—when in reality less virtuous, more experienced midwives who worked for a living might have been just as useful. In foundling homes Ivan Betskoi preferred feeding the babies cow's or goat's milk to hiring wet-nurses whose virtue was not beyond reproach. Tragically, this attitude exacerbated infant mortality.

Kuxhausen's study is carefully researched and well argued, and provides important comparisons with Western models and practices. It sheds new light on various aspects of *vospitanie* in eighteenth-century Russia, especially their gender implications, and is a valuable contribution to the field.

CHARLES UNIVERSITY, PRAGUE URSULA STOHLER

Taboo Pushkin: Topics, Texts, Interpretations. Ed. by ALYSSA DINEGA GILLESPIE. Madison: University of Wisconsin Press. 2012. xix+482 pp. $34.95. ISBN 978-0-299-28704-7.

The Poetics of Impudence and Intimacy in the Age of Pushkin. By JOE PESCHIO. Madison: University of Wisconsin Press. 2013. xi+160 pp. $29.95. ISBN 978-0-299-29044-3.

Pushkin's Historical Imagination. By SVETLANA EVDOKIMOVA. (Russian Literature and Thought) New Haven and London: Yale University Press. 1999. xviii+300 pp. £25. ISBN 978-0-300-18190-6.

On 5 June 2013 the Russian government watchdog Roskomnadzor ordered that three articles be deleted from the independent news portal <www.lenta.ru> because they contained 'obscene language in open access'. One was a sober, scholarly discussion of the origins of Russian swear words with Moscow State University researcher Igor Pilshchikov. Such prudery can be seen as a manifestation of an oppressive political climate which increasingly threatens intellectual openness and pluralism. It is welcome and timely, therefore, that the three books under review here (of which two make extensive use of Pilshchikov's work) constitute such a spirited and meticulously argued refutation of dogmatism in an area of scholarship that remains central to Russian identity—the life and work of Aleskandr Pushkin.

One might say that, in Russia, the Pushkinian is always political. In her Introduction to *Taboo Pushkin*, the most explicitly polemical work considered here, Alyssa Dinega Gillespie traces the to-and-fro history of the political exploitation and artistic liberation of Pushkin and exposes recent attempts to establish a Pushkin who is both very orthodox and very Orthodox; she observes, following Abram Tertz, that often '"Pushkin" [. . .] is a politically expedient fiction lacking intrinsic spiritual reality' (p. 9). The essays in this rich collection counteract this recent trend for hagiographical attitudes towards the national poet by demonstrating that those aspects of Pushkin's œuvre and biography that have been considered taboo—most notably the importance of the erotic—are a rewarding field of enquiry that deserve frank and unselfconscious scholarly scrutiny, not squeamish suppression. The book is divided into three sections: 'Taboos in Context', 'Taboo Writings', and 'Taboo Readings'. The first predominantly deals with Pushkin's life rather than his work, but nevertheless remains moored in close reading and dogged archival investigation, most notably in the case of 'Pushkin and Metropolitan Philaret: Rethinking the Problem', Oleg Proskurin's dismantling of arguments which posit that the poet's correspondence with Metropolitan Philaret was central to his biography. Nevertheless, the contributors do much more than create a counter-narrative in which Pushkin is cast as a *bien-pensant* liberal rather than a pious patriot: Irina

Reyfman's 'Pushkin the Titular Councillor', which shows the importance of government service to Pushkin's career, is symptomatic in its willingness to confront aspects of Pushkin that frustrate attempts to cast him as a proto-liberal; Katya Hokanson does much the same by revealing the nationalistic sentiments behind Pushkin's so-called anti-Polish poems and 'Ia pamiatnik sebe vozdvig nerukotvornyi'. The second section, 'Taboo Writings', engages with Pushkin's 'obscene' works: various essays—including Pilshchikov's despatch from the front line of contemporary culture wars regarding the disputed authorship of the erotic romp *Ten' Barkova*—make convincing arguments for the richness of these texts, but the highlight is Dinega Gillespie's new reading of 'Prorok'. Her argument for the importance of corporeality and sexuality to this canonical poem is persuasive rather than revelatory, but this is rather the point: as in many of the chapters, acute analysis reveals semantic multiplicity, not a single, definitive exegesis. The final section, 'Taboo Readings', continues this trend by finding new interpretations of established classics such as *Kapitanskaia dochka*.

Joe Peschio, author of the slim but highly informative *The Poetics of Impudence and Intimacy in the Age of Pushkin*, also contributes an essay to *Taboo Pushkin*. (He too announces his hostility to prudish Pushkinists in an impassioned epilogue, and cites Pilshchikov as a mentor.) Peschio brings a light touch to communicating the fruits of many hours spent in the archives researching the works and ways of the secretive literary societies Arzamas and the Green Lamp. It is testament to the historical power of taboo over Pushkin scholarship that Peschio has been able to uncover much that is new about these societies, despite the fact that their influence on their sometime member Pushkin was, if anything, overemphasized by Soviet critics keen to bolster the poet's anti-tyrannical credentials. After establishing the importance of *shalost'*—a mode of knowing impropriety in word and action that challenged authority by blurring the boundaries between domesticity, society, and the state—Peschio turns to a detailed analysis of the ways in which members of Arzamas made programmatic use of rudeness as part of a coded language of communication that helped to cement their sodality; he goes on to show that, in the later grouping the Green Lamp, a similar role was played by politically oppositional libertinism and allusive sexual banter. While it is something of a relief in the final chapter to leave behind the large cast list of the two societies and focus on Pushkin's breakout hit *Ruslan i Liudmila*, Peschio nevertheless ultimately underlines their importance by demonstrating the *poema*'s debt to the codes pioneered by Arzamas and the Green Lamp.

Such open-minded approaches to overlooked aspects of Pushkin recall Svetlana Evdokimova's *Pushkin's Historical Imagination*, published over a decade ago, and now a feature of undergraduate reading lists. Although Evdokimova takes as a focus Pushkin's interest in history and historiography—an underdeveloped area, but not a taboo one—she too strives to broaden our image of Pushkin and, what is more, to show how broad and non-doctrinaire Pushkin's own image of the world was. Evdokimova analyses Pushkin's engagements with history and the past, and discovers therein 'infinitely varied perceptions of history'; what is more, 'If there is anything that unites them, it is Pushkin's believing in, and striving for, the complementarity of multiple truths' (p. 15).

Evdokimova's scrupulous analyses of works in all Pushkin's many genres are grouped into three sections, dealing in turn with questions of history and national identity, history and narrative, and finally Pushkin's near-obsession with the role of Peter the Great in Russian history. Deep knowledge of the texts and the period provides new perspectives: particularly worthwhile are the readings of 'Hero' and of Pushkin's polemic with the radicalism of Aleksandr Radishchev in the unfinished *Puteshestvie iz Moskvy v Peterburg*. These qualities are complemented by a pleasingly wide range of reference, especially in the extended analogies that enliven the text; only on one occasion is this range distractingly broad—an excursus about Indo-European mythology in the midst of an exemplary analysis of *Mednyi vsadnik*.

Evdokimova reminds us of Pushkin's sensitivity to multiple interpretations of the past: 'Pushkin, I claim, did not believe in Truth, but in truths' (p. 14). In this respect, then, the scholars under consideration here, who reveal Pushkin to be a multi-faceted, contradictory figure, are his heirs as well as his interpreters. By leaning heavily on the texts themselves and without resorting to airy theoretical pronouncements, they serve as a sharp rebuke to attempts to sanitize Pushkin, and to the dogmatic politico-cultural system that motivates them.

UNIVERSITY COLLEGE LONDON   JAMES RANN

Stalin's Ghosts: Gothic Themes in Early Soviet Literature. By MUIREANN MAGUIRE. (Russian Tranformations: Literature, Thought, Culture, 4) Bern: Peter Lang. 2012. 331 pp. £45. ISBN 978-3-0343-0787-1.

Commenting in 1928 on a volume of short stories by Nikolai Ognev, the editor of the journal *Krasnaia nov'*, Aleksandr Voronskii, asked where 'this dreadful predilection for the graveyard and the tombstone' came from. Six years later we have Konstantin Fedin's confident pronouncement that the Russian fantastic novel 'had died and been sealed in its tomb'. Muireann Maguire's wide-ranging and thought-provoking analysis sets out both to answer Voronskii's question and to rebut Fedin's claim, with a study of 'the extended collision between Socialist Realism and the Gothic-fantastic between 1920 and 1940', and an examination of 'key scenarios or tropes from the Gothic tradition [. . .] in the context of Soviet and other Russian literature in this time period' (p. 7).

It might seem that Soviet Russian literature in its first two decades, with its apparent emphasis on positive heroes, realistic plots, and optimistic resolutions, is unrelated to the familiar Gothic tropes of haunted castles and predatory corpses, and only distantly concerned with the Gothic themes of instability, retribution, and deformity. Maguire begs to differ: 'The Soviet experiment', she writes, '[. . .] is easier to accept—even appreciate—when ironically historicized through the Gothic veil' (p. 21). With impressive attention to detail she sets out to show the extent to which early Soviet literature is in fact informed by the Gothic. After a chapter on the chronotope of the Gothic castle, emphasizing the obsession with property and its repossession, the analysis moves to Gothic bodies, highlighting the theme of parasitic degeneration. A chapter on Gothic death follows, taking as its starting-point Agatha Christie's image of 'the body in the library', because of the 'disruptive, derisive effect on Socialist Realist narrative produced by an unexpected corpse' (p. 155). We then move on to Gothic monsters, including sections on doubles, vampires, and the subgenre of 'Cheka Gothic'—an exploration of the inner contradictions arising from the activities of secret police agents; and finally to Gothic returns, focusing on the work of the four members of the 'Bulgakov cohort', a small group who 'stubbornly sustained the Gothic-fantastic mode within Russian letters' (p. 253): Bulgakov himself, Aleksandr Chaianov, Sigizmund Krzhizhanovskii, and Nikolai Ognev. The concluding section briefly explores examples of Gothic texts in the post-war Soviet decades, including works by Petr Aleshkovskii, Boris Akunin, Vladimir Sorokin, Dmitrii Bykov, and Viktor Pelevin.

It is not possible within the space of a limited review to do full justice to the scope and force of this analysis. If asked to choose some examples among such a wealth of material I would point to the analysis of Daniil Kharms's short story 'Starukha' (pp. 159–64), laying bare Kharms's extraordinary narrative world in which corpses form 'an actively malign social group' (p. 162); the ingenious argument explaining the absence of the vampiric figure of Gella in the final scene of Bulgakov's *Master i Margarita* (pp. 218–25); and the discussion of the novel by the Don Cossack ataman Pavel Nikolaevich Krasnov, *Za chertopolokhom*, a work 'that blatantly prefers the recreation of past culture to the Soviets' radical utopianism' (p. 235).

It will be clear from the above that the book looks not only at familiar texts such as Bulgakov's *Master i Margarita* and Isaac Babel's *Konarmiia*, but also at a whole range of works by less well-known authors, many of whom have never been translated into English. Throughout, the analysis is set within a historical context, with references to earlier Russian authors such as Pushkin, Gogol', and Dostoevskii, and above all to previous exponents of the Gothic in English literature, ranging from Walpole, through Ann Radcliffe, Mary Shelley, and Bram Stoker to H. G. Wells. I was struck in particular by the detailed comparison of M. G. Lewis's *The Monk* with Vladimir Zazubrin's *Shchepka* (pp. 201–04). Equally enlightening are the references to Darwin's theory and its consequences, and to Marx's exploitation of Gothic imagery (vampires, corpses, vengeful phantoms, and their ilk) in his assault on capitalism.

Maguire summarizes her position as follows: 'The prevalence of the Gothic genre within Soviet Socialist Realist fiction proves that the latter is a richer, more dialogical corpus of work than commonly assumed' (p. 306). It is a case that is bold and persuasive enough to give even the most sceptical pause for thought. There are some mistakes in the Cyrillic and a few other slips—notably, the translation of the Russian *gorstiami*—'in handfuls'—as 'guests' (p. 298). Nothing, however, can detract from the overall quality of a book that enlarges and enriches our knowledge and perception of early Soviet literature. *Stalin's Ghosts* therefore challenges as much as it informs, inviting the reader both to revisit the familiar and to explore the unfamiliar. We are taken down into a dark, subterranean, and often terrifying world, but it is a world that is shown through a sharply focused and illuminating lens.

EXETER   ROGER COCKRELL

Toxic Voices: The Villain from Early Soviet Literature to Socialist Realism. By ERIC LAURSEN. (Studies in Russian Literature and Theory) Evanston, IL: Northwestern University Press. 2013. xiii+170 pp. $45. ISBN 978-0-8101-2865-1.

In this intriguing study, Eric Laursen redirects scholarly interest in Socialist Realist literature away from its positive heroes and onto its villains. The assorted wreckers, daydreamers, and generally bourgeois voices analysed here include well-known types from Aleksandr Bogdanov's *Red Star*, Fedor Gladkov's *Cement*, Lev Kassil's *Shvambrania*, and Valentin Kataev's *Time Forward*; as well as the more ambivalent and controversial characters found in such non-Socialist Realist fare as *We*, *Heart of a Dog*, and *Bedbug*. Laursen acknowledges that he owes a debt to previous scholarship on Soviet Socialist Realism, citing Katerina Clark's ground-breaking *The Soviet Novel: History as Ritual* (Chicago: University of Chicago Press, 1981) as a particularly important contribution. Clark's interest in the hero's transition from a state of spontaneity to revolutionary consciousness is reiterated and thoughtfully developed, as are depictions of reality in its revolutionary development, and the teleological drive to educate and direct readers along the correct ideological lines. An initial—one is tempted to say 'spontaneous'—response to this redirection of interest might well question whether any substantial contribution to the subject can be made by merely shifting attention away from the hero, while maintaining Clark's preoccupations with master plot and function. According to another villainous voice from early Soviet culture (Russian Formalism and its offshoots), villains exist solely as obstacles to the eventual resolution of heroic narratives, and serve to articulate the qualities of the hero as much as those of the villain. To focus on the villain is, potentially, merely to reiterate the dominant characteristics of positive heroes and their plots.

Over the course of Laursen's study, it becomes apparent that there is considerable insight to be gained in turning attention to the villain. Indeed, this shift of attention has profound implications for how spontaneity, revolutionary consciousness, and the properties of teleological art are to be understood in early Soviet culture and beyond. Perhaps inevitably, any self-respecting study of Socialist Realism has to address the (still) controversial problem of continuity between Socialist Realism and its preceding cultural regimes. Laursen contends a degree of continuity-through-inversion in Soviet literary culture, whereby the ambiguous 'heroes' of texts such as Zamiatin's *We*, Olesha's *Envy*, and Bulgakov's *Heart of a Dog* serve as prototypes for the villains of Socialist Realism proper. Both Zamiatin's and Olesha's novels foreground the fate of the creative, writerly individual in a post-Revolutionary context that places practicality and ideological conformity at a premium; both texts imply that literature is inherently ambiguous and should resist conformity. Consistent with his continuity-through-inversion argument, Laursen implies that Socialist Realism could never entirely shed this 'toxic' baggage which such villains brought with them from pre-Socialist Realist culture. They are symptomatic of a broader *dystopian* anxiety in Socialist Realism that fears the potential failure to create the Communist future, and, by extension, limit its *telos* of constructing a 'true' revolutionary consciousness in the reader. This undesirable grain of doubt, so Laursen argues, can in part be ascribed to the generic qualities of satire and fantasy, and his treatment of the latter is of particular interest. Drawing on the work of Todorov, Laursen pulls off an intriguing inversion of his own, arguing that fantastic literature shares many features with Socialist Realism. Fantastic literature aims to present an alternate reality as logical and possible, and the reader 'is thereby estranged from the reality in which he or she exists, only to be provided with an explanation that makes this estrangement acceptable—the unnatural world is made natural' (p. 59). The ambiguity of this statement is telling. On the one hand, the alternative world made plausible is that anti-Socialist Realist world of the villain that threatens the attainment of the Communist future. Yet on the other hand, the fantastic here is Socialist Realism itself, which serves to estrange the reader from the immediate, affective truth of reality under Stalinism and naturalize the unnatural and improbable existence of the Communist future.

For all his deft and subtle treatment of these elements, there are other aspects of Laursen's study which are less persuasive. Throughout he uses metaphors of cleanliness, disease, and the purging of toxicity to describe Socialist Realism, but at times he fails to articulate why such metaphors are so pertinent to the novels under discussion. Beyond the mention of Todorov and the fantastic, he rarely feels obliged to contextualize his critical terminology of voice, genre, and bodily metaphors which are so crucial to his study; all of which might leave some readers longing for the incorporation of a Bakhtinian reading into this otherwise impressive and important study.

UNIVERSITY OF DURHAM   MAX ANLEY

ABSTRACTS

Petrarch's *De vita solitaria*: Samuel Daniel's Translation c. 1610   by Jessica Stoll

Petrarch's *De vita solitaria* enjoyed considerable success, but it took more than two centuries for it to be put into English. In his version of it, *The Prayse of Private Life*, Samuel Daniel recasts Petrarch's treatise. He focuses on Petrarch's classical examples, adds Latin *sententiae*, and simplifies Petrarch's variety of reference, anecdote, and biographical detail, in order to present **solitude** as a **moral** way of life free from desire.

**The Courtesan and the Bed: Successful Tricking in Middleton's *A Mad World, my Masters*
   by Kate Aughterson**

The courtesan and her bed are central to **Middleton**'s *A Mad World, my Masters*. The play represents **female sexuality** through theatrical and generic innovations: attention to space and **stage properties** and meta-theatrical playing with anti-theatrical discourses. Middleton's courtesan celebrates theatrical and sexual agency, where **body**, woman, and stage are metonymized through the bed. The bed as central stage property coalesces, figures forth, and symbolizes anti-theatricalists' worst fears, transforming them into a comic serenade to provisional urban female identity. The performance of material beds in **Jacobean comedy** illustrates intersections of gender, identity, and **theatricality** in **early modern drama**.

'The Senses of Primitive Man': Joseph Conrad, W. H. R. Rivers, and Representing the Other in 'The End of the Tether'   by Andrew Purssell

This article explores the interfaces between the representation of non-European, native peoples in **Joseph Conrad**'s 1902 short story **'The End of the Tether'** and the **anthropology** of **W. H. R. Rivers**. After outlining some of the ethnographic contexts impacting on Conrad's representation of **Malay** indigeneity, I focus on Rivers's ideas about **'primitive vision'**, arguing that these ideas, drawn from fieldwork conducted in parts of the world that Conrad knew from his sea years, and current and influential when 'The End of the Tether' was first published, can be felt in the representation of the other in Conrad's tale.

**Mediterranean Mediations: Language and Cultural (Ex)change in BnF, MS fr. 19152
   by T. S. Mendola**

The medieval romance *Floire et Blancheflor* exists in two major forms, a *conte oriental* and a *roman d'aventures*. The *roman*, attested in only one manuscript (**Paris, BnF, MS fr. 19152**), has received little scholarly attention. This article builds on previous scholarship which reads the codex as a sustained literary project with an overarching structure. I suggest, however, that previous work does not take the codex's final piece, *Floire et Blancheflor*, into consideration. A close reading of key passages in the *roman* reveals BnF, MS fr. 19152 as a work profoundly invested in **French vernacular literature**'s nascent relationship with its **medieval Mediterranean** Others.

Galdós, Shakespeare, and What to Make of *Tormento*   by Gareth J. Wood

This article explores the hitherto ignored **intertextual** link between **Galdós**'s novel *Tormento* and **Shakespeare**'s *Othello*. Drawing on Galdós's critical observations concerning Shakespeare and the **galley-proofs** of *Tormento*, the article argues that Galdós had *Othello* much in mind when characterizing the protagonists of his novel as well as shaping key scenes. The cultural, ethnic, and social tensions underpinning Shakespeare's Venice offer parallels with Galdós's pre-revolutionary Madrid. The article shows how Galdós uses *Othello* as a counterpoint to prurient responses to female sexual transgression that typified his contemporaries and argues against critics who have seen *Tormento* as a novel about female duplicity.

Medieval Humour? Wolfram's *Parzival* and the Concept of the Comic in Middle High German Romances   by Stefan Seeber

This article questions the common view that modern concepts of **humour** can easily be applied to the interpretation of medieval texts, and specifically examines the extent to which the idea of humour as Weltanschauung (as outlined in **Jean Paul**'s *School for Aesthetics*) is applicable. I offer a different approach to **Wolfram von Eschenbach**'s *Parzival*, based on a rhetorical theory of the ridiculous as expounded in the *Rhetorica ad Herennium*, **Cicero**, and **Quintilian**. On this basis I reconsider the relation between *delectatio* and *utilitas* in the romance.

After the *Flâneur*: Temporality and Connectivity in Wilhelm Genazino's *Belebung der toten Winkel* and *Das Glück in glücksfernen Zeiten*   by Anne Fuchs

Drawing on current debates on the '**culture of immediacy**' in the digital era, this articles analyses Wilhelm Genazino's **poetics of temporality**. While the modern *flâneur* transformed fleeting impressions into quasi-metaphysical moments, his contemporary successor is a stray self roaming an illegible urban jungle. In the context of a runaway world Genazino's figures attempt to exercise **temporal sovereignty** through five tactics of resistance: retreat into melancholy, the performance of private rituals, the fabrication of stories, the technique of the prolonged gaze, and slowness. For Genazino literature restores **interiority** and **intimacy** as essential conditions of **cultural connectivity**.

Evgenii Popov: A New Gogol' for a New Russia?   by David Gillespie

This article examines the recent writing of Evgenii Popov (b. 1946), especially the 2012 novel *@rbeit*, and attempts to place the writer in the **satirical** tradition of Russian prose. The comparison with the nineteenth-century writer **Nikolai Gogol'** seems apt as both writers depict Russian society as a **grotesque** and **absurd** reality where the relationship between individuals and the collective breaks down and life itself borders on the **phantasmagorical**. Disparities, nevertheless, exist: Gogol' expresses **anguish** for the future of Russia, whereas Popov's work attacks **injustice** and **corruption** in both **Soviet Russia** and the Russia of **President Putin**.

Thesaurus of the Unspeakable: *Thanatopraxis* in Kharkiv's Tales of Trauma   by Tanya Zaharchenko

Using three **contemporary short stories** from the city of **Kharkiv**, this article discusses a literary technique I call *thanatopraxis*, or exaggerated **death**, as a tactic used by **Ukrainian writers** to approach the phantoms produced by the previous epoch. A fusion of **deconstruction** and **naturalism**, *thanatopraxis* tackles the apparitions of death by combining a heightened degree of descriptive focus on a microcosmic level, and a general incomprehensibility of narrative on a macrocosmic level. Mingling tormented bodies with tormented texts, it engages with **suffering** in concentrated ways that render it more accessible: one dose at a time.

www.ingramcontent.com/pod-product-compliance
Lightning Source LLC
Chambersburg PA
CBHW052112010526
44111CB00036B/1828